Contributions to Security and Defence Studies

This book series offers an outlet for cutting-edge research on all areas of security and defence studies. Contributions to Security and Defence Studies (CSDS) welcomes theoretically sound and empirically robust monographs, edited volumes and handbooks from various disciplines and approaches on topics such as international security studies, securitization, proliferation and arms control, military studies, strategic studies, terrorism and counter-terrorism, defence and military economics, economic security, defence technologies, cyber-warfare, cyberdefence, military applications of artificial intelligence, security policies, policing and security, political violence, and crisis and disaster management.

All titles in this series are peer-reviewed.

Silviu Nate
Editor

Ukraine's Journey to Recovery, Reform and Post-War Reconstruction

A Blueprint for Security, Resilience and Development

Editor
Silviu Nate
Faculty of Social Sciences and Humanities,
Department of International Relations,
Political Science and Security Studies
Lucian Blaga University of Sibiu
Sibiu, Romania

ISSN 2948-2283 ISSN 2948-2291 (electronic)
Contributions to Security and Defence Studies
ISBN 978-3-031-66433-5 ISBN 978-3-031-66434-2 (eBook)
https://doi.org/10.1007/978-3-031-66434-2

This work was supported by Hasso Plattner Foundation through the grant LBUS-UA-RO-2023, financed by the Knowledge Transfer Center of the Lucian Blaga University of Sibiu; 455/01.02.2023

This Springer imprint is published by the registered company Springer Nature Switzerland AG
The registered company address is: Gewerbestrasse 11, 6330 Cham, Switzerland

Preface

The collective work entitled *Ukraine's Journey to Recovery, Reform and Post-War Reconstruction: A Blueprint for Security, Resilience and Development* provides a comprehensive investigation of the Russo-Ukrainian War's multifaceted implications and critical encounters for the country's post-war rebuilding process linked to European integration and broader economic interconnection process. Thus, Ukraine's peacebuilding potential emphasises the importance of strategic planning, rapid reforms, and adopting sustainable development principles. Particular attention is paid to managing post-war consequences by harmonising Ukrainian legislation with EU standards.

Focusing on charting Ukraine's journey after the war is highly topical and essential given the ongoing conflict, and it promises actionable recommendations for reforms, not just academic analysis, being functional for stakeholders involved in rebuilding Ukraine. Several chapters situate Ukraine's reconstruction in the broader geopolitics of Eastern Europe and the Black Sea region. At the same time, a wider lens is functional to explore potential for reshaping the Eurasian landscape, contributing to understanding the path towards sustainable peace, regional integration, and global stability. Resorting to an interdisciplinary perspective, the breadth of the sources investigated and the quality of the analyses make collective work significantly contribute to understanding ampler intricacies. There are no academic hypocrisies; the prospects for post-war dynamics logically and explicitly confront the imprint of belligerent actions with the complex legal landscape surrounding compensation mechanisms, the tort of armed aggression, and the procedural issues encountered in compensation cases. Contributors explore parallels between the current conflict and past experiences, drawing insights and patterns to enlighten reconstruction efforts and challenges.

Beyond great power competition, this research has the merit of confronting the alleged virtues of a "rules-based order". At the same time, contributors indicate that international norms are substituted for hegemonic ambitions, and weakened states are forced to play a cynical game of survival in the global anarchic system. Through the rigorous analysis of the multiple components—politics, military, economics, law, environmental, infrastructural, ideological, and cultural, the collective book suggests that power in international relations is not a one-dimensional concept, and success in geopolitical competition requires the ability to combine creative tools. Strategic communication plays an essential role in shaping public awareness and resilience; the Black Sea region is a geopolitical epicentre where hegemonic projects compete, while regional developments have a global impact, posing constant systemic remodelling, conditioned somewhat by fluctuating power ratios between nations.

The manuscript serves as a crucial resource for those committed to navigating the complexities of post-war reconstruction and fostering a more secure and prosperous future for the region and the world. The analytical portfolio is significant, indicating drivers and actionable policies for Ukraine's sustainable rebuilding. Collective insights are valuable to a larger audience, like policymakers, governments, and international institutions preoccupied with crafting reforms, policy development, and reconstruction blueprints in conflict-afflicted states. Thus, the book informs their interventions. Other categories of stakeholders consist of think tanks and academics studying geopolitics and the Eastern European region, especially conflict resolution and state building; business leaders and investors looking at economic revival and opportunities in post-war Ukraine across sectors like infrastructure, energy, and digitalisation; non-government organisations that channel humanitarian aid and drive social development programmes in Ukraine's civil society; security specialists interested in studying the intelligence apparatuses and military integration of conflict states into post-war order; advocacy groups and activists pushing Ukraine's membership bid for the EU and NATO; and researchers using Ukraine's post-conflict progression as a case study for models and frameworks like sustainable development goals.

Consequently, the research opens a significant analytical horizon for deciphering the fluidity of an active and continuous front implicitly positioned in the Black Sea region and Ukraine, characterised simultaneously by high risk and high opportunity.

Sibiu, Romania Silviu Nate

Contents

Global Power Shifting Tendencies Influenced by the Conflict's Outcome: Regional and Global Implications

Andriy Stavytskyy

Abstract The initiation of military operations by Russia against Ukraine in February 2022 sparked a full-scale war in Europe, impacting the global economy and geopolitical dynamics. This chapter delves into the underlying factors that ignited the conflict, with a particular focus on Russia's historical inclination towards expansion through warfare, its reliance on resource exports, and military capabilities, and its response to technological changes. The modern world's decreasing reliance on resources in favour of technological development poses a challenge to resource-rich countries like Russia, leading to efforts to maintain dominance through military aggression. Russia's economic dependence on resource exports, particularly energy, exacerbates its vulnerability to global market shifts. Understanding the multifaceted drivers of conflict is essential for addressing geopolitical tensions and fostering global stability. Mitigating the risk of future conflicts requires strategic diplomacy, economic diversification, and technological innovation to navigate evolving geopolitical landscapes.

On February 24, 2022, Russia carried out another aggression against Ukraine. Let's be honest, in the case of a blitzkrieg, European countries would not be able to change anything or react in time. However, Ukraine was ready to put up fierce resistance to aggression, which turned a momentary operation into a long-term war. After that, the main countries of the world could not help but react to the beginning of a full-scale war in Europe. Ukraine has common borders with the countries of the European Union, and therefore the consequences of the full-scale invasion of the Russian Federation strongly influenced the policy of the European Union.[1] This includes the

[1] Cumming, D.J. (2022). Management scholarship and the Russia -Ukraine war. *British Journal of Management,* (in press), 33, 1663–1667.

A. Stavytskyy (✉)
Lucian Blaga University of Sibiu, Sibiu, Romania

Taras Shevchenko National University of Kyiv, Kyiv, Ukraine

S. Nate (ed.), *Ukraine's Journey to Recovery, Reform and Post-War Reconstruction*, Contributions to Security and Defence Studies,
https://doi.org/10.1007/978-3-031-66434-2_1

reaction to the violation of the EU's basic values, the flow of migrants, a change in the energy paradigm, changes in production, an inflationary shock, etc.

The war significantly weakened the long-term prospects of the world economy. The main channel of the initial influence on the world economy was the market of raw materials. The prices of goods supplied by Russia and Ukraine, such as oil, wheat, fertilizers, various metals, have risen sharply. Rising food and energy prices exacerbate poverty and, in some cases, food insecurity, and add to already rising inflationary pressures. Capital outflows and a marked increase in borrowing rates are observed in many countries.[2] Monetary policy in developed economies became more rigid, which made less rich countries more vulnerable to financial stress.[3] There are already clear signs that the war and the associated spike in commodity prices will make it difficult for policymakers in some countries to strike a delicate balance between containing prices and supporting post-pandemic economic recovery.[4]

Prerequisites of War: Mentality

Several reasons for the initiation of military operations are noted in the political discourse. First of all, we are talking about the desire of the Russian Federation to be at a distance from NATO countries. In particular, this was noted in the actual ultimatum of V. Putin in 2021 on providing Russia with "security guarantees",[5] which demanded the refusal of NATO expansion, the withdrawal from the territory of countries that became NATO members after 1997, all armed forces and armed forces from have appeared there in recent years. Now it is already obvious that the acceptance of such demands, on the contrary, would only allow Russia to seize all the countries of the former Soviet Union, as well as certain NATO countries, in particular the Baltic countries. At the same time, the argument about the threat of NATO cannot be taken seriously, because even in the conditions of the war, Russia relatively calmly accepted the entry of Finland and Sweden into this organization. It is obvious that the problem does not lie in the defensive organization at all, but in what real tasks and goals Russia sets for itself. To answer this question, you need to do some research into the history of the country's development.

---

[2] *CentralBankRates. URL: https://www.cbrates.com/.*

[3] Guénette J.D., Kenworthy P., Wheeler C. Implications of the War in Ukraine for the Global Economy. EFI Policy Note 3. URL: https://openknowledge.worldbank.org/server/api/core/bitstreams/c0de65e6-cc96-5992-8f48-78417ce0e70e/content.

[4] How War in Ukraine Is Reverberating Across World's Regions—IMF Blog. URL: https://joserobertoafonso.com.br/wp-content/uploads/2022/03/How-War-in-Ukraine-Is-Reverberating-Across-Worlds-Regions-%E2%80%93-IMF-Blog.pdf.

[5] Russian December 2021 ultimatum. URL: https://en.wikipedia.org/wiki/Russian_December_2021_ultimatum.

Russia was created precisely during the war of 1478 when the Moscow principality annexed the Novgorod Republic. Even though constant wars and conquests were commonplace at the time, this annexation was fundamental: an authoritarian country annexed a mercantile republic with an elected system of government. It was very difficult to keep such opposite systems in one state, therefore the management of the country began to develop exclusively in the direction of strengthening repression, strengthening authoritarianism and oppressing the masses. Accordingly, each new tsar of this territory did not in any way think about ensuring the development of the people themselves, but only about increasing the possibilities of obtaining resources to maintain the repressive apparatus. Any successful entities that were next to Russia have historically been perceived precisely as an object for capture and parasitism.

In the fifteenth century, Russia waged aggressive wars against the Kazan Khanate and the Grand Duchy of Lithuania, in the sixteenth and seventeenth centuries against the Crimean Khanate, the Hetmanate, the Siberian Khanate, and the Ottoman Empire. In these wars, Russia significantly increased its territory, and as a result, the amount of its resources. At the same time, similar wars against Sweden, Denmark, Livonia, and the Polish-Lithuanian Commonwealth were unsuccessful, which made it impossible to expand the state to the West. However, already in the eighteenth century, after the victory in the Northern War of 1700–1721, the Russian Empire began to seize new territories in all directions. During the eighteenth and nineteenth centuries, this country captured the territories of modern Georgia, Azerbaijan, Armenia, Finland, Kazakhstan, Kyrgyzstan, Uzbekistan, Tajikistan, Sakhalin, Turkmenistan, Inner Mongolia, Tyva, part of Prussia, Austria, Dagestan, Amur Krai, Khabarovsk Krai, a large part of Poland As a rule, the capture was carried out by military means, after which puppet rulers were appointed, who "voluntarily" became part of the empire.

At the beginning of the twentieth century, the situation was not favourable for new conquests, because, in the first quarter of the century, Russia was mainly losing territories. In particular, Finland, Poland, Lithuania, Latvia, Estonia, part of Ukraine and Belarus were lost. However, as early as 1934, permanent operations to change the governments of neighbouring countries began. For example, this year a communist government was established in Xinjiang, later during the Second World War the territories of modern Ukraine and Belarus, Lithuania, Latvia, Estonia, and part of Finland were captured, and control was established over Poland, Czechoslovakia, Hungary, Albania, Yugoslavia, Romania, part of Germany, part of Japan. The bloody world war did not stop Russia's aggressive policy. In 1956, 1968, and 1979, troops invaded Poland, Czechoslovakia, and Afghanistan to establish the desired puppet government.

The collapse of the Soviet Union in 1991 significantly reduced the volume of the controlled territory, and a significant part of the gains of the nineteenth century was lost. But since 1992, Russia has returned to its favourite business: seizing neighbouring states. The main scheme remained the Finnish one, which was tested in 1940: saboteurs take over any settlement where a certain people's republic is proclaimed, which means the beginning of a "civil war", in which Russia intervenes in various ways. In 1991–1993, Russia made a puppet of part of Georgia—Abkhazia, in 1992—a part of Moldova—the Transnistrian Republic, in 1999—captured Ichkeria, in 2008—made a puppet of a part of Georgia—South Ossetia.

In 2014, Russia committed another act of aggression by seizing Crimea and creating puppet states in the east of Ukraine. Non-recognition of the annexation of the territory led to an open invasion of Ukraine in 2022. Thus, we see that, regardless of size, Russia has already formed an imperial mentality that requires constant expansion of controlled territory. If in the Russian Empire, it was simply the capture of neighbouring countries, in the USSR—the so-called spread of communism, in modern Russia—the introduction of the idea of the "Russian world", which requires the capture of any territories where there are Russian citizens or speakers of the Russian language. In principle, any other state falls under the idea of the "Russian world" in the same way as under the idea of communism. Therefore, it is not necessary to be surprised by the desire to be admired by Russia.

Russia's aggressive behaviour lies solely in its inability to ensure the development of the state and population in the long term. The system of parasitism in the Russian Empire, the USSR, and current Russia only led to corruption and technological, cultural and social backwardness. Moreover, this logic is also correct for its satellites. For example, East Germany, occupied by the USSR since 1945, 1990 was already 10–15 years behind Western Europe technologically, that is, about a third of the period of occupation. The greater the influence of Russia, the greater the decline. It is not for nothing that the post-socialist countries, which were satellites until 50 years ago, were able to relatively quickly build a more or less normal economy, still lagging behind Western countries. At the same time, the post-Soviet republics, which were under occupation for about 90 years, spend decades on the same path, not always having significant success. Thus, one of the components of aggression is constant technological and social backwardness, which creates a complex of inferiority in citizens, which they try to compensate for with a certain sublimation—a nuclear complex.

Prerequisites of War: Decreasing of Weight of Resources in the Modern World

The second major reason, which is somewhat related to the first, is the inability of Russia to show flexibility and adapt to new business conditions. Since the time of the USSR, a system has been formed in which Russia acts as the resource base of Europe, supplying oil, gas and other resources to the countries of the world. In recent decades, this country has focused on increasing supplies to Europe, which allowed it to increase its profits, therefore, as of the beginning of 2022, Russia was not only one of the world's largest exporters of natural gas and oil but also the main exporter of other goods to Europe.[6] For a long time, Russia received huge revenues from the export of oil, gas and other resources, which created a certain cushion for it, which allows it to solve several strategic tasks. Firstly, at the expense of significant incomes, an opportunity was created to provide the average standard of living of the population higher than that of neighbouring countries, especially the former republics of the USSR, which made Russia a desirable country for trade. Secondly, Russia created a significant dependence on the supply of energy resources, which to a large extent tied the economies of its neighbours to itself, and also created prerequisites for the possibility of influencing the political institutions of these countries. Such influence was not limited to the countries of the former USSR, because Russia strategically wanted to make the European market as dependent as possible on supplies, which could guarantee political stability in the event of war.

Russia had an extensive network of gas and oil pipelines and stable supply routes. Before the war, dependence on Russian oil supplies exceeded 20% in 14 countries, and for five of them (Slovakia, Lithuania, Poland, Finland, and Hungary) it exceeded 40%.[7] With gas, the degree of dependence was even higher: three countries depended on Russian gas supplies for 100%, and another three depended on more than half. In Germany, Italy and Poland, the dependence on Russian gas in 2021 was from 40 to 50%. It is these three countries that create almost 40% of the GDP of the countries of the European Union, and therefore the dependence was really critical.

If other resource-rich countries made powerful investments in the development of the economy and culture, Russia fell into the so-called Dutch disease, when the state budget depends on the export of several types of raw materials (oil and gas) for more than two-thirds. At the same time, the needs of the population in goods and services are met at the expense of imports, which makes it impossible to develop its own production.

Despite the relative degradation of the Russian economy, this situation generally suited everyone. European countries were guaranteed to receive relatively cheap gas and oil, and the leadership of the aggressor country strengthened its position in its own state. However, the situation began to change. The rapid development of shale oil and gas extraction technologies, the transportation of liquefied gas, and green energy have led to the understanding of a reduction in the impact on neighbours at the expense of energy carriers, which means a reduction in stability in Russia itself.

The degree of implementation of renewable energy sources is steadily increasing, on average since 2006 it has doubled across EU countries: from almost 11% to 22%. Scandinavian countries traditionally remain the leaders, where this share exceeds 83%. But the main thing is that the trend of increasing the use of renewable sources is unchanged, and therefore dependence on energy supply should decrease soon.

---

[6]Bhattarai, A., Romm, T., & Siegel, R. (2022, February 28). US economy appeared ready that surge, but Russia's invasion of Ukraine could send shock waves. The Washington Post. URL: https://www.washingtonpost.com/business/2022/02/25/economy-us-russia-ukraine-gas/.

[7]Izarova I., Drozd N., Kharlamova G., Terech O., Baklazhenko Yu., Stavytskyy A. The first 100 days of war. Through the eyes of the Ukrainian academia. Ed.: Delia Stefenel, Razvan Serbian, | Francheska Pop.—Sibiu: Editura Universitatii "Lucian Blaga"din Sibiu, 2023.—177 p.

Russia realized this back in the 2000s, when the shale revolution began, which called into question the possibility of long-term energy supplies to Europe. The active implementation of alternative energy sources only caused concern for the Russian leadership.

The started war led to the realization of accumulated problems and Europe's gradual rejection of energy cooperation with Russia, which will mean the formation of a completely new market structure in the world, and, accordingly, a new security system. After all, in the long term, the situation for Russia does not look so good. Various strategies for switching to alternative fuel sources have already been implemented in the EU many times, but the 2022 crisis only accelerated this process. In particular, the European Commission adopted a plan for the transition to renewable energy sources and the abandonment of Russia's energy resources, according to which it is planned to spend 300 billion euros on financing the missing links of the gas, LNG and oil infrastructure, accelerating and expanding the transition to clean energy. Accordingly, by 2030, the share of renewable energy sources should be 45%, and energy consumption should be reduced by 13%.

Despite the understanding of the impossibility of further focusing on the Russian Federation in ensuring Europe's energy security, it is almost impossible to give up supplies quite quickly. If oil from the Russian Federation for most countries can be replaced by similar supplies from the countries of the Middle East, then for landlocked countries, it looks quite difficult in the short term. Previously, they received oil through pipelines, and existing logistics routes cannot meet the demand. Accordingly, when the oil embargo was adopted, exceptions were expected for pipeline oil.

Similarly, with gas: the only alternative to pipeline gas is LNG. In 2021, Europe imported from the Russian Federation 17.4 billion m^3 of liquefied gas and 167.0 billion m^3 pipeline gas. Now these 184.4 billion m^3 have to be found in other countries of the world. However, supplies of this gas are significantly limited: firstly, by the availability and capacity of LNG terminals, and secondly, by the supply of LNG in the world. Australia, the USA and Qatar sell a total of 309.9 billion cubic meters or 60% of all liquefied gas. At the same time, 75% of gas from Australia and Qatar will be sent to Asia, which will not give it up. Taking into account certain actions of the Russian Federation to limit gas supplies, Europe will already face a significant gas shortage this year.

Thus, ensuring European energy security requires a fairly quick search for a replacement for almost 30% of the energy that was previously supplied by the Russian Federation and almost half is a gas replacement. It is not for nothing that European countries agreed on a 15% reduction in gas consumption during the war. The way out of the situation should be the development of LNG terminals and own LNG production, especially in new fields in Poland and Ukraine, accelerated development of renewable energy sources and bringing their share to at least 25% by 2030, temporary development of nuclear energy.

Thus, the further development of the concept of energy security in Europe should be related to the achievement of the above goals, the provision of energy logistics, as well as the process of unification of energy rules and tasks in European countries, which will allow full energy sovereignty.

Russia once again faced its standard problem: the current source of income will soon begin to decrease critically, and technologically the country once again lags behind the world. Accordingly, since the aggressor country does not want to implement global development trends, it is necessary to find another place for parasitism.

Given the fact that during its existence the Russian Federation was unable to build a self-sufficient economy based on the sale of resources, the time of its competitive existence should be shortened. Accordingly, the country's authorities are in a hurry to seize the largest possible amount of resources and production to ensure further demand for their products. Russia has entered the last phase of its existence, where without structural transformation it will not be able to sustain its activities. It is for this reason that this country is forced to hurry.

However, other industrial resources should not be underestimated, because the technology change significantly affects which resources are useful. In particular, metals necessary for the production of a key element of the transition to green energy (batteries) have soared in price 6 times since March 2021 and then halved. In general, for example, during the period from March 2021 to the summer of 2023, lithium in general grew by 5 times, and nickel by 1.5 times. Because of this, there was a desire to create a cartel conspiracy between countries that control almost 60% of explored lithium reserves. There is also the problem of China's monopoly position, which controls 58% of lithium processing capacity. Therefore, greater control over territories provides opportunities for additional control over resources.

Prerequisites of War: Military Backwardness

The world economy is developing rapidly, it is enough to note that the combined GDP of the countries of the world in 2021 was almost 8 times greater than the GDP in 1960.[8] It is obvious that this growth is due to two key factors. First, it is the development of technologies that contributed to more efficient use of resources, the creation of new goods and services, and the development of logistics. Secondly, the significant increase in the global population, which increased 2.6 times from 1960 to 2021.[9] These changes lead to the formation of a completely new structure of the economy, changing the role and influence of every country in the world. If we consider the development of the main players on the planet, it can be seen that the share of the US GDP in the planetary output from 1992 remained approximately at the level of 27–28% until 2007. It was in this pre-crisis year that there was a drop to 26.5%, which accelerated in the following years. Currently, the US produces only 23.6% of the global GDP, remaining at the top of the leaderboard. At the same time, China's role as the main geopolitical adversary of the USA is constantly growing. If

[8] GDP (constant 2015 USD). URL: https://data.worldbank.org/indicator/NY.GDP.MKTP.KD.

[9] Population (total). URL: https://data.worldbank.org/indicator/SP.POP.TOTL.

back in 1992, China produced a little more than 3% of the global GDP, then already in 2021 this share will increase to 18.2%. During this time, Russia produced from 1.5 to 2.5% of the global GDP, and over the past 15 years, this share has gradually but steadily decreased from 2 to 1.7%.

It is worth analyzing the role of NATO in the geopolitical confrontation between the three main states. If by 2021 its role had declined somewhat, then the beginning of the Russian Federation's war against Ukraine posed the question of NATO's existence and membership in it with new force. In 2022, three countries submitted applications to the alliance: Finland, Sweden and Ukraine. Finland's application was approved relatively quickly, but the situation with Sweden due to certain political problems forced the postponement of this country's membership, but there is no doubt that Sweden will soon become a new member of NATO. Accession to Ukraine is currently impossible due to the war. However, NATO is the main block in the world that is able to oppose the Russian Federation, which has both conventional and nuclear potential comparable to it. The table shows the share of GDP of NATO countries as of 2022 after the accession of Finland. This share has fallen from 56.6% to 46.1% since 1992, despite NATO's relatively steady expansion. In order to understand the role of new members, the share of NATO's GDP from the planetary GDP was calculated with the countries that were actually in the bloc on a certain date. As we can see, this share is from 97 to 99%, that is, the entry of new members, so their additional contribution as a whole is at the level of statistical error. Thus, regardless of the entry of new members of the bloc, it controls an ever-lower level of production. However, it should be noted that while China added 15% of global GDP during the period under review, NATO countries lost 10.5%, but NATO, China and the Russian Federation began to control 3.5% more than in 1992 (increasing from 62.5% to 66%). As you can see, there is currently no opportunity in the world to create another real military bloc that could compete with the existing ones. The rest of the world accounts for only a third of the world GDP.

One of the most important aspects of financial management in the security and defence sector is cost control. After the Second World War, these costs almost always decreased. If in the early 1960s, they accounted for almost 6.5% of GDP, then in 2021 they will drop to 2.2%. However, in nominal terms, they continue to grow, in particular, in 2021 they reached 2.1 trillion. Dollars. The largest spending in 2021 was seen in the US, China, India, the UK and Russia, which together accounted for 62% of spending. In 2022, Saudi Arabia replaced Great Britain in the top five. If we analyze it by world regions (Fig. 1), we can see certain trends, in particular, obvious constant trends for the growth of military spending in Asia and the countries of the Middle East.

According to SIPRI's assessment,[10] the largest 20 countries spend almost 87% of all military expenditures. At the same time, the distribution of such expenses across the countries of the world is rather uneven. For example, according to statistics, in 2020, Ukraine's defence expenditures amounted to 3.4% of GDP, which is one of

[10] SIPRI Military Expenditure Database. URL: https://www.sipri.org/databases/milex.

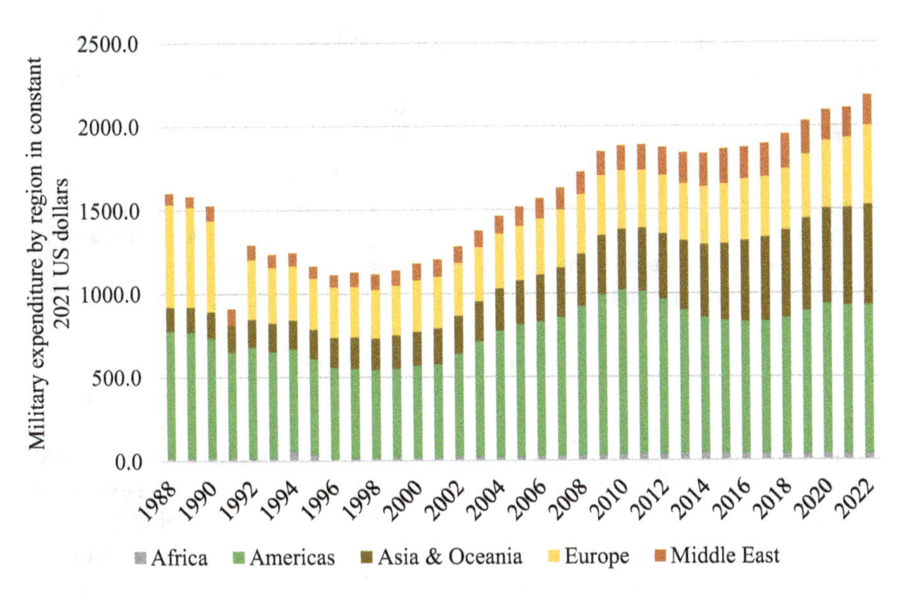

Fig. 1 Military expenditures by world region. Source: compiled by the author based on SIPRI Military Expenditure Database. URL: https://www.sipri.org/databases/milex

the largest indicators among the countries of Eastern Europe. At the same time, the full-scale invasion of the Russian Federation into Ukraine forced a significant increase in these costs. Currently, Ukraine has the highest percentage of relative defence spending. Ukraine's military expenses in 2022 increased 9.3 times and amounted to $80.3 billion, or 55% of GDP,[11] the Ministry of Finance, and NATO countries paid 86% of Ukraine's needs. The budget of the Ministry of Defense of Ukraine in 2022 was $37 billion, and together with spending on paramilitary formations, the costs amounted to $44 billion.[12] NATO countries allocated 32.4 billion dollars to Ukraine, i.e. up to 74%. The second part of the costs is the supply of weapons by allied countries. As of February 2023, they reached $7 2.4 billion.[13]

It should not be forgotten that economic power is a rather variable concept. Currently, there are two main leading countries in terms of economic power: the United States and China. However, The Economist magazine[14] notes that China is currently facing a number of serious problems that can seriously complicate its further economic development. First of all, we are talking about the demographic component. The size of the working population of China has been decreasing for

[11] The 2022 budget. URL: https://mof.gov.ua/uk/budget_2022-538.

[12] Trends in the world military expenditure, 2022. URL: https://www.sipri.org/sites/default/files/2023-04/2304_fs_milex_2022.pdf.

[13] Data Set Ukraine Support Tracker Data. URL: https://www.ifw-kiel.de/publications/data-sets/ukraine-support-tracker-data-17410/.

[14] How soon and at what height will China's economy peak? URL: https://www.economist.com/briefing/2023/05/11/how-soon-and-at-what-height-will-chinas-economy-peak.

about 10 years, and in 2022 the country's population reached its peak. Any attempts to increase the birth rate have not yet yielded results, so according to the UN, by the middle of the century, the number of the working-age population of China may decrease by more than a quarter. This, of course, will deal a significant blow to China's GDP growth. However, another significant problem is the constant decrease in labour productivity in the country. A long period of booming development and construction of houses, roads and railways is replaced by a period of diminishing returns on infrastructure spending. Also, increasing geopolitical tensions in the world lead to the withdrawal of investments and entire enterprises from China to the USA, Great Britain and others, which will further reduce labour productivity.

In such a situation, there are several possible solutions. The first in practice was shown by the countries of Eastern Europe, which implemented not only market mechanisms but also a democratic system, which led to growth even in conditions of population decline. The second method is practised by authoritarian countries that try to compensate for the outflow of the population or its decrease at the expense of new territories, new resources, and new technologies. It is obvious that China has chosen the second path, and therefore it will become more aggressive as the situation in the economy worsens. According to forecasts, by 2030, the country's naval fleet may exceed the American one by 50%, and by 2035, its nuclear arsenal will increase almost four times.

Prerequisites of War: Technological Changes

As already mentioned earlier, throughout its history, Russia has always faced technological backwardness. Another important aspect of the present should be added to this—the change in the phase of technological development. The book[15]examines the history of technological innovation. Although the author uses them to analyze the implementation of the green economy, his division into historical cycles can be useful for understanding geopolitical changes. The stages of technological development have a major impact on various areas of society, including industry, military affairs, energy, social change, and education. Table 1 shows six stages of technological development with a description of the relevant technological innovations and their impact on various areas.

Currently, we are at the beginning of the sixth stage, which determines the individualization of demand, production, training, and logistics. This means that standard resources cease to play the role they used to play.

The openness of the economy allows you to quickly adapt existing technological solutions to life, which was demonstrated by Ukraine, which in a rather limited time became one of the technological leaders in the banking sector, agriculture, and

[15] Stoknes PETomorrow's Economy. A Guide that Creating Healthy Green Growth. The MIT Press, 384 pp. ISBN: 9780262044851.

Table 1 Stages of technological innovation

Stage	Technological innovations	Military innovations	Energy innovations	Social changes	Changes in education
Wave One: Mechanization (1760–1830)	The creation of the first engines that allowed to mechanize primitive production, mainly with the help of water energy. Replacement of people with machines, development of the textile industry, factory production.	The development of steamships and steam engines, which significantly improved the transportation of troops and the provision of military operations.	Use of water energy. The beginning of industrial coal mining	The creation of a new class of people who were the owners of new capital, which was associated with new technologies: mills, spinning mills, weaving and mechanical factories.	Implementation of mass compulsory education, development of universities
Wave Two: Steel, Steam, Railways (1830–1900)	The creation of steam engines, which allowed the creation of railways, the transportation of large volumes of goods by land and the rapid development of industry, in particular, steel.	Development and improvement of firearms, including long-range	Mass use of coal for all spheres of life. Beginning of industrial production of electricity (1882).	The creation of monopolies in the field of transportation and steel production, the spread of their influence on political processes in countries.	Achieving almost complete literacy of the population, increasing diversity educational trajectories
Wave Three: Industry (1900–1945)	The introduction of mass production technology, which made incredible volumes of consumer goods available at ever lower prices. The beginning of the introduction of chemistry in industrial production.	The development of mass-produced weapons that used new energy (oil) technology: airplanes, tanks.	The beginning of oil production and its widest possible use for the transportation of people and goods. The use of electricity for mass production and improving the quality of life.	Industrial conglomerates have the greatest influence.	Development of research work, expansion of courses in social sciences and humanities, increase in the number of students and expansion of access to higher education.
Wave Four: Electronics,	Introduction of electronics, development of	The development of aircraft strength, the		TNCs become rich and politically influential	Standardization of education, its globalization,

(continued)

Table 1 (continued)

Stage	Technological innovations	Military innovations	Energy innovations	Social changes	Changes in education
Television, Aviation (1945–1990)	television and consciousness management technologies.	creation of high-precision and nuclear weapons.	Start of gas production, the introduction of nuclear energy.		the introduction of active international exchange of experience, academic mobility.
Wave Five: The Digital and Internet Wave (1985–Present)	Implementation of the internet, online trade, mass communication technologies	Improvement of high-precision weapons, implementation of systems for simultaneous control of troops and various equipment, creation of UAVs	New technologies for the production of shale oil and shale gas, liquefied gas, the beginning of the introduction of green energy and renewable energy sources	Digital content companies are the most profitable and influential in the world	The integration of technologies and the start of using online courses, the introduction of training programs that meet the requirements of the labour market, the creation of innovation centres and a change in the model of interaction between teachers and students.
Wave Six: Green (2015–2060)	Implementation of the Internet of Things, electricity conservation technologies, systems for sharing items and services.	Automation of management of technical means, implementation of artificial intelligence systems for management of robotic troops	Transition to renewable energy, abandonment of fossil fuels	Companies developing artificial intelligence systems, robots and drones, environmentally friendly technologies, climate control systems.	Activating the focus on an individualized approach to learning and research, using artificial intelligence and blockchain technologies, promoting the development of flexible and distance learning, expanding cooperation between universities and industry to improve the level of graduate training

					and ensure compliance with the requirements of the modern labour market.

Source: compiled by the author

online trade. This was demonstrated during the war, when even in the most difficult early days, the banking system never once stopped making payments or issuing funds, the shops continued to operate. At the same time, relatively closed economies, for example, the Russian Federation, create only technological clusters in large cities, without spreading technology throughout the country.

Key Take-Aways

1. The state formation on the territory of the modern Russian Federation constantly gravitates towards expansion at the expense of war, which is proven by its history. The mentality of the people requires constant conflicts, and therefore the only way to avoid future wars on the European continent is to divide Russia into several states that will not possess nuclear weapons. At least some of them should choose a democratic path of development with subsequent accession to the EU.
2. The role of resources in the modern world is gradually decreasing in favour of technological development. Resource-rich countries (such as Russia), sensing their backwardness, are trying to delay the inevitable collapse of their economy due to the loss of the monopoly on the supply of energy to European countries. Until the economy of such countries is diversified, they will pose a threat to all humanity.
3. The role of NATO has decreased over the past 30 years, in particular, the countries of the alliance began to control 10% less of the world's GDP than earlier. Today, their share is slightly more than 46%, which gives certain chances for the formation of a new block similar in strength to what China is doing. However, in the medium term, it will not be able to create an entity that will be able to challenge NATO.
4. The world is undergoing another technological transition, which complicates disputes between countries and leads to tectonic shifts. The new order will be associated with the development of artificial intelligence, planetary object management systems, climate control systems, and robotic troops. Countries that can adapt to changes will be leaders in the next 20 years before a new phase transition.

From Conflict to Stability: Intersecting Regional and Euro-Atlantic Security Logic in Ukraine's Reconstruction

Silviu Nate

Abstract Ukraine's post-war reconstruction is crucial but unmanageable without victory, a just peace agreement, or security guarantees. The conflict's roots trace back to the 2014 Maidan Revolution and Russia's subsequent actions, like the annexation of Crimea and the Donbas War.

Russia's inability to modernize and its leaders' imperialist mentality led to the 2022 invasion. Russia's war economy and ability to overwhelm with weapons and ammunition have allowed it to maintain high costs in Ukraine. Still, its relative decline is visible in economic, technological, and political realms, while changes in the international system's balance of power limit Russia's influence, causing aggressiveness and instability in its periphery.

Any possible U.S. disengagement from Ukraine jeopardizes its hegemonic decline and increases global instability. Ukraine's reconstruction must consider the competing regional and Euro-Atlantic security logic, balancing Ukraine's European aspirations amid Russia's efforts to reassert influence.

The chapter examines Ukraine's struggle, options, and implications for regional and Euro-Atlantic security. It analyses whether Russia is losing the great power competition, acknowledging that Western society has a decisive role in balancing and enhancing opportunities for Ukraine's reconstruction, including its interconnection with Central Asia and the Black Sea region. Consequently, Ukraine's integration into the Euro-Atlantic security architecture is critical to long-term stability.

S. Nate (✉)
Faculty of Social Sciences and Humanities, Department of International Relations, Political Science and Security Studies, Lucian Blaga University of Sibiu, Sibiu, Romania
e-mail: silviu.nate@ulbsibiu.ro

S. Nate (ed.), *Ukraine's Journey to Recovery, Reform and Post-War Reconstruction*, Contributions to Security and Defence Studies,
https://doi.org/10.1007/978-3-031-66434-2_2

Conflict Roots and Ukraine's Reconstruction Significance

Ukraine and the West face a dilemma: Ukraine's post-war reconstruction is unmanageable without victory, a just peace agreement, or a compromise between the parties that produces security guarantees for Ukraine. Therefore, we have in our sights a goal for stability blocked by the prospect of a long-term confrontation.

The symptoms of this war appeared immediately after the Maidan Revolution, also named the Revolution of Dignity, in February 2014, when former Ukrainian President Viktor Fedorovich Yanukovych was removed from power by force of protests. The street's demands were aimed at a European path for Ukraine by eliminating corruption and abuse of power, the influence of oligarchs, and human rights violations. Social emancipation and the force of political transformation in Ukraine was the turning point by which the Kremlin understood that it could no longer exercise unfettered political control. A series of tensions and events aimed to affect Ukraine's integrity followed, such as Russia's illegal annexation of Crimea and Moscow's support for pro-Russian separatists in the Donbas War. After 8 years of failures, on February 24, 2022, Vladimir Putin decided under the pretext of invoking Russia's right to preserve its "spheres of influence" to invade Ukraine massively. The imperialist mentality and the Russian civilisational model promoted by Moscow's geopoliticians and Russian political elites "inspired" the colonialist culture of controlling neighbouring states through abuse and subordination. Clarifying historical developments and the belief behind decisions is essential to understand that for Vladimir Putin, war is a primordial and ultimate means in his quest to control political regimes on the "periphery of the empire." Russia's inability to be attractive for the modernisation and development of neighbouring societies, an example of the emancipation and modernisation deficit, eventually attracted its regional hegemonic decline precisely, with post-Soviet societies preferring a European path open for opportunities and predictability.

By exhausting competitive means to be a significant global power and failing to perform domestically, Russia has entered a hegemonic decline with a periphery that turned its back on the Soviet legacy. While China exerts growing global influence, Vladimir Putin's fear of losing Russia's geopolitical predominance has prompted him to resort to the only option available, namely, to start a war, thus challenging the European security architecture and returning to the select group of global influential actors, thus protecting Russia's privilege to count in world affairs.

Throwing his boots on European ground would have given Putin much-needed negotiating leverage with the US for transatlantic security and China for conditioning or facilitating routes and access to Europe's economic market. In reality, the Kremlin's anti-Western ideological constructs are the same Soviet-styled myths to awkwardly justify its lack of domestic performance amid corruption that has kept alive political loyalties to Putin.

The war in Ukraine was projected from the start of the invasion on February 24, 2022, as the first phase of Russian expansion, and later, depending on the results, the Kremlin would adjust its tactics and subsequent moves. Therefore, the

Russian-Ukrainian war is not an isolated conflict but involves a broader dynamic with the potential to redefine the global order.

The significance of Ukraine's reconstruction stems not only from its military resistance to Russia but, above all, from the aspirations of Ukrainian society to freely choose its destiny for democracy in the great family of European nations. The *de facto* end of the Ukrainian Revolution and the liberation of Ukraine from the forced and unfriendly legacy inserted by Russia will be the very moment of reconstruction. Therefore, the prospects of stabilising and rebuilding Ukraine must consider society's desires, cancelling through the new architecture of interdependencies any subsequent possibility of Russia challenging Ukraine's sovereignty and placing it on an abortive Eurasian circuit.

Is Russia Losing the Great Power Competition?

From the historical perspective of the dissolution of empires and hegemonic decline, the phenomenon has been characterised mainly by the inability to provide the best military technologies and the financial burden of the cost of armaments.[1] In the first 2 years since its massive invasion of Ukraine, Russia has restructured its economy to a war economy, avoiding economic collapse, and even though it does not benefit from a significant technological ascendancy, through quantitative overwhelm of weapons, it has managed to maintain high costs for Ukraine and its supporters.

In terms of geostrategic location, Ukraine has a crucial position for European security, being able to ensure in the future, together with Poland and Romania, a security and defence corridor between the Black Sea and the Baltic Sea, thus contributing to strengthening NATO's eastern flank and the eastern security of the European Union. Russia is looking to Ukraine from the east as part of its Eurasian project, maintaining a buffer zone from the West. By controlling Ukraine and Belarus, Russia could challenge the European security architecture by pushing its so-called sphere of influence to Poland's eastern border at the risk of severing the Baltic states from the rest of Europe in the more distant future. These competing geopolitical and geostrategic perspectives between the West and Russia narrow the physical confrontation in Ukraine, reflecting equally the fact that the success of either side could influence, in one way or another, the redistribution of global power.

Although the cost of war to Russia might seem affordable, Putin has embarked on this confrontation with a duotone economy predominantly based on hydrocarbon exports and weapons production, which suggests some vulnerability. But precisely because all military and economic effort is channelled into Ukraine, a compensatory force limiting expansion is the gradient of loss of expanded influence.

[1]Mark Elvin, *The Pattern of the Chinese Past: A Social and Economic Interpretation* (Stanford University Press, 1973) pp. 20–21.

Amid the background of a failed expansion, collateral costs arise that are not cumulated with the much-desired benefits, so following poor results and the desire for hegemonic reassertion, Russia not only channels its resources in one place to achieve its objectives but its political influence and net benefits decrease compared to other points of its periphery such as the South Caucasus or Central Asia. Moreover, Finland and Sweden's decision to become NATO members negatively transcends Moscow's initial expectations at the time of the invasion.

Once the West's connectivity with states in Russia's traditional zones of influence increases, as it weakens, Moscow will experience difficulties maintaining control, and the periphery will present additional limits for her.

Changes in the structure of the system of international relations regarding the balance of power cause another symptom of Russia's hegemonic decline. The Kremlin's use of military force is equivalent to exhausting its ability to participate in achieving the balance of power; it tends to exert opposition to other powers in the form of counterbalancing military, political and economic alliances. In this case, energy blackmail unconventional and military measures are the only levers Russia has at its disposal to seek to regain a great power status. Historically, the balance of power has become an institutionalised coordinate of the transatlantic model and a fundamental reason European states have maintained their independence from imperial external attempts and interference.

Vladimir Putin's declarations of returning to the Cold War order indicate, on the one hand, the hegemonic decline of Russia in search of nostalgia for the Soviet Union, in which clear and diametrically opposed territorial, political, and ideological delimitations functioned. On the other hand, in the current times, the power structure has changed, disliking Russia, witnessing at the same time a process of fragile resettlement characterised by an unbalanced multipolarity in which the points of tension are much more numerous. In this case, polarity manifests itself not only in the spectrum of military power but also in the economic, political, and technological ones.[2]

Referring to the limits of the aggregation of political and economic power on the part of expanding states,[3] we can admit that Russia's great drama is that although it has benefited from the incorporation of other centres of power, a strong tendency to detach them, in the long run, has formed.

But Russia's war is not just fought militarily. The lack of consensus among non-dominant states and divergences are often due to one-way perspectives and interests in foreign policy, overshadowing the settlement of potential common risks. There are some instances in the political orientation of Hungary, Serbia, Austria,

[2]Zichen Wang, Jia Yuxuan, and Shangjun Yang, 'Joseph Nye Says China, U.S. Need to "Power with" Rather than "Power over" Other Countries', *CCG Update - Center for China and Globalization*, 2023 https://ccgupdate.substack.com/p/joseph-nye-says-china-us-need-to [accessed 1 March 2024].

[3]Bruce M Russett, 'Economic Theories of International Politics', *(No Title)*, 1968, pp. 306–307.

Slovakia, and sometimes Bulgaria when political fragmentations are exploited by a great power, namely Russia, in its attempt to expand its spheres of influence.

In theory, the imbalance of the system of international relations implies a lack of parity between the ability of dominant states to maintain the system through defence costs, the maintenance of spheres of influence, the application of law and the international economy, and the revenues necessary to finance these arrangements.

According to Adam Smith, war spending tends to grow ever faster[4]as civilisation ages, and hegemonic decline is closely linked to economic and technological performance depreciation. Therefore, the costs for the best military technologies and the loss of high-tech weapons on the front can become burdensome even for Russia. The effects of ageing or power sclerosis are visible in Russia's case. The increasing asymmetric interdependence with China causes the economy to be fragile. At the same time, vectorisation of global hydrocarbon export flows through India, and the exploitation of circumstantial situations is not always sustainable in the long run. Possible disruptions in the energy market may cause significant economic damage to Russia, while the effects of a corrupt domestic system based on political loyalties and rising war costs could push Russia from its geopolitical trajectory to the destructuring of power. As the sclerosis of power sets in, despair, struggle for survival, and fierce regaining of dominant power status transform from a relatively benign policy of reassertion to a more virulent policy of global power distribution.[5] However, Russia, and in the past, the Soviet Union, showed creativity and ambition to return to the global power game, emerging from the highly unfavourable conditions in which they found themselves, so its ability to problematise the architecture of international relations further should not be underestimated.

The hegemonic decline is generally associated with resource overuse and loss of means to exert influence, a situation that generates at least two options for Russia:

1. The inability to exercise control over some regions and states, thus keeping them below its level of development, and in this case, Russia's proximity zone, is conclusive by the pressure exerted in recent decades on the states of the South Caucasus, Central Asia, Ukraine, Belarus and the Republic of Moldova. Without modernisation, Russia could not propagate rapid economic growth rates and regional conditions favourable to trade or investment in the periphery. As a result, the dominant states had no economic surpluses to cover combined spending on consumption, protection, and investment.
2. The hegemon needs to avoid collapse, to accept its new unsatisfactory condition, incompatible with its "glorious past", and to emerge from the state of decline using any means at its disposal. In the absence of persuasive soft-power tools to exert influence, the declining hegemon considers the use of force an acceptable option. Behind Russia's actions is despair and the fear of collapse. This

[4]Adam Smith, *The Wealth of Nations [1776]* (na, 1937), pp. 653–658.

[5]Robert Gilpin, *War and Change in World Politics* (Cambridge University Press, 1981), p. 57.

perspective outlines premises for escalation and multiple threats in an attempt to re-enter the initial condition's parameters or gain influence and better results than historical ones.

Today, geopolitical competitors and systemic rivals resort to hybrid tactics and actions[6] to support their hegemonic ambitions, be they global or regional. The Black Sea area is an example of a specific confrontation that has gained tradition from which lessons learned can be drawn, especially for those who still believe that in a world of economic, technological, and informational interdependencies, Geographical distance would protect them from aggressors. Russia has exploited this kind of judgment, relying on the lack of European cohesion and encouraging European political fracturing by unconventional means. Western Europe's strategic autism and romanticised approaches to security were based on the reluctance to assume a strengthened deterrence posture; subsequently, Europe proved unable to project security in its eastern neighbourhood. The new reality Russia had prepared in advance was also based on the nefarious dependencies of influential European states that preferred energy supplies, *business as usual* with Moscow and political interference, ignoring the long-term effects.

The gravity of these mistakes has burdened the frontline states on NATO's eastern flank, which also secures the European Union's eastern border in relation to an area marked by instability.

For now, Russia is not willing to lose the new geopolitical competition. Still, the changes that occur due to power distribution between states are natural and inevitable. As a hegemon is in relative decline, new emerging powers challenge it for influence, and China contests Russia's position without direct confrontation. Maintaining dominance requires substantial resources and becomes increasingly costly as the hegemon's relative strength decreases. In the case of Russia, we acknowledge that hegemons tend to invest disproportionately in defence to maintain their status. The relative decline eventually leads to the deterioration of the political and economic order sustained by that hegemonic power, a situation that produces changes in its periphery, and the force gradient fades. Changes may be marked by instability or opportunities for smaller states to break out of the old condition or for larger powers to replace the position of the declining hegemon. From a different angle, Russia's increasing asymmetric interdependence on China will accelerate the collapse.[7] Still, it also shows that no matter how fast Putin runs for a strategic outcome, the direction seems wrong.

---

[6]Silviu Nate and Aurelian Rațiu, 'Defending the Truth and Counter Information Warfare in Europe', 2017, XXIII, 213–219.

[7]Silviu Nate, 'Simbolismul șters al Rusiei și pragmatismul „binevoitor" chinez sau întâlnirea Xi-Putin la Moscova', *Contributors*, 2023 https://www.contributors.ro/simbolismul-sters-al-rusiei-si-pragmatismul-binevoitor-chinez-sau-intalnirea-xi-putin-la-moscova/ [accessed 4 March 2024].

Euro-Atlantic Security and the Imperative to Defend Ukraine

Transatlantic stability after World War II resulted from a hegemonic peace assumed by the US. According to Charles Kindleberger,[8] the global economy's instability between the two world wars appeared due to the absence of a dominant power capable of stabilising the international system. Therefore, increased instability imposed the necessity of a leading power to influence the international system to achieve the success of cooperation. Between interwar Europe, the traditional global power of the British weakened, the world was in economic crisis, and the United States did not assume a central stabilising role. It might be a forced but partially true assumption that some characteristics and potential tendencies find similarity today. A military crisis provoked by Russia and possible US disengagement in Ukraine favours further instability in Europe, getting back to a few interwar correspondences, but particular explanations will follow.

Only after World War II did the United States assume a global hegemonic role out of altruism and necessity to avoid a new world conflagration, save democratic regimes, and limit further expansion of the Soviet Union. At the same time, the policy of containment through the famous George Kennan's Article X or The Long Telegram[9] captures an equally topical perspective on the Russian playbook. The stabilising effect of the US on the European continent was based on complete evolutionary hegemonic traits such as the ability to create and enforce international laws, the will to engage, and decisive global dominance in the economic, technological, and military fields. Finally, by supporting the main European economic centres through the Truman Doctrine,[10] the US won the geopolitical competition against the Soviet Union.

Europe's defence continues to depend fundamentally on the United States, amid the historical change of security paradigm and the European Union's soft-power profile, but also due to dependencies on the production of US military equipment. Beyond NATO's existence, Russia's war in Ukraine has brought to the surface the reality that Europe is being exposed to possible Russian aggression.

A decade and a half ago, Joseph Nye stated, *"The problem of American power in the twenty-first century is not one of decline but of recognising that even the most powerful country cannot achieve its aims without the help of others."*[11] His assumption suggests that the US military and technological supremacy are not questioned, but its hegemony would hardly be perpetuated without the support of the allies and

[8] Charles Poor Kindleberger, *The World in Depression, 1929–1939* (Univ of California Press, 1986) pp. 291–292.

[9] Lacey Helmig, 'This Day In History', *Truman Library Institute*, 2022 https://www.trumanlibraryinstitute.org/kennan/ [accessed 1 March 2024].

[10] Benn Steil, *The Marshall Plan: Dawn of the Cold War* (Oxford University Press, 2018).

[11] Joseph S. Nye Jr., 'American Power in the Twenty-First Century | by Joseph S. Nye, Jr.', *Project Syndicate*, 2009 https://www.project-syndicate.org/commentary/american-power-in-the-twenty-first-century [accessed 1 March 2024].

partners. Although some domestic academic and political debates in the United States advocate American isolationism, decoupling from Ukraine and implicitly from the Black Sea region could trigger American hegemonic decline. As explained earlier, such a situation would be associated with increased instability, leaving a strategic vacuum for the assertion of increased regional powers, thus weakening the gradient of American influence on the Eurasian route, with the risk of emerging new blocs and competing regional alliances that become more claimant and vindictive. The behaviour of certain states in Eastern Europe and the wider Black Sea region would become much more transactional in exercising an aggressive status quo. In contrast, hegemon-dependent states may enter a foreign policy crisis. This extreme scenario, incompatible with US national interests, could lead precisely to American decline by weakening the alliance system.

While it goes without saying that European states need to spend more on their defence, the delay in US support for Ukraine, along with heightened instability, may cause increased anarchy within the system of international relations. Moreover, it could fracture the transatlantic relationship on several levels of cooperation, weakening the alliance system, an objective fiercely pursued by Putin. Eloquent is the message of the first NATO Secretary General, Hastings Ismay, who genuinely formulated the purpose of NATO was *"to keep the Soviet Union out, the Americans in, and the Germans down"*.[12] Today, Germany is a predictable and solid ally, but Putin's plans to discredit the US's ability to contribute to European security is reversing the transatlantic principle. In a malicious sense, the Europeans' naivety before Russia's invasion of Ukraine may have even facilitated the implementation of the "*China in*" Europe principle. Finally, China's duplicitous diplomacy toward Ukraine's legitimate defence brought more clarity among Europeans on China's position.

The US is not a European country; still, isolationism is not productive for the United States, and stepping out of shaping the international system is much more costly than hardly staying involved. We are dealing with an existential issue because Europe cannot stand alone on its hard power in the long run.

Regarding handling relations with China, Secretary Blinken used the term "competitive coexistence",[13] and former Australian Prime Minister Kevin Rudd called it "managed competition."[14] According to Joseph Nye,[15] *competitive coexistence* should consider international cooperation to manage joint transnational issues. Since polarity also comes from areas other than military power, the new normality suggested in world affairs with China is doing two mutually contradictory things.

---

[12]NATO, 'Lord Ismay, 1952–1957', *NATO* http://www.nato.int/cps/en/natohq/declassified_137930.htm [accessed 1 March 2024].

[13]John Ruwitch, 'With Visit to China, Blinken Clears a Diplomatic Path, but It's Unclear Where It Goes', *NPR*, 20 June 2023, section World https://www.npr.org/2023/06/20/1183098899/antony-blinken-beijing-china-trip-analysis [accessed 1 March 2024].

[14]Kevin Rudd, *The Avoidable War: The Dangers of a Catastrophic Conflict between the US and Xi Jinping's China* (Hachette UK, 2022).

[15]Wang, Yuxuan, and Yang.

China will continue sympathising with democratic powers and authoritarian regimes to promote opportunistic projects. At the same time, the European Union should develop greater strategic thinking and agency along with the US by using its soft-power capability to strengthen strategic alliances, address the Global South countries, and get its engagement where possible.

Russia's war has great power competition implications and stakes that have generated and will generate turmoil in many Western chancelleries. The emergence of new tension points, such as the conflict between Israel and Hamas, the potential escalation between Venezuela and Guyana and the blatant blockade of Western trade maritime transit to the Suez Canal aggravated by Houthi rebels' attacks, tend to diversify the international agenda. Therefore, it is predictable Russia will pursue through direct channels or proxies such as Iran, provoking tensions in various regions to disrupt supply chains and hijack Western priorities for supporting Ukraine. In its desire to achieve broader goals, Russia could profit from increasing anarchy within the international system while seeking to dilute the US global power projection, from which China would benefit at some point.[16]

The Western Balancing Act and Ukraine's Reconstruction

Two years after the second invasion on February 24, 2022, Russia has learned to adapt strategically, has found formulas to resist economically, its current military recovery capacity is much faster than the historical one of the Soviet Union, and other military mobilisations could take place in Russia to increase troop numbers on the front. New conditions and the gaps in Western support for Ukraine determined the asymmetry of capabilities in the conflict and favoured Russia's initiative on the front. In the absence of institutionalised security guarantees, Kyiv must rely on the guarantee of Western support; otherwise, projections on Ukraine's reconstruction and energy and connectivity projects in the Black Sea will be nothing more than part of strategic autism.

Reconstruction must consider three major potentialities: (1) Putin's ambition to treat this conflict as a zero-sum game in which Russia desperately seeks territorial gain or exit on the Kremlin's terms, adding two possible scenarios (a) Russia wins partially or totally, or (b) Ukraine gains partially or totally; (2) Russia's weakening could include a different kind of Eurasian integration and interconnection with Western support; (3) In addition to internal reform and compliance with European Union rules, the reconstruction of Ukraine would become a central pillar for increasing economic and military resilience on the Eastern European flank.

[16] Silviu Nate, 'Navigating through the shadows of 'strategic autism' or some considerations on 2024's place on the map of global challenges', *Contributors*, 2023 https://www.contributors.ro/navigand-printre-umbrele-autismului-strategic-sau-cateva-consideratii-privind-locul-anului-2024-pe-harta-provocarilor-globale/ [accessed 29 February 2024].

Kenneth Waltz's thesis on the periphery of bipolar systems may be conclusive for Putin's desperation to throw himself "all in" into a zero-sum game. Since in a bipolar world, there are no peripheries, the geographical expansion in the spheres of interest of both powers also expands the range of factors included in their competition.[17] At the same time, amid polarity restructuring, Russia is entering into a visible geopolitical decline. Old benefits may migrate to the dominant strategic competitor, or, in the case of a multipolar world, it is unclear where new rivalries come from. John Mearsheimer considers that the emergence of a potential hegemon makes the other powers even more fearful.[18] At the same time, Russia looks with the specific concern of its weakened power to new potential forms of imbalance.

China's rise could prompt the Kremlin's power calculation to assiduously seek formulas to repair the power imbalance, applying riskier policies to that end.

The realist thought suggests that Russia may have pursued the total conquest of Ukraine and control of Belarus from the beginning of the invasion and aimed to implement a reinforced military corridor from the mouth of the Danube to the Baltic Sea. To the south, the broader stakes of the invasion of Ukraine are aimed at cancelling Western military, commercial and energy developments in the Black Sea and obtaining leverage for a return to the circuit of great powers. Russia aims to capture the entire Ukrainian coastline[19] to project its naval status quo in the northern Black Sea and access to the warm waters of the Mediterranean, thus gaining easy access to the Atlantic and Indian oceans. Such an outcome would lead to the almost exclusive division of the Black Sea between Russia and Turkey.

Russia's partial gain implies achieving military objectives in Donbas with complete occupation of the Donetsk and Luhansk regions. Following a strategic stalemate, Moscow could resume negotiations to freeze the conflict. This formula would entail heavy political and military costs for Kyiv by discrediting President Zelensky for accepting a territorial compromise; it could also involve the risk of regime change in Ukraine, intensely pursued by Moscow. The worst-case scenario would mean the Kremlin's imposition of a puppet regime in Kyiv and Ukraine's turning against Europe, respectively, strengthening Russia's wider influence and force gradient. Freezing the conflict is not a viable option, and this compromise cannot attract the expected security guarantees for Ukraine. At the same time, Russia will rebuild its forces to resume the offensive after a specific time.

The complete success for Ukraine is to regain its territorial integrity, which is unlikely while Putin is in power, ruthlessly pursuing his goals. A partial and satisfactory victory for Kyiv would consist of breaking the land corridor between Russian troops in the south and those in the east, allowing the Ukrainian army to

[17] Kenneth Neal Waltz, *Theory of International Politics*, Reiss (Long Grove, Ill: Waveland Press, 2010), p. 171.

[18] John J Mearsheimer, *The Tragedy of Great Power Politics* (WW Norton & Company, 2001).

[19] 'Putin's "Greater Novorossiya" - The Dismemberment of Ukraine - Foreign Policy Research Institute' https://www.fpri.org/article/2014/05/putins-greater-novorossiya-the-dismemberment-of-ukraine/ [accessed 2 March 2024].

remove the entire Russian force on the Crimean Peninsula subsequently. This corridor has been a strategic gain for Russia since the beginning of the invasion and remains a critical objective as long as it can maintain its control—being a logistical corridor for supplying Russian troops. By maintaining control over this logistics corridor, Russia pursues at least two major objectives: occupying the Ukrainian littoral and ensuring the naval status quo in the northern Black Sea. However, after 2 years of large-scale confrontations, Ukraine successfully pushed the Russian Federation's Black Sea Fleet eastward, reactivating its maritime export of goods.

There is, however, a dose of scepticism about Ukraine's success, substantiated by the delay in foreign support packages, the reluctance of Western states to share more advanced technology and the numerical human limits that affect the ability of its armed forces to recover most of the territories.

And precisely because Putin is unwilling to give up his goals, coalition members supporting Ukraine must also adopt a long-term strategy. Kyiv needs long-range weapons to strike deep on the enemy front, electronic warfare capabilities, drone reconnaissance and surveillance, and air supremacy capabilities. Recovering the occupied territories and the Crimean Peninsula, except for Donbas, would still be a partial but spectacular gain for Ukraine as it confronts one of the world's largest military powers. The recovery of Crimea would return to Ukraine the four continental maritime plateaus located in territorial waters around the peninsula, reactivating national energy prospects, with access to a hydrocarbon base estimated to provide 35% of Ukraine's natural gas consumption needs.[20]

Given the previous assessments, we can appreciate the trend of an attrition long-term war, while any "availability" on Putin's part to negotiate with Ukraine starts from the Kremlin's unilateral perspectives and its propensity to project uncertainty without assuming a well-established agreement between the parties that would include additional guarantees for Ukraine.

While debates about Ukraine's reconstruction continue among Western chancelleries, the initial priority is to provide the necessary military support and optimise the European defence industry.

In the east, Central Asia has been a space of interaction between Moscow and Beijing. Still, amid Russia's hegemonic decline and channelling of its resources into a retrograde war, certain Central Asian states are pursuing diversified development and interconnection opportunities. Over the past two decades, actors such as the US, the European Union and India have become active factors in the region, diversifying the area of interactions. The development of trade, energy, transport and digital infrastructure projects between Europe and Central Asia could contribute to the region's modernisation amid Russia's weakening influence. This prospect of Eurasian interconnection with Western support attracts several benefits for Ukraine, advancing the prospect of Kyiv's participation in the Three Seas Initiative, thus

[20] Ganna Kharlamova, Silviu Nate, and Oleksandr Chernyak, 'Renewable Energy and Security for Ukraine: Challenge or Smart Way?', *Journal of International Studies*, 9.1 (2016).

being a bridge between Central Asia, the South Caucasus and northern Europe. The new geoeconomic architecture would facilitate Ukraine's faster integration into the European and Eurasian economic circuit because it is on the route of interconnecting the Baltic Sea with the Black Sea, from Poland to Romania, with the prospect of being located in the future on NATO's strategic infrastructure circuit for defending the Eastern Flank. Ukraine could integrate transport networks that streamline military and commercial mobility while playing an essential role in North-South interconnection in the trade relationship with African states. The Republic of Moldova would benefit from this thinking by achieving increased economic and political resilience on its way to European integration.

To the West, Ukraine borders a predictable and appetising Europe, which has long been a wealthy and naive client for Russia, historically bringing Moscow multiple benefits throughout their relations. The constraints for changing the European mentality on security and interactions with Russia get Ukraine into a zone of more concrete objectives regarding its European future. As most strategic transnational infrastructure projects are realised over a longer time horizon, Ukraine's interconnection is part of the reconstruction process, complemented simultaneously with reforms and internal modernisation.

Romania is the most fervent supporter in the Black Sea region for Ukraine's Euro-Atlantic integration[21] while being a member of NATO and the EU. The use of Romanian facilities on the Danube to export grain and goods has shown the strategic importance of this European waterway for its low transport costs to the Black Sea and the continental European West. European investments in intermodal transport stations with rail, road and river access on the Danube would accelerate east-west and north-south geoeconomic integration, amplifying the reconstruction process. Also, the Black Sea's energy potential, cooperation with Turkey and the design of gas pipelines from Kazakhstan could cancel out Europe's negative energy dependencies on Russia. Modernisation in the European Union's eastern neighbourhood requires the development of critical transport, energy and digital infrastructure networks that should be protected through surveillance and monitoring mechanisms against hybrid threats.

[21] 'Joint Statement by the President of Romania Klaus Iohannis and the President of Ukraine Volodymyr Zelenskyy' https://www.presidency.ro/en/media/press-releases/joint-statement-by-the-president-of-romania-klaus-iohannis-and-the-president-of-ukraine-volodymyr-zelenskyy [accessed 3 March 2024].

Reframing the Black Sea Security Architecture in Ukraine's Reconstruction

The precondition for East-West interconnection is the guarantee of free navigation in the Black Sea; still, to materialise the broader geoeconomic ambitions, Cold War thinking is initially necessary so as not to be thrown by Russia into a scenario with new borders, stretching as far as Poland and Romania. An unwelcome risk would be to generate an additional European front for the US and its allies, deconcentrating part of its presence in the Pacific, and the so-called Chinese challenge would turn into the nightmare of China plus Russia.

At the same time, the Baltic Sea-Black Sea interconnection must consider commercial and military mobility to be included in NATO's Regional Plans,[22] considering multiple strategic benefits and a new enhanced posture that will take shape on the Eastern Flank.

Allies can develop and integrate specific defence industry cores in frontline NATO states such as Romania to produce and deliver weapons and ammunition needed to defend Ukraine.

The Black Sea security architecture's design should consider some potentialities. Natural barriers and geography were historically the most important of the compensatory forces limiting expansion. It is paramount for Ukraine to regain and control the Crimean Peninsula and, implicitly, both banks of the Dnieper River. Moreover, Turkey's sovereignty exercised over the Bosporus and Dardanelles straits[23] has significantly contributed to limiting the depreciation of the regional security environment. Russia sees the Black Sea and the Danube as buffer zones and exercise of its enlarged status quo, veritable natural barriers to protecting what it calls spheres of influence. At the same time, the West looks at these waters as an integrative and positively interdependent perspective.

Another compensatory force is given by the changes in the international system, namely the polarity repositioning tendencies, which indicate possible constructions towards a new global order. That is why resource availability is a crucial variable for exerting influence in international relations, no matter which competing side we are discussing. From this perspective, American isolationism cannot be a viable option, risking becoming a major source of systemic disorder, especially when it is not efficiently managed. Furthermore, Europeans do not have the capacity and strategic range for such a transformation.

As some countries expand their military and security commitments beyond the capacity to support their economies, they are entering a downward course.[24] In

[22] NATO, 'NATO's Military Presence in the East of the Alliance', *NATO* https://www.nato.int/cps/en/natohq/topics_136388.htm [accessed 3 March 2024].

[23] 'UNTC' https://treaties.un.org/pages/showDetails.aspx?objid=0800000280166981 [accessed 4 March 2024].

[24] Paul Kennedy, *The Rise and Fall of the Great Powers: Economic Change and Military Conflict from 1500 to 2000* (Vintage, 2010) pp. 95–96.

Russia's case, poor economic performance is a symptom of hegemonic decline, while the extreme strain of war may become the additional cause of its collapse. Excessive war spending and higher status eventually lead to a relative decline in economic power, and resources devoted to the military sector can no longer sustain innovation and growth. Ultimately, Russia's relative decline in economic power may have a self-undermining effect on its military strength and global influence. Putin is aware that the lack of a strong economy, which he could have achieved through expansion and army conditioning, will further erode Russia's power on the world stage. Not coincidentally, NATO Secretary General Jens Stoltenberg associated Russia's defeat with inflicting the highest possible costs for it to cease hostilities.[25]

Technology as a compensatory force is closely linked to economic power. When unable to achieve a major military technological ascendancy, Russia has traditionally tried to win the competition by the amount of weapons and ammunition engaged in the confrontation and by substantial human losses. Kennedy's "imperial overload" theory explains how extensive military engagements drained the resources of certain states, limiting long-term growth and hastening the decline of their relative power.[26] In this case, Russia's relative strength is conditioned by the commitment of Western states to support Ukraine.

Unfortunately, history suggests that relative decline, not peacefully transitioned, may eventually lead to war, and a new balance of power emerges in the wake of a major conflict. When the peaceful transition of a declining dominant power is not possible in search of global stability, the solution lies in the assumption of guarantees by another hegemon or the sharing of responsibility within a group of great powers. We understand that a peaceful transition of power is only possible through the firm commitment of the United States and its European allies to support Ukraine. The winning competition in the Black Sea by the West and the East-West interconnection would generate the premises of calibration for achieving long-term economic and security development parity between the Pacific and the Mediterranean Sea; at the same time, Ukraine is a critical piece of the global strategic puzzle. While Russia turns to Iran and North Korea to support its illegitimate war in Ukraine, the West can support structural change in the international system through new geoeconomic reconfigurations that will suggest the reliability of future strategic alliances.

The war in Ukraine is a consequence of Russia's hegemonic decline, and the violent power transition affects peripheral states,[27] which are feeling the effects of global balance change. Thus, the periphery has become a battleground for influence and power, and the international system is strained during these periods of structural change. Because the ability of periphery states is limited to repel Russia's demands, only one other dominant actor can maintain or reconfigure the force gradient. That is

[25] *NATO Secretary General on Modern Needs of the Alliance 75 Years After Its Founding*, dir. by The Heritage Foundation, 2024 https://www.youtube.com/watch?v=bM4hwUyHeaI [accessed 29 February 2024].

[26] Kennedy.

[27] Gilpin.

why the evolution in the Black Sea area is decisive for the future global power architecture and, as stated earlier, for the US and its allies, the costs of non-involvement are much higher than the costs of participating in the game. Prospects of Ukraine's accession to NATO arouses violent reactions from the Russian Federation, challenging the balancing act of the West and Russia. Still, at the same time, Ukraine's integration into the Alliance is the key to European long-term security.

SDGs Realization for the Renovation of Ukraine

Andriy Stavytskyy and Ganna Kharlamova

Abstract The chapter explores the post-war reconstruction of Ukraine and its integration into the European and global economy. It emphasizes the need for strategic planning to achieve peace and outlines steps for sustainable development until 2030. The paper discusses the necessity of rapid reforms to modernize the economy, prioritize clean and resource-efficient practices, and address environmental risks. Special attention is given to the management of post-war waste and the adoption of new principles for resource processing. The importance of harmonizing Ukrainian legislation with EU standards is highlighted, with a focus on reforms necessary for EU accession. The paper outlines a roadmap for achieving Sustainable Development Goals post-war. Key challenges include geopolitical shifts, the duration of the conflict, and the need for significant financial assistance. The chapter concludes with the potential for Ukraine to become a regional economic centre in case of SDG implementation with EU support and substantial financial aid for post-war recovery and integration.

In this section, the issue of the post-war reconstruction of Ukraine, its integration into the European and world economy, and an overview of the necessary steps that should be taken immediately after achieving the desired outcome of the war will be considered. It should be clearly understood that even the outcome of Ukrainian troops to the borders in 1991 is not yet a guarantee of the end of the war, because the aggressor country has long-term opportunities to support and incite a military conflict. However, even such a situation will allow the EU and NATO to make strategic decisions that will prevent further escalation. In such conditions, it will be possible to talk about a long-term peaceful coexistence, within which Ukraine will play a key role in the promotion of democratic values, the formation of a new circle

A. Stavytskyy · G. Kharlamova (✉)
Lucian Blaga University of Sibiu, Sibiu, Romania

Taras Shevchenko National University of Kyiv, Kyiv, Ukraine

S. Nate (ed.), *Ukraine's Journey to Recovery, Reform and Post-War Reconstruction*, Contributions to Security and Defence Studies,
https://doi.org/10.1007/978-3-031-66434-2_3

of democratic countries in the Caucasus and in the future—on the remnants of the aggressor country.

Accordingly, it is necessary to understand what exactly awaits Ukraine, and what opportunities Ukraine itself and its partners can create. What should be the concept of sustainable development and post-war renovation until 2030 in Ukraine? What specific steps should Ukraine take for the fastest recovery after the war and what financial resources are needed for this?

Ending the war with the aggressor country requires further rapid strategic reforms, which will allow the modernisation of the Ukrainian economy, making it clean, resource-efficient, competitive and separating economic growth from resource consumption, protecting the health and well-being of citizens, reducing the impact of environmental risks. The task becomes especially important in the conditions of the post-war reconstruction of Ukraine, which as a result of the military operations has accumulated a huge amount of waste, used parts of weapons, destroyed buildings, etc. It is obvious that the restoration of the country requires the application of new principles, including the processing of resources.

The future fate of Ukraine will be inextricably linked with the European Union. As a result, the coming years will be used to harmonize EU and Ukrainian legislation, to resolve the main issues that precede joining this organization. First of all, it is necessary to guarantee the implementation of reforms in areas in which Ukraine is significantly behind the EU. This should be helped by the EUR 50 billion long-term support plan for Ukraine,[1] which is aimed at supporting macro-financial stability, promoting recovery, as well as modernization of the country during the implementation of key reforms on the way to joining the EU. It will support the transition to a green, digital and inclusive economy that will gradually move closer to EU rules and standards, one of the most important of which is the achievement of the Sustainable Development Goals. Through a preliminary analysis, a road map for achieving these goals in Ukraine after the end of the war was developed (Table 1).

Summing up, it can be noted that Ukraine is conceptually facing a huge challenge that needs to be overcome after the war. It has to become the main geopolitical player in Eastern Europe. At the same time, Ukraine should provide a significant positive impetus to this region, because it is expected to restore economic and political control over about 20% of the territory, significant investments from the EU to restore the economy after the war, which will cause an increase in imports from neighbouring countries and the EU. The rate of growth of exports and imports from Ukraine will increase significantly at least during the next 3–4 years after the war due to the provision of various preferences and the demands of the reform of economic

[1] Ukraine: Commission proposes that set up a dedicated Facility to support Ukraine's recovery, reconstruction and modernization. URL: https://ec.europa.eu/commission/presscorner/detail/en/ip_23_3355.

Table 1 Roadmap of the SDGs implementation in Ukraine at the current stage

Objectives	Necessary steps	Necessary projects	Impact on subgoals	Obstacles	Recommendations for implementation	Vision of the development of Ukraine
Goal 1. Overcoming poverty	After the war, Ukraine will face a significant level of unemployment, bankrupt firms and enterprises due to the return to the peaceful life of more than a million military personnel In 2021, 1,956,248 economic entities were registered in Ukraine, of which 1,585,414 were natural persons-enterprises. On January 1, 2023, this number decreased to 1,464,953, that is, by 25.2%.[a] A state program to stimulate the development of small and medium-sized enterprises should be created, which will allow overcoming the consequences of military aggression and avoiding a catastrophic drop in the purchasing power of the population. An equally important part of the aid should be directed to the forcibly displaced people, as well as to migrants who have lost their homes. The state policy of reconstruction of cities and towns should overcome possible poverty in the country.	Small and medium-sized business development programs for 500,000 people. (Estimated cost of 3–5 billion euros). Program for restoration of private destroyed housing. (Estimated cost of 35–55 billion euros). Relocation program from affected regions (estimated cost 1–2 billion euros).	1.1, 1.5 1.3, 1.5 1.1, 1.2, 1.1.a, 1.b	The continuation of hostilities hampers recovery opportunities. Lack of funds to finance programs. The refusal of a significant number of displaced persons to return to Ukraine until the end of the war. Lack of reparations from Russia. A protracted period of war.	Develop a system for monitoring victims as a result of hostilities, which will allow for providing targeted compensation for recovery. Develop a monitoring system for the creation of small enterprises by persons receiving grants from European organizations for their better coordination. Conduct a series of trainings on initial steps for entrepreneurs.	After the war, Ukraine must not only restore the pre-war standard of living but also move quickly in the direction of growth at least to the level of its neighbours. Salary should become an adequate factor in assessing everyone's contribution to the country's development. The development of the restored real estate market should become a factor in restoring justice in society.

(continued)

Table 1 (continued)

Objectives	Necessary steps	Necessary projects	Impact on subgoals	Obstacles	Recommendations for implementation	Vision of the development of Ukraine
Goal 2. Overcoming hunger, development of agriculture	Ukraine has no serious problems with the development of agriculture. However, this industry suffered significant losses due to the destruction of crops, destruction of animals and birds. This requires restoring the animal population to pre-war levels. The supply of agricultural enterprises with equipment has worsened, which is associated with both a decrease in sales and physical losses of equipment as a result of hostilities or its theft by the occupiers.[b] However, one of the state programs should be aimed at demining rural lands and renovating the territories affected by the destruction of the Kakhovska HPP. Competition and opportunities in new markets will guarantee the absence of hunger in the country.	The program to restore the number of animals and birds on farms, in particular, the purchase of young animals, their vaccination, the construction of family-type livestock farms. (Estimated cost of 1 billion euros). Program for demining rural lands and renovation of territories affected by the destruction of Kakhovskaya HPP. (Estimated cost of 3850 billion euros[c]). The restoration program of the Kakhovka HPP and the Kakhovka reservoir. (Estimated cost of 3.8 billion euros).	2.1, 2.2, 2.3 2.4, 2.5 2.5, 2.a	Various lawsuits and conflicts between European countries and Ukraine regarding access to European markets. Demining takes a long time. Lack of funding or investment.	Determine the list of farms, poultry farms, agricultural enterprises affected by the destruction of animals. To involve the armies of NATO countries to clear the territories after the war. Apply public-private partnership to implement this project.	Ukraine should become a European leader in the introduction of new technologies to agriculture, which will provide not only the country itself, but also other food products. Ukraine effectively uses all rural land. The ecology of the Kherson region has been restored.

Goal 3. Strong health and Well-being	The consequences of the war will be a significant brake on Ukraine's economy for a long time to come. First of all, it is necessary to implement and finance a program for the rehabilitation and support of persons who were seriously injured or maimed during military operations. Mechanisms for the creation of state-of-the-art prostheses must be implemented, which will help such persons return to normal life. Secondly, a program of psychological rehabilitation of soldiers returning from the front has been created. It is necessary to achieve their full integration into peaceful life, restoration of family Well-being, observance of calm civil behaviour. The third direction should cover the implementation of a broad system of disease prevention in Ukraine, which will allow to significantly reduce mortality from diseases.	Program of bionic prosthetics. (Estimated cost of 1–2 billion euros). Military psychological rehabilitation program. (Estimated cost of 1–2 billion euros). Disease prevention system program. (Estimated cost of 1–2 billion euros).	3.8 3.4, 3.5 3.1, 3.2, 3.3, 3.8, 3.d	Lack of funding Lack of funding Indecision in reforms in the medical field.	Making investments in bionic prosthetics enterprises. Formation of groups of specialists for appropriate rehabilitation.	War veterans are fully integrated into public life. Life expectancy increases due to timely detection and treatment of diseases.
Goal 4. Quality education	First of all, it is necessary to approve a new modern classifier of professions in Ukraine, to develop all the necessary professional standards so that the requirements of the labor market can be brought	NUS implementation program (estimated cost 1–2 billion euros). Program for the development of	4.1 4.3 4.5, 4.6, 4.7 4.c	Bureaucratic obstacles and lack of wartime funding. The reluctance of many stakeholders to change their	Methodical assistance in the development of the strategy for the development of education in Ukraine until	Ukraine is becoming a leader in innovative education, digitization in education, attracting a

(continued)

Table 1 (continued)

Objectives	Necessary steps	Necessary projects	Impact on subgoals	Obstacles	Recommendations for implementation	Vision of the development of Ukraine
	closer to education. The motivation of those seeking higher education should be increased through a change in the financial model in which the state and the student are partners in co-financing higher education. Ukraine needs full implementation of the concept of the New Ukrainian School, aimed at forming skills for modern life. Vocational education needs comprehensive reform, which should make working professions truly prestigious in society. Under such conditions, there will be a constant request from applicants to improve the quality of education.	professional and technical education (estimated cost of 2–3 billion euros). Adult education implementation program (estimated cost 2–3 billion euros). Higher education reform program aimed at its optimization and efficiency improvement (estimated cost of 10–15 billion euros).		behaviour and funding directions.	205, synchronization of the EU legislation.	significant number of students from other countries, who may become permanent residents in the future.
Goal 5. Gender equality	In general, the situation with gender equality in Ukraine is improving and is satisfactory, its level fully corresponds to the corresponding situation in neighbouring countries. For this reason, only cosmetic legislative changes will gradually improve the state of equality.	Program for the synchronization of legislation with the EU on gender equality. (Estimated cost of 0.1 billion euros).	5.c	Insufficient initiative of women for active participation in public life.	Encouraging women's participation in public life through various programs and training.	Ukraine is a country of equal opportunities regardless of race, gender, religion, etc.

Goal 6. Clean water and proper sanitation	Ukraine faced the practice of destroying not only entire cities during the war but also the destruction of critical infrastructure. It is very important to restore these facilities based on smart development, guaranteeing a completely new modern level of water, air and waste treatment, which will guarantee the improvement of drinking water in the country. It is necessary to overcome the consequences of the destruction of the Kakhovskaya HPP, which led not only to the flooding of large areas, but also to the destruction of the ecosystem of the Kherson region, pollution of the Dnipro and the Black Sea.	Program of new water filtration in big cities (estimated cost of 30–50 billion euros). Program to provide clean water to Ukrainian villages (estimated cost 5–6 billion euros). Program for cleaning water bodies in Ukraine as a result of hostilities (estimated cost 10–15 billion euros). Program for creation of water quality monitoring in reservoirs of Ukraine (estimated cost 2–3 billion euros).	6.1, 6.2, 6.3, 6.4. 6.1, 6.2, 6.3 6.5, 6.6 6.6	Lack of funding	Creation of a compatible program with the EU regarding the implementation of filtration, water purification in Ukraine, the formation of a water supply system and the purification of reservoirs.	Water in apartments and houses can be used for drinking without boiling. All reservoirs are suitable for swimming.
Goal 7. Affordable and clean energy	Ukraine should become an important link in ensuring the energy security of the whole of Europe. In April 2023, the Cabinet of Ministers of Ukraine approved and implemented the Energy Strategy of Ukraine for the period until 2050.[d] According to it, the goals by 2050 are:[e] achieving the	Alternative energy development program (estimated cost 30–45 billion euros). The program for the construction of new nuclear reactors. (Estimated cost of	7.2 7.1 7.1, 7.a 7.3, 7.b 7.b	Lack of sufficient funding Protests against the construction of new nuclear plants Competitive struggle in the EU regarding the energy market	Define legislative norms for the participation of companies in the relevant programs, stimulate their participation at the expense of partial compensation of	Ukraine is an energy-independent country, an important gas hub in Europe, new buildings comply with the principles of climate neutrality.

(continued)

Table 1 (continued)

Objectives	Necessary steps	Necessary projects	Impact on subgoals	Obstacles	Recommendations for implementation	Vision of the development of Ukraine
	maximum level of climate neutrality, the maximum reduction of the use of coal in the energy sector, renewal and modernization of the energy infrastructure, increasing the efficiency of the use of resources in the energy sector, comprehensive integration with the markets of the European Union and the effective functioning of internal markets. Provision of the energy sector with its own resources, taking into account economic feasibility, development of alternative energy sources, new products and innovative solutions in the energy sector. By 2050, the country has the potential to increase the capacity of wind generation—up to 140 GW, solar—up to 94 GW, energy storage storage)—up to 38 GW, nuclear generation—up to 30 GW, CHP and bioenergy capacities—up to 18 GW, hydro generation—up to 9 GW.[f]	10–15 billion euros). Program for the creation of a gas hub in Ukraine (estimated cost 3–4 billion euros). Investment program for modification of energy networks to reduce losses during transportation (estimated cost 20–40 billion euros). Building energy efficiency program. (Estimated cost of 20–30 billion euros).		Unwillingness of certain energy companies to participate in the program. Not all buildings are maintained by certain companies, not all are ready to participate in the program	interest on investments and loans.	According to the strategy, natural gas consumption over the next 10 years will increase to 23 billion cubic meters of gas in 2035, and then decline to 10.4 billion cubic meters in 2050,[g] which will be achieved by gradually switching private consumers to electricity. Ukraine will increase its own gas production to 20 billion cubic meters in 2024. It is expected that industrial consumers will replace gas with hydrogen, in particular, by 2050 it is planned to produce up to 1.65 million tons

						of hydrogen per year. Also, part of the gas will be replaced with biomethane in the amount of up to 10 billion cubic meters per year. All coal-fired thermal power plants are planned to be decommissioned by 2035 and replaced by thermal power plants and thermal power plants based on natural gas and biomethane.
Goal 8. Decent work and economic growth	It is necessary to fundamentally change the concept of the tax sphere. It's no secret that Ukraine has a fairly high level of shadow economy, which is associated with various types of abuse. Taxpayers participate in schemes, and businesses and ordinary Ukrainians avoid paying taxes. It will be impossible to become a full member of the EU if dozens of tax evasion schemes exist. Ukrainians should get used to the fact that	The draft of the new tax reform, which will significantly change tax administration, will reduce direct taxation in favor of indirect taxation. (Estimated cost of implementation together with compensatory mechanisms is 30–35	8.1, 8.2, 8.3, 8.5, 10.4 8.5, 8.6, 8.8 8.9, 8.10	Lack of political will to make reforms due to the fear of a significant budget deficit. Insufficient speed of introduction of new technologies. Lack of reform of legislative acts regarding the impossibility of reconstruction of	Write down the terms of the tax reform during negotiations between Ukraine and the EU regarding accession. Conducting trainings for businesses on the possibilities of creating new jobs. Change the legislation that will allow the reconstruction of	Ukraine takes the leading places in the indices of ease of doing business, paying taxes, and developing tourism.

(continued)

Table 1 (continued)

Objectives	Necessary steps	Necessary projects	Impact on subgoals	Obstacles	Recommendations for implementation	Vision of the development of Ukraine
	paying taxes is a constitutional duty of every citizen.[h] The reform of the tax system should solve the issue of informal employment and improve the system of labour inspections. For this, changes should be made to the labor code, which will enable high mobility of workers, in particular, simple and understandable hiring of workers from other countries. According to the estimates of the Ministry of Finance, in 2022 Ukraine's GDP fell from more than $200 billion to $161 billion. However, Ukraine sets an ambitious goal[i] of increasing its dollar GDP by 6.2 times up to $1 trillion in ten years.	billion euros). The program for the creation of new high-paying technological jobs. (Estimated cost of 10–20 billion euros). Program for the creation of tourist recreation facilities in the Republic of Crimea (estimated cost of 10–15 billion euros).		recreation facilities in certain regions.	all means of recreation without unnecessary bureaucratic procedures.	
Goal 9. Industry, innovation and infrastructure	An important component of such support will be the laying of a new European-style railway track connecting Lviv, Lutsk, Uzhhorod and Chernivtsi with European hubs. Even before the start of the war, the Ukrainian leadership	The program of transition to the European railway communication (estimated cost 70–90 billion euros). Investment	9.1, 9.2 9.1, 9.3 9.1, 9.2, 9.3 9.c	Expensive cost of translation of paths. Weak profitability of the project at the first stage. The initial unwillingness of	The transition to the European railway should be written in the languages of Ukraine's accession to the EU. The first projects	Ukraine has high-speed passenger services (with an average speed above 200 km/h) on the following routes: Warsaw-

	planned to gradually introduce European railway standards. During the military operations, this issue became even more urgent. First, since Russia blocks access to Ukrainian ports, the railway has become a key route for the movement of import and export goods, and therefore the economic condition of Ukraine depends on its capacity. Second, given the significant dependence of Russia's ability to conduct military operations on railways, the transition to European-wide railways will create another obstacle to future wars.	program for the creation of high-speed rail connections in Ukraine and with foreign countries. (Estimated cost of 30–50 billion euros). Investment program for the construction of autobahns. (Estimated cost of 50–60 billion euros). Program for the maximum distribution of high-speed internet throughout the territory. (estimated cost of 5–6 billion euros).		Ukrainian citizens to widely use toll roads. Low profitability of the project in certain territories.	should be subsidized. It is necessary to carry out educational work among the citizens of Ukraine. The project may be partially subsidized.	Lviv-Kyiv-Poltava-Kharkiv, Luhansk-Donetsk-Zaporizhia-Dnipro-Kryvyi Rih-Odesa-Kyshiniv, Chernihiv-Kyiv, Vinnytsia-Odesa-Simferopol-Sevastopol. All regional centres are connected by paid or free autobahns (at least 2 lanes in each direction). 5G technology has been introduced and is widely used in Ukraine.
Goal 10. Reducing inequality	Before the war, this goal was achieved in Ukraine. However, the war led to a significant redistribution of people's incomes, devaluation of their savings. Thus, the level of economic inequality is expected to increase, which can only be solved by a balanced economic and tax policy. It is	Adaptation program for military personnel and war victims. (Estimated cost of 3–4 billion euros).	10.1, 10.2, 10.4.	The unwillingness of Ukrainian citizens to accept aid	Conducting educational events, staff training.	By 2030, Ukraine has overcome the consequences of the war with Russia, ensured a decrease in the Gini coefficient to the level of neighboring countries.

(continued)

Table 1 (continued)

Objectives	Necessary steps	Necessary projects	Impact on subgoals	Obstacles	Recommendations for implementation	Vision of the development of Ukraine
	recommended to carry out a large-scale tax reform that will stimulate economic growth and reduce unemployment.					
Goal 11. Sustainable development of cities and communities	According to the KSE estimate, the total amount of direct material damage caused by Russia to the infrastructure of Ukraine in just one year of the full-scale war reached almost $144 billion,[j] of which about $102 billion are houses, infrastructure, and factories. In total, more than 150,000 residential buildings were destroyed buildings, including private, multi-apartment buildings, and dormitories, were damaged or destroyed. Taking into account the ferocity of the fighting in March–June 2023, the destruction of the Kakhovskaya HPP, the flooding of a large area, the amount of damage can be multiplied many times over. It is also very important to change the legislation, according to which the connection to power grids, roads, and water supply will be	The program of restoration of buildings, damaged infrastructure, creation of new technological infrastructure, development of public transport, development of recreation systems in cities. (Estimated cost of 75–100 billion euros). The program for the destruction of long-term buildings by disposal or commissioning. (Estimated cost of 10–13 billion euros).	11.1, 11.2, 11.3, 11.5, 11.7 11.2, 11.3	Absence of plans to restore cities and create new infrastructure. Available regulatory acts.	Obtaining technological assistance from the EU as part of Ukraine's preparation for accession. Change the legislation to encourage either the destruction or the commissioning of long-term buildings that have lost their owners.	In the cities of Ukraine, it is more convenient to use public transport than to drive your own car, the time for a full trip by public transport between two arbitrary points in the capital does not exceed 30 minutes, all residents have access to recreational areas within walking distance.

	significantly simplified, which will allow to promote the development of settlement communities in the first place.					
Goal 12. Responsible consumption and production	Ukraine needs significant capital investments in the energy sector, which will allow to update energy supply networks and reduce electricity losses several times over. A huge amount of construction waste accumulated in Ukraine, because a significant number of cities are almost completely destroyed, this requires a special program for its processing. No less threatening are the remnants of military equipment, which not only pollute the environment but also carry the potential threat of explosions. For such regions, recovery should be based on the principles of the circular economy, using efficient technologies and methods of secondary use of materials. This will provide new opportunities for employment and support for economic development after the war. For example, the secondary use, repair and recycling sectors can be a source of jobs.	Smart waste recycling program. Before the war, about 420 million tons of industrial waste was generated in Ukraine every year, including 250 million tons of coal slag, 100 million tons of metallurgical slag, 11 million tons of household slag.[k] This means that the main emphasis should be placed on changing industrial production and the use of waste. Taking into account the fact that even before the war Ukraine accumulated 15 billion tons of waste, and the war significantly increased this amount, the	12.5, 12.6	The high cost of implementing the program. Implementing a circular economy after the war can be a difficult and rather expensive task due to the specifics of the situation, but taking these principles into account can contribute to a more sustainable and effective post-conflict recovery.	A change in legislation that will stimulate waste recycling.	In Ukraine, the level of waste recycling into new resources reaches at least 50%, energy production from waste processing ensures the functioning of small cities.

(continued)

Table 1 (continued)

Objectives	Necessary steps	Necessary projects	Impact on subgoals	Obstacles	Recommendations for implementation	Vision of the development of Ukraine
		only way out is the implementation of the state policy of regulating the circular economy. (Estimated cost of 20–30 billion euros).				
Goal 13. Mitigation of the consequences of climate change	Ukraine will require significant capital investments to restore the Kakhovka HPP, the ecosystem of the Kherson region, as well as other regions affected by military operations.	The program for the restoration of the ecosystem of the regions of Ukraine. (Estimated cost of 20–30 billion euros).	13.1, 13.2	Slow restoration of the ecology of the affected areas.	The goals of the program should be agreed upon during the accession negotiations between Ukraine and the EU.	Ukraine has achieved a steady trend to improve environmental standards of living.
Goal 14. Conservation of marine resources	After the war, Ukraine will face the need to overcome the consequences of the war in the Black and Azov Seas and coastal zones. It will also be necessary to restore the composition of the fauna in these seas. At the same time, we should hope for the implementation of joint projects with the countries of the Black Sea Basin.	Fauna restoration program of the Dnipro, Black and Azov seas. (Estimated cost of 2–5 billion euros).	14.1, 14.3	Reluctance to participate in the program of the countries of the Black Sea Basin	The goals of the program and its financing should be agreed upon during the accession negotiations between Ukraine and the EU.	Ukraine has clean water in the Dnieper, Black and Azov seas, the number of fish in the seas has increased by at least 30% compared to 2022.

Goal 15. Protection and restoration of terrestrial ecosystems	Similar actions should be carried out throughout the territory of Ukraine, in particular: Demining the territory, cleaning the territory from the remnants of military actions, restoring the landscape, planting trees and other plantations, increasing the fauna in nature reserves. It should be noted that this process will not be quick and will take at least the next decade.	The program for the restoration of flora and fauna of war-affected regions of Ukraine (estimated cost of 1–3 billion euros).	15.1, 15.3, 15.9	Lack of funds for restoration.	The financing of the corresponding program should be secured in the state budget during the post-war reconstruction.	Ukraine has territories that are safe for people and animals to live in, and the presence of forests allows the oxygen level in the air to be restored.
Goal 16. Peace, justice and strong institutions	Such state institutions as the constitutional court of Ukraine and the Supreme Court of Ukraine, which have acquired a negative reputation for corruption in recent years, should be strengthened. To this end, the real independence of NABU and other law enforcement agencies should be promoted, and the active citizenship of Ukrainians should be stimulated. The situation in Ukraine with state procurement is currently difficult. Even in the conditions of war, clearly dishonest and non-transparent procurements are carried out, which have no public benefit. Accordingly, a system of control and audit of public funds should be developed and	Draft legislation to strengthen the transparency of state bodies. (Estimated cost of 0.1 billion euros).	16.5, 16.6	Political resistance of certain forces.	Requirements for changes in legislation in this area must be agreed upon in order to receive financial assistance and loans.	Ukraine has transparent bodies with zero tolerance for corruption.

(continued)

Table 1 (continued)

Objectives	Necessary steps	Necessary projects	Impact on subgoals	Obstacles	Recommendations for implementation	Vision of the development of Ukraine
	implemented, especially in the defence and security sectors. Solving this issue is directly related to the further strengthening of competition protection and the state's anti-monopoly policy, which should contribute to the de-oligarchization of the economy.					
Goal 17. Partnership for sustainable development	Ukraine should fully complete the transition to a digital state, which will significantly reduce the level of bureaucracy and corruption. It is necessary to significantly change the approach to the collection of statistical information, which requires a significant reform of the state statistics Service of Ukraine and its integration with the relevant bodies in the EU. It will also be obvious that there will be a movement towards the implementation of normative acts regarding the integration of Ukraine into the EU.	Program of full digitization of official document flow, banking, requests to public services, transition to a cashless economy. (Estimated cost of 3–5 billion euros).	17.1, 17.13, 17.17	Lack of desire to implement projects in certain areas.	Stimulate digitization in all spheres of life by influencing education.	Ukraine is a "smartphone country", the transition to digital democracy is underway, the level of corruption and shadowing is falling due to the cashless economy.

Source: compiled by the author

[a] The number of economic entities in Ukraine. URL: https://dostup.pravda.com.ua/request/kilkist_subiektiv_ghospodariuvan_27#incoming-368906

[b] Sales of combine harvesters in Ukraine decreased by more than 2 times. URL: https://agravery.com/uk/posts/show/prodazi-kombajniv-v-ukraini-znizilis. . .

[c] Shmyhal told how much demining of Ukraine will cost. URL: https://www.slovoidilo.ua/2023/04/05/novyna/finansy/shmyhal-rozpoviv-yaku-sumu-obijdetsya-rozminuvannya-ukrayiny

[d] Decree of the CMU dated April 21, 2023 No. 373-r "On the approval of the Energy Strategy of Ukraine for the period until 2050". URL: https://zakon.rada.gov.ua/laws/show/373-2023-%D1%80#Text

[e] Energy strategy. URL: https://www.mev.gov.ua/reforma/enerhetychna-stratehiya

[f] Ministry of Energy of Ukraine. URL: https://mev.gov.ua/

[g] Davydenko B., Chaika O. Very strategic plans. URL: https://forbes.ua/money/duzhe-strategichni-plani-spozhivannya-gazu-10-mlrd-vidobutok-215-mlrd-kubiv-forbes-oznayomivsya-z-chastinoyu-zasekrechenoi-energostrategii-2050-08052023-13493

[h] New rules await Ukrainians: in order to join the EU, it is necessary to get rid of shadow salaries, the European Commission is satisfied with only a few sectors. URL: https://news.obozrevatel.com/ukr/abroad/putin-hrin-tobi-scho-mae-skazati-bajden-schob-zemlya-ne-zgorila-v-yadernomu-vogni-intervyu-z-fejginim.htm

[i] Ukraine aims to increase the dollar GDP by 6.2 times in ten years—a conference in London. URL: https://www.epravda.com.ua/news/2023/06/21/701428/

[j] URL: https://kse.ua/about-the-school/news/during-the-year-of-the-full-scale-war-the-total-amount-of-damages-caused-russia-to-ukraine-s-infrastructure-has-reached-almost-143-8-billion/

[k] Ruda M.V., Yaremchuk T.S., Bortnikova M.G. Circular economy in Ukraine: adaptation of European experience. URL: https://science.lpnu.ua/sites/default/files/journal-paper/2021/jun/23807/menedzhment121-214-224.pdf

relations. To strengthen economic growth, regulatory legislation should be modified and liberalized, which together with security guarantees (by NATO or other players) will lead to the emergence of a new European economic centre for the production, logistics and storage of goods, and especially energy. This will require Ukraine to change its policy from passive to proactive, becoming a full-fledged regional centre.

Key Take-Aways

1. After Ukraine's victory in the war, geopolitics should change significantly. Instead of total globalization, a period of regionalization is expected, in which regional centres will play a key role. Due to the introduction of new technologies, the replacement of Russia in the energy market, and digitalization, Ukraine has a chance to become one of such centres in Eastern Europe. The result will depend on the political will of the country's leaders and the speed of liberal reforms.
2. As part of achieving the SDGs, a road map with specific goals and programs for implementation has been developed for Ukraine. In part, these programs can be financed by both Ukraine and the EU as part of pre-accession assistance, and these programs can also be of an investment nature. The implementation of these programs will allow Ukraine to make significant progress in achieving the SDGs by 2030. However, a significant obstacle may be the prolongation of the war, which will exhaust the population and kill the potential for reforms.
3. A significant level of financial assistance should be provided to Ukraine to restore the economy. Such financing should include reparations from the aggressor country and financial assistance from the EU and the USA. Private investment in Ukraine is very important, which will stimulate the development and introduction of new technologies, which means faster integration of citizens into the European community.

From Crisis to Opportunity: Embracing Sustainable Development Goals and Artificial Intelligence in the Transformative Innovations World

Răzvan Sorin Şerbu and Bogdan Ştefan Mârza

Abstract This chapter explores the analytical junctions of Artificial Intelligence (AI) and Sustainable Development Goals (SDGs). The chapter highlights the important need for decisive actions in the face of a triple planetary crisis encompassing climate change, pollution, and biodiversity loss. It encourages for a commitment to leveraging AI to fulfill its promises, particularly in promoting digital equality, advancing the SDGs, and connecting AI for the greater good. The chapter explores the potential of AI, together with other high-potential technologies like virtual reality and digital twins, in driving sustainable operations and addressing pressing challenges. The discussion extends to the role of AI in reconstruction efforts for countries facing destruction, emphasizing the importance of systemic changes and practical applications of AI to optimize outcomes for millions of individuals. Through a nuanced understanding of the complex interdependencies between AI, sustainable development, and environmental supervision, the document highlights the transformative potential of AI in shaping a more sustainable and equitable future.

Introduction

The promising discourse surrounding the ramifications of artificial intelligence (AI) on economic dynamics and Sustainable Development Goals (SDGs) has garnered considerable attention. Moreover, the situation is complicated by new conflicts that make even harder the anticipation and planning process so necessary for reaching the sustainable development goals for a healthier world. Currently that

R. S. Şerbu (✉)
Management, Marketing and Business Administration, Lucian Blaga Universtiy of Sibiu, Sibiu, Romania
e-mail: razvan.serbu@ulbsibiu.ro

B. Ş. Mârza
Finance and Accounting, Lucian Blaga Universtiy of Sibiu, Sibiu, Romania
e-mail: bogdan.marza@ulbsibiu.ro

S. Nate (ed.), *Ukraine's Journey to Recovery, Reform and Post-War Reconstruction*, Contributions to Security and Defence Studies,
https://doi.org/10.1007/978-3-031-66434-2_4

are almost 2 years of war in Ukraine and 2 months of war in Gaza, and all of these without good news for seeing the light of peace very soon. All this uncertainty and damages will demand a lot of effort for reconstruction. Conscious this hypothesis, the reconstruction must be done alert and persuasive, taking in consideration the humanity benefits in both short and long term. Within this chapter, we will try to present certain facets that seems controversial and need more and more world attention. There exists a prevailing anxiety among the public that automated entities, commonly referred to as robots, may supplant human roles, precipitating a unsafe scene for human existence. Pessimistic speculations contend that these technological developments could exacerbate challenges to human survival, rendering our existence more arduous.

In the perspective of economic sustainability, it is imperative not to underscore the profound impact of new innovations including artificial intelligence that holds in navigation transformative advancements. Artificial intelligence (AI), as an innovative bond, can satisfies diverse sectors, offering unparalleled potentialities for sustainable development. As we move towards the peak of this technological era, it becomes increasingly obvious that AI's integrative applications can go beyond simple computational functionalities.

However, a confident outlook on the future conjectures, need substantial prospects for positive outcomes. I invite the readers to peruse this chapter, where constructive reflections are expanded upon. This journey aims to unravel the complexities underlying AI transcending dominant ambiguities and misconceptions. This chapter here, adopts an analytical approach, related to traditional practices in data science.

The Pursuit of SDGS Through AI

From the beginning it is imperative to recognize that the requirement for ensuring the optimal realization of AI lies collectively upon humanity. As we occur nearly a decade post the adoption of the 2030 Agenda for Sustainable Development, the SDGs face a trajectory deviating off course. A surge in poverty and hunger accompanies a triple planetary crisis—climate change, pollution, and biodiversity loss—pushing humanity to the edge. The critical crisis before us demands decisive choices. In this chapter, I support for a commitment to the scenario wherein AI fulfils its promises. In this journey it is important to associate with the cause of digital equality, the SDGs, and the pursuit of AI for the greater good. The early era of generative AI is, with the scenario of AI's future, yet to unfold.

The focal point of this chapter turns around the junction of AI and the realization of the SDGs in reconstruction of any country that suffers from destruction. Various methodologies are being explored to achieve sustainable operations, and AI stands as a prominent player in this landscape. This exploration is interwoven with other high-potential technologies such as virtual reality and digital twins, encompassing a broad and intricate domain.

Initiating our exploration, we mention that sustainability, conventionally depicted as a triad of societal, ecological, and economic domains, necessitates a mode of existence and operation that avoids jeopardizing future generations. Presently, the global situation is heavily influenced by material resources and tangible assets, demanding a radical shift in our approach to value creation. The imperative is to transcend any material-centric growth and embrace a paradigm where intangible assets, the intangible aspects shaping our lives and future, assume significance and consequence. In this regards we must focus more on circular economy and renewable resources.

Investigating into the economic landscape, the application of AI exemplifies a substantial market projection. Anticipations indicate a staggering market value exceeding billions of dollars within the next years. Notably, this sector represents the fastest-growing authority throughout a dynamically changing economic landscape.

Moving to the root of this chapter, the pursuit of SDGs through AI, particularly within the context of industrial development, demands more attention. Unprecedentedly, we confront a reduction in material resources, marking a departure from a trajectory spanning over two centuries. Examining the course of the last two centuries and three industrial revolutions, material mobilization, electrification, and automation have been the symbol. The present crisis necessitates a shift from the global economy fashioned in the 1970s towards a smarter economy.

Reaching the Sustainable Development Goals (SDGs) necessitates significant policy reforms informed by science and facilitated by technology. It requires a close integration of sustainable development, technological advancement, and digitalization. This involves embracing a comprehensive and responsible strategy, mobilizing extensive collaborative events across various contexts, involving diverse stakeholders and disciplines. It also involves leveraging technology, policy frameworks, and social factors as enablers. Additionally, compelling narratives for transformation are crucial, capable of effectively engaging policymakers, businesses, academics, and the entire civil society in the pursuit of this overarching plan for the well-being of humanity and the planet (Del Río et al., 2021).

This transformation underscores the inclusion of humans back into the assembly of activities, challenging the historical trend where machines had succeeded human roles. The predicted cooperation of machines, AI, and humans, holds essential significance in addressing SDGs, effecting changes in industry, infrastructure, and innovation. The future, as projected, accentuates the predominance of intangible assets as the foremost business opportunity.

Transformative Synergy in Integrating Military Expertise in Shaping a Post-War Sustainable Economic Development

The expertise that an army is acquire every moment, especially during a war, can and should be transfer to the development of an economy expressly in a post war time.

A similarity can be generated between priorities in the need of an army for military technology and innovation to meet the challenges of warfare and sustainable economy. The same principle applies to both, so the sustainable economy also needs those new technologies that plays a crucial role in finding solutions to environmental and resource problems.

While strategic investments in ICTs will not solve all the economic challenges facing post-conflict countries, a clearer view of how a mission's technology footprint can influence the economy of a host country can aid in the planning of missions that meet their security mandates while also playing a positive role in the economic development of the host country (Martin-Shields & Bodanac, 2018).

Technology is becoming extremely important nowadays for energy efficiency and many more. In the military context, technologies such as drones, and electronic warfare equipment are essential for efficient defending operations same as for the sustainable economy, innovative technologies can help increase energy efficiency, reduce carbon emissions, and optimize the use of natural resources. Technological development can help both security and sustainability. Army strategy emphasizes to keep pace a comparable technological development like the partners or adversary. In a sustainable economy, all the partners or adversary should sustain innovation and technological development that are essential to fight the climate urge and find sustainable solutions to environmental challenges.

After the ending of hostilities and the beginning of reconstruction, a strategic incorporation of the military defeat industry into sustainable economic endeavours emerges as a viable approach. The integration involves a nuanced exploration of possibilities aimed at aligning the industry's capabilities with the objectives of sustainable development.

Engaging in a transfer of technology and innovation constitutes a fundamental strategy. This initiative centres around adapting advancements originally designed for military applications, such as cutting-edge materials and communication systems, for deployment within the sustainable economy. This adaptation contributes to the evolution of eco-friendly technologies and reinforces the development of sustainable practices.

The industry's wealth of expertise in infrastructure development becomes a focal point for post-war reconstruction projects with a sustainability emphasis. Drawing upon the industry's efficiency in swiftly restoring essential infrastructure, this approach accelerates the transition to sustainable environments. The focus shifts towards green infrastructure and urban planning that is ecologically conscious.

To capitalize on the skill sets prevalent in the military defeat industry, implementing programs facilitating personnel transition emerges as a critical component. These programs aim to redirect individuals from military-focused roles to positions supportive of renewable energy, environmental conservation, and various other sustainable pursuits.

Additionally, assigning the military defeat industry to spearhead environmental remediation projects becomes a proactive strategy. Tasking the industry with addressing issues such as pollution and ecosystem damage resulting from conflict aligns with overarching sustainable development objectives.

The establishment of collaborations between the military defeat industry and private sector entities engaged in sustainability emerges as a potent avenue. Such partnerships leverage the strengths of both sectors, with the military industry contributing resources and capabilities to private initiatives aligned with environmental and social responsibility.

An allocation of funding from military research and development budgets to projects focused on sustainable technologies serves as a strategic redirection. This shift accelerates the progress of green technologies and renewable energy solutions, contributing significantly to the evolution of a sustainable economy.

Creating education and training programs within the military defeat industry emerges as a transformative strategy. These programs foster a culture of sustainability within the industry, enabling professionals to contribute more effectively to sustainable economic initiatives.

Furthermore, encouraging the industry to transition to renewable energy sources and adopt energy-efficient practices stands out as a proactive measure. Embracing sustainable energy practices within the industry sets a precedent for other sectors, contributing to the establishment of a more sustainable and resilient energy landscape.

Unfortunately, it must be acknowledged that no political solution guarantees Ukraine safety after the war. The war showed that even participation in various organizations would not guarantee the assistance or participation of other countries in military operations. It is obvious that the only means of protection remain to be the Ukrainian armed forces and diplomacy. It is the combination of the two that makes it possible to repel aggression and receive joint actions from allies (Silviu et al., 2023).

Through these integrated strategies, the military defeat industry can play a transformative role in post-war reconstruction, contributing its resources and capabilities to foster a society that embraces environmental consciousness and social responsibility.

Tech Fusion Shaping Tomorrow's Realities

Engaging in the practicality of realizing this vision, essential technologies like artificial intelligence, virtual reality, cloud, or digital twins emerge. Positioned as transformative agents, these technologies operate at the link of sustainable operations, innovation, and infrastructure. The imperative, within this transformative landscape, is to accentuate the real-time integration of objects, services, and human entities. Given the accelerating pace of change, real-time applications emerge as the cornerstone of future operations. Nevertheless, it is imperative to underscore that technology, in and of itself, does not shape the world; rather, its efficacy lies in the manner of its application. Therefore, a discerning approach is requisite to harness the potential of these technologies for reshaping work paradigms and business models.

Transitioning to this technology, virtual reality, originally, virtual reality entailed specialized hardware and software tailored for creating virtual environments, a trajectory propelled by NASA's advancements. However, the nomenclature "virtual reality" was popularized by Jaron Lanier and traced its origins to science fiction. Over the years, virtual reality has been erroneously associated with recreational applications, such as gaming, which belies its profound implications for transforming our understanding of reality. The expansive continuum of XR (extended reality) encapsulates the transition from wholly synthesized reality (virtual reality) to the coexistence of physical and virtual realities (mixed reality). This continuum empowers us to perceive and interact with both visible and intangible aspects of our environment.

In the lines that will follow will determine how cloud computing can withstand sustainability and green economy. In the cloud services industry, economics and green energy are closely linked, with an increased focus on sustainability. Many cloud services companies are investing in renewable energy sources, such as wind farms or solar installations, to power their data centres. This not only helps to reduce carbon emissions, but also to saving costs in the long run, as renewables can be more economical than traditional energy sources. Cloud services companies focus on optimising efficiency of their data centres to reduce operational costs. Technologies such as convection cooling, server virtualisation and intelligent energy management help save energy and money.

The green energy and cloud server economy case study illustrates how the industry technology industry is adapting to help reduce environmental impact and save costs in the long term, while maintaining operational efficiency and competitiveness. This transition reflects the importance of understanding the interaction between the economy and sustainability in today's digital world.

The other technology in focus, digital twins, emerges as a central player in addressing the challenges posed by the reduction of material resources. The historical trajectory of the last two centuries, marked by industrial revolutions, witnessed the primacy of material mobilization, electrification, and automation. The contemporary imperative is to transition from a physically growing global economy to a smarter economy, reinstating the centrality of human involvement. Digital twins, operating at the interface of data infrastructure and human experiences, offer a potent framework for orchestrating solutions to the challenges posed by sustainable development. The differentiation between the back end, housing data infrastructure and machines, and the front end, where human experiences and decision-making processes unfold, delineates the architecture of digital twin implementation.

Among the complexities of the twenty-first century, dealing with an increasing global population, surpassing nine and a half billion by 2050, the challenges include securing clean water, sustainable energy, and education. The environment struggles with issues of profound gravity, including environmental degradation, prejudice, poverty, and hunger. Inadequate thus far, attempts to redress these challenges induct hope in the transformative potential of AI. The opportunity that AI presents lies in its capacity to address multifaceted issues afflicting humanity, offering practical solutions that can benefit millions.

AI's Transformative Impact on Agriculture in Ukraine and Beyond

While AI may not be a panacea, it equips us with fundamental tools to establish systems that hold promise in mitigating critical issues. This involves leveraging AI's core capabilities to tackle persistent global predicaments such as hunger, scarcity, epidemics, and overall health and well-being. The current application of AI extends to age-old industries like agriculture, where it integrates diverse data sources—be it from combines, weather satellites, or fields—to enhance decision-making. Through AI, farmers gain the ability to synthesize vast datasets, enabling more informed choices in managing their operations.

AI's impact is akin to a tidal change morphing the very axis of our lives. I fundamentally believe that AI can act as a force for good across the world. Equally, I am not oblivious to the potential for its misuse. We have a great responsibility to ensure that AI can live up to its potential—whether it be job creation, medical advancement, transformation of industry processes, access to better education, or making our everyday lives easier through countless conveniences—both big and small (Lee & Qiufan, 2021).

We can notice that Ukraine is a key global agricultural centre and plays a critical role in supplying oilseeds and grains to the world market. With over 55 percent of its land designated as arable, agriculture in Ukraine employs an important percent of the population and stands as the cornerstone of its most vital exports.

Ukraine agriculture has been evolving since it achieved independence in 1991, following the breakup of the Soviet Union. State and collective farms were officially dismantled in 2000. Farm property was divided among the farm workers in the form of land shares and most new shareholders leased their land back to newly formed private agricultural associations. The sudden loss of State agricultural subsidies had an enormous effect on every aspect of Ukrainian agriculture (World Data Center for Geoinformatics and Sustainable Development, n.d.).

Agriculture functions as the foundational pillar of Ukraine's economic structure, providing sustenance for a substantial demographic segment. The nation's abundant arable lands, propitious climate conditions, and investment environment have not only sustained the domestic populace but have also propelled the exportation of food products to regions encompassing Asia, Africa, and the Middle East. Nevertheless, the dynamics inherent in Ukraine's agricultural sector are intricate, marked by the coexistence of large-scale agribusiness and family farming (Foreign Agricultural Service U.S. Department of Agriculture, n.d.).

Preceding the onset of hostilities of war, the agricultural domain in Ukraine witnessed prosperity. However, the advent of the Russian invasion has instigated disruption and posed challenges to the sector. The ongoing contest for resources and governmental support between corporate entities and family-based agricultural efforts persists, engendering inquiries into the future trajectory of Ukrainian agriculture. As Ukraine attempts to navigate the course of recovery, we extend an invitation to explore the impact of the new technological breakthroughs.

As we delve deeper into the potentialities of AI, it becomes evident that it does not mean to be a universal cure-all but rather furnishes essential instruments to address pressing challenges. Its utility lies in instigating systemic changes that could ameliorate issues with practical value. This pragmatic application of AI carries significance in optimizing outcomes for the 7 million people who stand to benefit from these technologies.

In the area of artificial intelligence, a current dialogue unfolds around its role in farming—an ancient profession now incorporating cutting-edge technology. AI facilitates the integration of disparate datasets, ranging from machinery inputs to satellite-derived weather information and field-specific data. The fusion of these diverse datasets, guided by artificial intelligence, empowers farmers to make informed decisions that resonate with modern technological advancements.

The implementation of AI as a solution involves the proactive dispensation of recommendations to farmers, delineating strategies to augment land productivity. AI's formidable prowess and latent potential lie in its adeptness at addressing challenges necessitating extensive computational and pattern recognition capabilities, complexities that often confound human comprehension. In the realm of pharmaceuticals, the trajectory of drug design is already witnessing transformative changes through the employment of molecular models. For instance, the identification of optimal drugs for addressing distinct problems, such as combating virus proteins, is achieved by conducting meticulous searches within molecular frameworks.

The United Nations summit, believing ambitious goals, stands poised to attain success through the leveraging of artificial intelligence—aptly deemed the dormant behemoth of beta. Within the expansive repository of global data lies the potential, upon refinement and adept tagging, to be harnessed in addressing multifarious challenges ranging from famine and human trafficking to disrupting cycles of economic destitution. The symbiotic relationship between progress in AI and advancements in diverse domains underscores its transformative potential. Enhanced machine learning algorithms not only contribute to predictive medical diagnostics but also extend their efficacy to refining self-driving vehicles, exemplifying the profound impact AI could exert, potentially shaping the contours of the nascent civilization it is ushering in at this very moment.

Unveiling Promising Opportunities Towards Sustainable Reconstruction: Collaborative AI Solutions

Explorations into the application of AI technologies unveil promising avenues, particularly in less celebrated and underexplored realms. These seemingly austere domains wield substantial influence on our collective future, specifically in the pursuit of a sustainable trajectory culminating in the achievement of net-zero targets over the ensuing decades. Among the often-overlooked sectors with substantial environmental footprints, agriculture takes centre stage, given its direct responsibility for approximately 10 percent of global greenhouse gas emissions. The proposition emerges to embark on the development of AI technologies geared towards enhancing agricultural stability.

In recent decades, the old construction industry has undergone swift digital technology advancements and witnessed the expansion of big data. Notably, there has been considerable focus on integrating AI, aiming to impart machines with human-like intelligence and reasoning capabilities. It has been observed that various AI techniques have generated substantial value in transforming the construction industry, fostering a more dependable, automated, self-adjusting, time-efficient, and cost-effective approach to Construction Equipment Management (CEM) (Pan & Zhang, 2021).

Unlike traditional computational methods and expert judgments, the promising field of AI excels in addressing intricate and dynamic challenges amid significant uncertainty and extensive data, thereby delivering more precise and compelling outcomes for tactical decision-making that can and will help Ukraine a lot in their decision-making process.

The conceptualization and development of AI systems mirror the mechanisms through which human learning and knowledge expansion occur. Initial requisites include the deployment of observational tools like cameras, sensors, and scanners to collect high-quality environmental data, echoing the human reliance on sensory inputs. Subsequently, the need arises for a mechanism facilitating the seamless dissemination of information across various systems, mirroring human communication via the internet and the cloud. The apex involves the establishment of an AI-based decision support system, capable of learning and deciding, akin to human decision-making but distinguished by its unparalleled capacity to automate processes and discern patterns across vast and diverse datasets—a domain where AI systems invariably outperform their human counterparts.

The inclination toward contributing to a more sustainable world, particularly for the prosperity and well-being of future generations, stems especially from a paternal love for children. In delving into the discourse of sustainability and development, the imperative surfaces for a development paradigm that caters to present needs without compromising the capabilities of succeeding generations. This involves a concerted effort towards both environmental stability and financial sustainability, with agriculture serving as a pivotal sector. The financial sustainability of interventions aimed at mitigating greenhouse gas emissions, spanning from the farm to the consumer's fork, assumes paramount importance.

Another facet of this AI-based decision support involves the seamless sharing of information across the entire supply chain. This facilitates the aggregation, analysis, and processing of larger datasets, providing comprehensive insights not only within a specific farm but across diverse agricultural landscapes. The third aspect centres on decision-making, necessitating the development of bespoke AI technologies, encompassing machine learning and artificial neural networks. These technologies, like to those employed in contemporary smartphones for image processing, can be trained using observed and shared data.

The past decade has witnessed a notable rise in the prevalence of digital technologies. This shift has prompted policymakers to transition their emphasis from the diffusion of these technologies to their utilization by governments, businesses, and individuals. In fact, digital technologies and the internet have emerged as primary drivers in the transformation of the contemporary world and its economy (Eduard & Ioana, 2017).

In emphasizing the reputation of AI's adaptability and efficacy in navigating novel and challenging scenarios, such as climate change and sustainability, it becomes apparent that AI's transformative potential extends beyond conventional paradigms. While the metaphorical comparison of data to the "new oil" may not universally resonate, the undeniable reality persists that artificial intelligence is poised to fundamentally redefine global business dynamics. In the book "AI Superpowers: China, Silicon Valley, and the New World Order" Kaifu Lee's assertion, quoting PricewaterhouseCoopers estimations, forecasts a substantial infusion of $15.7 billion into the global GDP by 2030 through the widespread deployment of AI (Lee, 2018).

The allure of AI, with its potent tools and methodologies, has captivated interest for an extended duration. Its potential to expedite progress in sustainability aligns with the United Nations' Sustainable Development Goals (SDGs). Some engagement with the early drafts of the SDGs, coupled with the environmental ethos instilled sometimes ago, set the stage for a sustained fascination with the interplay between human activities and the planet.

While the SDGs encapsulate a diverse spectrum of objectives, only three to five goals are directly tied to environmental concerns, namely climate action, life below water, and life on land. The interconnectedness of these goals with others, such as clean water, food security, job stability, and income equality, underscores the pivotal role each facet plays in fostering an individual's capacity to champion environmental causes.

Addressing the prevailing concerns about AI's environmental impact, especially in relation to carbon footprints generated by large data centres and model training, requires a nuanced understanding. Although the carbon footprint of training AI models surpasses that of an individual flight, the comparison is inherently flawed. Large-scale AI models, collaboratively developed by thousands, transcend the scope of individual actions. Nevertheless, acknowledging the public fear and misconceptions surrounding AI becomes crucial for informed discourse and dispelling unfounded fears.

Recent research concerns, such as those by earth.org and studies published in Nature, further delineate the 17 SDGs into three categories: environment, economy, and society. Contrary to concerns about AI's potential detrimental effects on certain aspects of sustainability, these studies shed light on the technology's affirmative role. The analysis suggests that AI can substantially enhance the prospects of achieving these goals, often outweighing any negative repercussions.

Conceptualizations of sustainable AI nevertheless did consistently reference the sustainable development framework associated with the SDGs, however, validating the use of that paradigm to elaborate the concept in the context of public sector governance (Wilson & van der Velden, 2022).

Exploring into specific impacts, the intersection of AI and climate change emerges as a realm where AI contributes significantly to global efforts. Notably, AI interventions, when applied across various regions, exhibit a substantial reduction of greenhouse gas emissions by an average of 4 percent, reaching up to 6 percent in certain regions. This noteworthy impact positions AI as a potent ally in the ongoing struggle to curb climate change.

The complex interplay between AI and employment dynamics adds another layer to the sustainability discourse. The question of whether AI will predominantly replace or create jobs hinges on industry, sector, and geographical context. While certain manual jobs may become obsolete, the evolving landscape also heralds the creation of new roles, such as AI explicators, model maintainers, and industry innovators. Thus, the impact of AI on employment is contingent upon a multitude of factors.

As the discourse on AI and sustainability unfolds, it becomes evident that while challenges exist, the potential for positive impact outweighs the drawbacks. Collaborative efforts, rooted in diverse skill sets and interdisciplinary collaboration, become paramount for co-creating solutions that transcend individual perspectives and foster a collective vision of a sustainable future.

Conclusion

In conclusion, the confluence of AI and sustainability represents a dynamic landscape, marked by both challenges and unprecedented opportunities. As we navigate this intricate terrain, the imperative is not just to acknowledge the transformative potential of AI but to actively engage in co-creating solutions that harmonize technological advancements with global sustainability objectives. The journey towards a sustainable future demands a collective commitment to innovation, collaboration, and a nuanced understanding of the intricate interdependencies that govern our relationship with the environment and each other.

Within the prerogative of sustainable development goals, the absence of AI-derived insights poses a substantial impediment, adaptation decision-making and course correction formidable tasks. To elucidate the transformative potential, specific use cases exemplify the profound alterations attainable through AI applications. Yet, considering Merriam-Webster's second definition of intelligence — the adept application of knowledge to enhance one's environment — prompts introspection into the practicality and necessity of integrating AI-driven wisdom.

The interconnection between sustainability and AI, indicates a collaborative effort. Stakeholders at the local level, including academia, corporate entities, and the public, must collaborate to cultivate a comprehensive understanding of how AI can authentically contribute to sustainability goals. The responsibility falls not only on the creators of AI models but also on the end-users to discern and rectify any inadvertent biases or restrictions, ensuring ethical and equitable deployment.

This chapter is also a call to action emerges, persuasive collaboration and interdisciplinary interconnection are necessary to link AI and sustainability. This appeal extends beyond theoretical discourse, emphasizing the imperative to transform research and theoretical competency into a sustainable reconstruction of any country after a war, with tangible products and companies that appreciate sustainability. The ultimate aspiration is not only to be a research inspiration but to actively participate in shaping discourse, contributing substantively, and effecting positive change through the development and implementation of AI-driven solutions.

On the synergy between artificial intelligence and sustainability, it is vital to highlight that the responsibility for development this connection rests not just on technological innovators but also on the broader spectrum of society. As we analyse this intellectual panorama, the imperative to cultivate an inclusive dialogue, one that transcends disciplinary boundaries, becomes increasingly evident.

The call to action at the local level extends beyond mere collaboration; it necessitates a concerted effort to bridge the gaps between academia, corporate entities, and the public transcending theoretical boundaries. This convergence of diverse perspectives aims not only to deepen our understanding of AI's potential contributions to sustainability but also to address ethical considerations and potential environmental ramifications.

In the spirit of develop this collective understanding, it becomes imperative to engage with ethical and environmental concerns surrounding AI. Through such engagements, a more profound understanding of the ethical dimensions of AI emerges, lay the foundations for informed decision-making and responsible implementation. However, the transformational potential lies not just in theoretical frameworks but in the translation of ideas into realities. By establishing a robust presence at this virtual table, Ukraine can assume a leadership role, contributing meaningfully to the global discourse on sustainable AI for reconstruction.

References

Del Río, G., Castro, M. C., Fernández, G., & Colsa, Á. U. (2021). Unleashing the convergence amid digitalization and sustainability towards pursuing the Sustainable Development Goals (SDGs):

A holistic review. *Journal of Cleaner Production, 280*, 122204. https://doi.org/10.1016/j.jclepro.2020.122204
Eduard, S., & Ioana, A. B. (2017). A comprehensive analysis regarding DESI country progress for Romania relative to the European average trend. In *Balkan Rrion Conference on Engineering and Business Education* (Vol. 3., No. 1, pp. 258–266). https://doi.org/10.1515/cplbu-2017-0034
Foreign Agricultural Service U.S. Department of Agriculture. (n.d.). https://www.usda.gov/oce/commodity/wasde
Lee, K.-F. (2018). *AI superpowers: China, Silicon Valley, and the new world order.* Harper Business.
Lee, K.-F., & Qiufan, C. (2021). *AI 2041: Ten visions for our future hardcover—Crown currency* (1st ed.).
Martin-Shields, C. P., & Bodanac, N. (2018). Peacekeeping's digital economy: The role of communication technologies in post-conflict economic growth. *International Peacekeeping, 25*, 420–445. https://doi.org/10.1080/13533312.2017.1408413
Pan, Y., & Zhang, L. (2021). Roles of artificial intelligence in construction engineering and management: A critical review and future trends. *Automation in Construction, 122*, 75–76.
Silviu, N., Stavytskyy, A., & Kharlamova, G. (2023). Index of the openness and transparency of budgeting and financial management of the defence and security sector: Case of Ukraine. *Sustainability, 15*(7), 5617. https://doi.org/10.3390/su15075617
Wilson, C., & van der Velden, M. (2022). Sustainable AI: An integrated model to guide public sector decision-making. *Technology in Society, 68*, 21–22. https://doi.org/10.1016/j.techsoc.2022.101926
World Data Center for Geoinformatics and Sustainable Development. (n.d.). http://wdc.org.ua/en/node/29

National Resilience and Post-war Reconstruction of Ukraine

Mykola Nazarov

Abstract Successful post-war reconstruction of Ukraine is possible due to critical analysis of the previous experience of state building and taking into account the main mistakes. In this chapter, we analyze the dynamics of the Ukrainian political regime over the past 15 years, key changes in the security and defense sector of the state as well as critical decisions in the economic and energy spheres. Despite significant changes in Ukrainian politics after the start of the war in 2014, it is necessary to note systemic problems in the economic, energy, and military spheres that prevented full preparation for repelling a full-scale invasion of the Russian Federation in 2022. Among the main vulnerabilities of Ukraine that can hinder the post-war reconstruction of Ukraine are negative demographic dynamics, authoritarian tendencies in the political system of Ukraine, a significant loss of industrial and energy capacities as well as a shortage of specialists in certain industries. One of the important tools for the successful post-war reconstruction of Ukraine can be the development of national resilience. Resilience in the most generalized view is the potential of communities and institutions to demonstrate the system's ability to maintain its functions, adapt and evolve. Strengthening resilience at the level of regions and territorial communities, especially front-line and deoccupied ones, is a priority task for the state.

Ukrainian Vulnerabilities Before the Start of a Full-Scale Invasion 2022

The full-scale Russian invasion of Ukraine on 24 February 2022 was the culmination of a deliberate multi-year strategy to weaken and split Ukraine. This strategy has always pursued the same goals: to turn Ukraine into a failed state, prevent its

M. Nazarov (✉)
Department of Psychology, Political science and Socio-cultural technologies, Sumy State University, Sumy, Ukraine
e-mail: m.nazarov@socio.sumdu.edu.ua

S. Nate (ed.), *Ukraine's Journey to Recovery, Reform and Post-War Reconstruction*, Contributions to Security and Defence Studies,
https://doi.org/10.1007/978-3-031-66434-2_5

integration into European and Euro-Atlantic structures, and ultimately merge the country (or most of it) with the Russian Federation (Stoicescu et al., 2023).[1]

In this section we will outline the key areas and tools that the Russian Federation used to achieve the goal of occupying Ukraine. We emphasize that the Russian Federation has always relied on a comprehensive approach to exerting influence in Ukraine: political tools have always been combined with economic pressure and supported by military levers of influence. Also, the Russian Federation actively worked in the international arena to discredit Ukraine, creating the image of a failed state, a country with which it makes no sense to work. After discrediting Ukraine on international platforms, the Russian Federation immediately tried to replace Ukrainian exports with its positions, where there was competition between countries. In our analytical text we will also note the counter-actions of Ukraine that were taken to neutralize Russian influence in Ukraine and offer policy recommendations based on Ukrainian experience in countering external influences.

Instruments of political and ideological influence have always been dominant in the entire palette of instruments of Russian Federation influence in Ukraine. The electoral base on which the pro-Russian political or public figure relied was mainly citizens of the eastern and southern regions of Ukraine, which border on the Russian Federation and have cultural and family ties with the citizens of Russian Federation. Based on the fact that politics in Ukraine is highly personalized, the Kremlin relied on leaders, not structures. Therefore, we will consider the key politicians and oligarchs who actively promoted the Russian agenda and outline the organizational structures (parties, media, religious organizations) with which these leaders are affiliated. It is important to note that the pro-Russian figures worked on a niche basis, focusing on politics, the public sphere, religion, and so on. As a result, each figure worked in his own field, but for a common goal.

Viktor Yanukovych served as President of Ukraine in 2010–2014. The Russian Federation publicly supported his candidacy in the elections in 2004 and 2009 as well as the Party of Regions in the parliamentary elections led by Yanukovych. One of the first laws was adopted, the Law of Ukraine "On the Fundamentals of Foreign and Domestic Policy" and declared the non-bloc status of Ukraine (Shapovalova, 2017).[2] Thus, at the start of his presidency, V. Yanukovych fulfilled de facto the main strategic goal of the Kremlin in relation to Ukraine—the rejection of integration of Ukraine with NATO.

The next important step in the context of implementing the interests of the Russian Federation in Ukraine through Yanukovych was the agreement on basing the Black Sea Fleet in Sevastopol until 2042. From the position of today, we are well aware of the importance for the Russian Federation of maintaining this military site

[1] Kalev Stoicescu, Mykola Nazarov, Keir Giles and Mattew D. Johnson, 'How Russia went to war: the Cremlin's preparations for its aggression against Ukraine' (2023), ICDS, <https://icds.ee/wp-content/uploads/dlm_uploads/2023/04/ICDS_Report_How_Russia_Went_to_War_Stoicescu_Nazarov_Giles_Johnson_April_2023.pdf/>.

[2] Aleksandra Shapovalova, 'Yanukovich statements on Ukraine–NATO relations' (2017), *The Politics and Complexities of Crisis Management in Ukraine*, DOI: 10.4324/9781315554402-5.

in Crimea for the implementation of a further strategy for the annexation of Crimea in 2014 and support for military aggression in 2022. The opposition and the public warned about this and clearly demanded the refusal to prolong the existing treaty (Davlikanova et al., 2023).[3]

After the victory of the "orange revolution" in Ukraine and the election of President Victor Yushchenko, the Russian Federation began to perceive Ukraine as an opponent. Consequently, the actions of the Russian Federation in the field of economy and energy were aimed at "punishing" Ukraine for its foreign policy choice. The strategy of the Russian Federation in this area can be summarized as follows: (a) use Russian capital to corrupt Ukrainian oligarchs and politicians; (b) liquidation in Ukraine of enterprises-competitors for the Russian industry; (c) contribute to the preservation of the corrupt oligarchic model of Ukrainian government (Singh, 2023).[4] In combination, these approaches should have led to the total economic dependence of Ukraine on the Russian Federation and, as a result, the impossibility of pursuing an independent domestic and foreign policy.

The power industry in Ukraine was actually controlled by Ukrainian and Russian oligarchs. The private electric power company VS Energy controlled nine Ukrainian Oblenergo until 2020, and the firm's de facto owner is Russian businessman Alexander Babakov. Russian-Ukrainian businessman Konstantin Grigorishin owns the Energy Standard company, which has shares in at least five Oblenergo. In addition to business interests, Russian oligarchs pursue political goals: through pricing policy, they attempt to put pressure on central and local authorities, realizing the general strategic line of the Russian Federation. It is worth adding that until recently the situation in the nuclear power industry was similar: Ukraine depended on the Russian Federation for the supply of fuel for reactors, waste management and the supply of some parts (Yakoviyk & Tsvelikh, 2023).[5]

The main points of application of the efforts of the Russian Federation in destabilizing the security and defense sector of Ukraine were the encouragement of corruption and the incorporation of its representatives into the security and defense sector of Ukraine. For many years, the Ukrainian authorities, under pressure from Russia, considered the issues of defense construction as secondary. Academician Volodymyr Gorbulin notes that the reform of the army was mainly marked by a reduction in its numbers and combat strength. There was no renewal of weapons and military equipment. In particular, the potential of the air defense system has decreased by more than an order of magnitude. The domestic military-industrial complex suffered large-scale destruction. Combat training was reduced to a

---

[3]Olena Davlikanova, Andriana Kostenko et al., 'The War of Narratives: The Image of Ukraine in Western, Russian and Ukrainian Media (1991–2022)' (2023), Kyiv: LLC «Vistka», 146p.

[4]Danny Singh, 'Ukrainian Desire for Political Autonomy and NATO Accession' (2023), *The Tripartite Realist War: Analysing Russia's Invasion of Ukraine*, DOI: 10.1007/978-3-031-34,163-2_4.

[5]Ivan Yakoviyk, Maksym Tsvelikh 'Energy Security of the European Union in the Context of Russian Aggression against Ukraine' (2023), *Problems of Legality*, DOI: 10.21564/2414-990X.160.274518.

minimum, military command and control bodies were losing effectiveness, and combat military training personnel were losing their effectiveness. Pacifist ideas were aggressively imposed that the Armed Forces of Ukraine and other military formations are only a rudimentary attribute of the state, which will never be used to protect Ukraine.

In the period 2010–2014, funding for defense needs was carried out in critically limited amounts at the level of 1% of GDP. The development of the Armed Forces was practically not financed. In 2010, the Joint Operational Command was disbanded, in 2011—the Command of Support Forces, which significantly complicated the use of forces and means of the Ukrainian Armed Forces. Under Viktor Yanukovych, the destruction of the Ukrainian air defense system was almost completed, and the most modern anti-aircraft missile systems and reconnaissance equipment were redeployed to the Crimea.

Thus, the security and defense sector of Ukraine until 2014 was subject to systemic processes of degradation both in terms of internal destruction and targeted external influence. Corruption and the deliberate destruction of the armed forces under the influence of the Russian Federation put Ukraine in a critical situation when it was necessary to respond to the annexation of Crimea and the outbreak of hostilities in the Donbass.

National Resilience During the War and Post-War Reconstruction of Ukraine

Researchers of the phenomenon of resilience have proposed a large number of definitions of individual resilience (Fletcher & Sarkar, 2013).[6] According to these studies, resilience is a process, personal disposition, outcome, or set of behavioral tendencies, and its multidimensional definitions include both aspects of exposure to adverse situations and subsequent positive adaptation. Consequently, it has been measured by various elements promoting resilience, such as increased resources (Hobfoll et al., 2008),[7] satisfactory performance on age-related developmental tasks (Masten, 2011),[8] or levels of distress symptoms.

[6]D. Fletcher, M. Sarkar, 'Psychological resilience: A review and critique of definitions, concepts, and theory'(2013), *European Psychologist*, 18, p.12–23.

[7]S. Hobfoll, D. Canetti-Nisim, R. Johnson & S. Galea, 'The association of exposure, risk and resiliency factors with PTSD among Jews and Arabs exposed to repeated acts of terrorism in Israel' (2008), *Journal of Traumatic Stress*, 21, p.9–21.

[8]A. Masten, 'Resilience in children threatened by extreme adversity: Frameworks for research, practice, and translational synergy'(2011), *Development and Psychopathology*, 23, p.493–506.

In addition to different definitions, researchers agree on two main issues: (1) resilience is a complex, multifaceted concept whose measurement causes considerable debate (Bonanno et al., 2015);[9] (2) the concept of resilience has often been used when discussing people's ability to withstand stress and adversity (Ajdukovic et al., 2015).[10]

Resilience is a characteristic of the individual and at the same time characterizes families and entire communities and states. Community resilience shows the interaction between individuals and their community and refers to the community's success in meeting the needs of its members and the extent to which people are supported by their community. National resilience, similar to individual resilience, is defined by scientists in different ways, and these definitions are quite similar to the definition of individual resilience.

In other words, national resilience represents a state and community ability to anticipate risk, limit impacts, and rapidly recover by surviving, adapting, evolving, and growing in the face of rapid change. Social resilience is directly related to increasing local potential: creating additional growth points in communities, increasing trust and social support on the ground.

Our study was conducted based in the Center for Social Research of Sumy State University during September–November 2022 and assesses the capabilities of territorial communities of Kyiv, Lviv, Zakarpattia, Mykolaiv, Sumy, Chernihiv, and Dnipropetrovsk regions for social resilience, restoration and development in conditions of martial law (Analitychnyi zvit (n.d.).[11] The target group is residents who currently live in the specified territorial communities, or lived there before the full-scale invasion, but are under evacuation at the time of the survey. The survey takes place by filling out a google form through the verification of interviewers. Separate groups of respondents were interviewed face-to-face or by telephone. A total of 1089 households living before the full-scale Russian invasion in the study areas were covered.

The war significantly affected the resilience of Ukraine, increasing the number of vulnerable groups—the unemployed, minor children, the elderly and internally displaced persons. Before the full-scale invasion, we did not consider emigration or having a child to be a vulnerability, but now we assess the situation differently. Half of the families in Ukraine have unemployed people (49.2%), and 46.9% have minor children. A little less than a third of households have elderly persons, as well as displaced persons. More than 10% of families include people with disabilities, and 12.4% are single persons. Such circumstances require complex solutions in approaches to the assessment and strengthening of the social stability of

---

[9] G. Bonanno, S. Romero, and S. Klein, 'The Temporal Elements of psychological resilience: An Integrative framework for the study of Individuals, families, and communities'(2015), *Psychological Inquiry*, 26(2), p. 139–169.

[10] D. Ajdukovic, S. Kimhi, and M. Lahad, (Eds.), 'Resiliency: Enhancing coping with crisis and terrorism' (2015), Amsterdam, the Netherlands: IOS Press. The NATO Science for Peace and Security Programme.

[11] Analitichnij zvit «Socialna stijkist teritorialnih gromad v umovah voyennogo chasu: spromozhnist do vidnovlennya ta rozbudovi»—https://essuir.sumdu.edu.ua/bitstream-download/123456789/90540/1/Kostenko_2022_2.pdf.

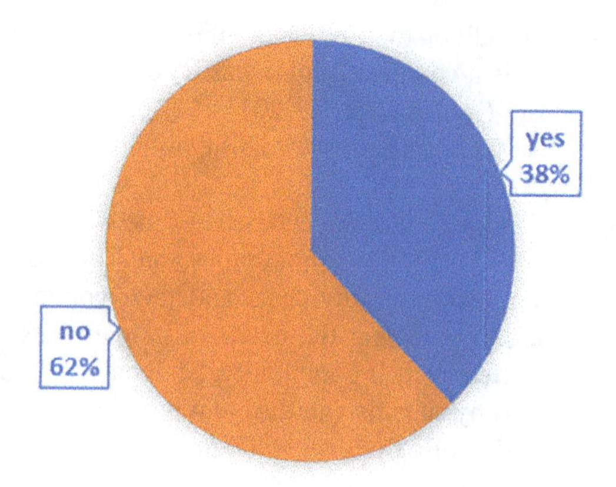

Diagram 1 Did any family members leave during the military invasion?

communities, because understanding the current vulnerabilities is necessary. It is also important to note that a third of Ukrainian families were separated due to the war, in particular, 37.8% of families had one of their family members leave (Diagram 1).

This indicator differs by region, depending on the proximity of the border with the Russian Federation, as well as the intensity of hostilities. Respondents noted the most departures of family members in Kyiv (46.6%), Mykolaiv (58.3%), and Chernihiv (43.6%) regions. These indicators are expected, because these areas suffered more than others from shelling and invasion in the first months of the war. The thesis about the vulnerability of families with minor children is also confirmed, because women left 25.9% of households, and children left in 24.6% (Diagram 2). A significant part of men of military age moved outside their regions/ communities to safer places (more than 10% of households).

Even in situations where hostilities have not yet ended, with certain threats to life and with great destruction, restrictions and disturbances that prevent a return to normal life, the population must assess the prospects and, in particular, the willingness of those who have left to return. Residents, as a rule, return to communities that are not in combat zones. Thus, 40% of households whose members left returned in full, while the other 9% returned partially. That is, half of the families separated by the war were fully or partially reunited. Thirty two percent of households whose members left are currently planning to return. And among families who left, 20% of family members have no intention of returning at all (Diagram 3). The number of people who choose not to return may be an indirect indicator of how successfully integrated in the new place.

Security criteria and employment prospects play a key role in the decision to return to Ukraine. A third of families whose members have gone abroad are willing to return only after the end of hostilities, 27% are willing to return if the security

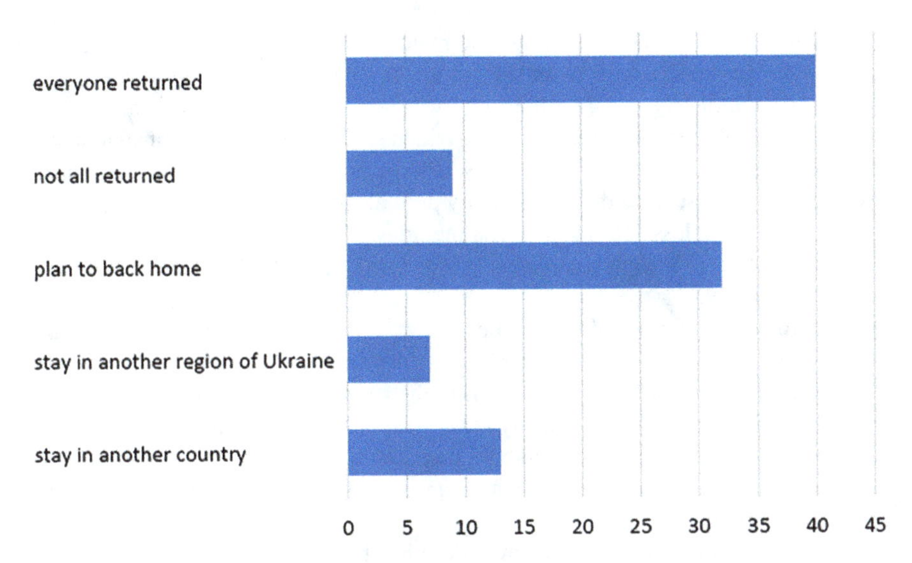

Diagram 2 Whom from your family members left home? (Respondents could choose several answer options so the sum exceeds 100%)

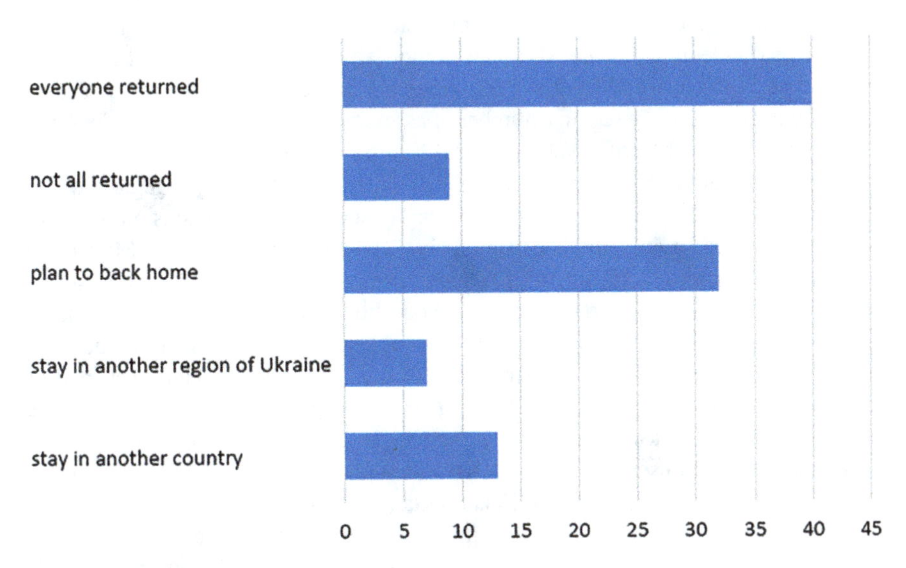

Diagram 3 Are family members planning to return or have they already returned? (Data refer to households whose members left)

situation in the community improves, and 16% have the opportunity to find work in their community. For 8% of surveyed households, the question of returning home is related to the prospects of completing their own affairs (education, treatment, work), which also indicates the strong influence of economic and social factors that will influence the decision to return to Ukraine.

In addition, 6% of households whose members left are ready to return if their housing is restored. It can be assumed that this is a part of the family members who partially or completely lost their housing. A general feeling of danger that does not go away is clearly revealed among all respondents. 13.7% of respondents felt unsafe at home, and 12.7%—in the community, although active hostilities are no longer taking place in most areas during the study period. According to respondents, about 65% feel more or less safe in their communities. Only every fifth respondent felt completely safe: 20.8% felt completely safe at home, and 22.4% felt completely safe in the community.

Therefore, the mentioned regularities speak rather about some uncertainty and fear in security issues. It should be noted that in May 2022, we recorded the following indicators: 50% of the residents of the studied communities feel in danger, 24.5%—have a feeling of uncertainty, 25.1% feel safe. Thus, the security situation has changed radically, first of all in those communities where we have the results of the study and can compare them, which are the territorial communities of Kyiv, Lviv, Mykolaiv, and Sumy.

It should be noted that assessments of the level of one's own security currently differ significantly in different areas. Residents of Sumy, Dnipropetrovsk, and Chernihiv regions feel relatively safe at home. More than a third of the surveyed Transcarpathian and Lviv regions feel completely safe at home. Instead, more than 30% of respondents from the Mykolaiv region answered that they feel unsafe at home. At this stage, we did not ask questions about the level of anxiety or expectations, but we assume based on a number of assessments that relate to both the sense of security and the state of psycho-physical health of the interviewees.

The socio-economic situation of households differs significantly by region, which requires a differentiated approach in planning support mechanisms in wartime conditions. More often, families from Kyiv (21% (against 15.1% in May)) and Lviv (24.9% (against 7.1% in May)) regions positively assess their current socio-economic status. While representatives of households from Sumy (14.5% (against 33.5% in May)) and Dnipropetrovsk (11.8%) oblasts more often state the position "not enough even for basic needs (food, utility bills, medicine)". Moreover, half of the respondents in these regions (54.6% and 50.7%, respectively) note that they have enough money for basic needs, but no more. In the risk group there is also a significant part of households that only have enough for basic needs from Mykolaiv (51% (against 47.5% in May)) and Zakarpattia (49.3%) regions.

Only 16.4% of surveyed households indicated that they have enough funds for all needs, and 34.3%—in the current conditions, they can afford to buy clothes and small appliances and have minimal savings. We can assume that a third of the population, who have savings, are able to cope with the challenges of war on their own for a certain period. It should be noted that as of May 2022, 10% of respondents indicated that they had enough funds for all needs, and 19.1% at that time could afford to purchase clothes and small appliances, noted the presence of minimal savings. Thus, from May to October, there is a tendency to improve the financial condition of people, and, therefore, access to means of livelihood. The rest of the households are either in the risk group, because they have enough funds only to meet basic needs, but no more (41.9%), or are in a difficult situation, because they do not have enough even for basic needs (food, utility bills, medicine) (7.4%) (Chart 6).

As of May, the data of the sociological survey showed that 41.1% of respondents have enough for basic needs, but no more, 29.8% do not have enough for basic needs. The above regarding the financial situation may be evidence of the need to change the emphasis in the mechanisms for ensuring the stability of communities from humanitarian aid to others (which does not exclude the need for humanitarian aid. 7.4%, who note the lack of funds for basic needs, as well as housing restoration programs as prerequisites for return people in the community). Due to the different socio-economic situation of families, humanitarian aid should be used only as an emergency measure for quick response to a difficult situation, or as a strategy to support the most vulnerable groups of families.

We believe that the revealed trend is the result of the action of certain state mechanisms, international aid, activity and solidarity of the people themselves, but also the habituation of people to war events, alarm signals, war news tapes. Based on the analysis of the documents of the Cabinet of Ministers of Ukraine, the Ministry of Social Policy, the Ministry of Development of Communities and Territories of Ukraine, five groups of state institutional mechanisms for strengthening the efficiency and stability of local self-government in wartime have been identified: (1) mechanisms of direct state action to ensure people's access to livelihoods, (2) mechanisms for maintaining basic conditions and well-being, (3) mechanisms for determining the needs of the population in social services at the community level, (4) mechanisms for strategic management, (5) mechanisms for public participation. The presented set of mechanisms appears, on the one hand, to be sufficiently systematic, on the other hand, the question of its completeness arises precisely from the point of view of the resilience of local self-government.

We proceed from the fact that in the government documents for the response to the full-scale Russian invasion, there is a significant focus on ensuring access to the basic means of livelihood of vulnerable population groups. At the same time, we would like to draw attention to two principles from the "UN Common Guidance on Helping Build Resilient Societies". It corresponds to the following: "No individual participant can offer comprehensive approaches to increasing resilience in the system and between systems. It is imperative that all stakeholders are engaged in their personal responsibilities and that a wide range of perspectives are jointly explored and agreed upon so that the resilience of the most vulnerable individuals and systems can be strengthened". In accordance with this principle, it is advisable to strengthen the mechanisms of public participation. Currently, state documents provide for public discussions, temporary consultation and advisory bodies, and participation. As an example, it should be noted that the discussion of the project "Strategy for recovery and development of the economy of the Sumy region for 2022-2024" was sufficiently participatory. However, at the level of territorial communities, participation in development strategies seems to be insufficiently implemented.

Conclusions

Resilience plays an important role in the sustainable functioning of society and enables managed recovery efforts. Social resilience represents both the individual qualities of a person and the collective (social) qualities of a community to withstand challenges and stabilize. The full-scale war of the Russian Federation against Ukraine actualized the socio-economic problems of Ukraine and created more vulnerable social groups of the population that need attention from both the state and the community. The prospect of Ukraine's post-war recovery depends on social stability, that is, the ability of communities to return to a state of equilibrium and reduce negative socio-economic factors. The post-war recovery of Ukraine will rely on processes directly in the communities: on the creation of "growth points" based on the communities, which will stimulate the entire state to recovery.

Existing systematic work on the development and implementation of state institutional mechanisms to strengthen the efficiency and stability of local self-government in wartime certainly ensures the social stability of communities and people in communities. At the same time, it seems that more emphasis is placed on humanitarian aid and provision of the basic needs of the population. Instead, it can be seen that the issue of ensuring citizens' participation in community decision-making processes, especially decisions of a strategic nature, requires special attention at the local level.

The principle of development local and national potential—resilience is primarily about the capacity and activity of people, communities, institutions and systems that are at risk. The success of resilience support depends on the degree of leadership roles taken by affected people, local and national authorities and institutions or systems. In this regard, it is appropriate to work not only on providing people with humanitarian aid and taking care of their psychological health, but also on training and creating conditions for the development of people, their competences, cohesion, responsibility and leadership. At the same time, in this case, on the one hand, we are talking about vulnerable people, on the other hand, people who take responsibility and work daily to develop the social and economic potential of the community.

References

Ajdukovic, D., Kimhi, S., & Lahad, M. (Eds.). (2015). *Resiliency: Enhancing coping with crisis and terrorism*. IOS Press. The NATO Science for Peace and Security Programme.

Analitychnyi zvit. (n.d.). «Sotsialna stiikist terytorialnykh hromad v umovakh voiennoho chasu: spromozhnist do vidnovlennia ta rozbudovy». https://essuir.sumdu.edu.ua/bitstream-download/123456789/90540/1/Kostenko_2022_2.pdf

Bonanno, G., Romero, S., & Klein, S. (2015). The temporal elements of psychological resilience: An integrative framework for the study of individuals, families, and communities. *Psychological Inquiry, 26*(2), 139–169.

Davlikanova, O., Kostenko, A., et al. (2023). *The war of narratives: The image of Ukraine in Western, Russian and Ukrainian media (1991–2022)* (p. 146). LLC «Vistka».

Fletcher, D., & Sarkar, M. (2013). Psychological resilience: A review and critique of definitions, concepts, and theory. *European Psychologist, 18*, 12–23.
Hobfoll, S., Canetti-Nisim, D., Johnson, R., & Galea, S. (2008). The association of exposure, risk and resiliency factors with PTSD among Jews and Arabs exposed to repeated acts of terrorism in Israel. *Journal of Traumatic Stress, 21*, 9–21.
Masten, A. (2011). Resilience in children threatened by extreme adversity: Frameworks for research, practice, and translational synergy. *Development and Psychopathology, 23*, 493–506.
Shapovalova, A. (2017). Yanukovich statements on Ukraine–NATO relations, The politics and complexities of crisis management in Ukraine. https://doi.org/10.4324/9781315554402-5
Singh, D. (2023). Ukrainian desire for political autonomy and NATO accession, The Tripartite Realist War: Analysing Russia's Invasion of Ukraine. https://doi.org/10.1007/978-3-031-34163-2_4.
Stoicescu, K., Nazarov, M., Giles, K., & Johnson, M. (2023). How Russia went to war: The Cremlin's preparations for its aggression against Ukraine, ICDS. https://icds.ee/wp-content/uploads/dlm_uploads/2023/04/ICDS_Report_How_Russia_Went_to_War_Stoicescu_Nazarov_Giles_Johnson_April_2023.pdf/
Yakoviyk, I., & Tsvelikh, M. (2023). Energy security of the European Union in the context of Russian aggression against Ukraine. Problems of legality. https://doi.org/10.21564/2414-990X.160.274518.

A First Look at the Geoeconomic Challenges of Rebuilding Ukraine

Antonia Colibășanu

Abstract The Ukrainian reconstruction project is a complex and ongoing endeavor, requiring a thorough evaluation of the initial stages of the process. The first stage involves assessing the war scenarios while addressing the societal harm done while fighting to counter Russia's aggression. The definition and implementation of victory will establish the primary goals for rebuilding Ukraine's socioeconomic and political future. This study employs theoretical frameworks for international conflict management to give an early knowledge of the present conflict, state players' goals, and methods of defining victory. The research identifies two crucial components that the West and Russia share in defining victory: (1) the avoidance of direct conflict between NATO and Russia's military force, and (2) the post-war reconstruction process, which includes not just Ukraine but also Russia. Using the geoeconomic framework to address the Ukraine reconstruction project, the research aims to establish the main layers of the peacebuilding process on both warring sides, which include economic (short and long term) support, financial infrastructure maintenance, and infrastructure investment. Finally, the paper discusses the difficult decisions and sacrifices that must be taken to assist Ukraine's reconstruction process, resulting in efficient and robust infrastructure that can adapt to changing conditions.

The Reconstruction Project and the Theory for Defining Victory in Ukraine

The Ukrainian reconstruction project is not just a protracted undertaking but also contingent upon the progression and eventual resolution of the war. Hence, prior to delving into the particular elements that contribute to shaping the post-war Ukrainian circumstances and the essential areas that require rebuilding once the fight

A. Colibășanu (✉)
Department of International Relations and European Integration, Romanian University of Political Science and Public Administration, Bucharest, Romania
e-mail: antonia.colibasanu@dri.snspa.ro

S. Nate (ed.), *Ukraine's Journey to Recovery, Reform and Post-War Reconstruction*, Contributions to Security and Defence Studies,
https://doi.org/10.1007/978-3-031-66434-2_6

concludes, it is imperative to evaluate the initial stages of the reconstruction process, commencing with an analysis of the ongoing methods employed in the battle. To clarify, the process of reconstruction starts by assessing the present and future lasting harm to the nation, including the societal harm that has to be addressed in order to rebuild the country while also countering the aggressive state.

Ukraine's recovery effort encompasses the challenge of sourcing resources to counter Russia's aggression, even in the midst of ongoing kinetic warfare. Given that these resources originate from outside of Ukraine and must be connected to the geographical context of the bordering region, the first stage of Ukraine's reconstruction process plays a crucial role in shaping the post-war rebuilding process. Currently, we can only focus on this particular stage, since the struggle persists, and both parties are still formulating conditions for their victory.

During the process of rebuilding Ukraine after the war, the definition and execution of victory will determine the main objectives for restoring the country's socio-economic and political aspects. Until then, we need to consider the theoretical framework provided by the study of international conflict management when discussing the Ukrainian reconstruction project. This framework provides for an initial understanding of the current international conflict, the motivations of state actors, and, through that, their way of defining victory which, in turn, may give effective strategies for sustaining Ukraine's reconstruction and eventually, for peace and prosperity in Ukraine and beyond, in Eastern Europe.

One of the most prominent theories in international conflict management is realism, which emphasizes the role of power and interests in international relations (Molloy, 2014). Realists contend that nations are largely driven by self-interest and that conflicts emerge from the quest for limited resources, territorial assertions, and the desire for supremacy over others. It is believed that nations frequently employ power politics, such as coercion and military force, in order to attain their objectives.

Structuralist theory argues that fundamental social, economic, and political frameworks of the international system are factors that may lead to conflict and explain its evolution. Their attention lies on variables such as inequality, injustice, and historical grievances that have the potential to influence the relationships between nations and intensify tensions. Given the growing social tensions during the last decade has resulted in political and international shifts, structuralism seems to explain much of current events (Donnelly, 2019).

Constructivists place significant emphasis on the influence of ideas, beliefs, and norms in determining the dynamics of international relations. They contend that our perception of the environment and our sense of ourselves can have an impact on our interactions with others. Constructivists think that engaging in dialogue, fostering collaboration, and establishing shared norms may effectively facilitate the transformation of disputes and foster the development of more harmonious relationships. They are the proponents of diplomacy i—which certainly is also undergoing major shifts as our world is changed by unconventional warfare, including through tactics shaping communication lines that were initially meant to support international dialogue and cooperation (Iommi, 2022).

While all three theories of international relations are certainly useful for understanding international conflict, all theoretical frameworks and empirical investigations on specific cases are derived not just from political science but also from the disciplines of social psychology, sociology, economics, and law. Processual theorists prioritize the examination of conflict resolution by stressing the sequential steps required to transition from conflict to resolution. In emphasizing the significance of a secure and favorable setting for negotiation, mediation, they are using all information available for building frameworks in which trust prevails—that is using cognitive analysis frameworks that allow for emphasizing with the parties. All this is necessary in order to begin and sustain reconstruction in a post-conflict environment. Therefore, all serious conversations about a reconstruction project must begin with a discussion of what victory means for each side, looking for the common denominator that may eventually transform the conflict into a peaceful situation.

Considering the three theories used in international conflict management and the main participants in the conflict: Russia and Ukraine, backed by the West, which is embodied by the US and the EU, there are several definitions for victory at the time of writing that need to be considered in outlining the long-term strategy for the Ukrainian reconstruction project. The analysis using the three theoretical frameworks first considers the definition for victory Russia and Ukraine have, as main belligerent parties and only then refers to the West, as an indirect but present party in the conflict.

Russia takes on a constructivist approach in defining its goals in Ukraine, much of which goes beyond Ukraine, referring to Russia's global role. The US, on the other hand, takes a realist approach towards the conflict, seeking to limit its direct involvement in the kinetic warfare and only indirectly supporting Ukraine, while working with the EU to do so. Russia's objectives in Ukraine may be analyzed in the context of its recently formulated foreign policy concept (Decree on Approval of the Foreign Policy Concept of the Russian Federation, March 2023). The paper presents Moscow's perspective on its ongoing efforts to curtail and counterbalance U.-S. dominance and influence worldwide. It also highlights Russia's resistance to a Western alliance led by the United States, which the document claims to undermine Russia. The Kremlin's strategic objectives involve forging alliances with and assuming leadership over other nations adversely affected by U.S. dominance, intending to change the global power structure completely. This means that Russia is not only defining victory beyond Ukraine's kinetic warfare but that it also doesn't regard Ukraine as its adversary.

Moreover, using the structuralist approach, Russia regards the war in Ukraine (Roth & Sauer, 2023) as an existential war, one that is redefining itself as a state and potentially, a global power. The new foreign policy concept mentions that "In response to the unfriendly actions of the West, Russia intends to defend its right to exist and to develop freely by all available means". This statement implies that Moscow has the intention to either influence a shift in U.S. policy or hinder the U.S. from accomplishing its stated objectives by obstructing them. This approach is compelling evidence Russia's new foreign policy concept is a break from the past, considering all its previous foreign policy documents published after the end of the

Cold War were calling for the establishment of a common security space with European countries.

Realism has Russia focusing on a key element: keep the war going until the West feels pressured enough and disunites in its support for Ukraine. While doing that, Russia must avoid a direct conflict with NATO as that is risky. Such a conflict may result in its defeat and may not give Russia a future to rebuild itself (Pinchuk, 2023) into a global power. Therefore, the current conflict will not only result in a post-war reconstruction of Ukraine but also in a post-war reconstruction of Russia, both of which depend on the way the conflict concludes. For Ukraine, on the other side, victory is dependent on territorial control. Its goals are relatively simple: obtain all territory taken by Russia since 2014, when Kyiv considers Russia has started the war against Ukraine's integrity, and receive reparation from Moscow. Using realism for discussing interests and goals for Ukraine is, however, incomplete: while Kyiv would ideally make Russia pay for the damages, the amount and the way to have it pay for it is unclear, especially since the post-conflict peacebuilding process needs to take into account the societal recovery which is still something that needs to be calculated. The application of the structuralist or constructivist theories gives little insight into other details of Ukraine's objectives, considering there is limited information as to how the country will look like at the end of the current conflict. Ukraine has been devastated with an uncertain recovery in sight, most of its ports closed, its economy entirely dependent on Western support, hundreds of thousands of men and women fighting, and millions of people, the vast majority of whom are women, have fled the country. The reconstruction project will need to sync up with a peacebuilding process that begins once the kinetic warfare is over (Norman & Mikhael, 2023).

Because the military support that the West gives to Ukraine is key to determining how the war ends, understanding Western goals is essential to see the way the West defines victory. While it is obvious that the Western concept of victory includes numerous definitions that certain nation-states have in terms of their geopolitical imperatives, as long as there is a unified Western front against Russia, the notion of a common Western victory is feasible. Four goals may be considered components of a common Western win. Using realism for identifying Western objectives, there are two main interests that the West needs to address in fighting in Ukraine. First, the West needs to help Ukraine to force Russia to withdraw from as much occupied territory as possible. Second, the West must avoid direct military confrontation between NATO and Russia, as that would translate into Western military and human expense that needs to be avoided. Not to mention that the West—and the US in particular—wants to limit its military presence worldwide.

The constructivist approach highlights another goal: the West needs to make sure Russia doesn't get emboldened to attack elsewhere, especially in a neighboring region of Europe such as the Balkans or the Caucasus—both potential flanks that may open up. For this reason, it needs to make sure it retains sufficient influence in Russia and in the non-allied regions—that the West ultimately needs to "win" over from Russian influence (Derviş, 2022).

Using the structuralist framework, from the Western perspective, the conflict in Ukraine should weaken Russia or should end on such terms that prevent Russia from invading Ukraine or another territory again. Socio-economically, Russia will likely need Western help should it be defeated in the current war—this is how the West not only increases its influence but also helps reconstruct the Russian system so that it is ideally not becoming antagonistic to its goals and its existence.

Therefore, there are two key elements that the West and Russia share in defining victory. First, there is the avoidance of direct confrontation between NATO's and Russia's military's might. Second, there is the post-war reconstruction process that not only refers to Ukraine, but also to Russia. Should Russia win the war, it will rebuild itself into a global power, while its social and economic features will be redefined. Should the West win the war, Russia will need to be restructured in such a way that in the future a similar conflict to that currently going on in Ukraine is avoided.

The Geoeconomic Framework: The Layers of Reconstruction

From a strategic perspective, reconstruction involves addressing the underlying causes of conflict and building sustainable peace and stability. It encompasses a broad range of efforts, including security, political, economic, social and psychological dimensions for both Ukraine and Russia (Harafonova & Stadniichuk, 2023). This is why the long-term approach to the reconstruction project needs to consider several layers or dimensions, all of them dependent on the way the war is evolving. Therefore, there are two major considerations to be taken into account when listing the dimensions of the reconstruction project for Ukraine. One refers to the momentum of drawing such a list—whatever theoretical framework we might consider, there are the current options that must be considered for building a sustainable environment for the state's survival and resistance during the conflict and, there are post-conflict options that need to be considered for long-term goals of Ukraine. The other consideration that needs to be taken into account is the effects that pertain to the peacebuilding processes as all dimensions must contribute to the long-term stability of Ukraine (Rist et al., 2023). Understanding, from using the international conflict management theories to define victory for each party currently at war, that the reconstruction of Ukraine goes hand in hand with that of Russia, we conclude that the West is a donor or at least a funding party (in case Russia manages to establish itself as a global power) on the long term.

Given the two considerations and the particular aspects of the reconstruction project in Ukraine, a list of the specific dimensions that need to be taken into account, together with an explainer about the timeline and the parameters to consider when discussing the dimension in question, is given in the Table 1 below. The also features geopolitical components for analytical framework: politics, economics and security as well as some specific considerations for the social and psychological

Table 1 Layers for Ukraine's reconstruction

Reconstruction layers/dimensions	Parameters to consider for each of the layer	Time of implementation
1.A. Economic (short term and long-term)	Supporting current employment levels, promoting socio-economic resilience Maintaining financial infrastructure integrated and functional at the international level Sustaining investments in infrastructure (health and educational infrastructure as well as physical critical infrastructure for energy and transport)	During the kinetic conflict, in areas less affected by the war and after the kinetic conflict ends, with a long-term focus
1.B. Economic (long term)	Creating a functioning market internally and sustaining the integration of the internal economy in the international economic flows Supporting the small and medium enterprises to create a stable economic system providing for internal needs Investments in all infrastructure needed for (re)building an economic system and integrating it into the world economy	Post-war reconstruction
2.A. Political (short term)	Maintaining a stable governing system that facilitates economic support Maintaining working state institutions for serving key functions, including the civil service and the judiciary	During the kinetic conflict
2.B. Political (long-term)	Establishing a legitimate and inclusive political system that represents the interests of all stakeholders Rebuilding and strengthening state institutions, including the police, judiciary, and civil service.	Post-war reconstruction
3.A. Social and psychological (short term and long-term)	Promoting community resilience and coping mechanisms for the society Providing access to education, healthcare, and essential service Addressing discrimination issues, especially in multiethnic settings	During the kinetic conflict and after the kinetic conflict ends, with a long term focus
3.B. Social and psychological (long-term)	Promoting reconciliation and healing among communities affected by conflict Addressing the psychological trauma of war and conflict	Post-war reconstruction phase

(continued)

Table 1 (continued)

Reconstruction layers/dimensions	Parameters to consider for each of the layer	Time of implementation
	Disarming and reintegrating former combatants into society	
4. Security	Ensuring the rule of law and upholding human rights Demobilization and reconsideration of the national military structure Creating a safe environment to avoid more violence and enable for the delivery of humanitarian supplies and the return to regular life.	Post-war reconstruction phase

Source: author's compilation, based on theoretical framework presented

aspects that need to be integrated within the reconstruction project for the Ukrainian society.

While the reconstruction process is multidimensional, the resources that need to be invested—both financial and political ones, are dependent upon global economic stability (Plotkinov, 2022). While the kinetic front is opened, the support each side takes is dependent on how they do in economic terms. Before Russia attacked Ukraine, forecasts predicted that global economic growth in 2022 would be approximately 4.5 percent (World Economic Outlook Update, January 2022: Rising Caseloads, a Disrupted Recovery, and Higher Inflation, 2022). The war was one of the primary causes that lowered economic growth in 2022 to just 3.5 percent (World Economic Outlook, October 2022: Countering the Cost-of-Living Crisis, 2022), and the IMF baseline forecast is that global economic growth will not surpass 3.0 percent in 2023 and 2.9 percent in 2024 (World Economic Outlook, October 2023: Navigating Global Divergences, 2023).

According to all analyses, the conflict has had the largest impact on Europe's economy, which has had to restructure itself, considering it needed to cut down the energy dependencies it had on Russia. At the same time, while the US has contributed the most to Ukrainian military resilience, Europeans have been the frontline for helping Ukraine remain economically stable, facilitating new trade routes when its ports closed, under Russian attack, and generally, funding the Ukrainian societal resilience (Jenkins, 2023).

The aforementioned layers of reconstruction demonstrate that resilience is both a component and a prerequisite for the reconstruction of a state, while the process of peacebuilding is a crucial component of statecraft (as shown in Table 1, on layers of Ukrainian reconstruction). Simultaneously, these components hold equal significance in the restoration endeavor of a nation that has endured the consequences of armed conflict.

Investing in resilience, according to the constructivist idea, is a way to facilitate the peacebuilding process (Fluri, 2020).

At the same time, while both of the two elements have four major dimensions or layers—economics, politics, security and socio-psychological, the effects and the interconnection between these layers, both for short and long-term, set the way the reconstruction project takes shape. The multifactorial environment has, however, a foundational starting point which usually refers to the economic dimension. This is because it is the economy that expresses the basic individual or community needs that shape, through the allocation of resources, the parameters that form the nation state and define its resilience, beyond basic security needs.

Assessing Priorities and Challenges in Ukraine's Reconstruction Process

The clash between Russian, Ukrainian, and Western perspectives on victory is a prescription for a long war. The only common point at the time of writing between Russia and the West is the fact that they both have an interest in avoiding an open military conflict between themselves.

All this points to the fact that the costs attached to the war are only going to grow as Kyiv is already completely dependent on Western funds and arms and there is little chance this will change in 2024. It's no secret that as long as the kinetic warfare continues the costs for keeping the country afloat are only growing. Considering the consideration of the reconstruction dimensions presented in the previous chapter, as the short-term support is growing and the risks are demanding, the long-term expense and considerations are increasing in complexity.

This is why priorities need to be assessed based on the particular challenges that they bring forth. At the same time, we also need to consider what was regarded as a priority since 2022 until the moment of writing, since based on the considerations above, whatever constituted support for the four dimensions considered, since Russia started the war on Ukraine is part of the reconstruction project as well.

Before Ukraine's Reconstruction Fund was discussed and implemented (Masters, 2023), the Ukrainian Recovery Plan was outlined in 2022 by the country's National Recovery Council. At the time, the current estimate of the damages to the Ukrainian economy was of "$100bn and growing" (Ukraine's National Recovery Plan, 2022). In September 2022, the World Bank assessed the recovery and reconstruction needs would cost about $349bn (World Bank, Ukraine's Reconstruction Needs, 2022).

A year later, the Ukraine Presidential Office and the country's ministry of the economy were helped by US JPMorgan and Blackrock to put together a national Development Finance Institution (DFI) dedicated to the goal of attracting investment for the country's reconstruction and modernization, which was requiring more than $50bn capital investment dedicated to only five key sectors for Ukraine's economic system. The sectors mentioned are infrastructure (with more than $20bn needed in investment), energy (with more than $10bn needed), manufacturing, agriculture and IT (Ukraine Reconstruction Fund—Description, 2023). The approach is much

Table 2 Financial support for non-military resilience of the Ukrainian state since February 2022

Donor and support package	Sum allocated
World Bank—first economic recovery development policy loan for Ukraine	$350 million
World Bank—support investment for EU's solidarity lanes	$100 million
UK—UK's updated commitments of a further $3 billion of guarantees to unlock World Bank lending to Ukraine	$3 billion
UK—other non-military assistance—supporting the rebuilt of energy and other critical infrastructure in Ukraine, including supporting the development of Ukrainian e-governance and fiscal capacity	$1.7 billion
EU—team Europe support for economic, social and financial resilience	€40.6 billion
EU—support funding for Ukrainian refugees dedicated programs	€17 billion
EU—solidarity lanes—quick improvements to existing infrastructure helping Ukraine's exports (grants)	€250 million
EU—EU solidarity lanes—support the infrastructure developments needed to increase further the capacity of the solidarity lanes	€50 million
EIB—European Investment Bank support for solidarity lanes	€300 million
EBRD—European Bank for Reconstruction and Development support for solidarity lanes	€300 million

Source: author's compilation

different than that of the Recovery plan published in 2022, which mentioned not only economic troubles for Ukraine, but also the need for the country to integrate into the EU as part of a long-term political and security imperative.

Moreover, in June 2023, the Ukraine Recovery Conference had become more complex than that organized in 2022 (Ukraine Recovery Conference Materials, 2022–2023, n.d.), confirming that the war has not only been much more damaging than initially thought but also that the recovery process had become a multi-factor problem for all involved. Apart from the country's Reconstruction Fund, the EU also announced a new Ukraine Facility program (European Commission—Ukraine's Facility, 2023) (Table 2).

In October 2023, the EU Commission announced its intention to renegotiate EU's multiannual budget to be able to support Ukraine's needs and add to the new Ukraine Facility €50 billion for 2024–2027 (EU Parliament News Press, 2023). In addition, the EU has also used the Solidarity Lanes initiative launched in 2022 to help Ukraine export its food products to the global market by investing heavily and supporting investment in the creation and improvement of European infrastructure (European Commission, Solidarity Lanes Press Corner, 2023). Each of the EU's programs needed update and political support—which is why the renegotiation of the EU's multiannual project is still questionable (Dennison & Zerka, 2023).

All of this indicates that the West—and the EU in particular, understands that it needs to be flexible when it comes to covering the needs for Ukraine's resilience and reconstruction (European Commission DG Neighbourhood Policy, 2023). At the same time, there is an obvious gradual growth in risk appetite, as "clean victory" and "clean peace" are improbable, nor are obvious benchmarks for transitioning from "recovery" to "modernization". While the work completed under the Ukraine Facility project will serve as the foundation for future discussions with a broader range of partner nations and financial institutions, it is clear that the scope of the reconstruction project goes beyond what the EU is thinking at the moment. While the EU Commission hopes to ensure EUR 50 billion in funds for Ukraine, it is also admitting that the actual reconstruction costs are anticipated to be between EUR 400 and 500 billion—an estimate made in June 2023 and which may already be outdated (EU Commission, Press Corner—Q&A on Ukraine Facility, 2023).

In some respects, reconstructing Ukraine may be more financially challenging than sustaining the conflict itself. The country has already faced levels of destruction unprecedented in Europe since World War II. However, the analysis of the Western support for Ukraine's resilience—as a first phase of the reconstruction project and as part of the Western definition of victory shows that it is dedicated to its success. Moreover, the EU seems to be most invested in the reconstruction process, judging by the sums invested.

European priorities align closely with the significant challenges that Ukraine and the South Eastern European region have encountered since February 2022. These challenges primarily revolve around the inadequate infrastructure that hinders the establishment of alternative trade routes in the Black Sea, which Ukraine relies on to export its goods to the global market. The necessity to cease operations at key Ukrainian ports due to the imminent Russian onslaught became apparent from the beginning of the war. As the conflict progressed and the Black Sea was officially designated as a region affected by war, the European Union recognized the pressing necessity to swiftly establish alternative infrastructure to facilitate Ukrainian exports.

Consequently, the majority of immediate, short term assistance for the reconstruction of Ukraine is allocated not to projects within Ukraine itself, but rather to infrastructure initiatives aimed at facilitating the transportation of Ukrainian trade. The rehabilitation project is expected to be advanced by funding Ukrainian resilience through initiatives that promote connectivity between Ukraine and the EU. These initiatives aim to enhance not just trade but also Ukrainian security and modernization, particularly in light of the ongoing kinetic conflict.

Moreover, investment in infrastructure in the EU's and NATO frontier countries is not only a way to sustain Ukraine's military resilience but also a way to grow Western deterrence. At the same time, investment in new energy projects such as the NuScale Small Modular Reactors (SMR) Project developed in Romania (Timpescu, 2023) may not only provide a cheap energy alternative to that of Russia in the region but also lay the ground for a joint Romanian-US endeavor to implement the technology in Ukraine.

All support for resilience within the framework of the reconstruction project ultimately has a foundational aspect that goes for the long-term implementation of strategic links between Ukraine and the West. The main challenge that the West has in supporting Ukraine through such investments is the irregular warfare that Russia conducts. While many are saying that Ukraine's reconstruction project resembles the Marshal plan for Europe after WWII, there is a big difference.

The post-World War II rebuilding in Europe and Japan did not face the threat of organized irregular conflict. However, even if a ceasefire is agreed upon, Ukraine may not have the privilege of enjoying this. Russia, harboring resentment, may persist in launching long-range missiles and drones at Ukraine. This is why the way victory is being defined by the parties is important—the full reconstruction of Ukraine, in tandem with that of Russia needs to support and be part of the peacebuilding process, after a settlement ends the war. Especially since Russia doesn't regard Ukraine to be its enemy, but the West. Hence, the rebuilding process necessitates making difficult choices and compromises between creating infrastructure that is both efficient and resilient, capable of adapting to changing circumstances. This is because the nature of the future Russian state that we will have to engage with after the conflict remains uncertain. Currently, it is evident that the West finds it challenging to trust Moscow once more. Consequently, this change in thinking leads to the West prioritizing resilience and deterrence in all of its investments.

References

Dennison, & Zerka. (2023, December 22). Europe's emerging war fatigue: How to shore up falling support for Ukraine. Foreign Affairs. Retrieved January 10, 2024, from https://www.foreignaffairs.com/eastern-europe-and-former-soviet-union/europes-emerging-war-fatigue

Derviş, K. (2022, August 26). What are the West's strategic goals in the Ukraine war? Project Syndicate. https://www.project-syndicate.org/commentary/ukraine-war-western-strategic-goals-russia-global-south-by-kemal-dervis-2022-08

Donnelly, J. (2019, January 22). Systems, levels, and structural theory: Waltz's theory is not a systemic theory (and why that matters for international relations today). *European Journal of International Relations, 25*(3), 904–930. https://doi.org/10.1177/1354066118820929

EU Commission, Press Corner—Q&A on Ukraine Facility. (2023, June). *A new Ukrainian facility – Q&A*. Retrieved January 10, 2024, from https://ec.europa.eu/commission/presscorner/detail/en/qanda_23_3353

EU Parliament News Press. (2023, October 17). *A long-term solution for Ukraine*. Retrieved January 10, 2024, from https://www.europarl.europa.eu/news/en/press-room/20231013IPR07125/a-long-term-solution-for-ukraine-s-funding-needs

European Commission. (2023, June). *EU Ukraine facility*. Retrieved January 10, 2024, from https://neighbourhood-enlargement.ec.europa.eu/system/files/2023-06/COM_2023_338_1_EN_ACT_part1_v6.pdf

European Commission DG Neighbourhood Policy. (2023, December 20). Multi-agency donor coordination platform for Ukraine meets to discuss Ukraine's budget needs for 2024, the Platform's membership and Ukraine's progress on reforms. European Neighbourhood Policy and Enlargement Negotiations (DG NEAR). Retrieved January 5, 2024, from https://neighbourhood-enlargement.ec.europa.eu/news/multi-agency-donor-coordination-platform-ukraine-meets-discuss-ukraines-budget-needs-2024-platforms-2023-12-20_en

European Commission, Solidarity Lanes Press Corner. (2023, October 11). 1 billion euro mobilised for solidarity lanes. European Commission-European Commission. Retrieved January 10, 2024, from https://ec.europa.eu/commission/presscorner/detail/el/statement_22_6825

Fluri, P. H. (2020). Stabilization missions–lessons to be learned from resilience-based peacebuilding. *Connections: The Quarterly Journal, 19*(4), 59–68. https://doi.org/10.11610/connections.19.4.04

Harafonova, O., & Stadniichuk, R. (2023). The essence and theory of social conflict. *Public Management and Administration in Ukraine, 33*, 14–17. https://doi.org/10.32782/pma2663-5240-2023.33.2

Iommi, L. G. (2022, September). The new constructivism in international relations theory. *International Affairs, 98*(5), 1783–1784. https://doi.org/10.1093/ia/iiac153

Jenkins, B. (2023, March 7). Consequences of the war in Ukraine: The economic fallout. RAND. https://www.rand.org/pubs/commentary/2023/03/consequences-of-the-war-in-ukraine-the-economic-fallout.html

Masters. (2023, June 19). *BlackRock and JPMorgan help set up Ukraine reconstruction bank.* Financial Times Retrieved January 10, 2024, from https://www.ft.com/content/3d6041fb-5747-4564-9874-691742aa52a2

Molloy, S. P. (2014, October 9). Pragmatism, realism and the ethics of crisis and transformation in international relations. *International Theory, 6*(3), 454–489. https://doi.org/10.1017/s1752971914000189

Norman, J. M., & Mikhael, D. (2023, September 13). Rethinking the triple-nexus: Integrating peacebuilding and resilience initiatives in conflict contexts. *Journal of Peacebuilding & Development, 18*(3), 248–263. https://doi.org/10.1177/15423166231200210

Pinchuk. (2023, December 13). *This is the world if Ukraine loses*. Retrieved January 11, 2024, from https://www.politico.com/news/magazine/2023/12/13/russia-ukraine-war-west-funding-00131638

Plotkinov, O. (2022, December 26). Post-war reconstruction of Ukraine in the context of fragmentation of the world economy. *Economy of Ukraine, 2022*(12), 3–12. https://doi.org/10.15407/economyukr.2022.12.003

Rist, L., Queiroz, C., & Norström, A. (2023). Resilience in peacebuilding: Misunderstandings, missed opportunities and some ways Forward. SSRN Electronic Journal. https://doi.org/10.2139/ssrn.4423837.

Roth, A., & Sauer, P. (2023, December 15). Putin says no peace until Russia's goals in Ukraine achieved. The Guardian. https://www.theguardian.com/world/2023/dec/14/vladimir-putin-peace-russia-ukraine-president.

The Kremlin, Decree on Approval of the Foreign Policy Concept of The Russian Federation. (2023, March). *Указ об утверждении Концепции внешней политики Российской Федерации.* Президент России. http://kremlin.ru/events/president/news/70811

Timpescu, R. (2023, October 2). Nuclearelectrica, NuScale's SMR project gets nod from Romanian authority. SeeNews. https://seenews.com/news/nuclearelectrica-nuscales-smr-project-gets-nod-from-romanian-authority-835563

Ukraine Reconstruction Fund – Description. (2023, June). Retrieved January 10, 2024, from https://uploads-ssl.webflow.com/621f88db25fbf24758792dd8/64931249dc66515444cf9379_BlackRock_FMA_Ukraine_Development_Fund_DFI_for_the_reconstruction.pdf

Ukraine Recovery Conference Materials, 2022-2023. (n.d.). Retrieved January 10, 2024, from https://www.urc-international.com/conference-materials

Ukraine's National Recovery Plan. (2022, June). Ukraine national recovery council. Retrieved January 10, 2024, from https://uploads-ssl.webflow.com/621f88db25fbf24758792dd8/62c166751fcf41105380a733_NRC%20Ukraine%27s%20Recovery%20Plan%20blueprint_ENG.pdf

World Bank. (2022, September 9). *Ukraine recovery and reconstruction needs estimated $349 Billion*. Retrieved January 10, 2024, from https://www.worldbank.org/en/news/press-release/2022/09/09/ukraine-recovery-and-reconstruction-needs-estimated-349-billion

World Economic Outlook, *October 2022: Countering the Cost-of-Living Crisis*. (2022, October 11). IMF. https://www.imf.org/en/Publications/WEO/Issues/2022/10/11/world-economic-outlook-october-2022

World Economic Outlook, *October 2023: Navigating Global Divergences*. (2023, October 10). IMF. https://www.imf.org/en/Publications/WEO/Issues/2023/10/10/world-economic-outlook-october-2023
World Economic Outlook Update, January 2022: Rising Caseloads, A Disrupted Recovery, and Higher Inflation. (2022, January 25). IMF. https://www.imf.org/en/Publications/WEO/Issues/2022/01/25/world-economic-outlook-update-january-2022

Common Issues of Compensation Mechanisms and the National and International Regulatory Sources on the Compensation

Kravtsov Serhii

Abstract Chapter 7 explores the intricate landscape of compensation mechanisms following the Russian military aggression against Ukraine declared on February 24, 2022. At the national level, legislative initiatives such as the draft law "On compensation for damage and destruction" and Cabinet of Ministers' Resolution No. 326 outline procedures for compensation application and damage assessment. However, international support is essential for implementation due to resource constraints. Internationally, Decree No. 346/2022 forms a working group to develop proposals aligned with international legal frameworks, including the creation of an international claims commission. Drawing insights from past conflicts, such as the Iran-United States Claims Tribunal, bilateral negotiations remain crucial, although Russia's reluctance poses challenges. In conclusion, the chapter underscores the urgent need for comprehensive legislative frameworks and international cooperation to address the multifaceted challenges of compensation in the aftermath of conflict. It calls for concerted efforts to ensure equitable and timely restitution for victims, laying the groundwork for long-term recovery and reconciliation.

On February 24, 2022, Russia officially de jure and de facto declared war against Ukraine, hiding behind the ridiculous goals of a so-called "special military operation." As a result of the active violent and illegal hostilities by the aggressor state, a lot of damage has been done to the property of regular citizens. Both private houses and entire high-rise buildings were destroyed, and administrative buildings of regional state administrations (for example, the Kharkiv and Mykolaiv Regional State Administrations), schools, kindergartens, and other infrastructure facilities sustained damage.

As of September, according to a damage assessment conducted jointly by the World Bank and the Ministry of Communities and Territories Development of

K. Serhii (✉)
Luxembourg Centre of European Law (LCEL) of the University of Luxembourg, Luxembourg, Luxembourg
e-mail: serhii.kravtsov@uni.lu

S. Nate (ed.), *Ukraine's Journey to Recovery, Reform and Post-War Reconstruction*, Contributions to Security and Defence Studies,
https://doi.org/10.1007/978-3-031-66434-2_7

Ukraine, Russia has caused $326 billion of direct damage to Ukraine. As the Prime Minister of Ukraine Denys Shmyhal noted, $105 billion out of this amount is needed to restore numerous destroyed infrastructure facilities. $17 billion is needed for rapid recovery, $3.4 billion of which Ukraine will receive already this year and the rest of it — in 2023.[1]

To date, establishing a unified compensation mechanism for the damage caused by the illegal actions of Russian troops remains a crucial issue on the agenda. At the national level, some regulations have already been prepared and submitted for discussion, which will help those who have suffered damage receive compensation for their destroyed property. Thus, in accordance with the draft law "On compensation for damage and destruction of certain categories of real estate objects as a result of hostilities, acts of terrorism, and sabotage caused by the military aggression of the Russian Federation", matters regarding the following are being regulated: recipients of compensation; procedure for submitting an application for compensation; ways of providing compensation; legal status and competence of the Commission for considering compensation issues, etc. In addition, the Resolution of the Cabinet of Ministers of Ukraine dated March 20, 2022, No. 326 "On approval of the Procedure for determining the damage and losses caused to Ukraine as a result of the armed aggression of the Russian Federation" defines the procedures for determining the damage and losses caused to Ukraine as a result of the armed aggression of the Russian Federation.

Yet, without the support of the international community, Ukraine's efforts to implement ideas for actual compensation to citizens who lost their property may be impossible due to the lack of resources.

On May 18, 2022, the Decree of the President of Ukraine No. 346/2022 "On working group to develop and implement international legal mechanisms to indemnify the damage caused to Ukraine as a result of the armed aggression of the Russian Federation" was adopted. Clause 2 of this Decree states that the working group shall develop and submit proposals regarding the means and legal instruments for compensation for damage and losses caused to Ukraine as a result of the armed aggression of the Russian Federation, including reparations, confiscation, contributions, as well as steps for their implementation with taking into account international legal mechanisms, international experience, and judicial practice.

The main idea of this working group is to create a Commission on international claims for compensation. Like most other claims commissions, the powers of the Commission shall be determined by an international agreement concluded between Ukraine and the concerned states. This commission shall be a "venue" where a wide range of issues will be considered in accordance with international economic and humanitarian law with regard to various groups of injured parties, including states, international organizations, and legal entities and individuals. The establishment of such an institution is not a new phenomenon in international humanitarian law, since

[1] https://www.ukrinform.ua/rubric-ato/3580685-koli-i-ak-mozna-bude-otrimati-kompensaciu-za-zrujnovane-rosieu-majno-analiz.html.

the military conflicts between Iran and the USA, Eritrea and Ethiopia ended with the establishment of special commissions, authorized to consider similar issues. However, this institution requires analysis in a comparative legal aspect.

As an example of the existence of a similar institution, it is possible to analyze the activities of the Iran-United States Commission (the official name is the Iran–United States Claims Tribunal). The Tribunal for the Settlement of Mutual Claims between Iran and the United States was established as one of the measures taken to resolve the crisis in relations between the Islamic Republic of Iran and the United States of America that arose out of the hostage crisis at the United States Embassy in Tehran in November 1979 and the subsequent freeze of Iranian assets by the United States of America. The Government of the People's Democratic Republic of Algeria acted as a mediator in the search for a mutually acceptable solution. After consulting the governments of both countries on the commitments each was willing to make to resolve the crisis, the Algerian government recorded these commitments in two statements made on January 19, 1981. Iran and the United States then joined the "General Declaration" and the "Claims Settlement Declaration", collectively "Algiers Declarations". According to the Algiers Declarations, the Tribunal has jurisdiction over claims by citizens of the United States against Iran and by citizens of Iran against the United States.

Analyzing the work of this Tribunal, it can be seen that the main emphasis is placed on the fact that both countries between which there were hostilities expressed a desire to regulate these issues regarding compensation for the damage caused as a result of military actions.

In the situation that currently exists in Ukraine, the aggressor country will not enter into such negotiations with regard to recognizing the fact of causing damage to Ukraine.

In addition, the International Court of Justice, in its decision of February 9, 2022, considered the issue of reparations as a result of the armed conflict between Uganda and the Democratic Republic of the Congo.[2] This decision, of course, shall not be considered as one that can be applied to the order of compensation for damage caused to Ukraine, which was caused by Russia's military aggression from 2014 to the present, but its analysis may be very useful for developing the key methodological aspects.

The crucial document, which is one of the main tools for compensation for the damage caused by Russia on the territory of the sovereign state — Ukraine, is the Agreement Between the Cabinet of Ministers of Ukraine and the Government of the Russian Federation on the Encouragement and Mutual Protection of Investments of November 27, 1998. This document is the object of research in international law enforcement practice. By using this Agreement, the Ukrainian side appealed to the ICC Court of Arbitration to recover damages caused by the Russian side to the Bank of Ukraine as a result of the annexation of Crimea. The claim was satisfied in full by

[2] Armed Activities on the Territory of the Congo (Democratic Republic of the Congo v. Uganda) https://www.icj-cij.org/public/files/case-related/116/116-20220209-JUD-01-00-EN.pdf.

the decision of international commercial arbitration. Disagreeing with this decision, the Russian side appealed to the Court of Appeal of Paris with a request to annul the arbitral award. And on March 30, 2021, such an application was granted. Reviewing this decision, the Court of Cassation of France canceled this decision on December 7, 2022, while adopting a new one, which refused to annul the arbitral award of the international commercial arbitration on the grounds that the arbitration was competent to consider this dispute and its decision is such that it meets the requirements both of the national procedural law of France and the New York Convention[3] (the Convention on the Recognition and Enforcement of Foreign Arbitral Awards).

With its criminal actions, Russia has caused intolerable consequences for Ukraine, which consist in damage to the lives and health of people, their property, destruction of infrastructure, etc. In such circumstances, the most difficult issue that remains not fully resolved is the presence of legislative regulation.

On March 20, 2022, the Cabinet of Ministers of Ukraine adopted Resolution No. 326, which approved the Procedure for determining the damage and losses caused to Ukraine as a result of the armed aggression of the Russian Federation. Despite the encouraging name, this regulation did not provide a methodology for recording the damage caused and determining the amount of the damage caused. The document only obliged state bodies to establish such methods within 6 months. Through this directive, the government has sought to encompass an extensive spectrum of domains through which damage and losses should be assessed. *This array of domains is notably comprehensive, spanning 22 categories, each containing a set of primary indicators subject to evaluation.* When these categories are conceptually grouped, several overarching classifications emerge. These encompass human losses (both civilian and military); material military losses intertwined with aspects concerning the state's internal security; depletion of housing stock and infrastructure facilities; the deterioration of public building assets (including educational, sports, social welfare, healthcare, cultural, and administrative structures); diminution of communal amenities, infrastructure, transport, and other networks, as well as energy infrastructure; ecological harm encompassing damage to land, depletion of subsoil and forest resources, degradation of water resources and atmospheric air, and impacts on natural reserves; loss of cultural heritage; and economic losses sustained by enterprises, institutions, and organizations.

In summation, it's evident that the damage stipulated by the governmental resolution aligns closely with societal demands, as observed through the examination of judicial precedents. This concordance underscores the government's commitment to addressing societal needs and its pursuit of the most efficacious mechanisms to achieve this objective.

On March 26, 2022, the Cabinet of Ministers of Ukraine adopted Resolution No. 380, which approved the Procedure for collection, processing, and accounting information on damaged and destroyed real estate as a result of hostilities, terrorist

[3]Cour de cassation, Première chambre civile, 7 décembre 2022, n° 21–15.390, Publié au Bulletin - Publié au Rapport https://www.courdecassation.fr/decision/63903c7f0f8a5205d45d7c87.

acts, and sabotage caused by the military aggression of the Russian Federation, which provided for the possibility of submitting information reports on destroyed/damaged immovable property through the Diia web portal. In accordance with this procedure, information reports on damaged or destroyed property were submitted according to the existing principle — without checking the relevant facts. In this regard, entering information into the state database about receiving a notification from the victim about the damage caused to him (her) cannot be considered a legal record of the fact of such damage.

On April 5, 2022, the Cabinet of Ministers of Ukraine adopted Resolution No. 423, which approved changes to the Procedure for conducting inspections of construction objects put into operation, which was approved by the Resolution of the Cabinet of Ministers of Ukraine No. 257 of April 12, 2017, namely, it was stipulated that inspections of damaged or destroyed buildings shall be carried out by the decision of the owner of the object or authorized bodies (bodies of local self-government or military administrations) by bringing specialists who have a qualification certificate for the right to perform inspection works in the construction of objects, as well as specialists with the qualification level "leading" or "category 1" specializing in "engineering and construction design in terms of ensuring mechanical resistance and stability":

- Design engineers;
- Consulting engineers;
- Construction experts.

On April 19, 2022, the Cabinet of Ministers of Ukraine adopted Resolution No. 473, which approved the Procedure for implementation of urgent works related to the elimination of consequences of the armed aggression of the Russian Federation, related to the damage to buildings and structures, which provided that the examination of damaged objects is carried out by the decision of the authorized bodies through the establishment of a commission, which includes specialists who have obtained higher education in the area of expertise "Construction and Architecture".

Based on the results of the conducted examination, the commission draws up an act according to the established template, which serves as the basis for entering information into the State Register of damaged or destroyed property, which does not yet exist at this time, but its implementation is provided for by the draft law No. 7385 of May 17, 2022.

On April 28, 2022, the Ministry for Communities and Territories Development of Ukraine issued Order No. 65, which approved the Methodology for the inspection of buildings and constructions damaged as a result of emergencies, hostilities, and acts of terrorism, according to which the inspection of damaged or destroyed buildings and structures is carried out in accordance with the Procedure for conducting inspections of construction objects put into operation, approved by Resolution of the Cabinet of Ministers of Ukraine No. 257 of April 12, 2017.

On May 18, 2022, the Ministry of Agrarian Policy and Food of Ukraine issued Order No. 295, which approved the Methodology for determining damage and losses caused to the land fund of Ukraine as a result of the armed aggression of the Russian Federation, according to which any documented information (survey reports, reports of commissions on determining the damages, reports on expert monetary valuation of land plots, primary accounting documents, information from the State Land Cadastre, land management documentation, etc.) shall form the information base for determining damage and losses, and the amount of damages caused to owners of agricultural land plots is determined by commissions created by local state administrations or local self-government bodies in the manner determined by Resolution of the Cabinet of Ministers of Ukraine No. 284 of April 19, 1993. At the same time, the value of residential houses, industrial and other buildings and constructions, including unfinished construction and lost profits, is included in the amount of such damages.

So, the government of Ukraine itself created a conflict regarding how exactly the fact of damage to property should be recorded:

- By the commission established by a self-government body in accordance with the Resolution of the Cabinet of Ministers of Ukraine No. 767 of September 2, 2020;
- By the owner or manager of the real estate object in accordance with the Resolution of the Cabinet of Ministers of Ukraine No. 257 of April 12, 2017;
- By the commission established by the authorized body in accordance with the Resolution of the Cabinet of Ministers of Ukraine No. 473 of April 19, 2022;
- By the commission established by the local state administration or local self-government body in accordance with the Resolution of the Cabinet of Ministers of Ukraine No. 284 of April 19, 1993?

At the same time, it remains unclear:

- Who and how should establish that the property was damaged as a result of hostilities, and not for other reasons?
- How should the owner or authorized bodies carry out inspections of objects located in the war zone or on territories occupied by the enemy?
- May other evidence be used to confirm the facts of the destruction or damage of property, in addition to the inspection reports drawn up by the relevant commissions — protocols of the inspection of the scene of the incident drawn up by investigators in accordance with the requirements of the Criminal Procedure Code of Ukraine; inspection reports of facilities drawn up by forensic experts; photo, video materials, witness statements, etc.?
- When determining the amount of damage, can generally recognized methods and standards for assessing the amount of damage be used, which involve the use of complex assessment methods, and not only the method of calculating the replacement cost of construction, the application of which is established by the abovementioned regulations?

The Ukrainian government partially recognized the existence of these problems: on June 14, 2022, the official website of the Cabinet of Ministers of Ukraine published information on the need to simplify the procedure for registering notices of destruction or damage to property and introducing a unified form of inspection report and a unified estimate of the cost of damages. However, this intention has not yet been realized.

On August 4, 2022, the official website of the Ministry of Economy of Ukraine published for discussion the draft Methodology for determining damage and the amount of damage caused to enterprises, institutions and organizations of all forms of ownership as a result of the destruction and damage sustained to their property due to the armed aggression of the Russian Federation, as well as lost profits from impossibility or obstacles in the conduct of economic activities.

This project contributes to addressing some of the controversial issues regarding the application of damage assessment methods, but does not at all address the problems related to the procedure for conducting surveys and recording the facts of damage or destruction of the victims' property.

As for the efforts of the international community to help in the establishment of a tribunal that will deal with issues of compensation for damage, it can be said that during 2022–2023 numerous international documents were developed and approved.

After the beginning of the full-scale invasion of the occupying country into the territory of independent Ukraine, a number of international documents were adopted, which called on the international community to do its utmost to resist the criminal actions of the "terrorist country".

These include the Resolution of the European Parliament of May 19, 2022 on the fight against impunity for war crimes in Ukraine (2022/2655 (RSP)),[4] the Resolution of the European Parliament of October 6, 2022 on Russia's escalation of its war of aggression against Ukraine (2022/2851 (RSP)).[5]

Also, in accordance with the Resolution of the European Parliament of January 19, 2023 "On the establishment of a tribunal for the crime of aggression against Ukraine" (2022/3017 (RSP)), the EU and its member states, as well as their partners and allies, are invited to start discussing the legal possibility of using sovereign assets of the Russian state as compensation for violations of international law by Russia in Ukraine, potentially by denying such assets the protection of sovereign immunity or by limiting such protection.

Are all damages subject to compensation, or is there potential differentiation? On January 26, 2023, the Parliamentary Assembly of the Council of Europe passed Resolution No. 2482. This resolution reiterates that the Russian Federation's armed

[4]European Parliament resolution of 19 May 2022 on the fight against impunity for war crimes in Ukraine (2022/2655(RSP)) https://www.europarl.europa.eu/doceo/document/TA-9-2022-0218_EN.html.

[5]European Parliament resolution of 6 October 2022 on Russia's escalation of its war of aggression against Ukraine (2022/2851(RSP)) https://www.europarl.europa.eu/doceo/document/TA-9-2022-0353_EN.html.

attack and large-scale invasion of Ukraine launched on 24 February 2022 constitute an "aggression" under the terms of Resolution 3314 (XXIX) of the United Nations General Assembly adopted in 1974 and are clearly in breach of the Charter of the United Nations. The Assembly emphasizes that the Russian Federation will be considered as continuing its aggression until the sovereignty, territorial integrity, unity and political independence of Ukraine within its internationally recognised borders are fully re-established. The Assembly recalls that the ongoing aggression is a continuation of the aggression started on 20 February 2014, which included the invasion, occupation and illegal annexation of Crimea by the Russian Federation.[6] This juncture is of paramount significance in delineating which damages, and over what time frame, are eligible for compensation on the international stage and thus in Ukraine. Is it the entirety of damages sustained from the entire period of aggression, spanning February 2014 to the present, or solely those incurred since the commencement of the full-scale invasion on February 24, 2022? The response to this question is unequivocal: Russia must unquestionably be held accountable for all damages accumulated over these 9 years of universally acknowledged aggression.

Furthermore, within the same Resolution, the Parliamentary Assembly of the Council of Europe strongly supports the creation of a special tribunal that its jurisdiction would be limited to the crime of aggression committed against Ukraine and would extend ratione temporis to the aggression started by the Russian Federation in February 2014.[7] Although the context involves the crime of aggression and a specialized criminal tribunal, the recognition of the ongoing period of Russia's aggression against Ukraine furnishes a foundation to seek compensation for all damages incurred during this duration.

The next step, which is aimed at creating a practical basis for legal grounds, became Resolution CM/Res(2023)3 establishing the Enlarged Partial Agreement on the Register of Damage Caused by the Aggression of the Russian Federation against Ukraine, Adopted by the Committee of Ministers on 12 May 2023. By this Resolution the Committee of Ministers of Council of Europe resolves to establish the Enlarged Partial Agreement on the Register of Damage Caused by the Aggression of the Russian Federation against Ukraine, governed by the Statute appended hereto that shall serve as a record, in documentary form, of evidence and claims information on damage, loss or injury caused to all natural and legal persons concerned, as well as the State of Ukraine (including its regional and local authorities, State-owned or controlled entities), caused on or after 24 February 2022 in the territory of Ukraine within its internationally recognised borders, extending to its territorial waters, by Russian Federation's internationally wrongful acts in or against Ukraine.[8] Notably,

[6]Resolution of the Parliamentary Assembly 2482 (January 26, 2023) https://pace.coe.int/pdf/af950f18903d947bda73c9e0a7689a2f41e9128cd2da8bd1bc2211277e4e666a/res.%202482.pdf.

[7]Resolution of the Parliamentary Assembly 2482 (January 26, 2023) https://pace.coe.int/pdf/af950f18903d947bda73c9e0a7689a2f41e9128cd2da8bd1bc2211277e4e666a/res.%202482.pdf.

[8]Resolution CM/Res(2023)3 establishing the Enlarged Partial Agreement on the Register of Damage Caused by the Aggression of the Russian Federation against Ukraine, Adopted by the Committee of Ministers on 12 May 2023.

the phrasing employed indicates the intent to encompass damages incurred on or after February 24, 2022, within this newly established Register. However, this language is semantically imprecise, engendering two possible interpretations. In the first interpretation, the phrasing "caused on" can be understood as encapsulating all damages accrued within the period spanning February 20, 2014, up to February 24, 2022. The second, more circumscribed interpretation is less optimistic for Ukraine, focusing exclusively on damages originating during the full-scale invasion period, specifically from February 24, 2022, up to the present. Nevertheless, when drawing from the content of the earlier Council of Europe Parliamentary Assembly Resolution, adopted several months prior, it is reasonable to deduce that the Register should also incorporate losses suffered by Ukraine up until February 24, 2022. This interpretation is both equitable and offers additional legal grounds for compensation.

Moreover, the United Nations General Assembly[9] which has repeatedly called for the immediate withdrawal of troops from the territory of Ukraine and the need to protect the civilian population plays an active role in promoting peace and facilitating the end of any military actions on the part of Russia. As for the need to implement a compensation mechanism, the UN General Assembly in its Resolution of November 14, 2022 also recognizes the need to establish, in cooperation with Ukraine, an international compensation mechanism for losses or damage caused as a result of internationally illegal acts of the Russian Federation in Ukraine or against Ukraine; recommends that member states, in cooperation with Ukraine, create an international register of damage, which would serve as a repository of documentary confirmation of evidence and information about claims for damage, loss or damage sustained to all relevant individuals and legal entities.[10]

This Resolution became the object of discussion both at the official level and in doctrinal circles. Some states (China, Russia, North Korea, Eritrea) have expressed their confusion about the legality of the Resolution, since, in their opinion, the General Assembly has exceeded its powers due to the fact that it is not a judicial body and therefore it cannot create an international mechanism that would determine internationally illegal actions of the state and would determine such compensation as necessary.

However, when justifying their position, the states that came out in support of the Resolution note that this international document does not entail the creation of any compensation mechanisms, but only declares the need for the creation of such a compensation mechanism. These suggestions correctly correspond to Art. 14 of the UN Charter, according to which the General Assembly may recommend measures for the peaceful adjustment of any situation, regardless of origin, which it deems likely to impair the general welfare or friendly relations among nations, including

[9]Resolution adopted by the UN General Assembly on March 24, 2022 (https://documents-dds-ny.un.org/doc/UNDOC/GEN/N22/301/70/PDF/N2230170.pdf?OpenElement).

[10]UN General Assembly (GA) adopted draft resolution A/ES-11/L.6 Furtherance of remedy and reparation for aggression against Ukraine https://documents-dds-ny.un.org/doc/UNDOC/LTD/N22/679/12/PDF/N2267912.pdf?OpenElement.

situations resulting from a violation of the provisions of the present Charter setting forth the Purposes and Principles of the United Nations[11]).

Therefore, it can be seen quite clearly that addressing the issue of creating a compensatory mechanism for reparation of damage caused by a terrorist country is not only the responsibility of the Ukrainian authorities, but also the international community, which is concerned with issues of peace and its own national security.

On March 16, 2022, the International Court of Justice of the United Nations passed a decision in the case "Ukraine v. Russia" (Allegations of Genocide under the Convention on the Prevention and Punishment of the Crime of Genocide) regarding temporary measures against Russia. Despite the unanimity in the adoption of this decision, the Court obliged the Russian Federation to immediately suspend military operations launched by it on February 24, 2022 on the territory of Ukraine; obliged the Russian Federation to ensure that no steps are to be taken to facilitate military operations by any military or irregular armed formations that may be directed or supported by it, as well as any organizations and individuals that may be under its control or management.[12] Despite the preliminary nature of this decision, the Court stated that it is binding and thus creates international legal obligations for Russia. By continuing active hostilities on the territory of Ukraine after the adoption of this decision, Russia defiantly neglects these obligations.

Therefore, by its active actions, Russia in the international legal context "unties the hands" of other countries to apply countermeasures to fulfill their obligations. In the classical doctrine of international law, such countermeasures are usually called "authorized repression".[13]

In the international legal understanding of the procedure for countermeasures and compensation for damage to Russia, attention should be drawn to the 2001 Articles on Responsibility of States for Internationally Wrongful Acts.[14] Although this instrument is not codified in form, it is effective and fully fulfils the objectives and objectives laid down in its substance. Thus, the UN General Assembly Resolution of 2019 provided for a special role of these articles, determining that they are an effective source of international law, to which a large number of both international organizations and international courts refer.[15]

---

[11]United Nations, Charter of the United Nations, 1 UNTS XVI, 24 October 1945, https://www.refworld.org/legal/constinstr/un/1945/en/27654.

[12]Allegations of Genocide under the Convention on the Prevention and Punishment of the Crime of Genocide (Ukraine v. Russian Federation) - The Court decides on the admissibility of the declarations of intervention filed by 33 States https://www.icj-cij.org/public/files/case-related/182/182-20220316-ORD-01-00-EN.pdf.

[13]Paddeu, F. (2018). Countermeasures. In Justification and Excuse in International Law: Concept and Theory of General Defences (Cambridge Studies in International and Comparative Law, pp. 225–284).

[14]UN. General Assembly. Fifty-sixth session. Resolution 56/83. Responsibility of States for internationally wrongful acts. 2001. UN Doc. A/RES/56/83. URL: https://documents-dds-ny.un.org/ doc/UNDOC/ GEN/N01/477/97/PDF/N0147797.pdf?OpenElement.

[15]UN General Assembly (GA) adopted draft resolution 74/180 Responsibility of States for internationally wrongful acts https://documents-dds-ny.un.org/doc/UNDOC/GEN/N19/431/90/PDF/N1943190.pdf?OpenElement.

That mechanism of countermeasures (the possibility of non-compliance with international obligations) provided for in the Articles for those countries which consider themselves the victim of Russian military aggression should be applied until the aggressor country complies with the laws on the use of force, international humanitarian law and other peremptory norms of international law, including diplomatic and consular privileges.

Speaking about national mechanisms of compensation for damage, attention should be focused on the analytical information that was received on the authors' request from the Ministry of Justice of Ukraine. Thus, according to official information, the Ministry of Justice of Ukraine ensures self-representation ***of the Government's interests in 275 court cases on claims of individuals and legal entities for compensation for damage caused by the aggressor country*** (by the Russian Federation) as a result of criminal actions on the territory of Ukraine in the period from 2014 to 24.02.2022 and from 24.02.2022 to 01.07.2023, where the defendant is the state of Ukraine represented by the Cabinet of Ministers of Ukraine or the Government of Ukraine. That is, analyzing the data obtained, it can be seen that the citizens of Ukraine are still trying to receive compensation for the damage caused as a result of the destruction of their homes by the aggressor country, namely from the state of Ukraine. But to what extent these attempts are justified will be discussed further in the analysis of procedural mechanisms.

The Ministry of Justice also notes that the Division for Enforcement of Decisions of the Department of the State Enforcement Service of the Ministry of Justice of Ukraine is conducting a consolidated enforcement proceeding dated 06.05.2019 on debt collection from the debtor—the Russian Federation, which as of 20.07.2023 includes ***199 enforcement proceedings*** (the number is not constant due to the current receipt of enforcement documents). There were no recovery of funds within the consolidated enforcement proceedings. These enforcement proceedings, which are mentioned by the Ministry of Justice of Ukraine, are the result of the recognition and enforcement of the decision of the international commercial arbitration (The Hague, Kingdom of the Netherlands) in the case of PTS No. 2015-36 on the claim of Everest Estate LLC and others against the Russian Federation represented by the Ministry of Justice of the Russian Federation on the territory of Ukraine. The current legislation allows a public or private enforcement officer to consolidate enforcement documents into one consolidated proceeding if the debtor is one and the same. This is clearly provided for in Art. 30 of the Law of Ukraine "On Enforcement Proceedings", according to which the execution of several decisions on the recovery of funds from one debtor is carried out by the state executor who opened the first enforcement proceedings against such a debtor, within the framework of consolidated enforcement proceedings.

Enforcement of several decisions on recovery of funds from one debtor is carried out by a private enforcement officer within the framework of consolidated enforcement proceedings.

That is, it can be seen that the claimants who initiated the procedure for enforcing the arbitral award on the territory of Ukraine at the expense of Russian property have become a "bridge" for other claimants.

In addition, during the analysis of the above-mentioned enforcement proceedings, through the prism of law enforcement practice, one can see a partial answer to the question that interests many people who have become victims of military aggression—what property of Russia remains on the territory of Ukraine that can be foreclosed?

In the Resolution of the Commercial Court of Cassation, reviewing the decision of the appellate court to appeal against the actions of the state executor on holding an auction for the sale of financial assets of Russian state-owned companies, it is noted that the Russian Federation is the owner of an indirect significant participation in the bank, since it indirectly owns its shares through the R&D "VEB.RF". The court of cassation, rejecting the arguments of the Russian companies, notes that the court of first instance, when deciding the issue of the legality of foreclosure on the property of R&D "VEB.RF" for the debts of the Russian Federation applied the doctrine of "raising the corporate veil" in the form of "alter ego" (provides for the reverse lifting of the curtain—bringing the participant of the legal entity to responsibility for its debts). And as a conclusion, it was recognized that on 04.03.2020, during the exchange trading, 99.7726% of the shares of PJSC "Prominvestbank" were sold for UAH 268,709,960.78. (EUR 6,717,749), in connection with which on 06.03.2020 an exchange contract for the purchase and sale of securities was concluded between the Ministry of Justice and FC Fortify LLC. These funds should be used to pay off debts within the framework of consolidated enforcement proceedings.[16]

[16]Resolution of the Commercial Court of Cassation dated 20.97.2022 in case 910/4210/20 https://reyestr.court.gov.ua/Review/105612017.

The Tort of Armed Aggression Principles Applied by the Russian Federation Against Ukraine and Its Post War Recovery

Roman Maydanyk

Abstract This chapter explores the intricate legal landscape surrounding the tort of armed aggression, focusing on the principles applied by the Russian Federation against Ukraine and the subsequent post-war recovery efforts. It underscores the urgent need for effective legal mechanisms to compel the aggressor state to provide compensation for the extensive damage inflicted. Reparations, spanning infrastructure reconstruction and individual restitution for human rights violations, are deemed essential components of transitional justice. However, existing international and national legal frameworks lack clear guidelines for establishing tort liability for damage caused by armed aggression. The paper advocates for a paradigm shift towards a reparative-tort model, emphasizing individual victim compensation alongside state reparations. It examines the evolving nature of property liability, encompassing both public and private torts of armed aggression. Furthermore, it outlines potential guiding principles for armed aggression tort and Ukraine's recovery, including provisions for counter-measures, asset constraints, and models for implementation in domestic and international law. The study concludes by advocating for the formulation of soft law acts to address these gaps and pave the way for more coherent legal frameworks and judicial practices in navigating the complexities of armed conflict compensation and recovery.

Introduction

One of the prerequisites for the early termination of the armed aggression of the Russian federation and recovery of Ukraine is the creation of effective legal mechanisms for compulsory compensation by the aggressor state for the damage caused to Ukraine, which necessitates a rethinking at the international and national levels of the legal provisions on property liability for damage caused by the armed aggression of the Russian federation against Ukraine and its post war recovery.

R. Maydanyk (✉)
Civil Procedure Department, Taras Shevchenko National University of Kyiv, Kyiv, Ukraine

S. Nate (ed.), *Ukraine's Journey to Recovery, Reform and Post-War Reconstruction*, Contributions to Security and Defence Studies,
https://doi.org/10.1007/978-3-031-66434-2_8

Reparations for the damage caused by this armed aggression should include both reparations in the context of infrastructure reconstruction of Ukraine and compensation to the state of Ukraine, as well as provide for reparations to specific individuals who suffered from gross human rights violations, war crimes, crimes against humanity and genocide committed during this Russian-Ukrainian armed conflict since 2014 and related to it (Busol, 2023).

Such a comprehensive approach is explained by the foundations of transitional justice and its fundamental principle of the centrality of the role and interests of all victims (UN Secretary-General, 2010).

Modern international and national law on compensation for damage caused by armed aggression does not contain clearly defined grounds and conditions of tort and other property liability for this type of tort and violation of international humanitarian law, given the historically established traditions of the prevailing international public law regulation of this type of property liability.

In this regard, a common approach is that "all combat-related damages should be compensated through 'national or international reparations programs' rather than through 'individual claims against any government'." (Wright, 1951, p. 550).

This approach creates a not always justified priority of the provisions of public international law on war reparations over national and international tort law for damage caused as a result of armed conflict.

As a result, this effectively excludes the possibility of compensation for jointly caused damage by the aggressor state and legal entities and individuals who contribute to armed aggression, as well as the recovery of accidental damage caused by armed conflicts, although it provides for provisions on intentional infliction of such damage to a certain list of civilians that are difficult to apply in practice.

The expediency of preparing guidelines for property liability for armed aggression as a prerequisite and prototype for an international convention and other international treaties on liability for this international crime is worthy of attention.

The Guiding Principles of armed aggression tort and Ukraine's recovery are a soft law act that will provide for provisions on the grounds and principles of compensation for damage caused by armed aggression, concept of counter-measure as a general ground for compensation of damage caused by armed aggression, the concept and conditions of the tort of armed aggression, and a model for its implementation in international and national law.

This study will provide a general characterization of property liability for armed aggression Russian federation against Ukraine (1) and then examine some guiding principles of the armed aggression tort guiding principles applied by Russian federation against Ukraine and its Recovery (2).

This study was conducted with a focus on the development of guiding principles on compensation of damage caused by armed aggression based on a comparison of the provisions of international law and national law of selected civil law (Ukraine, Estonia) and common law jurisdictions (US, UK, Canada).

General Provisions on Property Liability for Damage Caused by Armed Aggression

International Law on Property Liability for Damage Caused by Armed Aggression: From Sanctions to Reparations and Tort Compensation

Currently, there is a shift away from the understanding of international law as purely interstate relations in favor of international private relations and an individual model of compensation for damages.

In this regard, the international legal doctrine states that international law goes beyond interstate relations and regulates them in such a way as to ensure the protection of people.

The evolution of international law in favor of an individual model of compensation for victims of armed conflict, rather than the reparations model, despite the absence of a corresponding explicit provision in international treaties, should meet the current conditions.

The obligation to make reparations "is rooted in the general principles of state responsibility" (as expressed by the HRC in the Chorzów Factory case, 1928), in Article 3 of the Hague Convention (IV) of 1907 and in Article 91 of Additional Protocol (I) of 1977 to the four Geneva Conventions of 1949).

National Laws on Property Liability for Damage Caused by the Armed Aggression of the Russian Federation

Legal issues related to compensation for damage caused by the armed aggression of the Russian federation are becoming increasingly important and are determined by the parallel existing trends towards international unification and active implementation of methods of compensation at the national and international levels: appeals to national courts, national and international compensation commissions, the European Court of Human Rights, the International Court of Justice, and foreign arbitration courts.

The law of Ukraine is characterized by the legal idea of self-defense of the state and the recognition of the non-recognition of the sovereign immunity of the aggressor state for claims for compensation for damage caused by it and the resulting recognition of the "tort exception" of claims of the state of Ukraine, which uses self-defense, and private victims of armed aggression against the aggressor state (the Russian Federation) and its accomplices for compensation for damage caused by armed aggression, which is a gross violation of the aggressor state's international obligations, as well as international humanitarian and investment law.

In 2018, the Supreme Court of Ukraine (2018) concluded that responsibility for violations of the Constitution and laws of Ukraine, human and civil rights and freedoms in the temporarily occupied territory of Ukraine, in particular the Luhansk region, should be imposed on Russia as the occupying power in accordance with the norms and principles of international law (resolution of the Supreme Court of November 21, 2018 in case No. 2-o/381/134/16 (No. 381/2635/16-c)).

In our opinion, foreclosure on property owned or controlled by the aggressor state and property belonging to legal entities or individuals who are accomplices of armed aggression and alienated on the basis of court decisions on the grounds of threatening the national security, sovereignty or territorial integrity of Ukraine or contributing to the creation of such a threat, and court decisions on the recovery of damage caused by the aggressor state as a result of armed aggression in favor of injured individuals and legal entities are proportionate and necessary measures of individual self-defense of the state of Ukraine and self-defense of individuals and legal entities that have suffered damage as a result of armed aggression.

The United States has an established law enforcement practice of confiscating private Russian assets (Cohen, 2023; McCandless Farmer, 2023). The United States is the first foreign country to prosecute war crimes against its own citizens committed on the territory of Ukraine (Wendling, 2023).

US law is gradually shifting from imposing sanctions for armed aggression and liability for their violation to confiscating sovereign assets of the Russian Federation and private assets of Russian officials, as well as the government-aligned elites and those individuals and entities that directly or indirectly contribute to armed aggression against Ukraine.

The US Congress held a hearing of the Commission on Security and Cooperation in Europe (Helsinki Commission) on the confiscation of Russian assets in favour of Ukraine. The hearing was dedicated to the draft law "Restoring Economic Prosperity and Opportunity for Ukrainians Act". This draft law provides for the possibility of extrajudicial, i.e. administrative, confiscation of sovereign assets of the Russian Federation to compensate for the damage caused by the armed aggression against Ukraine (Boyarchuk, 2023).

The United Kingdom (UK) is going to introduce new laws that will allow ministers to maintain Russian sanctions until compensation is paid to Ukraine, thus introducing a way for frozen Russian assets to be donated to Ukrainian reconstruction (Viner, 2023).

The UK government is preparing proposals for the legislative implementation of a mechanism for using seized Russian assets to rebuild Ukraine, based on the idea that freezing Russian assets is not enough and that they should be used for reconstruction.

The British Parliament (UK Parliament, 2023) is considering a draft law on the confiscation of Russian state assets and support for Ukraine (Seizure of Russian State Assets and Support for Ukraine Bill).

Canadian law provides for a mechanism of compensation for damage at the expense of seized property of the Russian Federation and its residents. The Confiscated Property Management Act of Canada (SC 1993, c. 37) provides, inter alia, for mechanisms to replenish confiscated property accounts (Government of Canada, 1993). Canada has established accounts known as the Forfeited Property Working Capital Account and the Seized Property Revenue Account.

Estonia is working on a law that will allow the use of seized assets of the Russian Federation to compensate Ukraine for damages. Russia continues its war in Ukraine, and the devastation in Ukraine is growing every day. It is unfair that taxpayers in democratic countries should pay for the war damage caused by Russia (Perun, 2023).

The Government of Estonia noted that "in accordance with international law, unlawful losses must be compensated. The compensation for the damage caused by the aggressor, provided that Russia does not do so, will be the so-called advance from frozen assets. A prerequisite for the use of frozen assets is an international agreement with Ukraine or an international compensation mechanism to track losses and compensation. The first step is to create a war damage register in Ukraine at the Council of Europe. The Ministry of Foreign Affairs and the Ministry of Justice of Estonia have prepared a draft law on amendments to the Law on International Sanctions, which will be submitted for approval in the near future." (Government Communication Unit, 2023).

Reparations and Mixed Models of Property Liability for Damage Caused by Armed Aggression

International law knows two main models of war damage compensation: the post-war reparations model (reparations model) and the mixed model (reparations and tort model).

The model of post-war reparations is compensation for damage to the victim state of an armed conflict. The mixed model is a simultaneous compensation of damages to both the state-victim of an internationally wrongful act and its civilian population.

At present, Ukraine is mainly following the reparations model with elements of the tort model, which provides for the determination of the amounts and mechanism of compensation payment by the state commission for compensation for damage caused by armed aggression.

In exchange for the payment of compensation amounts, this commission receives a recourse claim for the return of the paid amount to the debtor whose fault caused the damage. Recourse is characterized by the fact that the legal relationship under which the person made the compensation has ceased, and therefore a new one has arisen—related to the recourse claim. The right of recourse arises out of relations for causing damage (i.e., non-contractual, tort relations) (Supreme Court of Ukraine, 2020; Rashevska, 2022, p. 1037).

In our opinion, it is necessary to move from sanctions to a reparative-tort model of property liability for damage under the rules of right on counter-measures and the tort of armed aggression.

However, regardless of which model, exclusively reparations or mixed, will be used in Ukrainian and international law, it is worthwhile to determine the conditions regarding the compensation of damages to victims, which is tortious in nature based on their individual or collective claims, as well as their correlation with interstate reparations.

The Nature of Property Liability for Damage Caused by Armed Aggression

By its legal nature, property liability for damage caused by armed aggression is a complex legal institution governed by private and public law (Havrylenko, 2018), combining public law elements stemming from the status of the state and private law elements reflecting the civil law status of individuals and legal entities that are parties to a tort obligation.

At the same time, given the main purpose of the obligation to compensate for damage, namely to restore the financial situation of the person who suffered damage, private law rules are preferable for its implementation.

The obligation of individuals and legal entities to compensate for damage is by its nature private law, and the obligation of the aggressor state to compensate for damage caused to the state that suffered from armed aggression is by its nature private law liability, unless otherwise follows from the nature of the forms of compensation (reimbursement), the damage to be compensated (reimbursed), the provisions of an international treaty and international customs, as well as applicable national law.

Public and Private Torts of Armed Aggression

Given the differences between public and private relations, property liability for damage caused by armed aggression can be conditionally divided into public and private torts of armed aggression.

Public Delict applies to interstate relations on compensation for property damage under the rules of reparations, which relate to compensation to the injured state, its individuals and legal entities for damage caused by the aggressor state, or in its interests and at its expense by third states.

At the same time, the reparation relations may be subject to the provisions on civil tort in cases provided for by the applicable international legal act or international customs.

Private (civil law) tort applies to the relations on compensation for damage between the aggressor state, persons who are aiding and abetting armed aggression or, in their interests and at their expense, third states, and individuals and legal entities that have suffered damage as a result of armed aggression.

A public tort provides for the obligation of the aggressor state and persons aiding and abetting armed aggression to compensate for damage caused by armed aggression to another state that has suffered from armed aggression, and a private (civil law) tort provides for the obligation of the aggressor state and individuals and legal entities aiding and abetting armed aggression to compensate for damage to injured individuals and legal entities, which may exist in parallel or in combination with each other.

Armed Aggression Tort Guiding Principles Applied by Russian Federation Against Ukraine And its Recovery

The Necessity and Scope of Armed Aggression Tort Guiding Principles Applied by Russian Federation Against Ukraine And its Recovery

Currently, there are no unified international legal acts on Armed Aggression Tort.

These relations are regulated by international legal customs and international legal acts on liability for damage caused by armed conflicts, which do not meet the current challenges of compensation for damage caused by armed aggression.

Eliminating this gap in the law should begin with the preparation of a soft law act in the form of armed aggression tort guiding principles applied by Russian federation against Ukraine and its recovery, which will facilitate the adoption of international legal acts and the formation of predictable judicial practice on these issues.

The Armed Aggression Tort Guiding Principles applied by Russian federation against Ukraine and its recovery could contain, in particular, provisions on: (1) concept of counter-measures; (2) constraint on the assets of the Russian federation and individuals and legal persons that are aiding and abetting the armed aggression; (3) the concept of armed aggression tort and the conditions of tortious liability for damage caused by armed aggression, (4) tortious liability for damages caused jointly by several persons as a result of armed aggression, (5) tortious liability and human rights violations as a result of armed aggression, (6) the standard of "due care" under armed aggression delict, (7) the implementation model of armed aggression tort in a domestic and international laws; (8) fundamentals of Ukraine's recovery; (9) key steps in reconstruction; (10) key reforms and monitoring of Ukraine's recovery plans; and (11) consolidated bond trust for compensation damage, caused by armed aggression and Ukraine's recovery;

Counter-Measures as a Universal Manifestation of Self-Defense Against Armed Aggression

The evolution of international law in favor of an individual model of compensation for victims of armed conflict in the legal doctrine is being discussed in the context of the expediency of its updating for the purposes of property liability for armed aggression, given the violation of the fundamental provisions of international law by an act of armed aggression, which gives rise to the right to self-defense in the form of counter-measures by the injured country and injured individuals, primarily residents of that country, to appeal directly to the aggressor state and related legal entities and individuals who contributed to the armed aggression, for compensation for damage caused by weapons.

In our opinion, it is advisable to introduce into international law and national law provisions on retaliatory measures as an inalienable right of any State as well as citizens and legal entities of this State to self-defense against armed aggression by another State.

A state exercising the right to self-defense against armed aggression has the right to counter measures against the aggressor state, individuals and legal entities that are aiding and abetting armed aggression, for the purpose of full compensation for damage caused as a result of armed aggression.

Damage caused by the state, or on its behalf or in its interests by individuals or legal entities, in the exercise by the state of the right to self-defense against armed aggression, including in a state of necessary defense or emergency, if their limits have not been exceeded, shall not be compensated.

Counter measures, which used by the state in the exercise of its right to self-defense, may be applied to the extent that they are proportionate to the damage caused by the armed aggression and do not violate human rights or the rights of protected persons under international humanitarian law.

A fair equilibrium (balance) between the interests of the injured state, individuals and legal entities that suffered damage as a result of armed aggression and the interests of the aggressor state, individuals and legal entities that are aiding and abetting armed aggression is considered to be maintained if the property of the aggressor state and individuals and legal entities that are aiding and abetting armed aggression is recovered, by way of arrest, confiscation, or in the course of execution of a court decision on the recovery of damage caused by armed aggression, according to the rules of sole, joint or several liability of the perpetrator(s) of the damage, or the application of a sanction established by law for an offense committed as a result of armed aggression.

Since the aggressor state and aiders and abettors of armed aggression compensate for damage caused as a result of armed aggression by foreclosing on their property in the course of execution of a court decision to recover damage under the rules of sole, joint or several liability of the perpetrator(s) of damage or the application of a sanction established by law for a crime of armed aggression, these perpetrators are not entitled to compensation within the value of the property seized from them, which is used to satisfy the claims for compensation.

Reparation and Tortious Liability for Damage Caused by Armed Aggression

In international law, the damage caused by armed aggression is compensated under the rules of reparations or tort liability. The legal uncertainty regarding the correlation of reparations with international torts and the scope of their application based on individual or collective claims of private legal entities and individuals weakens the effectiveness and prospects for full compensation and restoration of Ukraine as a state exercising self-defense.

The damage caused by the armed aggression should be compensated in accordance with the rules on payment of reparations, or tort liability, compensation for human rights violations, or other recoveries from the aggressor state, or other sources not prohibited by the law of Ukraine as an injured state, or the law of the country of recovery of property of the aggressor state or individuals and legal entities that contribute to the armed aggression, based on decisions of authorized national bodies (special commissions, etc.), bilateral or multilateral agreements between states.

Compensation payments to an injured state made during or after a war by one party—the state that committed the armed aggression, or by third states at the expense of the state that committed the armed aggression—to another party—the state that suffered from the armed aggression.

Reparations as a result of armed aggression are aimed at compensating for property damage and other harm caused by this armed aggression to the injured state, individuals and legal entities associated with it.

Other foreclosure against the aggressor state include the seizure and confiscation of its sovereign assets as a result of violation of sanctions imposed on the aggressor state for committing armed aggression, as well as recovery of damage caused by armed aggression based on a decision of a national court or international tribunal.

The Russian Federation, as the aggressor state, and individuals and legal entities involved in the armed aggression, who contribute to the armed aggression, are subject to property liability for property and moral damage caused by the armed aggression of the Russian Federation, as the aggressor state, against Ukraine, and the most serious crimes, under international humanitarian and investment law, including genocide, abduction of children, financing of terrorism, mass destruction of civilian infrastructure, other war crimes and crimes against humanity committed on the territory of Ukraine as an aggrieved state.

The Russian Federation, as the aggressor state, is obliged to pay property compensation (property reparations, compensation for damage) to Ukraine, as the injured state, for the restoration of everything destroyed by the armed aggression of the Russian Federation in Ukraine, as the injured state, on the basis of generally recognized principles of international law, international customs, international treaties between the injured state (Ukraine), the aggressor state (the Russian Federation), the guarantor countries, and other countries specified in this agreement.

Constraint of Sanctioned Assets of the Aggressor State and Legal Entities and Individuals Accomplices to Armed Aggression

International and national law requires an effective model for the recovery and management of the sanctioned property of the aggressor state and legal entities and individuals who are accomplices of the armed aggression, which will include legal and actual actions to search for, freeze, confiscate, enforce court decisions on compensation for damage caused by the armed aggression, and apply other methods of recovery of the property of the aggressor state and its accomplices.

This model could stipulate that Member States that have joined the Register of Damage should take possible measures within their domestic legal frameworks to find, freeze, seize and, where appropriate, confiscate and otherwise enforce the property of those individuals or legal entities that have been sanctioned in connection with the armed aggression of the Russian Federation against Ukraine, or are subject to enforcement of court decisions or international commercial or investment arbitration.

An international legal act should provide that the sovereign property of the Russian Federation and the property of legal entities and individuals who are accomplices of armed aggression located in the jurisdictions of the member countries of the Register of Damage may be arrested, confiscated, and enforced as part of the execution of a court decision on compensation for damage caused by armed aggression within the competence and on the basis of a decision of the competent authority of a member country of the Register of Damage, or a competent international court or other institution.

It will not be considered a violation of the right of ownership of sovereign assets to foreclose on property that will be acquired in the future after the imposition of sanctions on this property, the acquisition of which the owner could not reasonably expect. Thus, not the sovereign assets of the aggressor state themselves, but the property derived from them, which would not have been obtained by the aggressor state in the absence of sanctions on this property, may be directly used to compensate for the damage caused.

In this regard, unforeseen taxes that will be levied on sovereign assets in the future (Nardelli & Valero, 2023) or windfall revenues received from sovereign assets held in the form of securities (Mostrey, 2023) may be used without violating the property rights of the aggressor state, as such revenues, which are not actually sovereign assets at the time of their seizure, would not have been received if there had been no sanctions against Russia.

Noteworthy is the practice of recovering the assets of accomplices of the armed aggression of the Russian Federation into the state's revenue on the grounds of creating a threat to the national security, sovereignty or territorial integrity of Ukraine or facilitating the creation of such a threat in accordance with the provisions of the Law of Ukraine "On Sanctions" (Verkhovna Rada of Ukraine, 2014).

This method of foreclosure on the property of legal entities and individuals is applied to persons who have created a threat to the national security, sovereignty or territorial integrity of Ukraine or contribute to the creation of such a threat.

This method of foreclosing on the property of the aggressor state and persons who are aiding and abetting armed aggression is a statutory property liability on the grounds of a threat to national security, sovereignty or territorial integrity.

Unlike foreclosure on the property of the aggressor state and property belonging to legal entities or individuals who are accomplices of armed aggression, in accordance with a court decision on the grounds of a threat to national security, sovereignty or territorial integrity, another possible way to foreclose on this property is to enforce an obligation to compensate for damage caused by armed aggression on the basis of a court decision.

Concept of Armed Aggression Tort

The concept of the tort of armed aggression and the peculiarities of property liability for its commission are not provided for in international and national legal orders, which necessitates the application of general provisions on reparations, international torts and applicable national tort law to these relations.

One of the peculiarities of the tort of armed aggression is due to the multiplicity of persons in this tort obligation on the part of the debtors, which are the aggressor state and legal entities and individuals who contribute to armed aggression.

Legal entities and individuals who manufacture products, provide services, perform work, or commit other acts that contribute to armed aggression shall bear additional (subsidiary) responsibility for damage caused to individuals and legal entities as a result of armed aggression, if the conduct of legal entities and individuals who are aiding and abetting armed aggression can be attributed to the aggressor state in accordance with customary international law on state responsibility, either as a result of the transfer of elements of state power to legal entities or individuals, or as a result of these persons acting on the instructions or under the control or direction of the aggressor state, or if that state has recognized their conduct as its own.

Additional (subsidiary) liability for damage caused by armed aggression, in particular, is based on the doctrine of piercing the corporate veil, which protects the interests of the state and its individuals and legal entities that suffered damage from armed aggression by imposing additional (subsidiary) liability of the aggressor state to creditors on legal entities and individuals controlled by it.

In our opinion, the tort of armed aggression should be considered as a tort obligation to compensate for damage caused by armed aggression, either by the aggressor state alone or by conspiracy of several persons (conspiracy)—the aggressor state and legal entities and individuals—aiders and abettors of armed aggression, according to the rules of joint and several liability for damage caused jointly by several persons, or according to the rules of additional (joint) liability for damage caused as a result of independent actions that consistently caused damage, if the behavior of legal entities and individuals who are aiding and abetting armed aggression can be attributed to the aggressor state, or the rights of a subject of authority have been transferred to them, or these persons acted on instructions or under the control or direction of the aggressor state, or if the latter recognized their behavior as its own.

Conditions Armed Aggression Tort

The basis for the legal relationship of compensation for damage (civil liability of the offender) is the infliction of damage to the health or property of the victim by an individual or legal entity, and the conditions are, as a rule, the unlawfulness of the offender's actions, the causal link between the unlawful actions and the damage, the offender's fault, etc (Spasibo-Fateeva, 2014, p. 85).

As a general rule, there are four elements of liability in tort: wrongfulness, damage, causation and fault.

The question of whether the lawful or unlawful actions of aiding and abetting persons of armed aggression are recognized as an element (prerequisite) of liability for damage caused by armed aggression remains insufficiently clear.

In our opinion, the wrongfulness of a result rather than formal "illegality" of actions of a tortfeasor is the key for establishing tortious "wrongfulness".

Therefore, in the case of damage caused as a result of armed aggression, along with the causal link between the unlawful behavior of the aggressor state and the damage caused, it is necessary to establish a causal link between the actions of individuals and legal entities that are aiding and abetting armed aggression (regardless of whether such actions are lawful or unlawful) and the damage caused.

The actions of an individual or legal entity that are aiding and abetting of armed aggression are causally related to the unlawful actions of the aggressor state if the damage caused by this was the result of any interdependent, consistent joint actions, regardless of the existence of a common intent or the likelihood of damage as a result of armed aggression.

The Tort of Armed Aggression Committed Jointly by Several Persons

International law and national law do not provide for special provisions on the tort of armed aggression committed jointly by several persons.

In our opinion, the guiding principle on compensation for damage caused jointly by several persons as a result of armed aggression could be worded as follows:

Guiding Principle "Tort of Armed Aggression Committed Jointly by Several Persons"

1. Persons shall be deemed to have jointly caused damage as a result of armed aggression if they have caused damage by interrelated, consistent actions or omissions with any form of complicity, including aiding and abetting the direct perpetrator."
2. Damage caused jointly by several persons as a result of armed aggression is considered to be caused by the aggressor state and its auxiliaries by interrelated, consistent actions or omissions.

Acts or omissions that caused damage to other persons as a result of armed aggression do not necessarily have to coincide in time.

This rule applies to cases where it is impossible to establish which action and to what extent caused such a consequence.

In the case of damage caused by joint actions, there is a mutual interconnectedness of the actions of the causers, which consists in their interconnection in such a way that the exclusion of at least one of these actions from the complex of actions of the co-causers does not lead to the occurrence of damage caused by the joint actions of several persons.

3. Joint and several liability arises not only when the damage is caused by joint actions, but also when it is caused by joint inaction.
4. At the request of the injured person, the court may determine the liability of persons who jointly caused damage as a result of armed aggression in a share according to the degree of their guilt."

Human Rights Violations as a Ground for Tort of Armed Aggression

During armed aggression, the interaction of national tort law and international law results in the possibility of the emergence of a tort liability for compensation for damage caused by gross violations of international humanitarian law (hereinafter—IHL) by the aggressor state, including by the state exercising its right to self-defense (Primak, 2022, p. 169).

In this regard, depending on whether the aggressor state or the injured state has committed a gross violation of international humanitarian law, the aggressor state or the state exercising its right to self-defense should pay for the damage (Primak, 2022).

The norms of IHL are intended to define general criteria for the international legal illegality of an act committed by an offending state for negative consequences from the point of view of IHL.

For the purposes of tort liability for damage caused by armed aggression, the concept of human rights should be understood as both internationally recognised human rights (which apply to both individuals and legal entities) and the rules of international humanitarian law.

For the purpose of bringing to tort liability for damage caused as a result of armed aggression, human rights violations must be considered acts or omissions that indicate a direct violation of human rights or contribute to a violation of human rights.

Facilitating human rights violations may be manifested in actions that contribute to armed aggression, in particular in the actions of a business entity to manufacture products, perform work, provide services that are used or may be used for armed aggression, actions of an official or employee and/or a participant of a legal entity to manufacture products, perform work, provide services carried out directly and/or under their control, or an individual business entity.

If an individual or legal entity that is a business entity fails to prove that it has taken all measures in its power to respect human rights, it is considered an accomplice to a human rights violation for the purposes of tort liability for compensation for damage caused by armed aggression.

If it is proved in relation to an individual or legal entity that is not a business entity that these persons have not taken all measures in their power to respect human rights, they are considered to be an accomplice to a human rights violation for the purposes of tort liability for compensation for damage caused as a result of armed aggression.

Contributing to human rights violations may be expressed in actions that contribute to armed aggression, in particular, the production of products, provision of services, performance of works performed within the professional activities of a person contributing to armed aggression and used or that may be used for armed aggression.

If an individual or legal entity fails to prove that it has taken all measures in its power to respect human rights, it is deemed to be an accomplice to a human rights violation for the purposes of tort liability for compensation for damage caused by armed aggression.

The Standard of "Due Diligence" in Cases of Human Rights Violations by the Tort of Armed Aggression

The question remains open in international law and national law whether and under what conditions the standard of "due diligence" must be observed by the aggressor state and potential accomplices of armed aggression in the case of direct or indirect human rights violations resulting in harm to the victim.

Currently, there is no single approach to understanding the standard of "due diligence" in international law and national law of the respective jurisdictions.

In our opinion, it is advisable to introduce unified provisions on the standard of due diligence.

The duty of due care will include a general duty of all persons to take reasonable steps to prevent harm to others.

The standard of due diligence will be that the person knew or should have known about the violation of the rights of another person by his or her actions or omissions, if this follows from the standard of due diligence in civil relations expected of a reasonable party to those relations in comparable circumstances.

The legal significance of the introduction of the "due diligence" standard is that compliance with this standard will be recognised as a ground for exempting the tortfeasor from the obligation to compensate for damage for negligence, but will not exempt from liability for damage that occurs regardless of the tortfeasor's fault (so-called strict liability).

This approach will make it possible to extend the provisions of the standard of "due care" provided for by the rules of tort liability to the standard of "due diligence" applied in the event of human rights violations in armed conflict, taking into account the peculiarities arising from the content of international humanitarian law and the essence of human rights.

The aggressor state and potential aiders and abettors of armed aggression must comply with the standard of "due care" provided for by applicable law in the event of a direct or indirect violation of human rights resulting in harm to the victim.

The standard of due diligence applicable to human rights violations in armed conflict will presume that a person knew or should have known about human rights violations by his or her actions or omissions if it follows from the standard of care in civil relations in armed conflict expected of a reasonable participant in those relations in comparable circumstances.

A natural or legal person conducting business or non-business economic activities should be recognised as respecting human rights, including in situations of armed conflict, and not liable for direct human rights abuses or contributing to such abuses, if, in the exercise of the degree of care and diligence required of him or her by the nature of the human rights and the circumstances of their exercise, he or she has taken all measures to ensure due respect for human rights that a "reasonable" third party of ordinary skill could have taken.

The question of whether a breach of the standard of "due care" can be recognised as a ground for tort liability for damage caused by armed aggression needs a clear answer.

In our opinion, a breach of the "due care" standard may be a condition for tort liability for damage caused by armed aggression, if it is considered to be proper evidence of the guilt of the person who caused the damage, as a prerequisite for liability for the commission of the relevant tort in an armed conflict. However, a breach of the "due care" standard cannot be a condition for tort liability that occurs regardless of the fault of the tortfeasor (e.g., compensation for damage caused by a source of increased danger), since liability under these torts occurs even in the absence of the fault of the person who caused the damage.

Concluding Remarks

The manifest injustice in law related with Armed Aggression can be eliminated by introducing unified provisions on counter-actions of a state; which exercise self-defend against armed aggression, mixed (reparation and tortious) model compensation for damage caused by armed aggression, and the tort of armed aggression, taking into account the generally recognized principles and norms of international law and the specifics of applicable national law.

The question of how to develop a proper regime of guidelines on property liability for damage caused by armed aggression remains fundamentally important and open, in particular, should this involve unification through the conclusion of a convention or other international instruments at an international conference or the gradual development of international law?

In a civil law jurisdictions, the implementation of new types of torts is mainly the domain of written laws, such as the Civil Code or other laws interpreted and clarified by the courts, or the domain of judicial lawmaking in common law countries, if the introduction of such a tort does not follow from statutory law.

This provides certain arguments in favour of statutory law in the civil law countries by adopting special laws on compensation for such damage and amending civil codes on tort liability, as well as by formulating provisions on a special tort for compensation for damage caused by armed aggression by courts and statutory law in the common law countries.

The international legal development of property liability law for damage caused by armed aggression will be determined by the trend towards the formation of an international consensus and the preparation of an international commission for reviewing applications and conference of the member states of the international register of damage caused by the armed aggression of the Russian federation against Ukraine to adopt international convention or conclude bilateral agreements that will create effective mechanisms of compensation damage caused by armed aggression and stop massive violations of international law, ownership and human rights by the aggressor state and its accomplices, and Ukraine's recovery (Compensation for Damage due to the aggression of the Russian Federation, 2024; Register of Damage for Ukraine, 2024; Shkarlat, 2024).

References

Boyarchuk, T. (2023, December 8). Confiscation of Russian sovereign assets is being discussed at the highest level in the USA. *LB.ua*. Accessed June 25, 2024, from https://lb.ua/world/2023/12/08/588058_ssha_nayvishchomu_rivni_obgovoryuyut.html

Busol, K. (2023). Russian aggression and individual reparations: Needs of victims and options for their provision under international law. In K. Shunevych (Ed.), *The gender dimension of war: Results of analytical research* (pp. 102–114). Analytical Center YurFem.

Cohen, L. (2023, February 2). Russian oligarch ordered to forfeit $5.4 mln to U.S., Ukraine may get funds. *Reuters*. Accessed June 25, 2024, from https://www.reuters.com/world/europe/russian-oligarch-ordered-forfeit-54-mln-us-ukraine-may-get-funds-2023-02-02/

Compensation for Damage due to the aggression of the Russian Federation: The international commission for reviewing applications plans to start work by the end of 2025. *UNN*. (2024). Accessed June 25, 2024, from https://unn.ua/en/news.compensation-for-damages-due-to-the-aggression-of-the-russian-federation-the-international-commission-for-reviewing-applications-plans-to-start-work-by-the-end-of-2025

Government Communication Unit. (2023, June 15). Estonia is working on a solution for using sanctioned assets to compensate war damages to Ukraine. Government of the Republic of Estonia. Accessed June 25, 2024, from https://valitsus.ee/en/news/estonia-working-solution-using-sanctioned-assets-compensate-war-damages-ukraine

Government of Canada. (1993). *Seized property management act* S.C. 1993, c. 37. Accessed June 25, 2024, from https://laws-lois.justice.gc.ca/eng/acts/s-8.3/page-1.html

Havrylenko, O. O. (2018). Problematic issues of tort liability. *eNUOLAIR*. Accessed June 25, 2024, from https://dspace.onua.edu.ua/items/49baad47-5a2e-42d6-9f3f-776d1ab60675

McCandless Farmer, B. (2023, September 3). How U.S. prosecutors seize sanctioned Russian assets. *CBS News*. Accessed June 25, 2024, from https://www.cbsnews.com/news/russian-asset-seizure-60-minutes-2023-09-03/

Mostrey, L. (2023, October 26). Euroclear delivers robust performance in Q3.2023. *euroclear*. Accessed June 25, 2024, from https://www.euroclear.com/newsandinsights/en/press/2023/2023-mr-15-euroclear-delivers-robust-performance-q3-2023.html

Nardelli, A. & Valero, J. (2023, October 26). Russia's frozen cash earns €3 Billion as EU haggles over how to tap it. *Bloomberg*. Accessed June 25, 2024, from https://www.bloomberg.com/news/articles/2023-10-26/russia-s-frozen-cash-earns-3-billion-as-eu-mulls-how-to-tap-it-for-ukraine

Perun, V. (2023, June 15). Estonia is working on a law that will allow the seized assets of the RF to be used to compensate Ukraine. *LB.ua*. Accessed June 25, 2024, from https://lb.ua/world/2023/06/15/560736_estoniya_pratsyuie_nad_zakonom_yakiy.html

Primak, V. D. (2022). Tort liability of the state of Ukraine in the conditions of war. *Private International Law and Legal Problems of European Integration, 21*, 164–169. https://doi.org/10.32849/2409-9201.2022.21.19

Rashevska, K. Y. (2022). Models and mechanisms of reparation payments: International experience and ideas for Ukraine. In V. A. Bodak, M. P. Pantiuk, M. D. Haliv, V. I. Ilnytskyi, & M. Y. Vikhliaiev (Eds.), *The Russian-Ukrainian war (2014–2022): Historical, political, cultural-educational, religious, economic, and legal aspects* (pp. 1032–1041). Baltija Publishing. https://doi.org/10.30525/978-9934-26-223-4-129

Register of Damage for Ukraine (RD4U). (2024). Mandate and functions. Accessed June 25, 2024, from https://rd.4u.coe.int/en/mandate-and-functions

Shkarlat, K. (2024) Ukraine and US sign security guarantees agreement. *RBC-Ukraine*. Accessed June 25, 2024, from https://www.msn.com/en-gb/news/world/ukraine-and-us-sign-security-guarantees-agreement/ar-BB1obpz7?ocid=BingNewsVerp

Spasibo-Fateeva, I. (2014). *Civil code of Ukraine: Scientific and practical commentary* (Non-contractual obligations) (Vol. 11, V. ed.). Pravo.

Supreme Court of Ukraine. (2018, November 21). *Resolution of the Cassation Civil Court* case 2-o/381/134/16 (381/2635/16-c). Accessed June 25, 2024, from https://reyestr.court.gov.ua/Review/78378788

Supreme Court of Ukraine. (2020). Judges of the Supreme Court became the speakers of the online workshop on insurance disputes. Accessed June 25, 2024, from https://www.supreme.court.gov.ua/supreme/pres-centr/news/1019926/

UK Parliament. (2023). *UK seizure of Russian state assets and support for Ukraine bill*. Accessed June 25, 2024, from https://bills.parliament.uk/bills/3415

UN Secretary-General. (2010). Guidance note of the Secretary-General: United Nations approach to transitional justice. *UN Digital library*. Accessed June 25, 2024, from https://digitallibrary.un.org/record/682111?ln=en

Verkhovna Rada of Ukraine. (2014). *On sanctions law of Ukraine 1644-VII*. Accessed June 25, 2024, from https://zakon.rada.gov.ua/laws/show/1644-18

Viner, K. (2023, June 19). UK to change sanctions rules in move towards seizing Russian assets. Makes changes purpose of sanctions so that they will be maintained until Russia agrees to pay compensation. *The Guardian*. Accessed June 25, 2024, from https://www.theguardian.com/politics/2023/jun/19/uk-to-change-sanctions-rules-in-move-towards-seizing-russian-assets

Wendling, M. (2023, December 6). Four Russian soldiers charged with war crimes for torturing US citizen in Ukraine. *BBC*. Accessed June 25, 2024, from https://www.bbc.co.uk/news/world-us-canada-67641900

Wright, Q. (1951). War claims: What of the future? *Law & Contemporary Problems, 16*(3), 543–553.

Procedural Issues in Compensation Cases: Insights from Court Practice in Ukraine

Iryna Izarova, Oksana Uhrynovska, and Yuliia Hartman

Abstract This chapter delves into the procedural issues encountered in compensation cases arising from the armed aggression of the Russian Federation against Ukraine. It highlights the necessity of restoring violated rights through effective legal mechanisms, particularly focusing on compensation for damages via judicial proceedings. The study examines Ukrainian court practices since 2014, aiming to understand social demands and propose efficient dispute resolution methods. Financial constraints initially hindered justice, with victims reluctant to pay court fees. Legislative changes in 2018 exempted plaintiffs from fees in cases against Russia, prompting increased claims. The text categorizes damages into property and moral losses, detailing subtypes such as real estate forfeiture, loss of profits, and forced displacement. It also addresses the legal intricacies of property mobilization during war and the assessment of moral suffering. Moreover, it discusses the government's efforts to ascertain damages and losses comprehensively. The paper concludes by emphasizing the importance of substantiating claims and aligning legal precedents with principles of fairness and proportionality. Overall, the paper sheds light on the

---

This chapter is based on the publication by Izarova I, Hartman Y and Nate S. titled 'War damages compensation: a case study on Ukraine', published in F1000Research 2023, 12:1250 (https://doi.org/10.12688/f1000research.136162.1)

I. Izarova (✉)
Lucian Blaga University of Sibiu, Sibiu, Romania

Law Faculty, Department of Justice, Taras Shevchenko National University of Kyiv, Kyiv, Ukraine
e-mail: irina.izarova@knu.ua

O. Uhrynovska
Law Faculty, Department of Civil Law and Civil Procedure, Ivan Franko National University of Lviv, Lviv, Ukraine
e-mail: oksana.uhrynovska@lnu.edu.ua

Y. Hartman
East European Law Research Center, Kyiv, Ukraine

S. Nate (ed.), *Ukraine's Journey to Recovery, Reform and Post-War Reconstruction*, Contributions to Security and Defence Studies,
https://doi.org/10.1007/978-3-031-66434-2_9

multifaceted challenges and developments in compensatory procedures amid ongoing conflict.

Introduction: Prerequisites for the Development and Formation of Court Practice in Cases of Compensation for Damage Caused by the Armed Aggression of the Russian Federation Against Ukraine

The war in Ukraine has impacted everyone with its tragedies, yet each case is distinct: various rights were violated, so the losses suffered should be categorized based on specific criteria. Restoring the violated rights of citizens is an urgent task that should be implemented by the Ukrainian authorities in the post-conflict period.

It is the duty of the state to provide effective means of protection to those affected by armed aggression (referring to the ECHR[1] (Article 13 of the European Convention on Human Rights regarding the right to an effective remedy), which would contribute to the restoration of violated rights and obtaining fair satisfaction for their violation. One of such means of protection, guaranteed at both national and international levels, is compensation for the damage inflicted through judicial proceedings.

In this regard, we have planned to investigate the current Ukrainian judicial practice, which has been forming since 2014 when the armed invasion of the Russian Federation into the territory of Ukraine began, and up until now, with a focus on the practice of first-instance courts. By searching for court decisions through the web portal of the Unified State Register of Court Decisions of Ukraine, we have managed to summarize over 5500 different types of court decisions of which 3940 ones are first-instance court decisions and 1622 are appellate and cassation courts decisions in civil cases and approximately 1300 decisions in commercial proceedings.

---

[1] In this matter, the state must take all available legal and diplomatic measures with regard to foreign states and international organizations in order to continue guaranteeing rights and freedoms in accordance with the Convention (see Ilascu and Others v. Moldova and Russia, no. 48787/99, judgment of 8 July 2004, para. 333, Catan and Others v. Moldova and Russia, nos. 43,370/04, 8252/05, and 18,454/06, para. 110).

In the Court's judgment in the case of Sandu and Others v. Russia and Moldova of 3 December 2018, application no. 21034/05, paras. 40–46, the Court also concluded: "...to be effective, a remedy must be capable of directly remedying the impugned state of affairs and must offer reasonable prospects of success (see Mozer, cited above, para. 116)."

In the ECtHR judgment in the case of Sargsyan v. Azerbaijan, the Court, due to the failure of the Government of Azerbaijan to demonstrate otherwise, concluded the absence of effective remedies for Armenian refugees who were forced to leave their property and homes as a result of the Nagorno-Karabakh conflict and intended to seek restitution of their property or compensation for the loss of the opportunity to possess it.

This has helped us to identify the main social demands that individuals bring to the courts in order to understand how to effectively satisfy each of them and propose an individual approach to resolving certain disputes as more efficient ones.

Researching judicial practice is of great importance for the development by the state of other means of legal protection of violated rights, which include access to administrative bodies and other authorities, as well as mechanisms, conditions, and procedures in accordance with national legislation aimed at swift and effective compensation and resolution of disputes.

Before delving into the detailed examination of procedural issues that arose during our analysis of the judicial practices of Ukrainian courts, we wish to highlight an important fact. Despite the commencement of Russian aggression against Ukraine on February 20, 2014, the development of judicial procedures related to cases of seeking reimbursement for damages caused by the armed aggression of the Russian Federation only began in 2018. Strangely, for a considerable period (almost 4 years!), justice remained largely elusive for the majority of victims.

A significant impediment to the pursuit of justice was of financial nature, specifically the requirement for the affected individuals to pay court fees when submitting their claims for reimbursement. As all claims for damages are inherently linked to property matters, the standard court fee amounts to 1 percent of the claimed value, capped at five times the subsistence minimum for able-bodied individuals.[2] In 2014, this minimum was UAH 5880; in 2015 and 2016, it increased to UAH 6650; and in 2017, it reached UAH 7720.

Given the financial limitations experienced by the victims and their lack of assurance and confidence in a successful court outcome and subsequent compensation, the more practical and economical choice was to forgo the solitary available avenue for collecting damages. The elevated court fee rates for claims tied to property deterred victims from initiating claims for reimbursement due to the armed aggression of the Russian Federation.

However, a significant turning point occurred in January 2018 with the amendment of Clause 22, Part 1, Article 5 of the Law of Ukraine "On Court Fees". This addition stipulates the exemption of plaintiffs from court fee payments in cases involving lawsuits against the aggressor state, the Russian Federation, for compensation related to property and/or moral damages incurred during the temporary occupation of Ukrainian territory, armed aggression, armed conflict resulting in forced resettlement from Ukrainian territories, fatalities, injuries, imprisonment, unlawful deprivation of liberty, abduction, and violations of ownership rights pertaining to movable and/or immovable assets.[3]

---

[2]The Law of Ukraine «On the Court Fee» https://zakon.rada.gov.ua/laws/show/3674-17#Text.

[3]The Law of Ukraine "On the Peculiarities of the State Policy on Ensuring the State Sovereignty of Ukraine in the Temporarily Occupied Territories in the Donetsk and Luhansk Oblasts" https://zakon.rada.gov.ua/laws/show/2268-19#n174.

These legislative changes served as a catalyst, prompting victims to actively exercise their right to approach the court with claims seeking reimbursement for damages caused by Russia, starting from February 2014.

Types of Damages Caused by War as a Subject of Applying to the Court for Compensation

To accurately define an effective means of safeguarding violated rights, a crucial step involves comprehending the various forms of damage stemming from said violation and their distinct attributes. This rule takes on heightened relevance, particularly within the current context, when addressing the issue of compensating for damages inflicted by Russia's armed aggression against Ukraine. While determining the precise extent of damage sustained by individuals and legal entities during a large-scale invasion is challenging, it is unequivocal that this damage necessitates differentiation based on its inherent nature.

Ukraine, in collaboration with the international community, is actively engaged in devising potent mechanisms for redressing the damage caused by the war. This endeavor primarily seeks to distinguish the forms of damage, striving to align with the expectations of the affected parties. On May 12, 2023, the Council of Europe, through Resolution CM/Res(2023)3, dedicated to establishing the Enlarged Partial Agreement on the Register of Damage Caused by the Aggression of the Russian Federation against Ukraine, delineated the categories of damage to be encompassed within this registry. Among these categories are *attacks targeting civilians and civilian infrastructure, encompassing cultural and religious heritage, as well as the environment of Ukraine.*[4]

Ukrainian jurisprudence concerning damage compensation pursues a comparable trajectory, a path currently being actively shaped due to the widespread utilization of this particular recourse in the absence of alternative effective compensation mechanisms. Delving into an analysis of judicial precedents, it's evident that distinct types of damage and violated rights stand out, prompting victims to seek redress through legal channels.[5]

Foremost, a dichotomy emerges, segregating damage into two primary forms: *property damage and moral damage.* Each category carries distinct characteristics, especially pronounced within the context of a full-scale invasion. Notably, this division adheres to the classic demarcation outlined in the Civil Code of Ukraine,[6] thus reflecting the prevailing bifurcation observed in judicial practice.

[4]Resolution of Committee of Minister of Council of Europe CM/Res(2023)3.

[5]Izarova I, Hartman Y and Nate S. War damages compensation: a case study on Ukraine [version 1; peer review: 2 approved]. F1000Research 2023, 12:1250 (https://doi.org/10.12688/f1000research.136162.1).

[6]The Civil Code of Ukraine.

In cases involving reimbursement for damage caused by the armed aggression of the Russian Federation, property damage can be categorized into several subtypes. Among the most prevalent losses experienced by numerous individuals and legal entities is *the forfeiture of real estate.* This scenario encompasses two distinct directions. The initial of these pertains to occupation-related aspects. In such instances, the focus is *on property situated in temporarily occupied territories* that has either suffered damage, been partially or wholly destroyed, or has faced complete obliteration. Alternatively, there are situations where, due to varying circumstances, the proprietor has been unjustly deprived of their ownership rights, with the occupation itself being a significant factor. These cases pose challenges due to the inherent difficulty of quantifying the financial ramifications of the damage incurred. The owner and the legitimate Ukrainian authorities are unable to independently evaluate the extent of destruction or obtain inspection reports for razed structures, consequently hindering the pursuit of fair and comprehensive monetary reimbursement. Consequently, plaintiffs in these cases often approximate the amounts they wish to recover from the defendant, basing their claims on publicly available data regarding comparable properties found on the internet.[7]

An additional dimension of property damage concerns *harm inflicted upon assets within territory under the control of Ukrainian authorities*. This situation presents a contrasting scenario, as affected parties possess the capacity to accurately ascertain the scope of damage and anticipate full reimbursement.[8]

Moving on to the next category of property damage, as mentioned earlier in more detail, is *the loss of profits*. This form of damage has affected both individuals and legal entities. Within these circumstances, individuals sought reparation for income lost due to internal displacement, encompassing wages, social benefits, other potential earnings linked to property use (such as rent), income that went unrealized due to diminished production capabilities, suspension, or complete cessation of business operations, as well as the failure to fulfill obligations tied to supply contracts, among other instances.[9]

An unconventional category of damage is *the one stemming from forced internal displacement.* In legal claims, citizens petition for reimbursement of expenses incurred from renting housing in their enforced relocation locale, utility payments, and the arrangement of temporary accommodation. These expenses were

---

[7]The Decision of the Pecherskyy District Court of Kyiv City dated March 7, 2023 in case No. 757/13916/22-ц https://reyestr.court.gov.ua/Review/110940813.

[8]Decision of the Kyiv District Court of Kharkiv City dated May 12, 2023 in case No. 953/7268/22 https://reyestr.court.gov.ua/Review/111037088; Decision of Pecherskyy District Court of Kyiv City dated March 7, 2023 in case No. 757/13518/22-ц https://reyestr.court.gov.ua/Review/110940809.

[9]Decision of the Svatove District Court of Luhansk region dated April 6, 2020 in case No. 426/10700/19 https://reyestr.court.gov.ua/Review/88737292; Decision of the Prydniprovskyy District Court of Cherkasy City dated March 27, 2019 in case No. 711/17/19 https://reyestr.court.gov.ua/Review/81024789.

necessitated by circumstances brought about by the armed aggression of the Russian Federation.[10]

It's important not to overlook cases in which plaintiffs seek compensation for *destroyed movable property*. In the vast majority of instances, individual plaintiffs seek reimbursement for the value of a destroyed vehicle or other equipment. For legal entity plaintiffs, compensation pertains to obliterated vehicles and equipment (e.g., farmers incurring significant losses in relation to these assets), consumables, and goods housed in warehouses.[11]

While examining judicial practices concerning compensation for war-related damages, we identified a type of damage that had not previously received adequate attention. This type of damage can arise during a state of war or other exceptional periods, such as an anti-terrorist operation (ATO) which occurred between April 14, 2014, and April 30, 2018, and the joint forces operation (JFO) which transpired from April 30, 2018, until the commencement of Russia's full-scale invasion into Ukraine on February 24, 2022.[12] This particular damage is associated with *the forced appropriation (mobilization) of property from an individual's possession for military purposes*. This pertains to the legal provision that arises during the legal regime of martial law and certain other unique legal frameworks (such as ATO and JFO), which allow for the restriction of citizens' constitutional rights and freedoms, with the exception of certain constraints. Notably, property rights are not included in these exceptions. Consequently, under such circumstances, it is permissible to undertake the compelled transfer of property. This action involves divesting the owner of their right to ownership of specifically identified property, which may be privately or communally owned. This property is then transferred to state ownership for utilization within the parameters of the legal regime of martial law or a state of emergency. It is crucial to emphasize that prior to or after this process, full compensation for the property's value must occur.[13] If previous full compensation has not been carried out, this forced appropriation results in subsequent full compensation, as prescribed by the law.[14]

In one of the cases we analyzed, both the lower court and the appellate court awarded monetary compensation to the plaintiffs. This decision was reached based on the plaintiffs' contention that they lost the ability to use part of their house and garage due to the displacement caused by the dislocation of military units of the Ukrainian Armed Forces during the anti-terrorist operation in the Donetsk region, wherein soldiers were housed in their property. In such a scenario, the state is

---

[10] Decision of the Kyivskyy District Court of Poltava City dated March 14, 2023 in case No. 552/7314/22 https://reyestr.court.gov.ua/Review/109646640.

[11] Decision of the Vinnytsya City Court of Vinnytsya region dated January 24, 2023 in case No. 127/12775/22 https://reyestr.court.gov.ua/Review/108672416

[12] The Law of Ukraine "On the Legal Regime of Martial Law".

[13] The Law of Ukraine "On the Transfer, Forced Alienation, or Confiscation of Property under the Conditions of the Legal Regime of Martial Law or State of Emergency", adopted on May 17, 2012.

[14] The Law of Ukraine "On the Legal Regime of Martial Law".

obligated to provide compensation to citizens for the value of the requisitioned everyday goods. However, it's important to note that there currently exists no legislation regulating the procedure for compensating the value of mobilized property from the State Budget of Ukraine. The state has thus far not fulfilled its positive material and procedural obligations as outlined in Article 1 of the First Protocol to the Convention.[15] Specifically, it has failed to enact specialized legal measures concerning compensation for mobilized property during an anti-terrorist operation, as well as the protocol for determining the compensation amount.

It's noteworthy that a uniform approach to resolving the matter of compensating for damage caused by the forced appropriation of property for military purposes is yet to be established in judicial practice. Courts are awaiting clarifications from the Supreme Court on this issue. As of the time of writing this text, multiple cassation appeals have been filed by both primary plaintiffs and the Cabinet of Ministers of Ukraine, representing the interests of the State of Ukraine.[16]

Another distinct form of damage, contrasting with property damage—which is the most commonly litigated for compensation—is *moral damage*. Simultaneously, these represent the most poignant categories of cases, frequently intertwined with instances of death and disability. Within such cases, moral damage encapsulates the anguish experienced by individuals *due to the demise of a family member* (children, father, mother, husband, or wife), as well as the *distress stemming from acquiring a disability*.[17] Moreover, mental suffering arising *from the loss of a residence* (both physical and due to forced relocation) or irreplaceable personal belongings cherished for their sentimental value holds equal significance.[18]

For example, in the case of displaced persons from occupied territories involving the victim from Mariupol, the court, in determining the amount of moral compensation, referred to the "Rules of Court - Compensation for Damages" approved by the European Court of Human Rights. According to these Rules, which are used by the European Court of Human Rights in cases involving compensation for damages, in particular, paragraph 15, section 3 of these Rules establishes that applicants wishing to receive compensation for non-pecuniary damage have the right to indicate the amount that, in their opinion, would be fair. An applicant who considers

[15] Decision of the Pechersk District Court of Kyiv dated September 16, 2020 in case No. 757/14424/2-ц, Resolution of the Kyiv Court of Appeals dated June 2, 2021 in case No. 757/14424/2-ц.

[16] Decision of the Supreme Court of December 1, 2021 in case No. 757/14424/2-ц, proceeding No. 61-11257св21; Decision of the Pechersk District Court of Kyiv dated January 20, 2020 in case No. 757/64569/16-ц; Resolution of the Kyiv Court of Appeals dated December 3, 2020 in case No. 757/64569/16-ц; Decision of the Pechersk District Court of Kyiv in case No. 757/64415/17-ц.

[17] Decision of the Pohrebyshchensk District Court of Vinnytsya region dated January 28, 2019 https://reyestr.court.gov.ua/Review/79658736; Decision of the Leninskyy District Court of Kharkiv City dated November 20, 2019 in case No. 642/5977/19 https://reyestr.court.gov.ua/Review/86018545.

[18] Decision of the Suvorivskyy District Court of Odesa City dated July 8, 2020 in case No. 523/10292/19 https://reyestr.court.gov.ua/Review/90509334, decision of this court dated September 20, 2019 in case No. 523/11414/19 https://reyestr.court.gov.ua/Review/84980719.

themselves a victim of more than one violation of the European Convention on Human Rights and Fundamental Freedoms of November 4, 1950, may demand either a one-time sum covering all foreseeable violations, or a separate sum for each violation envisaged by the European Convention.

Therefore, taking into account the nature and extent of the moral suffering experienced by the plaintiff, which consists of a disruption of their established way of life and the effort required to regain a normal life, the court assessed as fair the amount of compensation for the inflicted moral damage as specified by the plaintiff in the statement of claim.[19]

Nonetheless, there are situations wherein individuals independently assert in their petitions to the court that their mental distress is a result of *following the news and the overall country's situation.*[20] The recognition by courts of such damage inflicted upon individuals and subsequent awarding of appropriate compensation (a practice that indeed exists!) paves the way for unscrupulous individuals to exploit the subject of war and the attendant moral distress. This could potentially result in the utilization of such a legal avenue for unjust enrichment, thus provoking a surge in court workload due to an influx of similar lawsuits.[21]

This analysis enables us to decipher the prevalent inclination in societal appeals to the court and the specific damages they primarily seek to rectify. Moreover, after scrutinizing this extensive array of court rulings, we can confidently affirm that any claimed damage must be meticulously substantiated. The underlying purpose for resorting to the legal process should be the genuine restoration of violated rights and the equitable compensation of victims as a protective measure. As courts develop their legal precedents, they must curtail any room for speculation regarding compensation matters, ensuring their resolutions are aligned with principles of fairness and proportionality.

Ukrainian government officials are actively engaged in addressing the task of delineating the various types of damage inflicted. On March 20, 2022, the Cabinet of Ministers of Ukraine approved a resolution outlining the Procedure for ascertaining the damage and losses sustained by Ukraine due to the armed aggression of the Russian Federation.[22] Through this directive, the government has sought to encompass an extensive spectrum of domains through which damage and losses should be assessed. *This array of domains is notably comprehensive, spanning 22 categories, each containing a set of primary indicators subject to evaluation.* When these

[19] The Decision of the Bilotserkiv District Court of the Kyiv Region dated January 10, 2023 in case No. 357/9325/22. Available at: https://reyestr.court.gov.ua/Review/108371522.

[20] Decision of the Busk District Court of Lviv region dated June 29, 2022 in case No. 943/1741/19 https://reyestr.court.gov.ua/Review/105182285.

[21] Izarova I, Hartman Y and Nate S. War damages compensation: a case study on Ukraine [version 1; peer review: 2 approved]. F1000Research 2023, 12:1250 (https://doi.org/10.12688/f1000research.136162.1).

[22] The procedure for determining damage and losses caused to Ukraine as a result of the armed aggression of the Russian Federation, approved by the Resolution of the Cabinet of Ministers of Ukraine on March 20, 2022. Available at: https://zakon.rada.gov.ua/laws/show/326-2022-п#Text.

categories are conceptually grouped, several overarching classifications emerge. These encompass human losses (both civilian and military); material military losses intertwined with aspects concerning the state's internal security; depletion of housing stock and infrastructure facilities; the deterioration of public building assets (including educational, sports, social welfare, healthcare, cultural, and administrative structures); diminution of communal amenities, infrastructure, transport, and other networks, as well as energy infrastructure; ecological harm encompassing damage to land, depletion of subsoil and forest resources, degradation of water resources and atmospheric air, and impacts on natural reserves; loss of cultural heritage; and economic losses sustained by enterprises, institutions, and organizations.

In summation, it's evident that the damage stipulated by the governmental resolution aligns closely with societal demands, as observed through the examination of judicial precedents. This concordance underscores the government's commitment to addressing societal needs and its pursuit of the most efficacious mechanisms to achieve this objective.

Separate discussions are taking place in academic circles regarding the compensation for Ukraine's *ecological losses*. This issue has arisen particularly sharply in connection with Russia's perpetration of the largest ecocide of the century on Ukrainian territory—the explosion of the Kakhovka Hydroelectric Power Station, the horrific consequences of which are difficult to imagine. In our opinion, the search for a solution to the issue of compensating for ecological damage includes the prospect of developing the institution of collective lawsuits by a group of plaintiffs regarding a single subject of claim, considering the vast territory affected by the ecocide and the number of victims. Such a procedure would reduce the burden on courts and increase the effectiveness of awarding fair compensation. However, until this issue is resolved in either legislation or, more importantly, in judicial practice.

Legal entities have a legitimate expectation of recovering funds corresponding to the inflicted damages from the defendant, beginning with their pursuit of legal action in court. Consequently, within these particular case categories, the focus is exclusively on the claimant's property interest. Considering its legal essence, no other forms of damage beyond property damage could have been inflicted upon them. The damages incurred by the plaintiffs are substantiated through diverse expert opinions, assessments, reports, and documents. For instance, reports detailing the examination of structural integrity, records outlining findings from surveys of impaired structures, expert conclusions derived from intricate judicial construction-technical and military examinations, as well as analyses of weaponry and traces along with their utilization circumstances.

In certain instances, the Russian Federation itself publicly acknowledged its role in the resulting destruction. Such admissions made by representatives of the Russian government are actively employed by plaintiff legal entities as supplementary evidence to establish the culpability of the Russian Federation for the harm inflicted upon their assets. An intriguing illustration in this context is exemplified by case No. 910/10517/22, adjudicated by the Commercial Court of Kyiv on December 22, 2022. The claimant, seeking the recovery of damages commensurate with their losses (this concerns the recovery of 21,561,390.70 euros, which is equivalent to 715,191,329.39 UAH), was the proprietor of the "RETROVILLE" ballistic missile defense system. Their premises were struck by a missile from the Kh-47 M2 "Kinzhal" hypersonic aviation missile complex. The Ministry of Defense of the Russian Federation corroborated that the "RETROVILLE" missile defense system was intentionally targeted and subjected to incendiary damage by the Russian Armed Forces.

This assertion can be verified from the content of a briefing delivered by Lieutenant General Konashenkov Igor Evgenovich, the head of the department of Information and mass communications of the ministry of defense of the Russian Federation, on March 21, 2022. It is pertinent to note that the strike was a deliberate act, with the BTRK (ballistic missile defense system) serving as the primary and principal objective of the missile strike. The intent behind the attack was the obliteration of what was believed to be the location of Ukrainian Armed Forces units within the confines of the "RETROVILLE" military complex. This interpretation classified the complex as a military facility. However, the data disclosed during the previously mentioned ministry of defense briefing regarding the presence of Ukrainian Armed Forces units on the premises of the destroyed property is unsubstantiated by the case records. In accordance with the expert evaluations provided, at the time of the missile assault and subsequent destruction, the "RETROVILLE" multifunctional shopping and entertainment complex did not possess a military character.[23]

Interestingly, the Procedure for determining the damage and losses inflicted upon Ukraine due to the armed aggression of the Russian Federation includes only one reference to moral damage. This pertains specifically to moral damage arising from the inability of the state's citizens to access Ukraine's *cultural heritage and cultural assets*, serving as a primary indicator for assessing *losses in the domain of cultural heritage*.[24] This suggests that the authorities highlight the significance of cultural harm to the Ukrainian populace, underlining its irreparable and irreversible nature. Unlike many material losses, cultural damage is largely unrecoverable. It is, therefore, striking that despite the magnitude of its occurrence, there has yet to be a single instance within domestic judicial practice involving a claim for compensation explicitly targeting damage to cultural heritage. According to information from the Kyiv School of Economics, as of February 2023, the cultural resources of Ukraine have suffered damages amounting to 1547 million US dollars.[25]

[23] The Decision of the Commercial Court of the city of Kyiv, dated December 22, 2022 in case No. 910/10517/22. Available at: https://reyestr.court.gov.ua/Review/108187407.

[24] The procedure for determining damage and losses caused to Ukraine as a result of the armed aggression of the Russian Federation, approved by the Resolution of the Cabinet of Ministers of Ukraine on March 20, 2022. Available at: https://zakon.rada.gov.ua/laws/show/326-2022-п#Text.

[25] KSE Institute data https://kse.ua/ua/about-the-school/news/zbitki-vid-ruynuvan-kulturnih-ta-religiynih-ob-yektiv-pid-chas-viyni-skladayut-ponad-1-5-mlrd/.

Grounds for Applying to the Court in Compensation Cases

What forms the foundation of the appeal and the cause for the infringement of rights—war or occupation? Are we referring to military operations or any actions taken during wartime? Does this pertain to all of Ukraine's territory or specifically to areas affected by hostilities? The Law on compensation of expenses specifies that it concerns losses "*as a result of hostilities, acts of terrorism, sabotage caused by the armed aggression of the Russian Federation against Ukraine*".[26] Generalization of judicial practice shows that the main reason for applications for compensation *is Russia's actual armed aggression against Ukraine, and the occupation of part of the territory of Ukraine, the conduct of hostilities, acts of terrorism, etc.* are already defined as its consequences and are derived grounds for such applications. On the other hand, the term "war" is not used either in judicial practice as a basis for going to court, or in national legal acts.

As it was mentioned in Basic Principles and Guidelines on the Right to a Remedy and Reparation for Victims of Gross Violations of International Human Rights Law and Serious Violations of International Humanitarian Law 2005 (hereinafter - Basic Principles),[27] for compensation, the damage must be *the result of gross violations of international law, human rights, and serious violations of international humanitarian law.*

Beyond the enumerated factual foundations for pursuing compensation through legal channels, the presence of legal justifications is equally imperative. Such justifications can be discerned from pertinent international and national legal frameworks. A classic rationale that triggers the engagement of one party towards another, or towards an authorized entity, arises from the existence of an obligation which the opposing party is bound to fulfill.

In our assessment, the Basic Principles, to which we frequently referred throughout our research, holds significance. Paragraph 16 within these Basic Principles stipulates that states should endeavour to establish national programmes for reparation and other assistance to victims in the event that the parties liable for the harm suffered are unable or unwilling to meet their obligations.[28] This codification of the

[26] The Law of Ukraine "On compensation for damage and destruction of certain categories of immovable property as a result of hostilities, acts of terrorism, sabotage caused by armed aggression of the Russian Federation against Ukraine, and the State Register of property damaged and destroyed as a result of hostilities, acts of terrorism, sabotage caused by armed aggression of the Russian Federation against Ukraine" dated February 23, 2023. https://zakon.rada.gov.ua/laws/show/2923-20/conv#n3.

[27] *Basic principles and guidelines on the right to a remedy and reparation for victims of gross violations of international human rights law and serious violations of International Humanitarian Law* (2005) *OHCHR*. General Assembly resolution 60/147. Available at: https://www.ohchr.org/en/instruments-mechanisms/instruments/basic-principles-and-guidelines-right-remedy-and-reparation.

[28] *Basic principles and guidelines on the right to a remedy and reparation for victims of gross violations of international human rights law and serious violations of International Humanitarian*

state's duty towards individuals impacted by the aggressive actions of an aggressor demonstrates that citizens possess valid grounds for initiating claims seeking compensation for damages stemming from the armed aggression of the Russian Federation. Specifically, these claims are directed towards the State of Ukraine, a sovereign entity entrusted with safeguarding and reinstating the violated rights of its citizens. It is the state's responsibility to devise effective mechanisms for redressing the damages suffered by its citizens, instituting swift and equitable procedures for their reparation, and ultimately providing compensation. This obligation is inherent to the "state-person" relationship. Simultaneously, within the "state-state" dynamic, a state that has inflicted damage and acted as the aggressor bears the obligation to fully indemnify the other affected state for the damages incurred.

Consequently, the state victimized by an act of armed aggression holds the right—and in our perspective, should—utilize all available legal means to demand comprehensive compensation for all incurred damages from the aggressor. However, this issue is resolved within a distinct procedural framework and falls under the purview of different branches of law, presenting itself as a promising avenue for future exploration.

Are all damages subject to compensation, or is there potential differentiation? On January 26, 2023, the Parliamentary Assembly of the Council of Europe passed Resolution No. 2482. This resolution reiterates that the Russian Federation's armed attack and large-scale invasion of Ukraine launched on 24 February 2022 constitute an "aggression" under the terms of Resolution 3314 (XXIX) of the United Nations General Assembly adopted in 1974 and are clearly in breach of the Charter of the United Nations. The Assembly emphasizes that the Russian Federation will be considered as continuing its aggression until the sovereignty, territorial integrity, unity and political independence of Ukraine within its internationally recognised borders are fully re-established. The Assembly recalls that the ongoing aggression is a continuation of the aggression started on 20 February 2014, which included the invasion, occupation and illegal annexation of Crimea by the Russian Federation.[29] This juncture is of paramount significance in delineating which damages, and over what time frame, are eligible for compensation on the international stage and thus in Ukraine. Is it the entirety of damages sustained from the entire period of aggression, spanning February 2014 to the present, or solely those incurred since the commencement of the full-scale invasion on February 24, 2022? The response to this question is unequivocal: Russia must unquestionably be held accountable for all damages accumulated over these 9 years of universally acknowledged aggression.

Furthermore, within the same Resolution, the Parliamentary Assembly of the Council of Europe strongly supports the creation of a special tribunal that its

Law (2005) *OHCHR*. General Assembly resolution 60/147. Available at: https://www.ohchr.org/en/instruments-mechanisms/instruments/basic-principles-and-guidelines-right-remedy-and-reparation.

[29] Resolution of the Parliamentary Assembly 2482 (January 26, 2023) https://pace.coe.int/pdf/af950f18903d947bda73c9e0a7689a2f41e9128cd2da8bd1bc2211277e4e666a/res.%202482.pdf.

jurisdiction would be limited to the crime of aggression committed against Ukraine and would extend ratione temporis to the aggression started by the Russian Federation in February 2014.[30] Although the context involves the crime of aggression and a specialized criminal tribunal, the recognition of the ongoing period of Russia's aggression against Ukraine furnishes a foundation to seek compensation for all damages incurred during this duration.

Subject of Liability in Cases of Claims by Legal Entities of Ukraine for Compensation of Damages Caused by Armed Aggression of the Russian Federation: Problems of Determining the Respondent's Obligation

Based on a broad assessment of Ukrainian judicial tendencies, it is evident that in most instances, the Russian Federation assumes the role of the defendant. This stems from the Russian Federation's unwarranted and extensive act of armed aggression against Ukraine, coupled with numerous genocidal acts targeting the Ukrainian populace. Consequently, the Russian Federation forfeits its right to claim judicial immunity, thus relinquishing Ukrainian courts' jurisdiction to adjudicate cases seeking compensation for damages resulting from such aggressive actions. The Supreme Court asserts that the aggressor nation in question operated beyond the bounds of legitimate self-defense, instead maliciously infringing upon Ukraine's sovereign rights within its borders. Hence, the Russian Federation is definitively barred from invoking judicial immunity in such cases. This stance, endorsed by the Supreme Court, fosters consistency in judicial practice regarding this particular category of legal matters.[31]

During the justification of the legal basis for lifting the judicial immunity of the Russian Federation, courts also refer to the relevant practices of the European Court of Human Rights (ECtHR). According to its precedent, in cases where the application of the rule of state immunity from jurisdiction restricts the right to access to court, the court must determine whether the circumstances of the case justify such a restriction. According to established ECtHR practice, limiting the right to a fair trial, particularly through the application of state immunity in civil proceedings, is considered compatible with Article 6(1) of the Convention for the Protection of

[30] Resolution of the Parliamentary Assembly 2482 (January 26, 2023) https://pace.coe.int/pdf/af950f18903d947bda73c9e0a7689a2f41e9128cd2da8bd1bc2211277e4e666a/res.%202482.pdf.

[31] Izarova I, Hartman Y and Nate S. War damages compensation: a case study on Ukraine [version 1; peer review: 2 approved]. F1000Research 2023, 12:1250 (https://doi.org/10.12688/f1000research.136162.1).

The Resolution of the Supreme Court as part of the panel of judges of the Third Judicial Chamber of the Civil Court of Cassation dated April 14, 2022 in case No. 308/9708/19. Available at: https://reyestr.court.gov.ua/Review/104086064.

Human Rights and Fundamental Freedoms (hereinafter referred to as the 1950 Convention) only if such a limitation: (1) pursues a legitimate aim, (2) is proportionate to the aim pursued, and (3) does not undermine the very essence of the right to access to court.[32]

The ECtHR has repeatedly recognized that 'granting immunity to a state in civil proceedings serves the legitimate purpose of observing international law to promote courtesy and good relations between states by respecting the sovereignty of another state.[33]'

Therefore, in the context of the cited ECtHR practice, the application of the judicial immunity of the Russian Federation in a case related to a claim for damages must serve a legitimate purpose, particularly promoting courtesy and good relations between states through adherence to international law. However, in the same vein, the armed aggression against Ukraine by the Russian Federation, violating fundamental principles and norms of international law, including the UN Charter, and the commission of international crimes in Ukraine by its armed forces, including the genocide of the Ukrainian people, negate the notion of promoting courtesy and good relations between countries through the respect for international law. This renders the application of the judicial immunity of the Russian Federation, which restricts the plaintiff's right to a fair trial, without a legitimate purpose.[34]

In ECtHR practice, it is established that 'a limitation will be incompatible with Article 6(1) of the 1950 Convention if there is no reasonable proportionality between the means used and the aim pursued.' Also, when considering the issue of access to court in the context of state jurisdictional immunity, it is necessary to ensure that the applied limitations do not restrict or diminish the access that remains for the individual in a manner that violates the essence of the right (access to court).[35] Otherwise, complete hindrance to the consideration of the case, without any fault on the part of the plaintiff, would contradict Article 6(1) of the 1950 Convention.[36]

Given that Russia is an aggressor state, refusing to acknowledge its responsibility for the invasion of Ukraine, which includes not only full-scale armed aggression but also any involvement of its armed forces in military actions in Donetsk and Luhansk regions since 2014, there is no reasonable basis to assume that the rights of the

---

[32] Ashingdane v. the United Kingdom (Application No. 8225/78), decision of 28 May 1985, § 57; Oleynikov v. Russia (Application No. 36703/04), decision of 14 March 2013, § 55; Fogarty v. the United Kingdom (Application No. 37112/97), decision of 21 November 2001, § 33; Cudak v. Lithuania (Application No. 15869/02), decision of 23 March 2010, § 55.

[33] Oleynikov v. Russia (Application No. 36703/04), decision of 14 March 2013, § 60; Cudak v. Lithuania (Application No. 15869/02), decision of 29 June 2011, § 52; Wallishauser v. Austria (Application No. 156/04), decision of 17 July 2012, § 60.

[34] Decision of the Commercial Court of Luhansk region dated June 29, 2023 in case No. 913/218/22 https://reyestr.court.gov.ua/Review/112209653.

[35] Ashingdane v. the United Kingdom (Application No. 8225/78), decision of 28 May 1985, § 57; Oleynikov v. Russia (Application No. 36703/04), decision of 14 March 2013, § 55.

[36] McElhinney v. Ireland (Application No. 31253/96), decision of 21 November 2001, Separate Opinion of Judge L. Loucaides.

plaintiffs, seeking protection through Ukrainian courts, could be safeguarded by bringing a lawsuit to a court where the Russian Federation would not rely on judicial immunity, i.e., a court of the Russian Federation.[37]

In cases related to the compensation for damage caused by the armed aggression of the Russian Federation, the determination of the respondent in lawsuits by legal entities is more variable due to the peculiarities of commercial proceedings. It should be noted that according to Articles 4 and 45 of the Commercial Procedural Code of Ukraine, a foreign state cannot be a respondent in a case considered under the rules of commercial proceedings.[38] Furthermore, according to Part 4 of Article 56 of the Civil Procedural Code of Ukraine, a state participates in a case only through the relevant state authority.[39] Therefore, analyzing the data contained in the Unified State Register of Court Decisions, the following respondent options can be observed:

- The Russian Federation represented by the Ministry of Justice of the Russian Federation (cases No. 916/2415/22, 905/799/22, 913/206/22, 910/12478/22, 922/784/23[40] and many others).

In decisions involving cases where the ministry of justice of the Russian Federation is designated as the defendant representing Russia, courts typically do not delve into the question of ownership concerning this defendant. This is because it is generally assumed that the jurisdiction of this ministry encompasses the responsibility of representing the state in foreign courts and other justice-related bodies. Nevertheless, considering the potential future execution of court rulings and the prospect of resorting to a foreign court for the recognition and enforcement of the Ukrainian court's judgment, meticulous attention to procedural specifics becomes crucial. This entails confirming the defendant's affiliation and the extent of its competencies.

As emphasized by the Cassation Commercial Court in its resolution dated 04.10.2022 for case No. 910/5210/20 (clause 5.4.), in engagements entered into by the state, the bodies through which it operates do not possess their own individual rights and obligations. Instead, they are imbued with authority (competence) to act as representatives of the state within pertinent legal relations.

The pronouncements of the Cassation of Commercial Court underscore the notion that state bodies are not autonomous entities but rather fulfill a representative

---

[37] McElhinney v. Ireland (Application No. 31253/96), decision of 21 November 2001, Separate Opinion of Judge L. Loucaides.

[38] The Commercial Procedural Code of Ukraine https://zakon.rada.gov.ua/laws/show/1798-12#Text.

[39] The Civil Procedural Code of Ukraine https://zakon.rada.gov.ua/laws/show/1618-15#Text.

[40] The Decision of the Commercial Court of Kyiv City dated July 12, 2023 in case No. 922/784/23 https://reyestr.court.gov.ua/Review/112483636; The Decision of the Commercial Court of Kyiv City dated October 27, 2022 in case No. 916/2415/22; The Decisions of the Commercial Court of Donetsk region in case No. 905/799/22; The Decisions of the Commercial Court of Luhansk region in case No. 913/206/22; The Decisions of the Commercial Court of Kyiv City in case No. 910/12478/22.

function on behalf of the state.[41] The role of these bodies most closely aligns with representing the interests of the Russian Federation in foreign courts. This classification of the Ministry of Justice of the Russian Federation as a representative entity is imperative due to the unique status of the state, which is exclusively capable of engaging in legal relationships through its duly authorized bodies.

Per the decree of the president of the Russian Federation No. 271 dated 28.05.2018, titled "On Amendments to the regulations on the Ministry of Justice of the Russian Federation," incorporated into the Regulations on the Ministry of Justice of the Russian Federation established by the decree of the president of the Russian Federation No. 1313 dated 13.10.2004, the following modifications were introduced:

a) Clause 1 was supplemented with sub-clause 5, reading: "5) functions to ensure, within the scope of their authority, the representation and safeguarding of the interests of the Russian Federation in foreign courts and international judicial (arbitration) bodies, including the European Court of Human Rights and the Court of Eurasian Economic Development."[42]

Given these circumstances, it is reasonable to infer that the Ministry of Justice of the Russian Federation is the competent body entrusted with the authorization to represent and safeguard the interests of the Russian Federation within this dispute. Consequently, it is the appropriate defendant in the case.

- The Russian Federation represented by the government of the Russian Federation (case No. 913/218/22[43]).

In its ruling, the court brought attention to the fact that throughout the proceedings of this case, the plaintiff fervently contended for designating the defendant as the aggressor state, specifically the Russian Federation, represented by the government of the Russian Federation. This argument was rooted in the stipulations of Article 25 of the Federal Constitutional Law of the Russian Federation No. 4-FKZ dated 06.11.2020, titled "On the government of the Russian Federation." As per this article, the government of the Russian Federation assumes the responsibility of representing the Russian Federation in foreign countries and international organizations.

Given the contextual backdrop, the court arrived at the determination that the plaintiff's identification of the defendant in the case as the aggressor state, namely the Russian Federation, was accurately substantiated. This identification is apt considering the Russian Federation's involvement in military aggression and territorial occupation of Ukraine. During the adjudication of this dispute, the representation on

[41] Resolution of the Commercial Court of Cassation dated 04.10.2022 in case No. 910/5210/20 https://reyestr.court.gov.ua/Review/106827716.

[42] https://yur-gazeta.com/dumka-eksperta/vidshkoduvannya-zbitkiv-zavdanih-voennimi-diyami-rf-u-nacionalnih-sudah-oglyad-aktualnoyi-sudovoyi-p.html.

[43] The Decision of the Commercial Court of Luhansk region dated June 29, 2023 in case No. 913/218/22 https://reyestr.court.gov.ua/Review/112209653.

behalf of the Russian Federation is undertaken by its government within a foreign court.

From the aforementioned exposition, it is discernible that the government of the Russian Federation, serving as the highest executive authority, is also the appropriate defendant in instances involving claims for compensation linked to damage inflicted by Russia's armed aggression against Ukraine.

- The Russian Federation represented by the embassy of the Russian Federation (case No. 911/1832/22[44]).

This mode of defining the defendant constitutes a classic approach in Ukrainian judicial practice. It was prevalent prior to the initiation of the full-scale invasion due to the presence of the Russian Embassy in Ukraine and the practical ability of its representatives to engage in the legal proceedings. Furthermore, the embassy was required to be informed about the commencement of proceedings against the Russian Federation, given that prior to the full-scale invasion by the Russian Federation, the principle of judicial immunity for states was upheld in Ukraine. Consequently, the authorized body had to grant consent for the state's participation in the legal process.

However, following the full-scale invasion into Ukrainian territory on February 24, 2022, Ukraine severed its diplomatic relations with Russia. This development subsequently rendered it impracticable to transmit requests and communications to the Russian Embassy in Ukraine from that point onward, due to the cessation of its operations within Ukrainian borders. Hence, we deduce that subsequent to the commencement of the full-scale invasion and the discontinuation of diplomatic relations with the Russian Federation, the Russian Embassy in Ukraine cannot be considered the appropriate defendant in cases involving claims for compensation for damages stemming from armed aggression.

- The Russian Federation represented by the office of the prosecutor general of the Russian Federation (case No. 925/903/22[45]).

To substantiate the rationale behind initiating the lawsuit against the Russian Federation via its general prosecutor's office, the plaintiff invoked (a perspective shared by the commercial court) the provisions articulated within subsection 3.1. of Article 1 of the federal law titled "On the Prosecutor's Office of the Russian Federation". This particular clause stipulates that the general prosecutor's office is entrusted with the responsibility of representing and safeguarding the interests of the Russian Federation in intergovernmental entities, foreign and international courts, as well as foreign and international arbitration courts. It is crucial to underscore that in this instance, the Economic Court of the Cherkasy Region unequivocally upheld the plaintiff's claim, amounting to UAH 154,940,212. However, it is worth noting that

[44] The Decision of the Commercial Court of Kyiv region dated February 8, 2023 in case No. 911/1832/22 https://reyestr.court.gov.ua/Review/109362636.

[45] The Decision of the Commercial Court of Cherkasy region dated December 19, 2022 in case No. 925/903/22 https://reyestr.court.gov.ua/Review/108025120.

within the final segment of the court's decision, as well as the court order, it was specified that the collection of the awarded sum should be carried out directly from the Russian Federation as a sovereign entity.[46]

- And even the Russian Federation represented by the president of the Russian Federation (case No. 910/9799/22[47]).

Certainly, the president of the Russian Federation bears the utmost responsibility for Russia's assault on Ukraine, and is obligated to endure the gravest and irreversible accountability as a war criminal—a matter diligently pursued by Ukrainian legal practitioners, diplomats, and the global community in unison. This subject holds significance and offers a potential avenue for extended research.

Nonetheless, it is imperative for the Russian Federation, acting through its president, to be held responsible for providing compensation for the inflicted damage. In light of this context, the defendant in such cases could be identified as the Russian Federation, represented by entities vested with the authority to act in foreign courts.

In our opinion, in commercial cases regarding the compensation for damage, it is most appropriate to address claims to the Ministry of Justice of the Russian Federation as the authority empowered to represent and protect the interests of the Russian Federation in courts of foreign states and international judicial (arbitral) bodies. In addition, it is possible to file claims to the Government of the Russian Federation as the representative of the state of the Russian Federation, since it is also endowed with the relevant representative powers.

However, it should be noted that in practice, the Russian Federation remains the actual respondent since its authorities act on its behalf and perform purely representative functions.

Model of Civil Liability of the State of Ukraine as the Defendant in Cases of Compensation for Damages Caused by Armed Aggression of the Russian Federation

An alternative approach to identifying the appropriate defendant has also emerged in judicial practice concerning compensation for damages, representing a complete departure from the first approach. We have encountered a substantial number of cases within the Unified State Register of Court Decisions where individuals have filed **claims against the State of Ukraine, represented by the Cabinet of**

[46] https://sud.ua/uk/news/blog/265867-problemni-pitannya-rozglyadu-sporiv-u-gospodarskomu-sudochinstvi-povyazani-z-vidshkoduvannyam-shkodi-zavdanoyi-rf.

[47] The Decision of the Commercial Court of Kyiv City dated September 29, 2022 in case No. 910/9799/22 https://reyestr.court.gov.ua/Review/106503401.

Ministers of Ukraine. In our view, this approach is warranted under specific circumstances, which we will elucidate subsequently.

Instances where the State of Ukraine is implicated as the defendant pertain to instances of inflicted moral damage (stemming from the loss of family members) and property damage (resulting from property destruction or damage) during hostilities, bombardments, and other terrorist acts perpetrated by illicit formations of the DPR and LPR, along with the Armed Forces of the Russian Federation, spanning the period of the ATO and JFO. Plaintiffs who sue the State of Ukraine draw from their entitlement to compensation for damage as outlined in Article 19 of the Law of Ukraine "On Combating Terrorism". Moreover, they invoke both negative and positive obligations of the state prescribed by the ECHR—primarily those linked to the right to life and property. It is noteworthy that the state's obligations to respect and safeguard human rights do not diminish even within the framework of armed conflicts.

The initial section of Article 19 in the Law of Ukraine "On Combating Terrorism" establishes a specific provision, whereby reparation for harm inflicted on citizens due to a terrorist act is to be financed from the State Budget of Ukraine in accordance with existing laws, with subsequent recoupment of this compensation amount from the affected individuals, following the procedure delineated by law. Additionally, restitution for damage incurred by an organization, enterprise, or institution as a result of a terrorist act is managed in consonance with the legal stipulations (as indicated in the second section of Article 19 of the aforementioned Law).[48]

Considering the substance of the aforementioned legal provisions, the realization of the entitlement to receive compensation is contingent upon the existence of a compensation framework, necessitating its formulation in a dedicated statute. Presently, Ukrainian legislation lacks a law that prescribes the procedure for seeking compensation from the State Budget of Ukraine for damage sustained to residential real estate properties owned by citizens.

In one of its decisions, the Supreme Court deduced that the legal right to compensation for damage, as laid out in Article 19 of the Law of Ukraine "On Combating Terrorism", does not inherently engender a valid anticipation of obtaining such compensation from the State of Ukraine. This conclusion stems from the requirement that for an "expectation" to be deemed "valid," it must derive from a legal precept or another legal instrument, such as a court judgment relevant to a property interest. (Please see the mutatis mutandis judgment of the ECtHR dated September 28, 2004, in the case of "Kopetskyi v. Slovakia" (Kopecky v. Slovakia), application No. 44912/98, §§ 49–50).[49]

However, despite the absence of grounds for compensation in accordance with the Law of Ukraine "On Combating Terrorism," courts must take into consideration that plaintiffs retain the right to seek compensation from the state for its failure to

[48] The Law of Ukraine "On Combating Terrorism".

[49] The Resolution of the Supreme Court dated February 24, 2021 in case No. 757/64572/16-ц https://reyestr.court.gov.ua/Review/95177274.

fulfill its positive material and procedural obligations. Given that the Convention is structured to safeguard practical and effective rights, any infringement by the state of its obligations under the convention may necessitate the award of compensation. Such compensation may take various forms and be established depending on the nature of the violation. The absence of pertinent provisions in Ukraine's legislation at the time when the disputed legal relations originated and during the course of the case's adjudication by the courts does not preclude an individual, who believes that a specific positive obligation concerning their rights has not been fulfilled, from demanding compensation from the state for this dereliction.

Courts should recognize that the legal foundation for awarding compensation, distinct from damage compensation, does not stem from the provisions of Article 19 of the Law of Ukraine "On Combating Terrorism" or Article 86 of the Code of Civil Protection of Ukraine. Instead, it rests on the state's failure to fulfill its positive obligation to devise and implement a specialized normative legal act in the country that pertains to the provision of monetary assistance and compensation to individuals injured during the anti-terrorist operation in the Donetsk and Luhansk regions.[50]

For each case involving a claim for compensation from the state of Ukraine due to damage (both property and moral) incurred as a result of terrorist acts during the periods of the anti-terrorist operation and the operations of the joint forces, the courts must ascertain the following: (a) the grounds for the claim (circumstances substantiating the claim); (b) whether the state of Ukraine, as defined by Article 1 of the Convention, possessed the authority to safeguard rights and freedoms within the territory where the alleged violation took place; (c) if such jurisdiction existed, whether the state fulfilled its contractual obligations pertaining to the aforementioned guarantee in the relevant territory (if there was non-fulfillment or inadequate fulfillment of a specific obligation, what precisely was it, the ensuing consequences, and the cause-and-effect connection between these factors and the non-fulfillment or inadequate fulfillment of the corresponding duty); (d) whether there is sufficient evidence to validate all of these facts (suitable, admissible, trustworthy, and substantial evidence).[51]

As the courts underscore, the issue in such cases isn't merely whether the plaintiffs experienced moral suffering, how to best quantify their suffering in monetary terms, or even to what standard compensation should adhere. Rather, the

[50]The Resolution of the Supreme Court dated February 24, 2021 in case No. 757/64572/16-ц https://reyestr.court.gov.ua/Review/95177274. Similar legal conclusions were reached by the Supreme Court in the decision dated March 25, 2020 in case No. 757/61954/16-ц, in the decision dated July 14, 2020 in case No. 757/49142/16-ц, in the decision dated November 3, 2021 in in case No. 243/11763/17, in the resolution dated December 6, 2021 in case No. 229/667/18, in the resolution dated January 20, 2023 in case No. 265/6582/16-ц.

[51]The Resolution of the Supreme Court dated July 27, 2022 in case No. 237/2571/17 https://reyestr.court.gov.ua/Review/105505183.

central question is whether the state of Ukraine bears responsibility for the plaintiffs' moral distress and property losses, and if so, the nature of the obligation that gives rise to this responsibility.[52]

Plaintiffs are required to substantiate that the state of Ukraine:

1) possessed the means to avert the risk of harm to them but failed to do so,
2) that it was aware of the potential danger,
3) and had the capacity to prevent and mitigate the risk to the plaintiffs but chose not to take action.

However, despite the plaintiff's obligation to establish the connection between the incurred damage and the state of Ukraine's liability for it, the courts' stance is somewhat perplexing. This sentiment was echoed by the Supreme Court's viewpoint that, under Article 2 of the Convention, the state isn't held accountable for every individual death within its borders. There's no reason to believe that such a universal responsibility for every individual's death was imposed on the state by other statutes within the current legislation of Ukraine, particularly within temporarily occupied territories. In this context, instances of individual deaths within the state-controlled territory, namely within the jurisdiction of the state as per Article 1 of the ECHR (particularly within its borders during periods of anti-terrorist operations and joint forces operations), do not automatically signify a breach of Article 2's safeguards for the right to life. The Supreme Court posits that acts of disrupting public order, peace, or causing property destruction or damage within Ukraine's borders (particularly during anti-terrorist operations and joint forces operations) are also insufficient grounds for attributing state responsibility under the Convention.[53] This stance is incendiary and harsh, disregarding the paramount societal value of human life enshrined in the Constitution of Ukraine.[54] Ukraine, as a state, has an obligation defined by international commitments to assume responsibility for each individual located on a territory under its control.

Commonly, in lawsuits against the State of Ukraine, only the State of Ukraine represented by the Cabinet of Ministers of Ukraine is identified as the defendant. As evidenced by judicial practice, the *State Treasury Service of Ukraine, the Anti-Terrorist Center under the Security Service of Ukraine, the Ministry of Defense of Ukraine, the Ministry of Internal Affairs of Ukraine, the Main Directorate of the National Guard of Ukraine, and the Security Service of Ukraine* are also named as co-defendants in this category of cases. Simultaneously, the Russian Federation, represented by the Government of the Russian Federation, is involved in some

[52] The Resolution of the Grand Chamber of the Supreme Court dated May 12, 2022 in case No. 635/6172/17.

[53] The Resolution of the Supreme Court dated July 27, 2022 in case No. 237/2571/17 https://reyestr.court.gov.ua/Review/105505183; The Resolution of the Supreme Court dated August 3, 2022 in case No. 759/17490/18 https://reyestr.court.gov.ua/Review/105704131.

[54] Constitution of Ukraine (article 3).

instances as a third party that doesn't independently assert claims pertaining to the dispute's subject matter.[55]

In accordance with the stipulations of Article 48 of the Civil Procedure Code of Ukraine, the state can participate as a party in civil proceedings, assuming a distinct role as a subject within civil proceedings due to its inability to directly exercise its rights in court.

Given the substantial responsibilities of the Cabinet of Ministers of Ukraine in overseeing counter-terrorism endeavors (namely, orchestrating anti-terrorism efforts and providing requisite resources), courts at all levels unanimously concur that designating the Cabinet of Ministers of Ukraine as the state's representative is an accurate characterization by the plaintiffs. We fully endorse this prevailing practice.

Moreover, Article 43 of the Budget Code of Ukraine affirms that the State Treasury Service of Ukraine directly manages the State Budget, underscoring the rationale for representatives from the State Treasury Service of Ukraine to act as defendants on behalf of the state in cases involving compensation for state-incurred damages.[56]

Other entities involved in counter-terrorism efforts, as enumerated in Article 4 of the Law of Ukraine "On Combating Terrorism"—including the Ministry of Defense of Ukraine, the Ministry of Internal Affairs of Ukraine, the Main Directorate of the National Guard of Ukraine, and the Anti-Terrorist Center under the Security Service of Ukraine—are primarily entities responsible for directly combating terrorism within their respective competencies.[57] These bodies, however, do not fulfill the role of state representatives within court proceedings, nor do they possess the authority to allocate budgetary resources for the purposes of restitution or compensation. Given these considerations, involving these entities as co-defendants in cases of compensation for damages incurred during Anti-Terrorist Operation (ATO) and Joint Forces Operation (JFO) is deemed inappropriate.

The practice surrounding the resolution of lawsuits against Ukraine is notably contentious, spanning across lower courts, appellate instances, and even the Supreme Court, with a spectrum of differing positions expressed therein.

Instances of lawsuits finding success in terms of full or partial compensation claims from the State Budget of Ukraine are not uncommon at the initial court level, and are sometimes upheld by the appellate court. Nevertheless, in cases where the Cabinet of Ministers of Ukraine submits a cassation appeal, the Supreme Court has consistently overturned such decisions, as evidenced in cases No. 237/2571/17 and No. 759/17490/18.[58]

[55]The Resolution of the Supreme Court dated November 3, 2021 in case No. 243/11763/17 https://reyestr.court.gov.ua/Review/100918843.

[56]Budget Code of Ukraine.

[57]The Law of Ukraine "On Combating Terrorism".

[58]The Resolution of the Supreme Court dated July 27, 2022 in case No. 237/2571/17 https://reyestr.court.gov.ua/Review/105505183; The Resolution of the Supreme Court dated August 3, 2022 in case No. 759/17490/18 https://reyestr.court.gov.ua/Review/105704131.

Furthermore, cases wherein the Supreme Court partially grants cassation appeals filed by the Cabinet of Ministers of Ukraine warrant attention. In these situations, the Supreme Court reduces the awarded amounts for property damage compensation, which had been previously determined by lower courts and affirmed by the appellate court. Such adjustments align with the compensation concept as interpreted by the European Court of Human Rights (ECtHR), as evidenced by case No. 243/11763/17.[59]

Distinct consideration should be devoted to cases where the initial and appellate courts dismiss plaintiffs' claims for compensation due to inflicted damage. The Supreme Court, however, has consistently nullified such judgments and has directed the State Budget of Ukraine to provide compensation to the affected individuals. This ruling is grounded in the state's failure to fulfill its positive procedural and material obligations as outlined by the European Convention on Human Rights (ECHR). It is worth noting that the Supreme Court, while deviating from ECtHR practice in determining compensation amounts, often assigns relatively small sums which may not be deemed equitable compensation for the incurred damage. Consequently, the practical realization of the right to compensation, as demonstrated in case no. 757/64572/16-ts,[60] may remain somewhat limited.

When determining the amount of compensation, courts consider that depending on the nature of the violation and its consequences for the victim, the specified compensation may significantly differ, taking into account the practice of the European Court of Human Rights (ECtHR). In the event of a state being found to have violated positive obligations, such as developing compensation mechanisms for interference, particularly in the right to peaceful possession of property, and conducting an objective and effective investigation into the interference with this right, there is no basis for concluding that such compensation should entail reimbursement of the actual value of the damaged (destroyed) property. However, for violations of negative obligations not to interfere with the aforementioned right, the state may be obliged to compensate for the damage inflicted on the property in full.

When deciding on the recovery of the corresponding compensation from the state, the court must be guided by the requirements of the Convention, other acts of national legislation, and, in order to effectively protect the convention right, establish, among other things, which type of convention obligations the plaintiff is seeking compensation from the state for, and whether the amount claimed is justified according to this violation.[61]

---

[59] The Resolution of the Supreme Court dated November 3, 2021 in case No. 243/11763/17 https://reyestr.court.gov.ua/Review/100918843; The Resolution of the Supreme Court dated January 20, 2023 in case No. 265/6582/16-ц https://reyestr.court.gov.ua/Review/108526423.

[60] The Resolution of the Supreme Court dated February 24, 2021 in case No. 757/64572/16-ц https://reyestr.court.gov.ua/Review/95177274#.

[61] Resolution of the Grand Chamber of the Supreme Court dated September 4, 2019 in case No. 265/6582/16-ц.

Since the Convention is designed to protect rights that are practical and effective, any violation by the state of its convention obligations may necessitate an award of compensation for it.

Such compensation may take various forms and be established, depending in particular on the type of violation (see, for example, the resolution of the issue of state responsibility for violating applicants' right to access their property: ECtHR decision of June 29, 2004, regarding the merits, and July 13, 2006, regarding just satisfaction in the case of "Dogan and Others v. Turkey", application no. 8803–8811/02 and others; ECtHR decision of June 16, 2015, regarding the merits in the case of "Chiragov and Others v. Armenia", application no. 13216/05, § 188–201; ECtHR decision of June 16, 2015, regarding the merits in the case of "Sargsyan v. Azerbaijan", application no. 40167/06, § 152–242).

Based on this consistent ECtHR practice, which is recognized under Article 17 of the Law of Ukraine "On the Implementation of Decisions and Application of the Practice of the European Court of Human Rights" as a source of law in Ukraine, legitimate expectations also arise for receiving compensation for property that was damaged/destroyed as a result of conducting an anti-terrorist operation, or in the language of the ECtHR, an armed conflict, on territory controlled by the Ukrainian government.[62]

[62] The Resolution of the Supreme Court dated January 20, 2023 in case No. 265/6582/16-ц https://reyestr.court.gov.ua/Review/108526423.

Implementation of the European Court of Human Rights Judgements as an Instrument for Recovery of Ukraine and its Accession to the European Union

Illia Chernohorenko

Abstract The chapter focuses on the potential role of implementation of the European Court of Human Rights (ECtHR) judgements in Ukraine's recovery and accession to the European Union. It first analyses pre-February 2022 challenges in implementation of the ECtHR judgements in Ukraine. It then evaluates the impact of the invasion on the implementation of the ECtHR judgements, particularly within the framework of Ukraine's aspirations for EU accession and the recovery plan encapsulated in the Ukraine Recovery Plan. Finally, it explores the interrelations between enforcement of the ECtHR judgements in inter-State cases against Russia and establishing a special mechanism of compensation for human rights violations caused by Russian aggression.

Introduction

Aristotle advanced scientific inquiry by introducing a classification of four causes—material, efficient, formal, and final.[1] As Kenny simplifies to a crude example of cooking a risotto, Aristotle's "material" causes of the risotto are the ingredients that go into it, the "efficient" cause is the chef himself, the recipe is the "formal cause", and the satisfaction of the clients of the restaurant is the "final" cause.[2] Aristotle's theorty of causes might bear relevance to the realm of Ukraine's justice sector recovery not only after but also during the unprovoked Russian aggression.[3] If to

[1] William Ross, *Aristotle. Metaphysics. Volume I* (Oxford University Press 1924) A 3. 983a24–983b17.

[2] Anthony Kenny, *Ancient Philosophy: New History of Western Philosophy* (Oxford University Press 2006) 1.

[3] *The omission of the term "post-war" by the author in the present paper is deliberate, as this term does not adequately encompass Ukraine's proactive approach to recovery and EU accession*

I. Chernohorenko (✉)
Faculty of Law, University of Oxford, Oxford, UK
e-mail: illia.chernohorenko@law.ox.ac.uk

S. Nate (ed.), *Ukraine's Journey to Recovery, Reform and Post-War Reconstruction*, Contributions to Security and Defence Studies,
https://doi.org/10.1007/978-3-031-66434-2_10

apply the named theory, human rights would epitomise the foundational "material cause" or "the ingridients"; both domestic and international institutions would embody the "efficient cause" or the "the chef"; the charted pathway delineated by the Council of Europe and the European Union on how to protect rights is a "formal cause" or "the recipe"; and effective protection of human rights, as a result, appears to be a quintessential and most important, by Aristotle, "final cause". With a focus on the latter, this chapter explores the potential role of implementation of the ECtHR judgements in the recovery of Ukraine and its accession to the European Union. For this purpose, the chapter examines the challenges inherent in the implementation of the ECtHR judgements in Ukraine preceding February 2022. Subsequently, it evaluates the impact of the full-scale invasion on the implementation process, focusing on the broader framework of Ukraine's aspirations for the EU accession and the recovery framework encapsulated in the Ukraine Recovery Plan or Lugano Plan.[4] Finally, the paper briefly delves into the interrelations between execution of the prospective ECtHR judgements in inter-State cases lodged against Russia and establishing a special mechanism to provide compensation for human rights violations caused by Russian aggression.

Implementation of the ECtHR Judgements and Justice Sector Challenges Before 24 February 2022

Within the Council of Europe (CoE), Ukraine, as its member state, must implement judgements rendered by the ECtHR. This obligation stems from the European Convention on Human Rights (ECHR). Article 46 of the ECHR expressly mandates member states to adhere to ECtHR judgements that highlight violations of the ECHR.[5] The oversight of the implementation process is entrusted to the Committee of Ministers (CM) of the Council of Europe, an intergovernmental entity comprised of representatives from all 46 CoE member states.[6] While retaining a certain degree of flexibility in determining the methods and approaches for implementing the judgements as envisaged by the so-called margin of appreciation doctrine,[7] Ukraine has a legal obligation to address violations found by the ECtHR in two distinct avenues. Firstly, individual measures might be needed to restore affected

---

during the ongoing armed conflict. In contrast to the notion of recovery transpiring solely after conflict cessation, the author acknowledges the significance of both wartime and peacetime as pivotal junctures for recovery and progression towards its recovery and the EU accession.

[4] Ukraine's Recovery Plan (July 2022) https://www.urc-international.com/urc2022-recovery-plan accessed 10 August 2023.

[5] Convention for the Protection of Human Rights and Fundamental Freedoms (European Convention on Human Rights, as amended) (ECHR) art 46.

[6] Ibid.

[7] Paul Greer, *The Margin of Appreciation: Interpretation and Discretion under the European Convention on Human Rights* (Council of Europe 2000) 5.

victims' status to situation existing before the breach (*restitutio in intergrum*). These are often compensatory measures awarded, known as 'just satisfaction' encompassing pecuniary and non-percuniary damage. Moreover, individual measures include reinitiating legal proceedings, returning confiscated property, freeing unlawfully detained individuals, and restoring individuals to their previous occupations. Secondly, Ukraine might need to adopt so-called general measures centred on proactively preventing future violations. These measures may necessitate amendment of existing or introduction of new domestic legislation, adoption of new policies or procedures, or enhancement of conditions, such as the amelioration of detention facilities. In essence, these measures underscore domestic advancements in laws, policies, and practices with the overarching goal of averting future breaches of human rights.[8]

In practice, after the ECtHR judgements become final, states shall promptly inform the CM through "action plans" about intended or completed measures, followed by "action reports" upon full execution. Subsequently, the CM ensures ongoing supervision of the ECtHR judgements implementation and persists until all required actions are taken, culminating in a final resolution.[9] Since January 2011, the execution of action plans has followed a dual-track approach. The standard procedure applies to most cases, while an enhanced procedure addresses urgent individual measures or significant structural issues. In the meantime, cases are categorised as 'leading', 'repetitive', or 'isolated', aiding supervision. Leading cases reveal new systemic problems, while non-leading cases are 'repetitive' (with already identified issues) or 'isolated' (linked to specific circumstances).[10] Repetitive cases are paired with leading cases, sharing general measures. When leading case execution is acknowledged, so are associated repetitive cases. When individual measures are needed, updates to the group's action plan usually include this information.[11]

Despite being an obligation under the ECHR, the execution of ECtHR judgements is an increasingly pressing concern, exacerbated over the past three decades. The failure to implement the ECtHR judgements stands as a primary catalyst for the accumulation of cases and the resultant delays within the Court's processes.[12] As of the onset of 2022, the CM was confronted with a cumulative total of 1300 pending leading cases, each emblematic of systemic or structural human rights problems across Europe. Among these, 106 cases, accounting for 8%, were against Ukraine. Of the 216 new leading cases opened in 2021, 14 cases, equating to 6.5%, concerned

---

[8] European Implementation Network, Implementation of Judgements of the European Court of Human Rights: A Handbook for NGOs, injured parties and their legal advisers (January 2020) https://www.einnetwork.org/ein-handbooks accessed 15 August 2023, 5.

[9] Council of Europe Committee of Ministers, The supervision process https://www.coe.int/en/web/execution/the-supervision-process accessed 15 August 2023.

[10] EIN (n 8) 6.

[11] Ibid., 7.

[12] George Stafford, 'The urgent reforms needed to improve the implementation of judgments of the European Court of Human Rights', (2023) EHRLR 2023 2, 135.

Ukraine.[13] That being said and partially explained by the fact that Ukraine holds the third position with a substantial count of 10,403 cases pending before the European Court of Human Rights against it. This equals 14% of the overall 74,650 pending applications in 2021.[14]

Among hundreds of leading cases against Ukraine, three of the most serious issues have come to the forefront: the excessive length of court proceedings, the non-enforcement of domestic judgements, including those delivered against the State, and the challenges related to the independence of the judiciary. In the meantime, a number of additional challenges persist. Indeed, the challenges confronting Ukraine's justice sector are multifaceted, as specified below.

First, a significant concern revolves around the non-execution of national court decisions, a persisting issue predating and postdating the Russian agression. The European Court of Human Rights explicitly highlighted this challenge in the group of cases *Zhovner v. Ukraine*, *Yuriy Mykolayovych Ivanov v. Ukraine*, and *Burmych and Others v. Ukraine*.[15] These instances outlined the systemic problem of delayed or unimplemented decisions rendered by domestic courts, including those adverse to the State or its affiliated entities. The challenge of non-enforcement of court decisions within the Ukrainian legal system presents a compelling issue demanding urgent attention. Remarkably, the accumulated value of court-ordered debts left unpaid in Ukraine at some point exceeded a staggering quarter of the nation's Gross Domestic Product (GDP).[16] This alarming statistic underscores the gravity of the problem and its far-reaching implications for economic stability and the rule of law within the country.[17] One pivotal facet contributing to this predicament is the restricted capacity of creditors to pursue their claims against state-owned enterprises effectively. This challenge is partly attributable to the presence of special legal provisions, the so-called moratoria regime, that effectively impedes the enforcement of judicial decisions and pre-empts the initiation of bankruptcy proceedings against state-owned enterprises.[18]

Another salient issue emerges concerning the excessive length of judicial proceedings. The ECtHR's observations, as evidenced in cases such as *Svitlana Naumenko v. Ukraine*[19] and *Merit v. Ukraine,*[20] lay bare the prolonged duration of

[13]Council of Europe Committee of Ministers, 15th Annual Report of the Committee of Ministers 2021 https://rm.coe.int/2021-annual-report/1680a9c848 accessed 01 August 2023.

[14]European Court of Human Rights, Annual Report 2021 https://www.echr.coe.int/documents/d/echr/annual_report_2022_eng-2 accessed 01 August 2023.

[15]Burmych and Others v. Ukraine (striking out) [GC], nos. 46852/13 et al., 12 October 2017.

[16]Pravo-JUSTICE, The Alchemy of "Moratoria" <https://www.pravojustice.eu/post/alhimiya-moratoriyiv> assessed 25 August 2023.

[17]Robert Buckland, Illia Chernohorenko, 'The ECHR remains a beacon for the people of Ukraine and Europe' (4 April 2023) The Times https://www.thetimes.co.uk/article/the-echr-remains-a-beacon-for-the-people-of-ukraine-and-europe-dx06s5pxr accessed 05 August 2010.

[18]Ibid.

[19]Svetlana Naumenko v. Ukraine, no. 41984/98, 9 November 2004.

[20]Merit v. Ukraine, no. 66561/01, 30 March 2004.

civil and criminal proceedings respectively. This protracted legal process, characterised by extended delays, has significant implications for Ukraine's judicial system's overall effectiveness and efficiency.

Furthermore, the imperative of ensuring court independence cannot be overlooked. The *Volkov v. Ukraine*[21] case serves as a vivid illustration of this concern, wherein the dismissal of Supreme Court judge Oleksandr Volkov in 2010 raised questions about political independence and impartiality. This situation, compounded by the *Agrokompleks v. Ukraine* case,[22] which highlighted the absence of adequate measures to counter undue influences on judges holding administrative positions, underscored the vulnerability of Ukraine's legal system to external pressures. Notwithstanding significant progress achieved over the recent decade on strenghening judical independence, the group of cases continues to remain under the enhanced supervision of the CM. As highlighted in the CM June 2023, commendable strides were made between 2014 and 2018 in reforming the systems governing judicial discipline and careers, achieved through a collaborative effort with the Council of Europe. The integration of constitutional amendments in 2016, accompanied by implementing legislation and pragmatic institutional measures, marked pivotal milestones in this reform trajectory. However, the persistence of certain unresolved issues warrants further attention.[23] To this end, the CM reiterated stance underscores the centrality of foundational principles such as the separation of powers, the structural autonomy of the judiciary, and the non-removability of judges, all of which are indispensable pillars of judicial independence.[24]

In the meantime, property rights violations present a formidable challenge as well. Notable cases such as *Koval and Others v. Ukraine*[25] reveal unauthorised actions by law enforcement agencies leading to the confiscating of property ownership documents and unlawful seizure of property. These occurrences raise profound questions about protecting property rights and the integrity of Ukraine's legal framework. Moreover, constraints on the freedom of peaceful assembly constitute a pertinent concern. As indicated by the *Vyerentsov v. Ukraine* case,[26] the absence of distinct regulations for organising assemblies, rallies, and demonstrations contrasts Article 185-1 of the Code of Ukraine on Administrative Offenses. This discrepancy underscores the need for greater alignment between legal provisions and practical applications. Equally important are the instances of illegal actions by law enforcement agencies. In the *Kaverzin v. Ukraine* case,[27] instances of torture leading to coerced self-incrimination highlight the challenges of upholding human rights within law enforcement practices. Moreover, the *Khaylo v. Ukraine*[28] and

[21] Volkov v. Ukraine, no. 8794/04, 17 January 2006.

[22] Agrokompleks v. Ukraine, no. 23465/03, 6 October 2011.

[23] CM/Del/Dec(2023)1468/H46-38.

[24] Ibid.

[25] Koval and Others v. Ukraine, no. 22429/05, 15 November 2012.

[26] Vyerentsov v. Ukraine, no. 20372/11, 11 April 2013.

[27] Kaverzin v. Ukraine, no. 23893/03, 15 May 2012.

[28] Khaylo v. Ukraine, no. 39964/02, 13 November 2008.

Fedorchenko and Lozenko v. Ukraine cases[29] underscore the need for robust investigations into crimes committed by law enforcement personnel. Furthermore, challenges related to detention conditions warrant attention. In cases such as the *Nevmerzhitsky group,*[30] *Melnyk v. Ukraine,*[31] and *Yakovenko v. Ukraine,*[32] substandard detention conditions prevail in pre-trial facilities, prisons, and police positions. These conditions not only raise concerns about the treatment of detainees but also point to systemic shortcomings within Ukraine's penal system.

In turn, unfairness in criminal proceedings constitutes a notable issue. The *Balitskiy v. Ukraine* case[33] exposes violations of the right against self-incrimination and the right to a fair defence. In a similar vein, the *Veniamin Tymoshenko v. Ukraine* case[34] sheds light on the discrepancy between legal provisions and their practical implications concerning collective labour dispute resolution. Moreover, the *Karpyuk and Others*[35] case highlights the disproportionate deprivation of liberty for organising mass protests, underscoring potential flaws in the balance between public order and individual rights.

Last but not least, the ECtHR's judgement in the well-known *Gongadze case*[36] has not yet been fully implemented, as indicated by a recent decision by the CM.[37] In turn, to implement general measures in this case, the CM called upon the Ukrainian Government to revise its legislation to align with the standards set by the Council of Europe.[38]

Therefore, before the full-scale Russian invasion in February 2022, the challenges besetting Ukraine's justice sector had long been conspicuously intricate and diverse. The spectrum of structural and systemic issues, ranging from the persistent non-execution of national court decisions to discernible injustices within criminal proceedings, had unequivocally underscored the urgency of enacting legal reforms that safeguard fundamental human rights. In turn, the unprovoked aggression in February 2022 had engendered a heightened significance in the execution of judgements of the ECtHR, as expounded upon in subsequent analysis.

---

[29] Fedorchenko and Lozenko v. Ukraine, no. 387/03, 20 September 2012.

[30] Nevmerzhitsky v. Ukraine, no. 54825/00, ECHR 2005-II.

[31] Melnyk v. Ukraine, no. 23436/03, 28 March 2006.

[32] Yakovenko v. Ukraine, no. 15825/06, 25 October 2007.

[33] Balitskiy v. Ukraine, no. 12793/03, 3 November 2011.

[34] Veniamin Tymoshenko and Others v. Ukraine, no. 48408/12, 2 October 2014.

[35] Karpyuk and Others v. Ukraine, nos. 30582/04 and 32152/04, 6 October 2015.

[36] Gongadze v. Ukraine, no. 34056/02, ECHR 2005-XI.

[37] CM/Del/Dec(2022)1428/H46-41.

[38] CM/Del/Dec(2020)1390/H46-30.

Implementation of the ECtHR Judgements in the Context of the EU Accession and Recovery Plan

Accession to the European Union

On 28 February 2022, Ukraine submitted its application for EU membership merely 5 days after Russia's unprovoked aggression commenced.[39] Subsequently, the European Commission (the Commission) defined seven concrete steps, on the understanding of which the Commission granted Ukraine the candidate status.[40] On 15 December, the European Council has decided to open accession negotiations with Ukraine.[41] Both the candidacy status and the negotiations are based on the so-called Copenhagen criteria, established in 1993, encompassing institutional stability, democracy, the rule of law, fundamental rights protection, a functional market economy, and the ability to engage with EU obligations.[42] Notably, two out of four Copenhagen political criteria—namely the rule of law and fundamental rights protection—interact, if not depend, on the implementation of the ECtHR judgements. It emphasises, therefore, the integral role of the European Court of Human Rights judgement implementation in Ukraine's path toward European Union accession, as detailed below.

Firstly, the imperative to reform the judiciary and safeguard media freedom, pertinent to the *Volkov* and the *Gongadze* cases, respectively, finds resonance in the explicit articulation within the seven precise steps to be taken by Ukraine, as defined by the European Commission. Regarding the judicial reform, the Commission explicitly urged Ukraine to enact and enforce legislation concerning the selection procedure for Constitutional Court judges, incorporating a pre-selection phase rooted in evaluating their integrity and professional competence, aligning with recommendations from the Venice Commission. The Commission also pressed for the conclusive integrity assessment of candidates aspiring to be members of the High Council of Justice, an evaluation executed by the Ethics Council, alongside the nomination of a candidate to establish the High Qualification Commission of Judges of Ukraine.[43] The re-launch of the Higher Council of Justice and its reconstitution to align with Venice Commission guidelines was precisely the essence of general measures within the scope of implementing the *Volkov case*, as outlined by the

[39] Versailles Declaration (11 March 2022) <https://www.consilium.europa.eu/media/54773/20220311-versailles-declaration-en.pdf> assessed 27 August 2023.

[40] European Commission, Commission Opinion on Ukraine's application for membership of the European Union (17 June 2022), 407 final https://neighbourhood-enlargement.ec.europa.eu/system/files/2022-06/Ukraine%20Opinion%20and%20Annex.pdf assessed 27 August 2023.

[41] European Commission, European Leaders decide to open accession negotiations with Ukraine and Moldova in a historic summit (18 December 2023) https://ec.europa.eu/commission/presscorner/detail/en/statement_23_6628 assessed 25 December 2023.

[42] Ibid.

[43] Ibid.

Committee of Ministers.[44] Furthermore, the Committee of Ministers urged swift action by the authorities to ensure the full functionality of the High Qualification Commission of Judges.[45]

Turning to media freedom, the Commission's call to action emphasised Ukraine's need to counter the sway of vested interests by adopting a media law that harmonises Ukrainian legislation with the EU's audio-visual media services directive, thus empowering an autonomous media regulator.[46] This step resonates distinctly with the Council of Europe Committee of Ministers in the *Gongadze case*. Precedingly, the Committee of Ministers had called upon the authorities to align legislative frameworks with the standards outlined by the Council of Europe, specifically the Committee's Recommendation on safeguarding journalism and the security of media practitioners (CM/Rec (2016)4), without restricting protection solely to formally recognised journalists.[47]

In tandem with the conspicuous interdependence between the European Commission's stipulated measures and the corresponding ECtHR judgements, the Commission directly confronts the issue of non-implementation of the ECtHR judgements within its analytical discourse before outlining the concrete steps to be taken. It underscores that Ukraine faces a substantial backlog of 501 European Court of Human Rights judgements, all subject to enhanced supervision by the Committee of Ministers yet remaining pending in terms of *effective implementation*. To this end, the Commission stressed that the majority of these cases follow an entrenched pattern, converging upon violations of the right to a meaningful remedy, excessive durations of criminal proceedings, instances of deplorable ill-treatment leading to substandard detention conditions, prolonged pre-trial detentions, and encroachments upon the rights to both liberty and security.[48]

The foremost formal membership negotiations encompass the integration of established EU laws, preparations to ensure effective application and enforcement, and the execution of a spectrum of reforms spanning judicial, administrative, economic, and other realms. Upon the consummation of negotiations and the concurrent completion of accompanying reforms to the satisfaction of both parties, Ukraine gains the opportunity to accede to the European Union.[49]

Notably, one of the crucial fields to negotiate is envisaged by Chap. 23 of the EU Acquis.[50] This Chapter delves into the EU judiciary and fundamental rights policies. Its primary aim is to sustain and elevate the Union as a realm of freedom, security,

---

[44] CM/Del/Dec(2023)1468/H46-38.

[45] Ibid.

[46] European Commission (n 38).

[47] CM (n 36).

[48] European Commission (n 38).

[49] European Neighbourhood Policy and Enlargement Negotiations (DG NEAR), Steps towards joining < https://neighbourhood-enlargement.ec.europa.eu/enlargement-policy/steps-towards-joining_en> assessed 27 August 2023.

[50] Ibid.

and justice. A pivotal component within this chapter is the establishment of an autonomous and efficient judiciary, underscored by impartiality, integrity, and the delivery of judgements at an elevated standard.[51] These attributes are vital for upholding the rule of law. The achievement of this goal mandates a resolute commitment to eliminating external influences over the judiciary, alongside the allocation of substantial financial resources and comprehensive training. In the meantime, member states must uphold fundamental rights, as enshrined within the acquis[52] and the Fundamental Rights Charter.[53]

Accordingly, as the EU Fundamental Rights Charter is based on the European Convention on Human Rights,[54] to successfully conclude negotiations on Chap. 23, Ukraine is, in any case, compelled to either implement or exhibit substantial advancement towards the implementation of a number of the ECtHR judgements.

Ukraine Recovery Plan

The Ukraine Recovery Conference 2022 (URC2022), hosted in Lugano from 4–5 July 2022, served as a platform for discussing and strategising Ukraine's recovery and reform agenda. URC2022 significantly focused on specific reform priorities, aiming to facilitate stability, prosperity, and digital transformation within Ukraine. These priorities included eradicating corruption, enhancing justice and the rule of law, empowering municipalities through decentralisation, promoting reintegration and cohesion, fostering a robust banking and financial sector, ensuring transparency in state-owned enterprises through improved corporate governance, spearheading the green transition, and investing in human capital.[55] During the Conference, the Ukraine Recovery Plan was presented.[56] It consists of a number of chapters, and the "Justice" chapter plays a pivotal role.[57]

However, it's important to note that the Plan has not been formally adopted as an official document; thus, in fact, its implementation has not commenced. Nevertheless, it serves as a crystallisation of the envisioned path towards Ukraine's recovery, encompassing its justice sector. Effectively, it functions as a blueprint that could be

---

[51] European Neighbourhood Policy and Enlargement Negotiations (DG NEAR), Chapters of acquis <https://neighbourhood-enlargement.ec.europa.eu/enlargement-policy/conditions-membership/chapters-acquis_en> assessed 27 August 2023.

[52] Ibid.

[53] European Union Charter of Fundamental Rights.

[54] European Commission, Why do we need the Charter? < https://commission.europa.eu/aid-development-cooperation-fundamental-rights/your-rights-eu/eu-charter-fundamental-rights/why-do-we-need-charter_en> assessed 27 August 2023.

[55] URC 2022, Recovery Plan (June 2022) https://www.urc-international.com/urc2022-recovery-plan assessed 25 August 2023.

[56] Ibid.

[57] Ibid.

repurposed either as an official Plan, pending adoption or as a foundational framework for upcoming policy documents. The Justice Recovery Plan prominently cites the ECtHR judgements, stressing the essential need for their implementation. Meanwhile, although the Plan does not explicitly mention ECtHR judgements in certain cases, it does mirror Committee of Ministers resolutions tied to ECtHR judgement execution.

To begin with, the Plan explicitly recognises the significance of implementing ECtHR judgements as a pivotal component for advancing justice sector reforms, especially within the context of the persistent challenge of court judgement non-enforcement. The Plan highlights that the European Court of Human Rights has identified the systemic nature of the issue of non-enforcement of national court decisions. The underlying factors encompass deficiencies in national legislation, imposition of enforcement moratoria, and inadequate enforcement mechanisms. The protracted duration of enforcement procedures or instances of non-enforcement of court judgements represent substantial structural concerns under the purview of the Council of Europe's Committee of Ministers in relation to Ukraine. The Plan also mentions that the Committee of Ministers oversees a total of 635 cases pertaining to this matter.[58]

Moving forward, the Plan precisely defines the core issue at hand—the improper execution and non-enforcement of legally binding court decisions. In response to this challenge, the Plan delineates a strategic approach to ensuring the enforcement of ECtHR judgements against Ukraine (Ivanov, Burmych case group), which notably encompasses the incorporation of recommendations endorsed by the Committee of Ministers of the Council of Europe. This objective is subsequently broken down into distinct tasks aimed at achieving comprehensive reform: (a) implementation of an automatic enforcement mechanism for court decisions issued against the State; (b) elimination of moratorium measures that hinder the execution of court decisions; (c) establishment of a robust and efficient judicial oversight mechanism for monitoring the execution of court rulings; (d) implementation of an effective protocol for determining or altering the method or sequence of executing non-property judgements; (e) enhancement of the procedural framework governing the enforcement of decisions that necessitate specific actions from the debtor or their abstention from certain activities.[59]

The issue of non-enforcement of court judgements is not explicitly singled out in the Plan concerning the implementation of ECtHR judgements. The Plan also recognises another problem within the infrastructure of the punishment execution system—the assurance of safety and suitable detention conditions for convicts and prisoners. In this vein, the Plan highlights the imperative to align the conditions of detainees in accordance with both recommendations of the Committee of Ministers of the Council of Europe. To this end, the Plan notes that non-implementation of the ECtHR judgements costs the Ukrainian Government a price. Around 2.5 million

[58] Ibid.

[59] Recovery Plan (n 52).

euros have been disbursed from Ukraine's State Budget for the execution of European Court decisions in this category of cases, indicating a discernible upward trend.[60]

In conclusion, the assessment of the recovery framework reveals that while the draft Justice Recovery Plan might not encompass the full spectrum of structural issues as identified by the ECtHR judgements in leading cases under the supervision of the CM, it does give direct attention to the two key concerns of non-enforcement and inadequate detention conditions. Therefore, it becomes apparent that the Recovery Plan recognises the implementation of ECtHR judgements as a crucial instrument for driving Ukraine's recovery efforts.

Implementation of the ECtHR Judgements in Inter-State Cases and a Special Compensation Fund

Not only does the implementation of the ECtHR judgements against Ukraine hold the potential to secure Ukraine's recovery, but also the implementation of potential judgements against Russia in inter-State cases lodged by Ukraine and other States. These inter-State cases might play a role in Ukraine's recovery as they aim to address systemic human rights violations committed by Russia. Eventually, such cases are to deliver justice to those who have suffered these violations. To achieve this, the case typically progresses through three stages: the assessment of its admissibility, the examination of its merits, and the award of justice satisfaction.

In general context, over the past 70 years, the Council of Europe member states have brought 32 situations to the former Commission and the ECtHR, alleging breaches of the Convention and its Protocols by other High Contracting Parties.[61] What's particularly noteworthy is the recent surge in these applications, with half of the total number arising in the last 7 years. Russia stands out among the targets of these applications, being the subject of a quarter of them.[62]

Regarding inter-State cases lodged by Ukraine against Russia, the two inter-State cases are currently under consideration by the ECtHR Grand Chamber. The first case revolves around events in Crimea, encompassing three inter-State applications previously submitted in 2014, 2015, and 2018. This case was declared partly admissible on 16 December 2020, marking the completion of the case's first stage.[63] The other case within the Grand Chamber pertains to the armed conflict in Eastern Ukraine, including the tragic downing of flight MH17. Moreover, this case also delves into Russia's aggression in Ukrainian territory since 24 February 2022. A

[60] Ibid.

[61] ECtHR, Inter-State applications <https://www.echr.coe.int/inter-state-applications> assessed 27 August 2023.

[62] Ibid.

[63] Ukraine v. Russia (re Crimea) (dec.) [GC], nos. 20958/14 and 38334/18, 16 December 2020.

substantial volume of related individual applications, nearly 8500, have been brought before the Court. These individual applications appear to be linked to the events in Crimea, Eastern Ukraine, the Sea of Azov, and Russia's unprovoked full-scale aggression on Ukrainian since 24 February 2022.

As previously mentioned, following the completion of the merits stage, the ECtHR may issue a just satisfaction award to the victims of human rights violations that prompted the initiation of the inter-State case. Article 41 emphasises that just satisfaction must be granted to the injured party in cases of violations.[64] However, while the legal framework is well-established, the practical implementation of just satisfaction awards in inter-State cases, in contrast to individual cases, has proven challenging. In fact, just satisfaction awards in inter-State cases have been rarely paid historically. A glance at the rate of just satisfaction actually paid in inter-State cases reveals a disheartening reality. Notably, in cases like *Cyprus v. Turkey*, *Georgia v. Russia* (I) and *Georgia v. Russia* (II), no payments have been made at all.[65]

It, thus, appears that Russia declined to provide payment to Georgia in sums of EUR 10 million and EUR 129 million, respectively, before its expulsion from the Council of Europe. Now, with its exposure, the likelihood of Russia compensating for human rights violations in cases ruled by the ECtHR concerning Ukraine appears to be diminished to zero. As a result, for justice to be delivered, the need to devise mechanisms to enforce judgements in the face of non-compliance by respondent States, particularly Russia, becomes imperative.

In the meantime, to address the issue of compensation, the President of Ukraine established a Working Group responsible for developing and implementing international legal mechanisms to compensate Ukraine for damages resulting from the armed aggression of Russia. Subsequently, the members of the group developed a concept comprising four key components: (a) an international commission for compensation claims, (b) a compensation fund; (c) a register of damage; (d) an international agreement to establish the procedure.[66] In May 2023, the Council of Europe Summit took a significant stride forward by establishing a register of damages for Ukraine, serving as an initial measure toward implementing an international compensation mechanism for victims affected by Russian aggression.[67] Before the summit, Leach mentioned that the concept of linking the execution of ECtHR judgements in inter-State cases with establishing a compensation fund was under consideration as well. However, no further specifics on this matter were disclosed and debated.[68]

[64]ECHR (n 5).

[65]CM/Del/Dec(2023)1468/H46-28, CM/Del/Dec(2023)1468/H46-28.

[66]Chiara Giorgetti, Markiyan Kliuchkovskyi, and Patrick Pearsall, 'Launching an International Claims Commission for Ukraine' (2022) EJIL: Talk! Blog of the European Journal of International Law. https://www.ejiltalk.org/launching-an-international-claims-commission-for-ukraine/ assessed 27 August 2023.

[67]Resolution CM/Res(2023)3.

[68]Donald, Alice, and Philip Leach, 'Responding to Seismic Change in Europe - The Road to Reykjavik and Beyond' (2023) European Human Rights Law Review 111.

The concept of a special fund holds promise as a potential resolution for enforcing just satisfaction awards in inter-State cases initiated by Ukraine against Russia, particularly given the necessity for innovative approaches in this context. However, while this idea shows potential, its development remains incomplete, and any progress may be complex.

A primary obstacle pertains to the legal framework mandated by the ECHR for implementing ECtHR judgements. Article 46 of the Convention necessitates the respondent state's compliance with these judgements. However, while Article 46 mandates respondent states to adhere to ECtHR judgements, it doesn't preclude the use of a special fund for the implementation of the ECtHR judgements.

A second query surfaces the question: why should just satisfaction be paid from a specialised fund in cases brought by Ukraine and not in cases lodged by, for instance, Georgia? What rationale drives the Committee of Ministers to craft effective solutions for one armed conflict and not extend them to others? An evident response is that the special fund could only be devised to address human rights violations in Ukraine. In the meantime, there is no inherent obstacle to establishing a parallel fund for Georgia. Objectively, the lack of functional mechanisms for one inter-State case shouldn't hinder a viable resolution for another.

The third concern revolves around synchronising the proposed compensation mechanism, which involves a registry of damages and a special claims commission utilising resources from the special fund, with the implementation of the ECtHR judgements. Beyond the mechanical aspects, one conceptual dimension emerges. The register of damages and subsequent claims commission are intended to redress harm occurring after 24 February 2022.[69] Nevertheless, ECtHR judgements are expected to encompass damages before and after this date (until 16 September 2022).[70] A pertinent query arises regarding whether the legal framework establishing the special fund might inadvertently restrict its scope to only address cases occurring post-February 24, 2022. This aspect warrants consideration and further discussion.

To conclude, the implementation of the ECtHR judgements stands as a pivotal instrument in Ukraine's path towards recovery and its accession to the EU. In this regard, enforcing landmark cases against Ukraine would fortify the rule of law and bolster the protection of fundamental rights, thus, fulfilling the political criteria for EU membership and facilitate Ukraine's recovery. Furthermore, the prospective execution of just satisfaction awards in inter-State cases against Russia would provide redress for human rights violations and, thus, might contribute to Ukraine's overall recovery efforts as well.

Nonetheless, while the "receipt" to borrow from Aristotle's framework, appears evident in the context of implementing judgements against Ukraine, the challenge remains in enforcement of potential just satisfaction awards that the ECtHR is to

[69] CM (n 66).

[70] Six months after its exclusion from the Council of Europe, the Russian Federation ceases to be party to the European Convention on Human Rights on 16 September 2022.

render against Russia in the future. Establishing the possibility of paying such awards from a dedicated special fund within or outside of the emerging compensatory mechaism could present a pragmatic and innovative solution. The solution which ultimate goal is achieving the effective protection of human rights as the final and, thus most important, final cause, as articulated by Aristotle.[71]

[71] Ross (n 1).

Reconstruction and Preparation for Ukraine's Accession to the EU

Melania-Gabriela Ciot

Abstract The evolution of the international arena indicates clearly that the state actors are competing for a better position on the New International Order. This perspective will bring political, social, economic, but also cultural and sustainable dimensions to the prospective analysis of evolutions. The invasion of Ukraine accelerated the reconfiguration of the Contemporary International System, with impact on the foresight developments of EU. The support of the European Member States to Ukraine manifested through different instruments, policies, and institutions, in several key areas: infrastructure, economic diversification, education and skill development, governance and policy, social development and inclusion, international collaboration, and resilience building. The present study will investigate the challenges for the EU's enlargement policy in the context of the war from Ukraine, focusing on the accession process, its preparation, negotiations, and management of the process. The study ends with some recommendations regarding the building of the administrative and resilience capacity to better support the complex process of reconstruction of Ukraine.

Introduction

In a recently published book of Mearsheimer and Rosato (2023), entitled *How States Think: The Rationality of Foreign Policy*, the authors argued that Putin's decision to invade Ukraine could be interpreted in the light of "straightforward balance-of-power theory", with the membership to NATO of Ukraine as the "red line" (Yarhi-Milo, 2023). Different by the realist interpretations of the states' actions and reactions on international scene of the twentieth century's scholars of international relations field, the perspectives and analysis of both authors, belongs to one of the newest trend in international relations—the psychological one. By analyzing

M.-G. Ciot (✉)
Babeş-Bolyai University, Cluj-Napoca, Romania
e-mail: melania.ciot@ubbcluj.ro

S. Nate (ed.), *Ukraine's Journey to Recovery, Reform and Post-War Reconstruction*, Contributions to Security and Defence Studies,
https://doi.org/10.1007/978-3-031-66434-2_11

how leaders make decisions, which are the idiosyncrasies that influenced a certain decision, the analysts and scholars will understand, frame and prospect better the evolution of a specific crisis.

In the case of Ukraine, there are emotional and cultural elements that could enriched the frame of interpretation. Some scholars mention the emotional reason or fixation of Putin to control Ukraine or the cultural similarities between the two countries as important. But what seems rational for a leader may not be rational for a state. That is why, when the future of a state or the evolution of a situation is discussed, the rationality of interpretation could be seen from different angles.

According with Mearsheimer and Rosato (2023) (Yarhi-Milo, 2023), the decision to invade Ukraine is Putin's answer to NATO's expansion and, if it is to consider Putin's idiosyncrasies, his perception as being a looser, also avoiding a domino effect for other countries in the region. There are other cases in our international history to appeal to, to underline the significance of idiosyncrasies that were ignored in the decisions and their negative consequences—as Chamberlain decision from 1938 regarding the annexation of parts of Czechoslovakia or 1982 decision of Argentina to invade Falkland Islands.

A historical dimension of the interpretation of the situation from Ukraine has an important value for the prospections on the reconstruction and of its impact on the region, especially Central and Eastern European (CEE). The entire area was troubled in the years that followed the communist regimes (Puşcaş, 2023), and this was not entirely because of the new paths of social reconstruction that the states from the area will follow, but merely because of the concerns regarding the evolutions of the "Great Eastern Power", which exerted the dominance in the region in the years that followed the Second World War. After 1989, many European capitals, especially the ones from the Western Neighborhood of former Soviet Union were looking with concern and even fear to the East. Some of the states from CEE constituted Visegrad Group (Czech Republic, Poland, Slovakia and Hungary), tutelage from the West, but some other states—as Romania and Bulgaria—did not find quickly a solution for regulating their relations with the East and Western Europe. Then the Balkan wars and the conflicts from Middle East focused the attention of United States and Western states. It was a "triangle of dangers", with massive implications for the regional security for Europe, European Union, and of course, Romania (Puşcaş, 2023).

It is clear that we are now in a competition phase between the Great Powers for the restructuring of the International World Order, which could not manage properly the complexity of global interdependencies. Expressions as „monetary wars", „commercial wars", „economic wars", „cultural-religious wars", even „New Cold War" have been said and written, remembering us that the Great Powers are willing to opt for confrontational relations (Puşcaş, 2023). But now, the non-state actors are entering into the scene/battle with an important role to play in the post-conflict period—economic and peace reconstruction in the region. It is important also for the International System, in that phase, to establish future rules to be followed by global, state and non-state actors (multinational companies and non-governmental organizations) (Puşcaş, 2023).

But the end of twentieth century, with the enlargement of NATO and of European Union in the CEE brought security guarantees for the region, whose importance has increased, in the actual context. The future of Ukraine is clear set now: the membership of European Union, so the interpretations of its future reconstruction and evolution should be done from a European perspective—a sustainable one.

Reconstruction and Sustainable Development of Ukraine—A European Perspective

The brutal aggression of Russia on Ukraine determined the European Member States and institutions to express their solidarity with emergency economic, military, and humanitarian assistance for Ukraine and Ukrainians and political decisions, by adopting a solid package of sanctions against Russia. The reconstruction of Ukraine needs a strong support of EU Member States and institutions in several key areas: infrastructure, economic diversification, education and skill development, governance and policy, social development and inclusion, international collaboration, and resilience building. By adopting a holistic and sustainable approach, Ukraine can not only recover from its current challenges, but also build a foundation for long-term prosperity and social well-being, aligning with the European values and standards.

The European institutions, especially the European Commissions developed a strong support for Ukraine, under the Team Europe approach, on several areas: financial, humanitarian, emergency, access to the Single Market, cooperation, and reform for the alignment with EU path, budget, and military (European Commission, 2023a).

The second half of 2021 brought the increased prices in energy prices in EU and worldwide, because of war from Ukraine, and increased concerns regarding security and energy supply, due to Russia's decision to suspend gas delivery to several EU states. To diminish the weaponization of fossil fuels by Russia, EU launched *REPower EU action plan*, supporting EU to become independent from Russian fossil fuels till 2030 (European Commission, 2023b).

Since the beginning of Russian invasion of Ukraine, the EU has financially supported Ukraine with €67.7 billion (European Commission, 2023a) and it is working for an additional support for recovery of €1 billion (European Commission, 2023b, 2023c). In January 2023, a *Multi-agency Donor Coordination Platform* was launched to support the international coordination of donors and financial institutions for Ukrainian economic recovery, with an operating office in Brussels and Kviv (European Commission, 2023d). On economic cooperation and access to the Single Market for Ukraine, the EU's Commission proposed the extension of proposal to suspend import duties beyond June 2023, a roadmap for access to the Single Market—*A Priority Action Plan for 2023–2024* -, and a roaming facility for affordable or free calls between EU and Ukraine—an extension with 6 months (European Commission, 2023c).

The sustainable approach on the reconstruction of Ukraine is materializing in the Solidarity Lanes platform, meant to facilitates the agricultural export and bilateral exports, by establishing alternative logistics routes using all transport modes (European Commission, 2023e). Since the beginning of war in Ukraine, 4 million Ukrainians registered for temporary protection (European Commission, 2023c). Strengthening the cyber resilience of Ukraine is important, and EU supported with equipment and software of €10 million and resilient digital transformation (European Commission, 2023c). The Ukrainian civil society was supported through the Civil Society and the Human rights and Democracy Thematic programs, and the European Peace Facility sustained military equipment delivered to Armed Forces (€5.6 billion mobilized) (European Commission, 2023c).

Another dimension of Ukraine's support was the conferences destinated for international community mobilization: *The Ukraine Recovery Conference* (21–23.06.2023) or *International Expert Conference on Recovery, Reconstruction and Modernization of Ukraine* (October 2022), both at the initiative of European institutions and some of the Member States (European Commission, 2023a).

Challenges for the EU Enlargement Policy in the Context of the War in Ukraine

The actual international context challenged the European establishment regarding the implementation of policies and the decision-making process, inclusive the coalition building and alliances formation. Reports of the analysts, of think thanks accredited the necessity of reforming the EU and its policies, enlargement being on top of the agenda. The geostrategic reason is imperative for the inclusion of new Member States into the EU—for stability and security of the continent, but policies, mechanisms and procedures of EU institutions should be adapted.

The EU and Member States will have to come with solutions for the long-term consequences of the successive crisis (energy, security, economic) in areas such security and defense capabilities, rebuilding and reconstruction of Ukraine, acceleration of energy transition/independence from Russian oil and gas, refugees and humanitarian action and EU enlargement process (Sandoval Velasco et al., 2023). The above-mentioned authors synthetized these concerns regarding the economic, fiscal, and financial impact on the following (Fig. 1):

Emerson (2023) made an interesting estimation of Ukrainian proportion from the EU's budget, based on the Poland and Romanian cases (Table 1):

The estimation of Ukraine proportion is €18.9 billion, that means an increase of 10.5% of EU budget for 2023 (of €179.8 billion, excluding NGEU) (Emerson, 2023). It looks like the Ukraine's accession will be a "relatively manageable prospect" (Emerson, 2023).

Regarding the process of enlargement, the biggest challenge is an enlargement in a war situation. Some opinions proposed different forms for adapting accession, as:

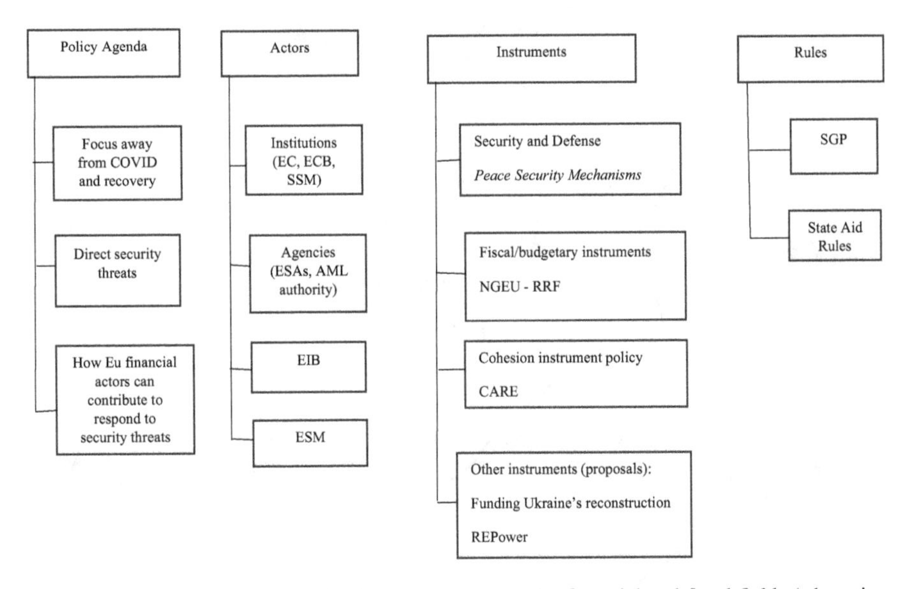

Fig. 1 The impact of war from Ukraine in EU's economic, financial and fiscal fields (adaptation after Sandoval Velasco et al., 2023, p. 5)

Table 1 Proportion of Ukraine from EU's budget, based on Poland and Romanian cases (adapted from Emerson, 2023, p. 5)

	UA based on Poland	UA based on Romania	UA based on average PL + RO
Agriculture	11.9	8.8	10.4
Cohesion	10.2	7.8	9.0
Other receipts	1.0	0.6	0.8
Total receipts	23.3	17.3	20.3
Contributions	−1.5	−1.3	−1.4
Net balance	21.7	16.0	18.9

phased, *accelerated*, *gradual* or *staged* accession. One proposal, delivered by the Group of Twelve experts introduced a differentiation, based on the principles of opt-outs (for deepening integration or extending QMV) and EU values respect: *inner circle* (deep integration—eurozone and Schengen), *EU* itself, *Associate Members* (participation in the Single Market and adherence to common principles) and *European Political Community* (EPC—political cooperation without bound to EU laws) (Fig. 2).

The management of enlargement process is discussed in the report, with accession negotiations organized in clusters and phasing out as a possibility for candidate countries to implement European policies and access some programs. For the next wave of accession, the Group proposed a *regatta* variant, organized around merit-based principle, considering also the potential bilateral conflict. The importance of this study consists in the setting of the vision of the future development of enlargement policy, which became more important at European level due to its geostrategic

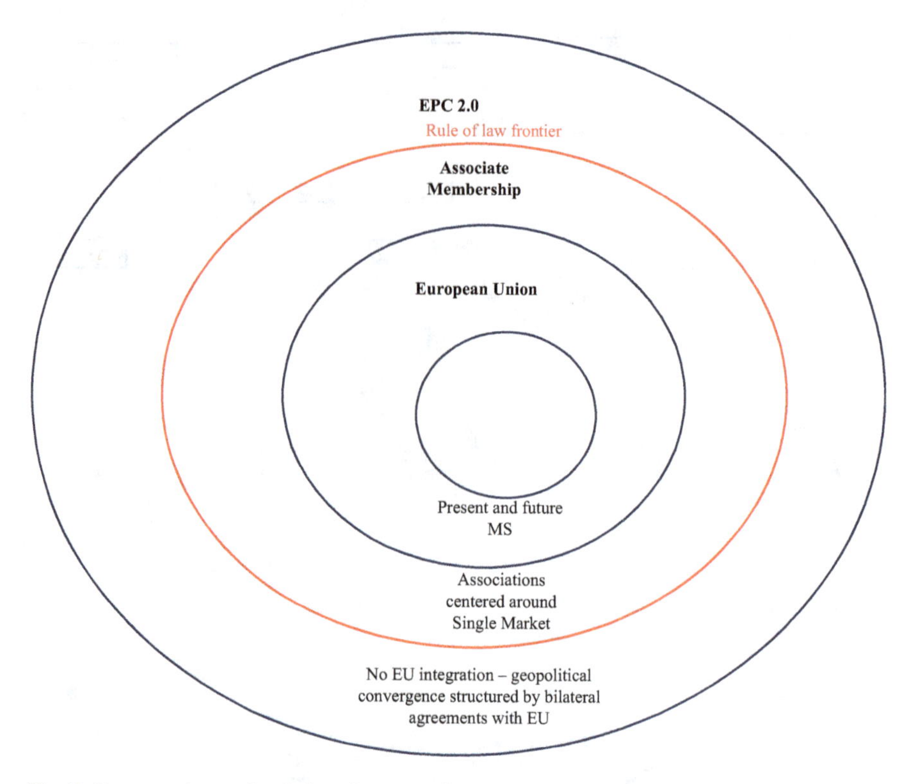

Fig. 2 European integration (adaptation upon Costa, Costa et al., 2023, p. 42)

significance. The future Presidency of Council of EU for the first semester of 2024 will belong to Belgium, and enlargement will be at the core, on 19th of April the Enlargement summit will be organized, to celebrate 20 years from the 2004 "big bang" enlargement of EU (Pugnet, 2023).

Other challenges for the enlargement policy are the sanctions policy adopted by the EU, with effects on Common Foreign and Defense Policy (Portela, 2023), which hurried the implementation of strategic autonomy of EU, especially in the energy policy, consolidating in this way the European Green Deal (focusing on energy policy).

Accession to the EU: Preparation, Negotiations and Management of the Process

The EU's accession process represents the most important process of transformation and development of a country and its society. For the CEE region it is the only chance of modernization and enrollment on the right path of its belonging—European values and principles. But the accession means a lot of opportunities for the countries, not an "abundance basket", situations that will be created and fruited in that countries and in Europe by the political decision-makers (Puşcaş, 2017). Also, for the EU, the enlargement means a better management of diversity, stronger common policies, and mechanisms, especially in regards with decision-making processes and more powerful institutions.

The current methodology of accession is based on the Methodology launched in February 2020 and reinforced by the November 2023 Package (European Commission, 2023f). It stated that accession is and will be a merit-based principle, dependent on the progress achieved by each candidate. The *ab initio* condition for candidate countries is to embrace the EU values and to reform the institutions and national legislation to respond to the European set of values and principles.

The principles of current methodology of accession are:

- ***More credibility***—of the candidate countries must become more credible on their commitments to deliver fundamental reforms;
- ***A more dynamic process***—clustering of currently 35 chapters of the *acquis* into six logically connected thematic policy clusters.
- ***Stronger political steer***—both sides should show more political leadership and should live up to their respective commitments.
- ***Predictability, positive and negative conditionality***—the annual enlargement package as an instrument of checking the progress or lack of it (European Commission, 2023g).

The accession process is a complex sinergy between two other processes: (1) the EU association process based on association-type of agreement and the (2) the EU accession negotiation process (Mrak & Zuber, 2022). The first one indicates the framework that need to be designed, so the relations between EU and the candidate country are developing, promoting the deepening of political ties and economic integration. For Ukraine, the Association Agreement (AA) was signed on 27 June, 2014 and ratified on 1 September 2017. The second process indicated the complex negotiations which the candidate country has with other EU Member States and institutions, especially the Council of EU, focusing on the transposition of *aquis* into national legislation and reform or establish of new institutions.

The current accession process indicated that the candidate country needs to fulfill the Copenhagen criteria (1993) regarding: (a) the stability of institutions, guaranteeing democracy, the respecting of rule of law, human rights and respect for and protection of minorities; (b) a functioning market economy and the ability to cope with a competitive market within the EU and (c) the ability to take on the obligation of membership, the capacity to implement rules, standards and policies (EUR-Lex, 2023)—indicating the building of the administrative capacity.

According with the Enlargement Methodology from 2020, the process is organized in six clusters, each containing a certain number of chapters, in total 35 chapters (Table 2). The „Fundamental" cluster will open the first and will be provisionally closed the last, progresses on this cluster will influenced the entire pace of negotiations. The table below details each cluster on chapters:

Table 2 Clusters and chapters of EU's accession process (adaptation after European Commission, 2022, p. 2)

Cluster	Chapter
Fundamentals	Judiciary and fundamental rights (Chap. 23) Justice, freedom, security (Chap. 24) Public procurement Statistics Financial control
Internal market	Free movement of goods Free movement for workers Right of establishment &freedom to provide services Free movement of capital Company law Intellectual property law Competition policy Financial services Consumer and health protection
Competitiveness & inclusive growth	Custom union Education & Culture Science & Research Enterprise & Industrial policy Social policy & employment Economic & monetary policy Taxation Information society & media
Green agenda & sustainable connectivity	Environment & Climate Change Trans European networks Energy Transport policy
Resources, agriculture & cohesion	Agriculture and rural development Food safety, veterinary & phytosanitary policy Fisheries Regional policy & coordination of financial instruments Financial & budgetary provisions
External relations	External relations Foreign security and defense policy

Negotiation of each cluster is open, after the candidate country has fulfilled the opening benchmarks. Each chapter will be negotiated individually.

The main steps of the accession process could be organized into three main stages, as: (a) pre-accession negotiation; (b) accession negotiations and (c) post-accession negotiations (European Commission, 2022; Mrak & Zuber, 2023):

1. **Pre-accession negotiations**:

    a. Country submits an application to the Council (EU Member States). For Ukraine, it was 28th February 2022.
    b. Commission submits an Opinion on the application. In the case of Ukraine, it was on 17th of June.

c. EU Member States decide unanimously to grant the country candidate status—the European Council decision. The decision was taken on the European Council from 23–24th of June 2022.
d. The accession negotiations are opened when the EU Members States decide unanimously that. The decision was delivered by the European Council on 14th of December 2023.

2. **Accession negotiations**:

a. First Intergovernmental Conference (CIG) of the candidate country with the EU institutions represents the start of the accession negotiations. Commission proposes a draft negotiating framework as a basis for the talks—*Negotiating Framework for the candidate country's EU accession negotiations*. The Member States agree on the negotiating framework. For Ukraine case, it is expecting to be the highest demanding task for EU, because of the territorial integrity situation of Ukraine.
b. During negotiations, the candidate country prepares to implement EU laws and standards. For every progress on negotiating chapter and clusters, all EU Member States must agree that all requirements are met in each case.
c. Screening process, through which the European Commission is evaluating the country's legislation on each chapter and the progress that have been made, aiming at finding solutions for adapting the domestic legislation to the *aquis*. It reports to the Council of EU and propose the opening of negotiations or conditions to be met—benchmarks—before opening the negotiations.
d. If the opening benchmarks are met by the candidate country for all the thematic chapters from a cluster, the candidate country is invited to present its negotiating position for all chapters from that specific cluster. The common position of the EU is drafter by the European Commission and approved by the Council of EU. Closing benchmarks are part of the common position of EU and are concentrated on implementation and administrative capacity.
e. Provisional closing of each chapter of negotiations—a higher degree of harmonization with EU standards.
f. Conclusion of accession negotiations—last several years and ends when the candidate country and the EU reach an agreement on all chapters that were negotiated.
g. Once negotiations on all areas are finalized, Commission gives its Opinion on the readiness of the country to become a Member State.
h. Based on this Opinion, EU Member States decide unanimously to close the negotiation process—the European Council decision. The European Parliament must also give its consent.

3. **Post-accession negotiations.**

a. Drafting and approval of the Accession Treaty—it must be approved by the European Council with unanimity and the European Parliament with consent.

b. Ratification of Accession Treaty—after the Accession Treaty is signed, it must be ratified by the national parliament of candidate country and of Member States.
c. Accession to the EU—is the moment when the acceding country become full member of EU, with all rights and obligations.

A very complex and not easy process, which requires a national effort of a country. After accession was completed, the integration process will start, the implementation of the negotiated agreements, taking into consideration the derogations and transition periods which were negotiated.

The European Commission Package of Enlargement from November 2023 received many critics, especially from the experts and academic communities because it failed in providing a supple and sophisticated vision on the enlargement, but the East European Trio enlargement recommendation towards Ukraine, Moldova and the European perspective on Georgia were well received. According with Emerson and Blockmans (2023), the package shows its geopolitical reasons and logic, based on the EU values, but the Growth Plan has not been designed for the Eastern Trio, only for Western Balkans, while the €50 billion of Ukraine's Facility build on the same logic as for Western Balkans, will have to be designed for Moldova and Georgia.

The above-mentioned authors elaborated an interesting analysis in which they scored with ranks from 1 to 5 the performance of potential and candidate countries to the EU on the clusters and chapters for accession negotiation, as: (1). Early level of preparedness for membership; (2). Some level; (3). Moderate level; (4). Good level and (5). Very advanced level. For Ukraine, the evaluation indicated for *Fundamentals* cluster an average score of 2,21, meaning a low level; for *Internal market* cluster the score was 1,8—lower than the previous cluster, indicating a low level; for the third cluster—*Competitive*, the rank was 2,6, almost a moderate level; for the fourth cluster—*Green agenda*, the score is 2,5—similar with the previous one—indicating a moderate to good level; for the fifth cluster—*Agriculture, cohesion, budget* -, a score of 1,8, which is similar with the second cluster and for the sixth cluster—*External agenda*, a score of 3,8—the best score from the evaluation, toward a good level. On a general view on the performance, the average score for Ukraine is 2,28—a low level, which means that improvements in all areas should follow. The proposal for Ukraine to open the accession negotiations is a huge encouragement, that could designed the pathways of future reconstruction.

Recommendations for Accession Preparation of Ukraine—Building Administrative Capacities

The path to EU accession provides a unique opportunity for Ukraine to align its policies with European standards, fostering collaboration, shared values, and regional stability. As Ukraine navigates this course, it is essential to prioritize environmental conservation, invest in education and skill development, and engage local communities to build a resilient and prosperous nation.

There are several proposal for the enlargement policy renewal, and the new Eastern Trio represents the window of opportunity. The revision from 2020, has not delivered the expected results and the status quo remain unsatisfactory. Innovation in accession process could be a set of structured stages, where progress to another stage should bring funding and participations in the EU's institutions, in relation with the benchmarks for each chapter (Emerson & Blockmans, 2022).

Several proposals of reform of enlargement policy have been made, among which gradual or accelerated accession, rather than "in" or "out", till all the conditions of EU membership are met is preferably. A more structured accession, with a more staged accession, more transparent procedures, will assure a step-by-step integration in EU institutions and mechanisms. An assessment mechanism with ranks for each benchmark (Emerson & Blockmans, 2022).

One recommendation that could work for the improvement of the accession process and enlargement policy is a distinct financial instrument as the Next Generation EU type, that could support the acceleration of the internal reform of the candidate countries, in the field as rule of law, socio-economic (Emerson & Blockmans, 2023) and administrative capacity, based on reform rule. The integration to Single Market should be accelerated for Ukraine as future candidate country taking into consideration the socio-economic status and the strategic autonomy that the country need to develop in the future (Gopinath, 2023). Regional cooperation and cohesion policy with pre-accession funds should be invested in cross-border projects. The security dimension of the accession is underlined by the new status that Ukraine will gain after it will become member of EU, as Eastern external border. Negotiating and ratifying complementary agreements for the Association Agreements with EU in different areas of cooperation, at bilateral level between Ukraine and EU Member States, could prepare the administrative capacity for the future EU membership. Elaboration of a Growth Pact by Ukraine in collaboration with European Commission and with the approval of Council of EU, will assure a sustainable approach of the development and modernization of Ukraine. The accompanying parallel project for sectoral domains as Green Deal, energy sector, cyber security are good solutions.

Another recommendation is to establish a quantitative and qualitative ranking system with the Commission, especially for the clusters regarding democracy, rule of law, which needs a particular approach. This will bring a greater transparency and a better cooperation with Commission, increasing internal administrative capacity and trust from the European partners.

The Staged Accession proposal (mentioned by Emerson & Blockmans, 2023), included the reform of the unanimity voting procedure and replaced with the qualified majority voting as well as the ranking scores for progresses. The unanimity voting means the consolidation of the negotiation capacity for the candidate country and for the Member States, but a specific mechanism for the particular case of accession, could be designed and discussed. Also, the formal opening and closing of the chapters could be eliminated or redesignated for a faster mechanism of approval, and with the introduction of a score of ranking and the establishing of threshold, the solution will be sustainable. Introducing the status of *Affiliated membership* could be an intermediate solution, with a status for the candidate countries that are not meeting the Copenhagen criteria, to open accession negotiations, but expressed and have the political will for the European path of development.

The involvement of Ukrainian civil society in collaboration and cooperation projects with European partners regarding training of human resources in different areas will increase the administrative capacity, but also the trust of the partners. Ukraine represents an important element of consolidating the transatlantic alliance, in a times when Trump and trumpism are looking for a dangerous comeback. The European perspective is a necessity for the countries in the region, where Russia's and China's influence are present. The Ukrainian model of European accession will be a good example for the states in region, where pro-Russia sympathies still exist and for China, it will have an easier access for influence in the region.

Conclusions

The enlargement policy represents a geostrategic opportunity for an investment in peace, stability, security, and prosperity (European Commission, 2022). Accession is based on a rigorous conditionality and merit-based principle. Rule of law, functional market economy, fight against corruption and organized crime are the main areas of fundamental and complex reforms of the candidate countries. Building the administrative capacity, as well as reconciliation and good neighborly relations and cooperation are important pillars to be followed in the process.

The Enlargement Package from November 2023 is a new and important step forward for the enlargement policy, including for the first time the Eastern Trio, envisioning the European path of it.

The costs of non-enlargement must be evaluated, and it will be realized that the costs will be more than for the enlargement. For the wider geopolitical development of the EU and its Eastern neighborhood and for the transatlantic alliance in support for Ukraine, the European perspective for Ukraine need to be present. The accelerated or gradual accession should be based on conditionality and merit-based principle, with clearly defined benchmarks for pre-accession and accession stage, that will consolidate the possibility for alignment with *aquis* and EU institutions. The civic support of accession will assure the building of administrative capacity, consolidating cooperation and trust with European partners.

EU represents a transformative journey towards sustainable development, economic resilience, and enhanced societal well-being. By embracing a comprehensive strategy that integrates green technologies, fosters innovation, ensures good governance, and promotes social inclusion, Ukraine can not only recover from existing challenges but also emerge as a model for a modern, sustainable European nation.

International cooperation and support, particularly from the EU, will play a pivotal role in realizing Ukraine's aspirations. Together, with a commitment to sustainability, inclusivity, and a shared vision for the future, Ukraine's reconstruction and accession to the EU can contribute not only to the well-being of its citizens but also to the broader ideals of a united and prosperous Europe.

References

Costa, O., Schwarzer, D., Berès, P., Gressani, G., Marti, G., Mayer, F., Nguyen, T., von Ondarza, N., Russack, S., Tekin, F, Vallée, S., & Verger, C. (2023). *Sailing on high seas: Reforming and enlarging the EU for the 21st century*. 18 September 2023. Retrieved December 7, 2023, from https://institutdelors.eu/en/publications/sailing-on-high-seas-reforming-and-enlarging-the-eu-for-the-21st-century/

Emerson, M. (2023). *The potential impact of Ukrainian accession on the EU's budget—and the importance of control valves. Policy Papers*. International Center for Defense and Security, September 2023. Retrieved December 2, 2023, from https://cdn.ceps.eu/wp-content/uploads/2023/11/ICDS-Policy-Paper-Impact-of-Ukrainian-Accession-on-the-EU-Budget.pdf

Emerson, M., & Blockmans, S. (2022). *Next steps for EU enlargement – Forwards or backwards?* Stockholm Center for Eastern European Studies. 23 November 2022. Retrieved November 26, 2023, from https://www.ceps.eu/ceps-publications/next-steps-for-eu-enlargement/

Emerson, M., & Blockmans, S. (2023). *The 2023 enlargement package—Major political proposals and glimmers of a staged accession approach*. 21 November 2023. Retrieved November 26, 2023, from https://www.ceps.eu/ceps-publications/the-2023-enlargement-package/

EUR-Lex. (2023). Accession criteria (Copenhagen criteria). Retrieved December 8, 2023, from https://eur-lex.europa.eu/EN/legal-content/glossary/accession-criteria-copenhagen-criteria.html

European Commission. (2022). *EU accession step by step*. October 2022. Retrieved November 27, 2022, from https://neighbourhood-enlargement.ec.europa.eu/system/files/2022-10/eu_accession_process_clusters%20%28oct%202022%29.pdf

European Commission. (2023a). *Recovery and reconstruction of Ukraine*. Retrieved December 4, 2023, from https://eu-solidarity-ukraine.ec.europa.eu/eu-assistance-ukraine/recovery-and-reconstruction-ukraine_en#ukraine-facility

European Commission. (2023b). Flash Eurobarometer—EU challenges and priorities for 2023. September. Retrieved December 4, 2023, from https://europa.eu/eurobarometer/surveys/detail/3092

European Commission. (2023c). *EU solidarity with Ukraine. #StandWithUkraine*. November 2023. Retrieved December 4, 2023, from https://eu-solidarity-ukraine.ec.europa.eu/index_en

European Commission. (2023d). *EU Solidarity with Ukraine*. 2 February 2023. Retrieved December 4, 2023, from https://eu-solidarity-ukraine.ec.europa.eu/eu-ukraine-standing-together_en

European Commission. (2023e). *EU-Ukraine Solidarity lanes the joint coordination platform*. September 2023. Retrieved December 4, 2023, from https://eu-solidarity-ukraine.ec.europa.eu/eu-assistance-ukraine/eu-ukraine-solidarity-lanes_en

European Commission. (2023f). *Communication from the Commission to the European Parliament, the Council, the European Economic and Social Committee and the Committee of the Regions. 2023 Communication on EU Enlargement Policy. COM (2023) 690 final*. 08.11.2023. Retrieved December 4, 2023, from https://eur-lex.europa.eu/resource.html?uri=cellar:5d77752b-7eee-11ee-99ba-01aa75ed71a1.0001.02/DOC_1&format=PDF

European Commission. (2023g). *Revised enlargement methodology: Questions and Answers*. 5 February 2020. Retrieved December 4, 2023, from https://ec.europa.eu/commission/presscorner/detail/en/qanda_20_182

Gopinath, G. (2023). *Europe in a fragmented world.* Retrieved December 7, 2023, from https://www.imf.org/en/News/Articles/2023/11/30/sp-fdmd-remarks-bernhard-harms-prize

Mearsheimer, J.J., Rosato, S. (2023). *How States Think: The Rationality of Foreign Policy*. New Haven: Yale University Press

Mrak, M., & Zuber, P. (2022). *Ukraine's EU accession process in the field of regional and local development. Policy Paper.* & October 2022. Retrieved November 27, 2023, from https://u-lead.org.ua/storage/admin/files/a61fb22a9aa444242239b717acbee6b9.pdf

Mrak, M., & Zuber, P. (2023). *Negotiations as an integral part of the EU accession process. What is of main relevance for Ukraine?* 23 July 2023. Retrieved November 26, 2023, from https://voxukraine.org/en/negotiations-as-an-integral-part-of-the-eu-accession-process-what-is-of-main-relevance-for-ukraine

Portela, C. (2023). Easing, suspending and phasing out. The forgotten potential of sanctions relief, European Union Institute for Security Studies. Conflict Series. Retrieved December 4, 2023, from https://op.europa.eu/en/publication-detail/-/publication/1d2ad068-875c-11ee-99ba-01aa75ed71a1/language-en

Pugnet, A. (2023). *Belgium aims to close negotiations on EU open files, focus on bloc's future.* Euractiv. 8 December 2023. Retrieved December 8, 2023, from https://www.euractiv.com/section/eu-council-presidency/news/belgium-aims-to-close-negotiations-on-eu-open-files-focus-on-blocs-future/

Pușcaș, V. (2017). *România și calea de viață europeană.* Editura Școala Ardeleană.

Pușcaș, V. (2023). Al doilea Război al Crimeii?. In *Piața Financiară*, November, pp. 48–51.

Sandoval Velasco, M., Beck, T., & Schlosser, P. (2023). The impact of the Ukraine crisis in the EU economic and financial union. Policy Paper. https://cadmus.eui.eu/handle/1814/74815.

Yarhi-Milo, K. (2023). Why smart leader do stupid things?. In *Foreign Affairs*, November–December. Retrieved November 18, 2023, from https://www.foreignaffairs.com/reviews/why-smart-leaders-do-stupid-things

Transformation of Public Policy in Ukrainian Book Publishing as a Basis for Resisting Russian Cultural Expansion During and After the War

Maryna Zhenchenko

Abstract This paper examines the transformation of public policy to strengthen Ukrainian book publishing and counter Russian cultural influence. Employing a mixed-methods approach, it combines analysis of legislative changes and industry reports with expert interviews involving key stakeholders such as publishers, editors, and government officials.

The findings reveal a discernible trend that has intensified since the Russian invasion in 2014: a decrease in the presence of Russian books in the Ukrainian market and a simultaneous rise in support for Ukrainian publishing. Legislative alterations, including restrictions on importing Russian book products and active promotion of Ukrainian literature, underscore this shift. Moreover, the government has initiated programs to bolster Ukrainian publishers and bookstores. The Ukrainian Book Institute (UBI), a state institution, has received augmented funding for initiatives such as library book replenishment, to enhance the accessibility of Ukrainian literature. Additionally, new industry associations have been established to further professionalize the sector.

Despite these efforts, the publishing industry has been significantly impacted by the ongoing war. The adoption of digitization, particularly through e-books and audiobooks, holds promise for the industry's future. However, challenges persist, including the absence of a reliable system for collecting data on e-book sales, which impedes informed decision-making.

Crucial tasks for government organizations and the publishing community in post-war reconstruction include bringing state standards for book publishing into line with European legislation; providing state support for the publication and distribution of Ukrainian books (especially e-books and audiobooks), and continuing state programs to promote reading in the Ukrainian language. Additionally, efforts to popularize Ukrainian books globally and promote Ukrainian culture,

M. Zhenchenko (✉)
Maksymovych Scientific Library; Department of Editorial and Publishing Technologies and Producing, Educational and Scientific Institute of Journalism, Taras Shevchenko National University of Kyiv, Kyiv, Ukraine
e-mail: mizhenchenko@knu.ua

S. Nate (ed.), *Ukraine's Journey to Recovery, Reform and Post-War Reconstruction*, Contributions to Security and Defence Studies,
https://doi.org/10.1007/978-3-031-66434-2_12

science, and education through Ukrainian fiction, non-fiction and academic book translation programs are imperative.

Introduction

The book market in Ukraine plays a vital role in the country's creative economy and information security. Throughout the war, the development of public policies to restore and strengthen the Ukrainian book publishing system has become increasingly important. These reforms are crucial for safeguarding national interests, effectively countering Russia's aggressive information policy, and promoting the development of Ukrainian culture, science, and education, independent of the influence of Soviet and Russian narratives.

This paper will focus especially on a public policy regarding publishing books for the trade book market.

Public policy on publishing school textbooks, as well as publishing open monographs and open e-textbooks for university education and science, in line with the National Open Science Plan ratified by the Cabinet of Ministers of Ukraine on 8 October 2022 (Decree № 892-p), requires a separate study.

Background. Forming Public Policy in Book Publishing Before the War: 1991–2013

Overview of Ukrainian Legislation on the Book Publishing Market

In 1997, the main legislative document on book publishing was approved—the Law of Ukraine «On Publishing».

This law regulates the procedures for organizing and conducting publishing activities, the production and distribution of publishing products, and the relationships and functioning of publishers, printing houses, and booksellers. Its aim is the promotion of national and cultural development of the Ukrainian people, citizens of Ukraine of all nationalities, strengthening of their spirituality and morality, access of members of society to universal values, protecting the rights and interests of authors, publishers, producers, distributors and consumers of publishing products.

It also outlines the fundamental principles of the State policy in publishing which is determined by the Verkhovna Rada of Ukraine and is founded on the principles of publishing freedom, countering monopolization, strengthening the material, technical, organizational, legal, and scientific infrastructure of publishing, and ensuring the social and legal protection of its employees (Article 5).

According to article 4, «Legislation on publishing» the Law «On publishing» relations in publishing are regulated by the:

- **Constitution of Ukraine** (1996): Fundamental Law of Ukraine which provides for the right to «everyone to entrepreneurial activity that is not prohibited by law» (including in book publishing—M. Z.) (Article 42), and stipulates that «citizens shall be guaranteed the freedom of literary, artistic, scientific, and technical creative activities, protection of intellectual property, their copyright, moral and material interests arising in connection with various types of intellectual activity» (Article 54).
- **Economic Code of Ukraine** *(2003)*: «Shall determine fundamentals of economic activity in Ukraine and regulate economic relations arising in the process of organisation and exercising economic activity between economic entities, as well as between these entities and other parties to economic activity» (Article 1). This document, therefore, regulates the activities of book publishing, printing and distributing companies, which are part of the creative economy.
- **Laws of Ukraine:**
  - ***On Information*** *(1992, 2011—new edition)*: defines the prohibition of censorship and interference in the professional activity of journalists and media, «control the content of disseminated information, in particular for disseminating or preventing the dissemination of the complete information, withholding socially necessary information, imposing a prohibition to cover certain topics, display certain persons or disseminate information about them, prohibition to criticise the public authorities, except for the cases determined by law, an agreement between a founder (owner) and employees, editorial's articles of association» (Article 24).
  - ***On Mandatory Copies of Documents*** *(1999)*: regulated the general principles of the state policy of filling the National Information Fund of Ukraine with mandatory copies of documents; regulating the information relations connected with the functioning of the system of mandatory copies of documents; define the duties and rights of those creating and receiving documents (Article 2).
  - ***On Copyright and Related Rights*** *(1994, 2001—new edition)*: «shall protect personal non-proprietary rights and proprietary rights of authors and their successors related to the creation and use of works of science, literature and art—copyright, and the rights of performers, manufacturers of phonograms and videograms and broadcast organisations—related rights» (Preface). Defines the Powers of the Institution in the protection of copyright and related rights, which «shall ensure the formation and implementation of state policy in the field of copyright and related rights protection» (Article 4).
  - ***On State Secrets*** *(1994, 1999—new edition)*: Article 31 «Restrictions on the publication of secret information» obliges publishers to comply with the norms of this Law and other legal acts on state secrets when preparing materials for publication, distribution in the press and other media.
  - ***On State Support of Book Publishing in Ukraine*** *(2003)*: Defines that the state policy in book publishing is based on the recognition of the mental, scientific, educational, cultural and creative function of books in society and

the principles of freedom in book publishing, opposing its monopolization, strengthening the material, technical, organizational, legal and scientific foundations of book publishing, and guaranteeing social and legal protection of its employees (Article 5).

- ***Other regulatory legal acts.***

First Steps Towards the Institutionalisation of Ukrainian Book Publishing

After Ukraine regained independence in 1991, a new publishing landscape was started creating. This process involved the establishment of new commercial publishing houses, printing houses and bookstores, as well as the creation of a new state and non-profit institution aimed at shaping public policy and developing Ukrainian book publishing. Brief information on these institutions follows.

1994, the **Ukrainian Publishers & Booksellers Association** (UPBA) was registered by the Ministry of Justice of Ukraine on June 17, 1994, as the *Ukrainian Association of Non-State Publishing Houses.* In September 1996, it was re-registered as the *Ukrainian Association of Publishers* Charitable Organization, and in 2000 it once again changed its name to the Charitable Organization (CO) *Ukrainian Publishers & Booksellers Association.*

1994, the **Publishers' Forum**, a non-governmental organisation, was established. It is the creator of the iconic Lviv Publishers' Forum fair and later the BookForum festival, and aims to develop the Ukrainian book market and integrate it into the global publishing context.

In 1995, the **Ukrainian Library Association,** an independent all-Ukrainian non-governmental organisation with individual and collective membership started its work. It is a voluntary association of people professionally involved in library, bibliographic and information activities and all those interested in their development.

2011, the Mystetskyi Arsenal cultural, art and museum complex hosted the International **Book Arsenal** Festival for the first time, bringing together Ukrainian and foreign publishers, writers and illustrators to present their works, hold discussions and take part in lectures and meetings.

The 11th Book Arsenal Festival—prevented in 2022 by Russia's attack—was successfully held in Kyiv in 2023 from 22 to 25 June, with about 28,000 visitors.

Because of the ongoing Russian-Ukrainian war, the festival offered a limited format, but attracted a significant number of guests — President Volodymyr Zelenskyy and the First Lady attended the festival, as well as international guests, including Gvantsa Jobava, Vice President of the International Publishers Association. «My visit here is a gesture to say: we are here now, in solidarity, when you endure this difficult situation when you are at war. Meanwhile, you are so brave that you decided to hold a book fair during the war, and it is so inspiring. Your festival is a sign that even in these dreadful conditions, books and reading still matter,»

Gvantsa said in a conversation with the Chytomo team (CHYTOMO is the largest independent media covering publishing and contemporary literary and cultural processes in Ukraine.—M. Z.) (Baturevych, 2023).

Yulia Kozlovets, director of Book Arsenal, told the audience at the opening of the festival on 22 June 2023: «Preparation for the festival took place during the times that you and I experienced together: blackouts, bombings, airstrikes. At that time, we were doing our thing. Each of us, walking through the Art Arsenal today, thinks about our gratitude to the Armed Forces of Ukraine, which allow us to do our work and be who we are» (Porter, 2023).

War-Related Public Policy in Book Publishing Changes: 2014–2023

Legislative Changes in the Ukrainian State Policy on Book Publishing from 2014 to February 2022

«Even though Ukraine regained its independence 30 years ago, the formation of the national book market began only 6 years ago (after the Revolution of Dignity in 2014.—*M. Z.*) and continues to this day», emphasized the authors of the study survey on the development of the national publishing market «30th Anniversary of Independent Book Publishing in Ukraine», conducted by the cultural and publishing project Chytomo and the NGO «Publishers' Forum» with the support of the Ukrainian Cultural Foundation in 2021 (Baturevych & Khmelovska, 2021).

The Law «On Publishing» provided for the possibility of publishing books in the Russian language for the needs of the Russian population in our country. This provision of the law facilitated the expansion of Russian-language literature on the Ukrainian book market and created significant competition for publishers of books in Ukrainian.

Marjana Savka, editor-in-chief and co-founder of Lviv's Old Lion Publishing House, tells Publishing Perspectives that «in every year since Ukraine's independence" in 1991, «we have lost to Russian publishers both in sales and in obtaining licenses for world bestsellers. Only after 2014, when the ban on the import of Russian books into Ukraine came into force, were our publishers able to become owners of our market. At that point, we saw a breakthrough: new publishers, genres, a lot of translated literature» (Gerden, 2021).

In December 2016, Ukraine passed a law called «On Amendments to Certain Laws of Ukraine on Restriction of Access to the Ukrainian Market of Foreign Printed Products with Anti-Ukrainian Content». This law made changes to the «On Publishing» law, and these changes are worth noting especially two key points:

1. Adding a new paragraph to the second part of Article 28 «Restrictions on Publishing Rights» which says on

prohibited in the field of publishing to publish, produce and/or distribute products containing material (statements, appeals, etc.), the content of which is aimed at eliminating Ukraine's independence, changing the constitutional order by force, violating the sovereignty and territorial integrity of the state, undermining its security, illegally seizing state power, propagating war, violence, communist and/or national socialist (Nazi) totalitarian regimes and their symbols, inciting inter-ethnic, racial, religious hatred, committing terrorist acts, violating human rights and freedoms and public health.

2. Addition of a new article 28[1]. Importation from the territory of the aggressor state, the temporarily occupied territory of Ukraine of publishing products that can be distributed in the territory of Ukraine, which provide for obtaining the relevant permit for importation into the customs territory of Ukraine and distribution in its territory of publishing products originating or manufactured and/or imported from the territory of the aggressor state, the temporarily occupied territory of Ukraine.

   The analysis and evaluation of publishing products for classification which may not be distributed in the territory of Ukraine, shall be carried out by the Council of Experts of the Central Executive Body, which ensures the formation and implementation of the state policy in the sphere of information, comprising representatives of state authorities, industrial associations, trade unions, public experts, publishers, leaders of culture, art, science and education, social psychologists, media experts and other information specialists (Part 4 of this Article).

An important milestone in the development of state policy in the book publishing sector was the adoption in January 2016 of the Law of Ukraine «On Amending Certain Laws of Ukraine on Improving the System of Public Administration in Book Publishing». This law regulates the objectives, functions, structure, rules of participation in implementing of state support programmes for book publishing and the financing of the newly created state body, the Book Institute of Ukraine, and adds relevant new parts and chapters to the acts of Ukraine «On State Support of Book Publishing in Ukraine», «On Publishing», «On Library and Librarianship» and «On Culture».

In 2018–2021, the Ukrainian Book Institute implemented programmes to replenish library collections at the expense of the state budget:

- In 2018—714 titles from 91 publishers were purchased for 986,449 copies;
- In 2019—551 titles from 80 publishers for 669,609 copies;
- In 2020—720 titles from 90 publishers for 350,000 copies;
- In 2021—684 titles from 86 publishers for 331,077 copies.

Thanks to this program, publishers have received funding to create new publishing projects, and over 500 public libraries across Ukraine—free new books for Ukrainian children and adults.

Institutional Development on Book Publishing Industry

Since 2014, Ukraine has witnessed the establishment of various public and state institutions that have actively contributed to the development of national book publishing.

In **2014**, the **Ukrainian Institute of National Memory** was founded as the central executive body responsible for implementing state policies aimed at restoring and preserving the nation's historical memory. Its impact on the book industry has been notable through its efforts to popularize Ukraine's history, celebrate prominent figures, and publish a series of books that expose the atrocities committed by the communist totalitarian regime in Ukraine.

In **2017**, the **Ukrainian Book Institute** was established and emerged as a governmental entity under the Ministry of Culture and Information Policy of Ukraine. Its mission is to shape state policy in book publishing, promote book reading in Ukraine, support the book industry, provide incentives for translations and popularize Ukrainian literature abroad.

In **2019**, the Ukrainian Editors' Association began its work as a non-profit public organisation with the main goal of bringing together professionals in the editorial field. Its task is to coordinate the efforts of individuals, organisations and institutions interested in improving the level of language and publishing culture in the book industry, as well as to provide methodological, informational, analytical, scientific and practical assistance in the professional activities of editors.

In **2020**, the **National Intellectual Property Office** was created and entrusted with several key tasks:

- Acceptance and consideration of applications for state registration of copyright in works of science, literature and art, as well as for the registration of agreements relating to the rights of authors to works, their registration;
- Issue of certificates on registration of copyright to the work; publications in the official bulletin on the copyright and related rights;
- Implementation of international cooperation in the field of the legal protection of intellectual property and representation of interests of Ukraine in the protection of copyright and related rights in the World Intellectual Property Organisation and other international organisations by the law;
- Informing and providing explanations on the implementation of state policy in the field of copyright and related rights (article 4^1, Law of Ukraine «On Copyright And Related Rights).

Changes in Public Policy on Book Publishing After February 24, 2022

On 19 June 2022, 306 deputies of the Verkhovna Rada supported the law 2309-IX «On Amendments to Certain Laws of Ukraine on the Establishment of Restrictions on the Import and Distribution of Publishing Products Related to the Aggressor State, the Republic of Belarus and the Temporarily Occupied Territory of Ukraine». This law introduced stricter regulations on the import of publishing products from Russia, which were defined by an earlier legislative act adopted in 2016.

The new edition of the Article 28[1] of the Law «On Publishing» (2016) limits the import of publishing products from Russia and the Republic of Belarus and prohibits the distribution and import of book publications that include works by citizens of the aggressor state (see Table 1 for more details).

The second important law adopted on the same day, 19 June 2022, was the Law of Ukraine «On Amendments to Certain Laws of Ukraine to Stimulate the Development of Ukrainian Book Publishing and Book Distribution». It provided for important amendments to several laws of Ukraine, in particular:

- Replacement of Part Nine of Article 5 of the Law of Ukraine «On Publishing» with a new part of the following content:
  The State shall provide support to publishing subjects, and create favourable conditions for the development of national book publishing by the Law of Ukraine

Table 1 Comparison of the content of part one of Article 281 of the Law of Ukraine «On Publishing» in the 2016 and 2022 revisions

2016	2022
Article 28[1]. Importation from the territory of the aggressor state, the temporarily occupied territory of Ukraine of publishing products that can be distributed in the territory of Ukraine *Publishing products originating from or are published and/or imported from the territory of the aggressor state, the temporarily occupied territory of Ukraine, may be imported into the customs territory of Ukraine and distributed on its territory, subject to the presence of an appropriate permit, except for publishing products imported by individual citizens in hand luggage or checked baggage in a total amount of no more than 10 copies.*	***Article 28[1]. Importation and distribution of publishing products related to the aggressor state, the Republic of Belarus, and the temporarily occupied territory of Ukraine*** *It is **prohibited** to import into the customs territory of Ukraine and/or distribute on its territory publishing products originating from or published, and/or imported from **the territory of the aggressor state, the Republic of Belarus, the temporarily occupied territory of Ukraine** (except for the distribution of publishing products, originating or published in the temporarily occupied territory of Ukraine before its temporary occupation), **as well as book publications containing works whose authors are or were in any period after 1991 citizens of the aggressor state**, except former citizens of the aggressor state who are (or at the time of death were) citizens of Ukraine and do not have (at the time of death did not have) the citizenship of the aggressor state.*

«On State Support of Book Publishing in Ukraine», including by reimbursing the actual expenses of distributors of publishing products (book products) for renting real estate used by the publishing subject as a specialised bookstore.

- Addition of the Law of Ukraine «On State Support of Book Publishing in Ukraine» a new *Article 82 «Activities of the Ukrainian Institute of Books to Support of Distributors of Publishing Products (Book Products)»*, which defines the requirements for distributors of publishing products to receive state subsidies, and a new *Article 83 «Activities of the Ukrainian Institute of Books on Implementation of the Programme of Providing Citizens of Ukraine with Annual Support as a Certificate for the Purchase of Books»*.
- Addition of Article 26 of the Law of Ukraine «On Supporting the Functioning of the Ukrainian Language as the State Language» of the following content

1. Books in Ukraine are published and distributed in the state language and/or languages of the indigenous peoples of Ukraine, the official languages of the European Union.
2. Book may be published and distributed in languages other than those specified in the first part of this article in the following cases:

   a. A book, published in Ukraine or imported into Ukraine by the procedure established by law, contains only works in the original language or translated into the state language, languages of the indigenous peoples of Ukraine, or official languages of the European Union;
   b. The book was published by order of the state authorities of Ukraine in the interests of national security, repelling Russian aggression against Ukraine and is not subject to sale or distribution in any other way through the book distribution network in Ukraine;
   c. The book was published before January 1, 2023, except for books whose distribution is prohibited by the Law of Ukraine "On Publishing".

3. The requirements of parts one and two of this article apply to books in electronic form, including audio files.

In the context of state support for book publishing, the active work of the Ukrainian Book Institute deserves special attention. As stated on the official website of the state institution:

> *We keep on working despite the war. Although almost all of our employees have left Kyiv, we are still doing everything we can to make Ukrainian books known and accessible in the world, to make our Ukrainian voices louder.*
>
> ***We get the world acquainted with Ukrainian literature! —***
>
> *During the war, we are doing it even more intensively, as international book fairs provide us with withstands even though our funds envisaged for those events have been reallocated to the Armed Forces of Ukraine. We actively cooperate with other cultural institutions in Ukraine and all over the world so that decision-makers in the book industry could hear Ukraine and our appeals. Our foreign colleagues prevent russia from presenting*

its books, and they listen to us, whenever we tell them about Ukrainian publications and show great interest in our translation rights catalogues.

We help publish new books! —

We have come to understand that so many Ukrainian children leaving homes have lost books, a part of the strongest connection with one's home, so we have initiated the project of book publishing for refugee children abroad. We have found foreign partners, ready to fundraise, print book layouts provided by Ukrainian publishers for free and distribute books free of charge among refugee support centres where children can read and find something familiar and dear to their hearts.

We translate Ukrainian authors into foreign languages! —

We are currently unable to support projects where expenses are needed, as all the funds are being allocated to the Armed Forces of Ukraine. Although, during difficult times of war, foreign partners are on our side, encouraging a total boycott of russian books initiated by us and inviting us to their organizations. In particular, the UBI has already become a member of the ENLIT international translators' community.

We restock public libraries! —

We cannot spend money on books, as those funds are needed to protect our people, but we are researching catalogues of Western public libraries and looking for anti-Ukrainian books. We are calling on libraries to withdraw those books so that Ukrainian culture, literature and history could be represented by our authors, rather than by lying russian narratives.

We research the book market! —

Despite the ongoing war, we believe in our Victory and have started to prepare. We keep abreast and gather information from publishing houses and libraries about their losses and needs so that we could develop a strategy for the industry's recovery and start implementing it right after the Victory.

We do our best so that you could read! —

So that you could read about Ukraine. So that people could understand us, Ukrainians, translate our books and read all over the world.

An important contribution to protecting Ukrainian culture from Russian expansion is also the decision of the Ministry of Culture and Social Policy of Ukraine to remove Russian literature from Ukrainian library collections and replace it with high-quality Ukrainian literature and books from Ukrainian publishers. This process began in 2022 and is based on methodological recommendations developed and approved by the Ministry's specially created Council for the Development of Library Affairs, which includes leading library experts from all corners of Ukraine.

Ukrainian publishers' books will be used instead to replenish library funds. Despite facing financial difficulties and suspending the implementation of the state programme to replenish library funds in 2022, funds were still allocated in 2023 to publish, print and deliver 134 book titles to the libraries of Ukraine. These book projects were a winner of the art competition announced by the Ministry of Culture in 2023. There were selected according to three priority thematic directions:

1) Artistic and popular-scientific books for different age groups of readers: the history of Ukraine of different periods in the Context of the Struggle for the Development of Statehood, sovereignty and Independence; our heroes: Biographies of prominent Ukrainians (all historical periods); achievements and prospects of the unconquered Ukraine, development of Ukraine as an independent state;

2) Books for children and adults aimed at national-patriotic education, promotion of democratic values, cultural diversity and intercultural dialogue, gender equality, the inadmissibility of violence, development of leadership skills, ecological self-awareness, responsibility for the environment, critical thinking;
3) Books commemorating the heroic deeds of war veterans in defence of the sovereignty, territorial integrity and inviolability of Ukraine.

Roadmap for Changing Public Policy on Book Publishing in Post-War Ukraine: Towards Integration into the European Publishing Community

The formation of state policy in book publishing during the war and in the postwar period should simultaneously take place in several directions:

1. Harmonisation of state standards in book publishing with European legislation and current Ukrainian and international publishing practices.
2. State support for the publishing and distribution of Ukrainian books.
3. Digitalisation of the publishing industry: state policy on creation, distribution and accounting of e-books and audiobooks.
4. Implementation of state programmes to support reading.
5. Continuation and deepening of the Translate Ukraine State Grant Programme.

Harmonisation of State Standards in Book Publishing with European Legislation and Current Ukrainian and International Publishing Practices

Ukraine has several regulatory documents on standardisation in publishing:

1. National Standards of Ukraine:

   DSTU 4861:2007. Information and Documentation. Edition. Basic Information (ISO 8:1977, NEQ; ISO 1086:1991, NEQ; ISO 7275:1985, NEQ);

   DSTU 3814:2013. Information and Documentation. Editions. International Standard Book Numbering;

   DSTU 7157:2010. Information and Documentation. Electronic Editions. Main Types and Basic Information;

   DSTU 3017:2015. Information and Documentation. Editions. Main Types. Terms and Definitions of Concepts;

   DSTU 8344:2015. Information and Documentation. Editions. Main Elements. Terms and Definitions of Concepts.
2. Industry standards of Ukraine:

SOU 18.1-02477019-09:2015. Edition. Publishing Design and Printing. Quality indicators;

SOU 18.1-02477019-11:2014. Edition for Children. General Technical Requirements;

SOU 18.1-02477019-07:2015. Printing Industry. Textbooks and Study Guide for School. General Technical Requirement;

DSanPiN 5.5.6-138—2007. State Sanitary Norms and Rules. Hygienic Requirements for Printed Products for Children.

We mentioned only the main standards, the full list of publishing standards is available on the website of the Book Chamber of Ukraine.

Unfortunately, in practice, many publishers do not adhere to current publishing industry standards. There are several reasons for this:

1. The texts of the standards are not publicly accessible, Ukrainian publishers can only purchase a paper or electronic version of the standards by placing an order on the website of the **National Standardization Body**, but the cost of the standards ranges from 20 to 50 Euro, which is quite expensive considering the financial capabilities of Ukrainian publishers, especially in conditions of war.
2. The use of publishing standards is optional and failing to comply with the relevant standards does not entail any administrative or financial obligations for publishers.
3. The standards in publishing are not updated often enough to keep pace with changes and innovative publishing development needs. As a result, these standards become outdated. Take, for instance, the DSTU 7157: 2010. Information and documentation. Electronic editions. This standard has not been updated for 13 years and therefore does not fully cover many modern electronic books.

Special attention should be paid to the National Publishing Standards of Ukraine. These implement the intergovernmental standards (GOST) through reprinting. The Interstate Council for Standardisation, Metrology and Certification (ICSC), a regional organisation for standardisation and regulatory documentation in the CIS countries, developed these standards. In fact, they are copies of the Russian national standards, published in the Russian language and adopted by the «cover method».

We propose the following solutions to the problems outlined above:

1. Cancellation of the national standards developed by the Russian Book Chamber and preparation of Ukrainian national standards instead.
2. Expansion of the technical committee «Information and Documentation», which develops standards in book publishing, by adding new members from professional associations, particularly the Ukrainian Publishers & Booksellers Association, the **Ukrainian Editors' Association**, and teachers of the «Publishing and Editing» education program at Ukrainian universities.
3. Conduction a survey of publishers on current practices in using standards and the feasibility of standardising certain aspects of publishing.

4. Identification of standards that need to be updated, holding a broad discussion in the professional publishing community and bringing them in line with international standards and current practices in the European book area.
5. Amending the Law «On Publishing» to require publishers to comply with certain standards, such as the DSTU 4861:2007. Information and Documentation. Edition. Basic Information (ISO 8:1977, NEQ; ISO 1086:1991, NEQ; ISO 7275: 1985, NEQ).
6. Implementation of the principle of the state policy on standardisation regarding «accessibility of national standards and codes of good practice as well as information about them for users» (Article 4, Paragraph 7, Part Two of the Law of Ukraine «On Standardisation»).

State Support for the Publishing and Distribution of Ukrainian Books

Similar to other countries, Ukraine's publishing industry experienced significant losses during the COVID-19 pandemic. In the article titled «Discounts, Free Popcorn and Gifts: How Bookstores and Cinemas Compete for Zelensky's Grant», author Ihor Orel reports that the Ukrainian book market's pre-pandemic value was estimated at UAH 2.5 billion. Since 2020, sales have declined by 30–50%, as stated by Oleksandra Koval, Director of the Ukrainian Book Institute. Notably, one in five bookstores closed in 2020 (Orel, 2021).

A significant turnaround occurred with the introduction of the «eSupport» state program at the end of 2021. This initiative granted UAH 1000 to each vaccinated Ukrainian citizen, which could be redeemed over 4 months for purchasing cultural products such as books and films. It allocated an impressive UAH 11 billion to the program for 2021–2022. This endeavour resulted in UAH 1.2 billion in sales for bookstores and publishers within 2 months. The book industry sustained itself during the initial months of the war through the residual impact of this program.

A similar mechanism to support publishers by providing citizens of Ukraine with assistance as a certificate for the purchase of books was introduced by Article 83 of the Law of Ukraine «On Amendments to Certain Laws of Ukraine to Stimulate the Development of Ukrainian Book Publishing and Book Distribution» which was adopted on July 10, 2022.

According to the law, the certificate can only be used to buy books in the official language of the state. Citizens of Ukraine are issued the certificate free of charge upon the acquisition of a birth certificate and a citizenship passport if they are 14 years of age or older; the cost of the certificate is 0.3 times the minimum subsistence amount for able-bodied persons established by law; in 2023, the cost of the certificate will be UAH 833.

In addition, Article 82 of the Ukrainian Law, «On Publishing», offers state subsidies to distributors of publishing products to cover expenses for renting real estate (buildings, structures or premises), including separate premises used as specialist bookstores.

These programs should have been implemented on January 1, 2023. However, as stated on the official website of the Ukrainian Book Institute, during the period of martial law, Ukraine's economy is facing unprecedented challenges. The available financial resources of the state are primarily directed towards repelling armed aggression, ensuring the uninterrupted functioning of the budgetary sphere, addressing the vital needs of territorial communities' residents, implementing territorial defence measures, and safeguarding public safety. As a result, the Law of Ukraine «On the State Budget of Ukraine for 2023» did not allocate funds for implementing these programs. Implementing these programs will be considered by the Government after the conclusion or cancellation of martial law in Ukraine (Official position of the Ukrainian Book Institute on granting certificates and subsidies, 2023).

It is noteworthy that Ukrainian publishers and book distributors are not waiting for government support, but are already opening new publishing houses and bookstores during the war:

- *In Kharkiv, while some bookstores remain closed, the Knygoland chain (part of The Ranok Corporation), has against all odds, opened the largest bookstore in Ukraine with a floor space of 650 square meters.*
- *The fifth «The Old Lion Bookstore-Café» has already opened in Lviv, and the publishing house plans to open several more bookstores in Lviv and other cities.*
- *Why? Because bookstores are not only a business. Bookstores are a social responsibility for those who are willing to «rebuild Ukraine». Bookstores could also be a dream project that can't be postponed any longer. New bookstores are being opened by book chains, publishers, and entrepreneurs from other realms — whether IT or the event promotion industry»* (Baturevych, 2023).

Digitalisation of the Publishing Industry: State Policy on Publishing, Distribution and Accounting of E-Books and Audiobooks

The authors of the «Report Based on the results of the all-Ukrainian sociological research «Reading in the Context of media consumption and life construction», prepared for the governmental organization Ukrainian Book Institute by Infosapience LLC in 2020 recommended «to promote electronic and audiobooks in Ukraine—both paid and free, as among these types of books Russian-language content is much more prevalent than among printed books» (Volosevych & Shurenkova, 2020, p. 24).

As part of the research on digital transformations in the publishing industry, the author of this article surveyed book publishers through the personal distribution of questionnaires during the Book Arsenal event (April 2016 and May 2017) and through online surveys with the support of the Ukrainian Association of Publishers and Booksellers and the Book Chamber of Ukraine (June—November 2017). In total, representatives of 136 Ukrainian publishers responded to the survey questions. Only 33.1% of these publishers released e-books from time to time. Fewer than ten publishers regularly released new titles in both print and digital formats. At the same time, among 66.9% of the surveyed publishers focused only on printed books, 49.4% planned to diversify their activities in the future by entering the digital book market (Zhenchenko, 2019, p. 273).

The lack of sales statistics is one problem for the Ukrainian book market. As a result, the exact amount of revenue generated by the sale of electronic publications is not known. According to the monograph «Digital Transformations of the Publishing Industry», the Ukrainian ebook market shows similar trends to Eastern European countries such as Slovenia, Bulgaria and Hungary, where revenue from electronic publications did not exceed 1% of total book sales in 2018 [(Zhenchenko, 2019), p. 274].

Similar figures presented by the authors of the study «Publishing in Ukraine: A Review of the Sector, Final Report 2020»: «Most publishers estimated their e-book revenue to be between 1–3% of turnover» [(Shercliff, 2021), p. 24].

The major obstacle to the development of e-book publishing not only is electronic piracy but also the lack of places for selling legal e-books and audiobooks with protected digital content. Publishers also noted the following issues during the survey:

- *'We are just starting to work with e-books, but there are no safe spaces to sell them. There's a huge level of piracy.'*
- *'Audiobooks, there is a lack of places to sell them.'*
- *'We publish and sell e-books and people do buy a little, but we don't make much money.'* [(Shercliff, 2021), p. 24].

The second, no less important problem is the absence of an e-book accounting system. Data collection and statistical accounting of various aspects of publishing in Ukraine is carried out by the Book Chamber of Ukraine according to the requirements of the international standard ISO SO 9707:2008 Information and documentation—Statistics on the production and distribution of books, newspapers, periodicals and electronic publications [(Gorobets, 2018), p. 4].

In 2014 the State Committee for Television and Radio Broadcasting approved the form 1-B (books) «Report on the publication of book products», which contains information on the title, ISBN, the language of the publication, its volume, circulation, manufacturer's data, date of distribution of the mandatory copy, name of the budget programme (if the books were published at the expense of the budget programme), but this form is focused on the accounting of printed publications only. The Book Chamber of Ukraine compiles statistics on e-book publishing only based on mandatory copies of local e-books on CD-ROM, which does not correspond to modern technologies of e-book production.

We propose the following solutions to the above problems:

1. Adding information on the publishing of paper books in electronic and audio formats to the reporting in Form 1-B.
2. Encourage at the state level the creation and development of digital platforms for distributing e-books and audiobooks by Ukrainian publishers.
3. Developing mechanisms for public e-book procurement from publishers to fill Ukraine's digital libraries.
4. Improving Ukrainian legislation in electronic publishing and anti-piracy by the best practices of European legislation.

Implementation of State Programmes to Support Reading

The Ukrainian Book Institute researches reading habits in Ukraine. In 2020, two all-Ukrainian types of research were conducted: «Reading in the Context of media consumption and Life Construction» and «Reading in the Context of media consumption: impact of Lockdown on Ukrainians' reading behaviours».

The study «Reading in the Context of Media Consumption and Life Construction» found that «one-third of Ukrainians prefer to read books in Ukrainian. And this share has increased significantly—32% against 24% in 2018» (Volosevych & Shurenkova, 2020, p. 71).

During the war, book prices increased and the purchasing power of the population decreased significantly, as a result of which the demand for book products decreased. Against this background, the Cabinet of Ministers of Ukraine adopted Resolution No. 190-r on 3 March 2023, approving the Reading as a Life Strategy for the period until 2032 and an operational plan for its implementation from 2023 to 2025, which includes several key actions by the Ministry of Culture and Information Policy of Ukraine and the State Committee of Television and Radio of Ukraine.

- Introducing European standards for the provision and monitoring of compulsory free copies by publishers.
- Preventing the distribution of counterfeit book products.
- Promoting the creation and dissemination of the Ukrainian narrative and the popularisation of the cultures of Ukraine's partner countries.

Continuation and Development of the Translate Ukraine State Grant Programme

Translate Ukraine—is a programme of the Ukrainian Book Institute which partly compensates the expenses of the publisher on the translation and publishing of Ukrainian literature in foreign languages.

The Institute supports the projects of translations of literary works or anthologies of literary works written in Ukrainian and published by Ukrainian publishers. The number of applications for participation in the Translation Support Program from one publisher is unlimited.

By the Regulation, Ukrainian publishers can participate in the Translation Support Program for translations of Ukrainian literary works into other languages. Applications for translation of Ukrainian literary works that have already been translated and published on the applicant's book market in the relevant foreign language are not accepted for participation in the Program.

This programme enabled 53 literary works to get translated into 21 different languages, including English, German, Italian, French, Slovak and Polish, as well as Arabic, Hebrew, Mongolian, Macedonian and others, in 24 countries. A total of £114,000 has been allocated to the programme to support the translation of works by Ukrainian authors. According to the official website of the Ukrainian Book Institute, these 53 translations represent 30% of the total translations of Ukrainian literature to be published in other languages in 2020.

Conclusions

Even in the difficult times of war, with limited state funding for creative industry programmes, Ukrainian state institutions are actively working to establish a state policy for book publishing, recognising that the Ukrainian book serves as a crucial tool on the cultural front. Important tasks for the post-war restoration of book publishing for state organisations, professional associations and the publishing community include updating publishing standards and the system of statistical accounting of book products, especially in the field of e-books and audiobooks; seeking grant support from international organisations for the restoration and development of Ukrainian publishing houses and book distributors; creating new digital platforms for e-book publishing and distribution of digital publishing content; promoting reading practices among children and teenagers and increasing the visibility of Ukraine and Ukrainian literature in the international cultural space promoting reading.

References

Baturevych, I. (2023). The will to rebuild: Why the Ukrainian publishing industry keeps on going, Chytomo, 18, July 2023. [Online]. https://chytomo.com/en/the-will-to-rebuild-why-the-ukrainian-publishing-industry-keeps-on-going/

Baturevych, I., & Khmelovska, O. (2021). 30 years of independent book publishing in Ukraine, *Chytomo*, 19, November 2021. [Online]. https://chytomo.com/30-rokiv-knyhovydannia/ [In Ukrainian].

Gerden, E. (2021). Ukrainian publishers review industry numbers from 2020, *Publishing* Perspectives, 27, Січень 2021. [Online]. Доступний у https://publishingperspectives.com/2021/01/ukrainian-publishers-say-they-fear-disastrous-numbers-from-2020-covid19/

Gorobets, O. (2018). Book publishing in the context of the digital economy: A statistical analysis. *Scientific Bulletin of the National Academy of Statistics, Accounting and Audit, 4*, 28–37. https://doi.org/10.31767/nasoa.4.2018.03. [In Ukrainian].

Official position of the Ukrainian Book Institute on granting certificates and subsidies, *Official website of the Ukrainian Book Institute*, 11, January 2023. [Online]. https://ubi.org.ua/uk/news/kategoriya-2/oficiyna-poziciya-ukra-nskogo-institutu-knigi-schodo-nadannya-sertifikativ-ta-subsidiy [In Ukrainian]

Orel, I. (2021). Discounts, free popcorn and gifts. How bookstores and movie theatres compete for Zelensky's 'thousand', *Forbes*, 07, June 2021. [Online]. https://forbes.ua/news/luchshiy-podarok-kniga-kak-knizhnye-i-kinoteatry-konkuriruyut-za-tysyachu-zelenskogo-30122021-3081 [In Ukrainian]

Porter, A. (2023). In Ukraine: Kyiv's book arsenal festival draws 28,000, *Publishing* Perspectives, 27, June 2023. [Online]. Доступний у. https://publishingperspectives.com/2023/06/ukraine-kyivs-book-arsenal-festival-draws-28000/

Shercliff, E. (2021). Publishing in Ukraine: A review of the sector, Final Report 2020, April 2021. [Online]. https://drive.google.com/file/d/1KIlCvSeFpGg6w9d61qmIQtmJm0B4oZXL/view

Volosevych, I., & Shurenkova, A. (2020). Report based on the results of the all-Ukrainian sociological research 'Reading in the context of media consumption and life construction', Prepared for Governmental organization Ukrainian Book Institute by InfoSapience LLC, Kyiv, 2020. [Online]. https://ubi.org.ua/uk/activity/doslidzhennya/doslidzhennya-2020

Zhenchenko, M. (2019). *Digital transformations of the publishing industry*: A monograph (2nd ed.). Zhnets Publishing House. https://www.zhnets.com.ua/zhenchenko-maryna-tsyfrovi-transformatsiyi-vydavnychoyi-galuzi-kyyiv-zhnets-2019-2-ge-vyd-zmin-409-s/ [In Ukrainian]

The Digital Battlefield: Exploring the Intersection of Ukraine's War, Digitalization and Economic Development

Eduard Alexandru Stoica, Ioana Andreea Bogoslov, and Alina O'Connor

Abstract Nowadays, technological progress undoubtedly represents a competitive advantage in almost all the human being spheres of action, both at the individual and collective level. With multiple recognized beneficial influences, digital transformation is, among others, a key factor in the evolution of the modern economy and society. However, understanding the multifaceted effects of the technological tools involvement in crisis conditions requires a more in-depth approach. Thus, through the lens of Ukraine's war experience, the present chapter aims to examine notable aspects related to the intersection of conflict, digitalization, and economic development.

Exploring the perspective of the last decades, the analysis of the existing evidence depicts the undeniable efforts of Ukraine in the direction of digitalization, materialized in noteworthy results that demonstrate, among others, the benefits of technological progress in the face of situations characterized by risk and uncertainty. Under the war conditions, the use of digital resources proved to be one of the key means implied to reduce the crisis effects at multiple levels. However, the paradigmatic shift in dynamics through the use of technology has also brought new challenges, highlighting the urgent need for states to adapt their national strategies to the digital age.

Finally, the analysis investigates and proposes possible policy directions and strategies to support the digital transformation of Ukraine in the short, medium, and long term. Drawing lessons from Ukraine's experience, the obtained results support the need for a coordinated global response to address the challenges posed by the evolving nature of conflict in the digital age.

E. A. Stoica (✉) · I. A. Bogoslov
Faculty of Economic Sciences, Lucian Blaga University of Sibiu, Sibiu, Romania
e-mail: eduard.stoica@ulbsibiu.ro; andreea.bogoslov@ulbsibiu.ro

A. O'Connor
Georgetown University, Washington, DC, USA
e-mail: ao382@cornell.edu

S. Nate (ed.), *Ukraine's Journey to Recovery, Reform and Post-War Reconstruction*, Contributions to Security and Defence Studies,
https://doi.org/10.1007/978-3-031-66434-2_13

Digitalization Initiatives Pre-War: Exploring Early Efforts in Ukraine to Embrace Digitalization for Economic Growth and Development

Ukraine, the largest country in Europe by land area, has historically been a nexus of culture, trade, and innovation. In the recent years leading up to the Russian-Ukrainian conflict, the nation was rapidly emerging as a digital powerhouse in Eastern Europe. The transformation in question has captured different sectors, from IT and software development to digital governance and e-services.

Before 2022, Ukraine embarked on an ambitious path of digital transformation, underpinned by the government's strategic initiatives (Minitch, 2015). The comprehensive plans aimed to overhaul Ukraine's technological landscape, focusing on the digitalization of public services, enhancement of digital infrastructure, and promotion of digital literacy among the population. A central point of interest was the introduction of e-governance services, designed to foster transparency, reduce bureaucratic red tape, and make public services accessible to citizens. Furthermore, the plan prioritized cybersecurity measures to safeguard digital assets and user privacy, recognizing the critical role of security in building a digital economy. Investments were also directed into innovation hubs and IT education, nurturing a climate conducive to technological advancement and digital entrepreneurship. Through these rigorous efforts, Ukraine sought to accelerate its digital transformation, aspiring to boost economic growth, improve societal well-being, and position itself as a competitive player in the global digital economy.

The country became home to thousands of IT companies, with numerous tech startups emerging every year. The startups were often characterized by their innovative approach, tackling both local and global issues, which acquired international attention and investment. The pre-war period saw Ukrainian developers and entrepreneurs contributing to global tech innovation, with several Ukrainian-founded companies gaining prominence internationally.

The government, understanding and realizing the potential of the digital economy, had also started to invest in the smart infrastructure. Initiatives aimed at digitalizing traditional industries were launched, seeking to integrate cutting-edge technologies such as blockchain, AI, and IoT into sectors like agriculture, manufacturing, and public services. These efforts were not only modernizing the country's core infrastructures, but were also intended for fostering transparency, efficiency, and economic development.

Moreover, educational reforms in the tech sector became a priority, with a strong emphasis on STEM (acronym derived from *Science*, *Technology*, *Engineering*, *Mathematics*) education, from primary to tertiary education, and beyond. The country saw a surge in digital literacy programs, coding boot camps, and partnerships between educational institutions and tech companies, preparing a skilled workforce ready to contribute to the digital economy.

Several digital transformation policies were also being implemented, with the government taking steps towards e-governance. These initiatives included digital passports, electronic petitions, and online public services that were simplifying bureaucratic processes, reducing corruption, and making governmental services more accessible to citizens.

Per Ukraine's national recovery council representatives (The National Council for the Recovery of Ukraine from the Consequences of the War, 2022), prior to the commencement of the large-scale aggression, Ukraine held a prominent position among European nations in the advancement of open data sphere, securing the sixth position in the 2021 European Open Data Maturity rating. Approximately 7 million Ukrainians engaged with services built upon open data each month. In fact, the contribution of open data to the GDP fluctuated between 0.8% and 1.3%.

Despite the existing evidence, the perspective of scientific research on the efforts regarding the digital transformation in Ukraine before the war, with the aim of economic growth and development, could be easily distinguished. The specific context of pre-war digitalization initiatives in Ukraine could be considered, to some extent, narrowly explored in the scientific research world. In this respect, the advanced search in the Web of Science Core Collection database, based on the Boolean search query *TS = ("digital transformation" OR "digitalization") AND TS = ("economic growth and development" OR "economic growth" OR "economic development") and TS = ("Ukraine")*, which returns only 39 scientific publications indexed until the beginning of the year 2022, the time of the beginning of the war, could be considered as a preliminary reference point. Undoubtedly, the search carried out and previously mentioned is characterized by limitations related to the terms included, the use of a single database and others.

It can be observed that the subject in question was more a matter of interest for Ukraine, an aspect highlighted through the countries/regions contributing to the scientific research on the phenomenon (Fig. 1—from grey (zero contributions) to dark blue). Therefore, a local concern such as the digitalization of Ukraine for development and economic growth, was directly discussed, before the war, by scientific representatives at the national level.

Widening the search area in scientific research before 2022, outlines a state of the art reflecting a dynamic and complex landscape where digital transformation is at the forefront of national development strategies in Ukraine. The transition is comprehensive, affecting economic structures, security, and societal interactions at all levels. While the path is characterized by challenges requiring adaptive policies and proactive measures, the overarching sentiment is one of cautious optimism, recognizing digital transformation as a vehicle for sustainable growth and global competitiveness in the Ukrainian context.

Halimon's research positioned digital transformation as not merely an operational strategy, but a national imperative (Halimon, 2021). The digital economy was depicted as a dynamic ecosystem driven by innovation and the active implementation of information and communication technologies across all sectors. The paper in question suggests that the digital economy's integration with traditional economic models is blurring the lines, creating a paradigm where digital systems and internet-based solutions are becoming the norm. This integration is fostering a

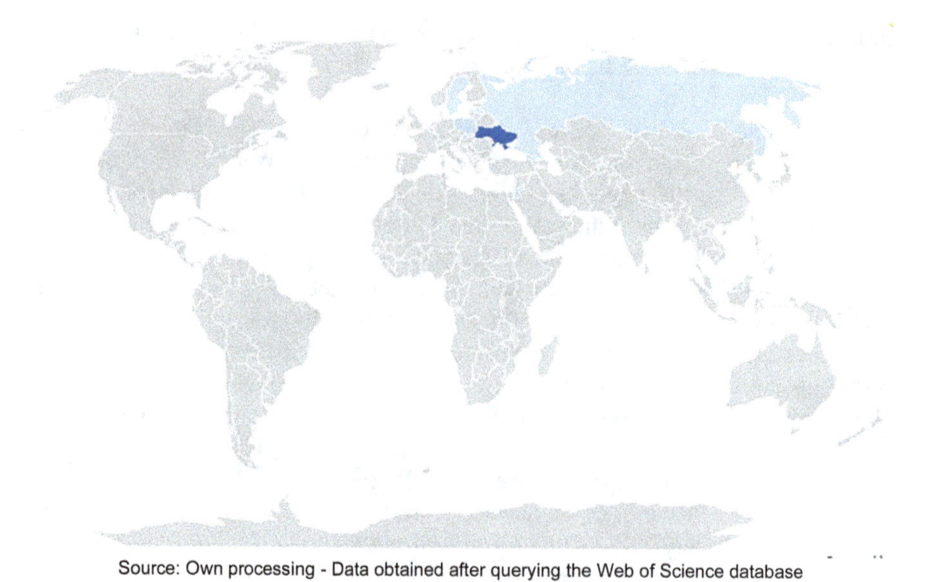

Fig. 1 *Countries/regions contributing to the scientific research at global level.* Source: Own processing—Data obtained after querying the Web of Science database

hypercompetitive environment, demanding rapid adaptation and the adoption of new business models.

The study by Avanesova and Kolodiazhna, "The essence, content, and role of digital transformation in development socio-economic systems" (Avanesova & Kolodiazhna, 2021) expands the discourse to the systemic implications of digital transformation. It is no longer confined to the technological realm but is a critical factor in the socio-economic evolution at micro, meso, and macro levels. The research emphasizes that the digital transformation, once a priority for innovative front-runners, nowadays represents a mass phenomenon, essential for regional and national success. The emergence of service integrators is highlighted as a significant trend, laying the foundations of a shift in economic structures and business strategies.

Osetskyi et al. introduced a nuanced element of the digital economy in Ukraine, where digital platforms are revolutionizing how goods and services are exchanged (Osetskyi et al., 2021). This sharing economy, facilitated by the digital transformation, creates new business models that merge the tangible and intangible, goods and services, in a reciprocal exchange system. The paper emphasizes that this is not without its challenges, as the models navigate the complexities of virtual reality and digital interactions, demanding a re-evaluation of traditional economic theories and practices.

Spivakovskyy et al. brings a critical perspective to the discourse, examining the repercussions of digital transformation on national economic security (Spivakovskyy et al., 2021). The digital economy, while offering growth opportunities, also presents challenges such as digital inequality, changes in labor market dynamics, data security issues, and potential industrial espionage. The paper calls for a balanced approach, recognizing the need for mechanisms to mitigate the adverse effects of digital transformation on economic stability.

Analyzing the digital technology landscape in Ukraine compared to the global context, Samoilovych, A., et al. underlined the advancement in internet accessibility among the Ukrainian population, and also highlighted the qualitative differences in digitalization processes between Ukraine and more developed nations (Samoilovych, 2021). Despite its progress, Ukraine faces a digital divide that requires strategic measures to reinforce its digital economy and align with global standards.

The previously discussed trajectory towards a digital future of Ukraine, based on both the direct observation, and on the scientific research, faced a severe setback as geopolitical tensions escalated into conflict. The war disrupted the nation's economy, infrastructure, and social fabric, predictably impacting the technological sector that was once poised for substantial growth and global integration. The period that followed required Ukraine to navigate through various challenges and find new pathways to revive and sustain its digital progress.

Digital Economy: Assessing Digital Businesses' Emergence and Contribution to Ukraine's Economic Landscape

The digital landscape in Ukraine has undergone a transformative journey, particularly in the last decade, with a significant surge in the emergence of digital businesses. This evolution highlights a pivotal shift in the country's economic paradigm, illustrating the growing influence of digitalization in shaping the nation's commercial forefront. Introducing digital businesses has not only diversified Ukraine's industrial tapestry but has also propelled its status as an emerging hub for innovation and digital entrepreneurship in Eastern Europe. Additionally, the emergence of digital businesses and their contribution to Ukraine's economic landscape represents a multifaceted subject that encompasses numerous aspects of the digital economy.

Before 2014, Ukraine witnessed a surge in digital transformation due to various factors such as increased mobile and internet penetration, a young and tech-savvy population, and governmental initiatives promoting digitalization. The process has led to the emergence of numerous digital businesses across different sectors, with demonstrated potential for further development.

Undoubtedly, Ukraine's IT sector has become a significant component of its economy, with a substantial increase in software development companies, many of which serve overseas clients. This sector's growth was generally ascribed to a highly skilled workforce, competitive costs, and a favorable geographical location.

Similar to the other global states, the digital economy in Ukraine has been significantly propelled by the growth in e-commerce. Factors such as improved

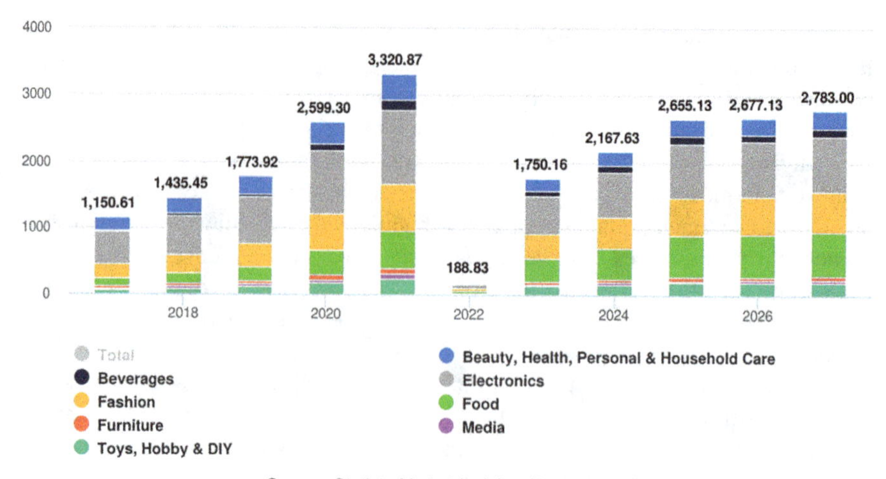

Fig. 2 *E-Commerce—Revenue evolution (Ukraine—million USD).* Source: Statista Market Insights (Statista, n.d.)

digital payment systems, increased trust in online shopping, and the global pandemic's push towards online services have fueled this sector.

As expected, in 2022, when the war started, the e-commerce sector in Ukraine experienced a downturn (Fig. 2), highlighting a deviation from the global trend of sustained growth. This decline was caused by a confluence of factors that disrupted the online retail market in the country. Economic instability, exacerbated by fluctuating currency rates and inflation, significantly eroded consumer purchasing power, making it difficult for individuals to engage with non-essential online purchases.

Additionally, logistical challenges, including disrupted supply chains and increased shipping costs, hindered the efficient operation of e-commerce platforms. Cybersecurity concerns also played a crucial role, as a spate of digital payment frauds and data breaches that undermined consumer confidence in online transactions. This phase of contraction in Ukraine's e-commerce highlighted the sector's susceptibility to macroeconomic pressures and the critical need for robust digital infrastructure and consumer protection mechanisms, in order to boost the resilience against future disruptions. Though, according to Statista, the forecasts highlight a moderate growth for the coming years (Statista, n.d.).

Moreover, Ukraine has seen a burgeoning startup scene, with increasing local and international investments in Ukrainian startups. Tech incubators, accelerators, and government programs are supporting innovative digital business ideas, contributing to job creation and economic diversification.

The country has established a notable position in the worldwide digital market by exporting various digital services, such as IT outsourcing and freelancing, which have substantially boosted its Gross Domestic Product (GDP). At the same time, the Ukrainian government has launched several initiatives to support digital businesses, such as simplified tax regimes, e-governance projects, and digital infrastructure development, creating an enabling environment for digital businesses to thrive.

Despite the growth, digital businesses face challenges including cybersecurity threats, regulatory hurdles, and the need for more comprehensive digital skills training. Addressing these challenges is vital for sustaining growth.

The rise of digital businesses has had a positive impact on Ukraine's economy, contributing to its GDP, fostering innovation, and creating employment opportunities. Looking ahead, continuous investment in digital infrastructure, education, and regulatory reforms are essential for maintaining momentum and ensuring that the digital economy is inclusive and sustainable.

Summarizing, the contribution of digital businesses extends beyond direct economic impact, as it also play a significant role in job creation, skill development, and the internationalization of Ukraine's market. Digital businesses introduced a new dynamism in the traditional market setup, driving competitiveness, and fostering a culture of innovation, therefore attracting foreign investment and global recognition. The multifaceted impact has profound implications for Ukraine's socio-economic development, positioning it on a trajectory of sustainable growth and integration into the global digital economy. Nevertheless, consistent efforts in overcoming existing challenges and leveraging opportunities for comprehensive development are required.

The Impact of Conflict: Ukraine's Digitalization Initiatives Amid Crisis

In times of crisis, allocating the resources becomes a critical challenge for any nation. Amid the ongoing war in Ukraine, the focus on digitalization—a pivotal aspect of modern governance and infrastructure—has sparked a debate: *Has the digitalization agenda taken a backseat amidst the immediate demands consequent to the conflict, or have efforts been resiliently maintained?*

The Nexus of Digitalization and Crisis Response

The general consensus argues that crises can serve as catalysts for accelerated digitalization efforts. The imperative for efficient communication, resource tracking, and crisis management systems might intensify the drive for digital solutions. Therefore, maintaining or even increasing digitalization efforts during a crisis can be seen as an investment in the long-term resilience and adaptability of the nation.

The war in Ukraine has presented unprecedented challenges, prompting a reexamination of the country's strategic goals. Digitalization, once viewed as a long-term goal, has now emerged as a critical component of the crisis response.

The digitalization of essential services, communication networks, and information systems has become urgent for maintaining continuity in governance, ensuring public safety, and facilitating efficient response mechanisms.

The adoption of digital technologies, from cybersecurity measures to data analytics, was instrumental in enhancing the country's resilience. Ukraine's experience underscored how digitalization was not merely a trend, but a necessity imposed by the critical demands of the situation.

Under the influence of the conflict, Ukraine's digital infrastructure has become the backbone of crisis response mechanisms. From natural disasters to geopolitical tensions, the country has leveraged technology to enhance preparedness, coordination, and communication. Robust digital networks enabled swift information dissemination, helping authorities and citizens alike to stay informed and to make timely decisions.

Digitalization has also facilitated innovative approaches to humanitarian assistance in Ukraine. Drones equipped with advanced imaging technologies were employed for real-time assessment of disaster-stricken areas, aiding in the efficient allocation of resources. Additionally, blockchain technology was explored to enhance transparency and traceability in the distribution of aid, reducing the risk of corruption.

Furthermore, digitalization has empowered Ukrainian citizens to actively participate in crisis response efforts. Social media platforms and mobile applications served as vital tools for disseminating information, organizing volunteers, and fostering community resilience. These platforms created a networked society capable of immediate collective action in times of emergency.

Ukraine's experience with crisis response through digital means has also paved the way for increased international collaboration. The sharing of best practices, technological expertise, and collaborative efforts in developing innovative solutions for crisis management are becoming integral components of Ukraine's approach to handling complex challenges.

One of the key benefits of digitalization in crisis response is the ability to make data-driven decisions. Advanced analytics and artificial intelligence play a crucial role in processing vast amounts of data to identify trends, predict potential crises, and optimize resource allocation. Ukrainian authorities are increasingly relying on these technologies to enhance their decision-making processes and improve overall crisis management strategies.

Navigating the Disruption of Initiatives During Wartime Challenges

The conflict in Ukraine has not only had extreme humanitarian consequences, but has also significantly impacted the country's economic landscape, with far-reaching consequences for its digitalization initiatives. Prior to the conflict, Ukraine was actively pursuing digitalization as a key driver of economic development. Initiatives ranging from e-governance to tech innovation were poised to propel the country into the digital age. However, the war has thrown a wrench into these plans. Ongoing digitalization projects have faced setbacks, as the focus shifted to more immediate concerns, such as humanitarian aid and infrastructure repair. The digital initiatives designed to boost efficiency and competitiveness now find themselves at the mercy of a conflict that threatens to stifle progress.

The war has not spared Ukraine's thriving IT sector and burgeoning innovation ecosystem. Start-ups, research, and development activities, as well as foreign investments, have all experienced disruptions. The volatile conditions and uncertain future have led to a contraction in the technology and innovation space, posing challenges for the resurgence of a dynamic, forward-looking economy.

Moreover, in an era where digital connectivity is integral to economic activities, the conflict has raised concerns about the cybersecurity landscape. The increased use of digital platforms during times of conflict brings with it the risk of cyber threats. According to the OECD Secretary-General, the availability of the Internet and the standard of data transmission has diminished since the commencement of the war, attributable to both cyber assaults and physical damage inflicted upon the nation's digital infrastructure (OECD, 2022). The urgency of addressing cybersecurity challenges becomes apparent as the nation navigates the fragile balance between maintaining digital operations and safeguarding against potential cyber-attacks.

On the other hand, even if the practice of telecommuting and the usage of cloud servers, both domestically and internationally, enable numerous businesses to sustain their operations, the ongoing processes of migration and military service are amplifying an enduring shortage of IT specialists in the country, an aspect also highlighted by OECD through its relatively recent publication (OECD, 2022).

The economic impact of the conflict in Ukraine extends beyond its borders, with ripple effects felt globally. International trade and economic relationships have been strained, requiring coordinated efforts for stabilization. As Ukraine grapples with the aftermath of conflict, the focus shifts to government responses and strategies for economic recovery. International assistance, collaboration, and a resilient approach to rebuilding are crucial components in steering Ukraine's economy towards a more stable and digitally enabled future.

The previously mentioned examples illustrate the multifaceted impact of the conflict on Ukraine's economy, encompassing both traditional industries and the digitalization agenda. The challenges posed by the war require strategic planning and international collaboration to facilitate economic recovery and the resurgence of digitalization initiatives.

The Dual Role of Digitalization in Ukraine

Based on these aspects, it can be stated that digital progress could be viewed and treated individually, from two key interrelated outlooks. The dual perspective

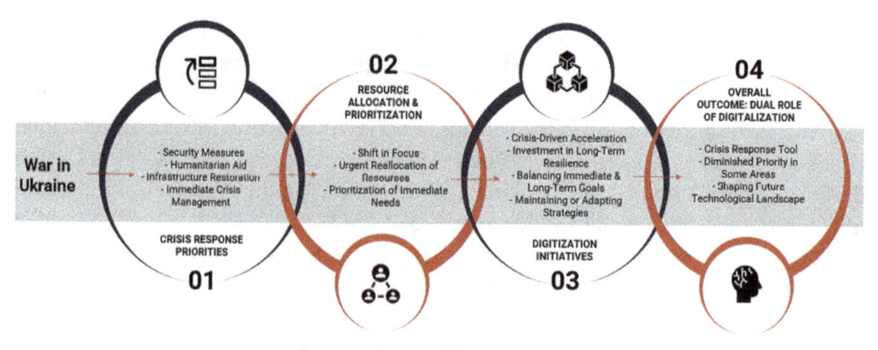

Source: Illustrated by the authors

Fig. 3 *Dynamics between crisis response priorities and the pursuit of digitalization.* Source: Illustrated by the authors

acknowledges the undeniable benefits of digitalization as a crisis response tool, while also recognizing that, depending on the specific circumstances, it might not always be prioritized at the same level as other urgent needs during a major crisis. This balancing act underscores the complex decision-making process governments and organizations face when allocating resources and determining priorities in the midst of significant challenges.

In the context of the war in Ukraine, the dynamics between crisis response priorities and the pursuit of digitalization unfold in a complex interplay, as synthesized illustrated by the schematic diagram below (Fig. 3).

The previous diagram begins with the overarching theme of the war in Ukraine, a situation that naturally demanded a focus on immediate and pressing crisis response priorities. These priorities include security measures, humanitarian aid, infrastructure restoration, and the overall management of the ongoing crisis, representing the first tier of the diagram.

The next layer delves into the critical juncture of resource allocation and prioritization prompted by the demands of the war. As the focus shifted towards addressing urgent needs, the reallocation of resources was needed, with an emphasis on prioritizing the immediate concerns brought about by the conflict. This involved a notable shift in attention, funds, and manpower toward security measures, humanitarian aid, and rapid infrastructure restoration.

Simultaneously, the impact of the resource reallocation on digitalization initiatives should be acknowledged. While some sectors may experience a crisis-driven acceleration of digitalization efforts, recognizing the need for efficient communication and crisis management systems is important. For others the digitalization may be perceived as a less important priority amid the immediate and tangible threats of war, the dichotomy in question being illustrated by the third tier of the diagram.

The final layer underscores the overall outcome: the dual role of digitalization in the war in Ukraine. On one hand, digitalization serves as a crucial tool for crisis response, enhancing communication, resource tracking, and overall efficiency. On the other hand, in certain sectors, digitalization takes a backseat as a less important priority, yielding to the urgency of immediate needs.

Stabilizing the possibilities to satisfy the basic needs of the community has opened up the focus on the evolution for directions of interest, among which digitalization represents a priority. Thus, the initial temporary situation only acted as a stagnation in progress, but the subsequent necessity led, in Ukraine, to an emphasis in terms of the focus on digitalization, determining a compensatory relationship at the temporal level, compared to the evolution recorded before the war.

The nuanced relationship between crisis response priorities and digitalization efforts, as depicted in the schematic diagram, highlights the intricate balance that nations must navigate during times of conflict. The ultimate impact consists in shaping the future technological landscape, influenced by the lessons learned and decisions made during the challenging period of war in Ukraine.

Navigating the Digital Horizon: Key Directions for Ukraine's Digitalization in the Short, Medium, and Long Term

As a result of understanding the recent context regarding the digital progress of Ukraine, under certain circumstances, perspectives of the future can be seen, considering optimistic or at least constant conditions. Translated into reality, the aforementioned statement also represents the focus of the existing organizational and decision-making organizations, both at the national and international level.

As Ukraine charts its course into an increasingly digital future, the nation stands at the intersection of innovation and opportunity. Embracing digitalization is not merely a technological imperative; it is a strategic decision that holds the potential to reshape the country's socio-economic landscape. To obtain a better understanding of the potential favorable and technologically advanced future, exploring short-term wins, medium-term strategies, and long-term visions, becomes compulsory. Certainly, the perspectives are intricate, and delineating a successful plan can be deemed an exceedingly challenging endeavor. Nonetheless, certain fundamental aspects can be elucidated concerning the outlook for Ukraine's digital future.

In the short term, the focus must be on building the essential digital infrastructure that establishes the bedrock of a thriving digital economy. This includes expanding high-speed internet access to rural areas, enhancing cybersecurity measures, and promoting digital literacy. Pursuant to OECD (OECD, 2022), as infrastructure undergoes reconstruction, Ukraine should contemplate the installation of fiber cables to extend connectivity to more individuals, even if service providers may not be immediately operational, especially in rural areas. In this regard, the regulatory body (NCCR) could incentivize broadband providers to expand fiber deployment within networks, gradually phasing out xDSL (Digital Subscriber Line) technologies as deemed suitable.

Additionally, streamlining e-governance services can foster transparency, efficiency, and citizen engagement. By investing in these fundamental aspects, Ukraine can quickly lay the groundwork for more sophisticated digital advancements.

Based on the data provided by the national recovery council representatives, anticipated benchmarks for Ukraine in the mid-term, encompass a targeted IT contribution of 10% to the country's GDP structure, reflecting a robust integration of technology into the economic landscape (The National Council for the Recovery of Ukraine from the Consequences of the War, 2022). The strategic plan aims for the complete implementation of electronic public services, ensuring a seamless and comprehensive digital experience for the public. Furthermore, the goal is to achieve full coverage for critical information infrastructure facilities, fortifying the nation's security measures. As part of a broader digital transformation, the objective is to migrate 30% of state information resources to cloud-based platforms, enhancing efficiency and accessibility. Finally, an ambitious connectivity goal is set, aiming to provide 95% of the population with access to high-speed Internet, fostering widespread digital inclusion. These indicators collectively represent a forward-looking vision for Ukraine's technological and digital advancement by 2025.

Concurrently, in the medium-term, sustainable digital transformation in key sectors such as healthcare, education, and agriculture, should be considered. Implementing smart technologies, data analytics, and artificial intelligence can enhance productivity, efficiency, and quality of services in these spheres of action. This not only ensures the well-being of the population but also contributes to economic growth. The medium-term strategy should also align with the broader goal of creating a resilient and sustainable digital society.

Looking further into the future, Ukraine should position itself to harness emerging technologies such as blockchain, the Internet of Things (IoT), and quantum computing. Research and development in these areas can propel the nation into new frontiers of innovation, opening doors to unprecedented possibilities. Long-term digitalization strategies should include a strong focus on education and skill development to prepare the workforce for the jobs of the future.

In the long term, Ukraine's digitalization efforts should extend to global collaborations. By actively participating in international initiatives, partnerships, and standards-setting bodies, Ukraine can contribute its expertise and learn from global best practices. This not only enhances the nation's global standing but also creates opportunities for cross-border innovation and knowledge exchange.

The digitalization journey is a dynamic and ongoing process that requires strategic vision, adaptability, and continuous investment. By navigating these key directions in the short, medium, and long term, Ukraine can carve a path toward a favorable digital future. As Ukraine welcomes the era of digital transformation, the country stands at the threshold of transformative opportunities that have the potential to elevate it to a position of global leadership in the digital age.

Conclusion

The progress of the last years, before the war, highlighted Ukraine's efforts to increase digitalization, with undoubted results, the benefits of which were felt once the conflict broke out. The extreme situation, characterized by risk and uncertainty, served as a means of using technological resources for specific purposes, specifically directed as responses to the crisis.

Based on the present analysis of the digital battlefield in Ukraine, the fact that the conflict has witnessed a paradigm shift with the integration of digital technologies were highlighted. However, cyberattacks, disinformation campaigns, and the weaponization of information have become integral components of modern warfare, presenting unprecedented challenges and opportunities for both state and non-state actors.

The aspects discussed underscore the critical need for nations to adapt their national security strategies to account for the evolving nature of warfare in the digital age. As Ukraine's experience demonstrates, a comprehensive approach that combines traditional military capabilities with robust cybersecurity measures is imperative to safeguarding a nation's sovereignty and integrity.

Examining the economic dimensions, the research shows the interconnectedness of digital warfare and economic development. The disruptions caused by cyberattacks and the harmonization of economic systems highlight the vulnerability of nations in an interconnected world. Simultaneously, opportunities arise for innovation, resilience-building, and the development of a cyber-resilient economy that can withstand and recover from digital threats.

The international community plays a crucial role in mitigating the impact of digital warfare. Collaborative efforts, information sharing, and the establishment of norms and regulations in cyberspace are fundamental for creating a secure environment. The lessons learned from Ukraine's experience emphasize the need for a coordinated global response to address the challenges imposed by the intersection of conflict, digitalization, and economic development.

The current analysis serves as a call to action for continued research into the dynamic relationship between digitalization, conflict, and economic development. Future studies should delve deeper into the evolving tactics of cyber warfare, assess the effectiveness of existing frameworks, and propose innovative solutions to address emerging challenges. Additionally, there is a pressing need for ongoing efforts to enhance the preparedness of nations in the face of evolving threats in digitalization.

Concluding, the intersection of Ukraine's war, digitalization, and economic development unveils a multifaceted landscape that demands comprehensive, adaptable strategies from policymakers, military leaders, and the international community. The lessons drawn from the analyzed context, focused on Ukraine, will undoubtedly inform future discussions and actions in the ever-evolving digital battlefield.

References

Avanesova, N., & Kolodiazhna, T. (2021). The essence, content and role of digital transformation in development socio-economic systems. *VUZF Review, 6*, 129–139. https://doi.org/10.38188/2534-9228.21.2.15

Halimon, T. (2021). Imperatives of the digital economy development in Ukraine. *Socio-World Social Research & Behavioral Sciences, 6*, 39–46. https://doi.org/10.36962/SWD0604(01)2021-39

Minitch, L. (2015). Digital agenda for Ukraine. Government of Ukraine. Retrieved from http://www.e-ukraine.org.ua/media/Lviv_Minich_2.pdf

OECD. (2022, July 1). Digitalisation for recovery in Ukraine. Retrieved from OECD – Organisation for Economic Co-operation and Development: https://www.oecd.org/ukraine-hub/policy-responses/digitalisation-for-recovery-in-ukraine-c5477864/

Osetskyi, V., Kraus, N., Kraus, K., & Grinchenko, B. (2021). Sharing economy: Dialectic development of reciprocal exchange in the conditions of virtual reality and digital transformation. *Economic Theory, 2*, 5–27. https://doi.org/10.15407/etet2021.02.005

Samoilovych, A. G. (2021). World experience and Ukrainian realities of digital transformation of regions in the context of the information economy development. *Financial and credit activity problems of theory and practice, 3*(38), 316–325. https://doi.org/10.18371/fcaptp.v3i38.237462

Spivakovskyy, S., Kochubei, O., Shebanina, O., Sokhatska, O., Yaroshenko, I., & Nych, T. (2021). The impact of digital transformation on the economic security of Ukraine. *Studies of Applied Economics, 39*(5), 1–10. https://doi.org/10.25115/eea.v39i5.5040

Statista. (n.d.). *eCommerce – Ukraine*. Retrieved September 23, 2023, from Statista – The statistics portal. https://www.statista.com/outlook/dmo/ecommerce/ukraine

The National Council for the Recovery of Ukraine from the Consequences of the War. (2022). Draft Ukraine recovery plan – Materials of the "Digitalization" working group. Government Portal. Retrieved from https://www.kmu.gov.ua/storage/app/sites/1/recoveryrada/eng/digitization-eng.pdf

Environmental and Energy Security on the Way to Rebuilding Ukraine on the Principle of Zero Carbon Footprint

Svitlana Delehan and Hanna Melehanych

Abstract This article explores state of Ukraine's energy security in view of the changing geopolitical landscape and new strategic risks as a result of Russia's military actions against Ukraine; green certification of Ukraine's civil and industrial infrastructure based on the principle of life cycle assessment in the context of European integration in times of war; the integration of international green certification standards, including LEED, BREEAM, and the WELL Building Standard, into the post-war reconstruction efforts in Ukraine. It highlights the comprehensive assessment criteria of LEED and BREEAM, emphasizing energy efficiency, water management, materials usage, and innovation. A comparison of these standards is also made. Additionally, it discusses the unique focus of the WELL Building Standard on occupant health and well-being. The article underscores the potential of these standards to guide the selection of environmentally friendly construction materials, efficient energy systems, and sustainable waste management practices. Furthermore, it discusses the benefits of incorporating these standards, such as enhancing building competitiveness, improving indoor environmental quality, and promoting human health and productivity. This integration represents a significant step in Ukraine's alignment with European standards and the adoption of new ecological practices, fostering its integration into the European Union and signaling its commitment to sustainable development.

Svitlana D.
Centrefor Interdisciplinary Scientific Research, Uzhhorod National University, Uzhhorod, Ukraine
e-mail: svitlana.delehan-kokaiko@uzhnu.edu.ua

Hanna M. (✉)
Department of International Studies and Public Communications, Uzhhorod National University, Uzhhorod, Ukraine
e-mail: hanna.melehanych@uzhnu.edu.ua

S. Nate (ed.), *Ukraine's Journey to Recovery, Reform and Post-War Reconstruction*, Contributions to Security and Defence Studies,
https://doi.org/10.1007/978-3-031-66434-2_14

The State of Ukraine's Energy Security in View of the Changing Geopolitical Landscape and New Strategic Risks as a Result of Russia's Military Actions Against Ukraine

The war in Ukraine has resulted in numerous human and material losses, significant damage and destruction of civilian, industrial and military infrastructure. According to official data alone, almost a million residential buildings, tens of thousands of non-residential buildings, thousands of kilometers of roads, railways, bridges, etc. have been destroyed or damaged as a result of the war in Ukraine. The construction industry has suffered significant damage, partially losing its raw material base and production. Russia's aggression against Ukraine has led to an unprecedented global energy crisis, which has a positive effect on countries' efforts to abandon fossil fuels and switch to renewable energy sources as soon as possible. It is important to note that reconstruction Ukraine should not be about returning to the state we had before the war, but about creating a new, modern, innovative and environmentally friendly environment. It is important to note here that the European Green Deal should be the framework for this. Due to its relatively large territory for Europe, Ukraine has significant potential for wind, solar and biomass energy production. In addition, Ukraine's aspirations to move from EU candidate status to full member state status encourage Ukraine to contribute to the EU's low carbon and net zero emission goals. Ukraine's recent connection to ENTSO-E offers a means to export renewable electricity while generating export revenue and reducing the EU's carbon intensity (Evensen et al., 2022).

In addition to the challenges of the war, green reconstruction is also driven by all international and European security standards, including environmental and energy security. After all, the growing global demand for alternative energy, climate change and rising energy costs are challenging all countries and their organisations to manage energy resources efficiently. Energy efficiency, energy conservation and environmental principles are key aspects of today's world for advanced countries, businesses and society in general, which is reflected in construction and planning. In the context of the war in Ukraine, there are even more arguments in favour of supporting alternative energy sources, because not only does it not harm the environment during the production process, but it also does not cause significant damage to the environment in the event of man-made disasters or terrorist activities. The example of the Russian Federation's activities on the territory of Ukraine, in particular the occupation of the Zaporizhzhia nuclear power plant, is a vivid example of this.

At the same time, Ukraine has committed itself to ensuring the gradual decarbonisation of its economy both for reasons of combating climate change and reducing energy dependence. In accordance with the provisions of the global climate agreement "Paris Agreement" (Paryzjka ughoda, n.d.), adopted in December 2015 in Paris and ratified by the Law of Ukraine No. 1469-VIII "On Ratification of the Paris Agreement" dated 14.07.2016, Ukraine, as a party to the agreement, is obliged to make its nationally determined contribution to achieve the goals of sustainable low-carbon development of all sectors of the economy and increase the ability to adapt to the adverse effects of climate change. Decarbonization of the energy sector economy means reducing CO_2 emissions per unit of energy produced. During this time, Ukraine has adopted a number of regulatory documents and taken many actions to achieve this goal. Since independence, this process has been quite successful in recent years. As of February 2022, Ukraine's energy sector was one of the most powerful in Europe, and it remains so today, despite significant damage as a result of the Russian invasion. In particular, Ukraine was among the top 10 countries in Europe in terms of installed power generation capacity, and ranks third among gas producers, with the largest underground gas storage facilities in Europe. Ukraine has one of the highest shares of carbon-neutral generation in Europe. Around 70% of electricity is generated by nuclear, hydro and renewable generation (Malinovska & Vysochenska, 2023).

Russia's attack on Ukraine has had complex and unpredictable effects on climate change issues in general, as well as on the implementation of the Paris Agreement. At the same time, it makes it necessary to accelerate the transition to sustainable energy. Due to the war, the value of renewable energy sources has transformed from an environmental to a security and economic issue in country. In 2021, Ukraine's renewable energy sector fought for the right to operate under fair conditions guaranteed by the state, but in 2022 it is preparing to become one of the foundations of Ukraine's post-war reconstruction and further increase the country's energy independence.

Thanks to the successfully implemented renewable energy projects in Ukraine, annual CO_2 emissions were reduced by more than 10.3 million tonnes as of 2021, which is equivalent to the emissions from more than 2.2 million cars. For example, electricity generation by industrial wind farms alone saved 1.8 million tons of coal and 1171.4 thousand m^3 of natural gas in 2021 and reduced approximately 3.1 million tons of CO_2 emissions (Konechenkov, n.d.).

Unfortunately, we have to state that Ukraine's wind and solar power generation has decreased by more than half compared to its pre-war level. That is, energy security is one of the most important issues for Ukraine in times of war, and it is necessary to take into account various aspects of organizing energy supply for the country's needs, which directly or indirectly affect the functioning of the fuel and energy complex and planning its development in the long term. One of the key ways to ensure Ukraine's (and, by extension, Europe's) security is to develop renewable energy sources.

The most widely used approach to describe energy security is the one used in the Asia Pacific Energy Research Centre study. It is proposed to distinguish four aspects that should be studied in terms of their impact on energy security, namely: resource adequacy; technical reliability; economic viability; and environmental acceptability. This approach has gained wide popularity and has become a model for forming a set of four groups of parameters for analyzing energy security. Later, greenhouse gas emissions and the use of renewable energy sources were added to the description of energy security (Sukhodolya et al., 2021). In the process of rebuilding Ukraine, it is the latter that should be emphasized in particular. After all, with the transition to renewable energy sources, energy as such will cease to be an instrument of political or military influence from one country to another.

Russia is shelling Ukrainian infrastructure every day, causing more and more damage. At the same time, Ukraine is already formulating a plan for post-war recovery, including in the area of secure renewable energy. Energy independence and the Green Deal are among the key areas and projects of the Recovery Plan, which aims to accelerate sustainable economic growth. In addition, since the beginning of the full-scale war, various projects (local and not yet systemic) have been implemented in different regions, using different approaches for the future sustainable development of the country. The existing projects will ensure energy saving and potentially energy independence of Ukraine, provided that these projects are scaled up.

In June 2023, UNDP released a new report assessing the damage to Ukraine's energy sector. According to the report, Ukraine's power system continues to operate in an emergency mode, affecting both the power grid and power generation. The report shows that 42 out of 94 (45%) key high-voltage transformers in government-controlled areas have been damaged or destroyed by rocket attacks or drone strikes since the beginning of the current phase of the war. Thus, the actual loss of outdated coal-fired generation should be seen as an opportunity to accelerate the green transition and decentralisation of the sector.

The report offers a set of clear and practical recommendations to help make the energy sector more sustainable and environmentally friendly than before. The recommendations include:

1. Dispersal of generation capacity across the country and decentralisation of the power system to increase its resilience and adaptability.
2. Introducing modern, highly manoeuvrable and more environmentally friendly generating capacities to enhance the manoeuvrability of the power system.
3. Increasing the share of renewable energy sources in the power system, utilising the great potential of clean and sustainable energy.
4. Initiate a gradual reduction and eventual phase-out of coal use in line with Ukraine's commitments to reduce CO_2 emissions.
5. Exploring further opportunities to increase the efficiency of nuclear and hydropower capacities and maintain an optimal energy balance (Livingplanet, n.d.).

Other issues that need attention include inefficient district heating and an old and poorly insulated housing stock, which should benefit from large-scale investment in energy efficiency and new heating approaches, especially heat pumps. Ukraine also sees an important role for hydrogen in its new energy system, although there are some concerns about the relative value and efficiency of such systems. Important decisions for Ukraine in the future will concern what energy efficiency measures are promoted and adopted. They will also relate to the role of nuclear, wind, solar, heat pumps, biofuels and hydrogen, and where and when to make each of these changes (Evensen et al., 2022).

Thus, it is clear that one of the main ways to increase the environmental acceptability of energy production is to increase the share of environmentally friendly renewable energy sources. Before the outbreak of hostilities, Ukrainian solar and wind power plants, which already produce electricity cheaper than European electricity, were a key to Ukraine's energy security and allowed the country to profit from increased exports to Europe (Konechenkov, n.d.).

In the first half of 2024, a new digital platform, the National Decarbonisation Platform (NDP), will be launched in Ukraine to facilitate the country's large-scale energy efficiency transformation and the widespread implementation of green reconstruction projects. Conceptually, the platform will act as a multifunctional IT tool and will become an accessible and effective guide for everyone to the world of energy efficiency transformation and decarbonisation. The platform will help every user from anywhere in Ukraine—municipalities, businesses, and ordinary households—to choose the most effective modern energy-efficient or green solution on favourable terms, with government support and the participation of global industry leaders. Users of the platform will have a wide range of options for green and energy-efficient solutions, from energy-efficient boilers and energy storage for the home to large-scale solutions based on solar panels, heat pumps or fuel cells from leading global manufacturers.

In summary, energy security should be directly attributed to the areas that implement one of the fundamental national interests—sustainable development of the national economy, society and state to ensure the growth of the standard of living and quality of life of the population, which is especially important in times of war. These are the principles and foundations that Ukraine will not abandon, even through all the challenges of war.

Green Certification of Ukraine's Civil and Industrial Infrastructure Based on the Principle of Life Cycle Assessment in the Context of European Integration in Times of War

A long-term study of global warming has revealed that modern cities, including buildings and structures, are one of the main sources of environmental pollution. Expert data shows that buildings around the world consume about 40% of all primary energy, 67% of all electricity, 40% of all raw materials and 14% of all drinking water supplies, as well as produce 35% of all carbon dioxide emissions and almost half of all solid waste. Therefore, in rebuilding, we can prepare cities for climate change as much as possible, while greatly reducing their own impact on the micro and macroclimate and making them more resilient. This includes both expanding the network of open green spaces and increasing the number of green spaces, promoting biodiversity, and implementing waste, rainwater and meltwater management systems using modern sustainable building solutions.

Historically, against the backdrop of high consumption of non-renewable resources and the emission of significant amounts of carbon into the atmosphere, it has become clear that it is important to introduce green standards and practices in construction. This has proven to be not only environmentally sound, but also a strategically important step in ensuring long-term energy sustainability and resource conservation.

The environmental criteria of environmental certification and labelling systems are considered to be the most transparent and reliable standards for assessing the life cycle and environmental benefits of a procurement item.

In Ukraine is only formulating legislative requirements for the environmental safety of building materials and the entire construction process, which should include the development of bylaws and regulations that will disclose the specifics of ensuring the environmental safety of various types of building materials at all stages of their manufacture and sale, which will meet the requirements for systematizing such legislation in the construction industry. The creation of an environmental safety system is a new element of national security, which should be based on an organizational, legal, socio-political and economic mechanism. The post-war reconstruction of Ukraine will require a fundamentally new approach and qualitatively new technologies in construction and urbanism. The issue of legal support for the environmental safety of building materials will become relevant both at the level of technical regulation and at the level of technical support and implementation.

The general principles of sustainable construction are defined in the ISO 15392 standard. They are based on the principles of maintaining a balance of economic, environmental and social aspects in the construction of buildings and other construction works.

Ukraine continues to implement the EU Energy Efficiency Directive and the Energy Performance of Buildings Directive in accordance with the EU-Ukraine Association Agreement. The EU Energy Efficiency Directive obliges central authorities to procure only products, services and buildings with high energy efficiency performance, if this is consistent with economic efficiency, economic viability, greater sustainability, technical suitability and sufficient competition.

These provisions of European law have been implemented in Ukrainian legislation through the provisions of the Law of Ukraine "On Public Procurement", updated in 2019, and the Law of Ukraine "On Energy Efficiency", adopted in 2021 (Livingplanet, n.d.).

Today, legal provisions on environmental safety fill most of Ukraine's legislative and regulatory acts and thus have a comprehensive, cross-sectoral, cross-cutting, universal impact on the regulation of various legal relations, especially in terms of environmentally hazardous, risky activities.

On 23 July 2018, the Law of Ukraine "On Energy Efficiency of Buildings" came into force, the requirements of which are in line with the provisions of Directive 2010/31/EU on the energy consumption of buildings. This Law will bring Ukraine closer to the emergence of zero-energy buildings that meet international standards and will allow for significant savings on utilities. The Law introduces mandatory energy certification and determination of building classes in accordance with the

European methodology. In particular, construction projects and already constructed buildings must undergo energy efficiency certification to determine the actual performance and assess whether these indicators meet the established minimum requirements for energy efficiency of buildings.

Based on the results of the assessment, each building is assigned a certain class. Furthermore, if a building improves its energy efficiency class, it receives government support.

The following are subject to mandatory energy efficiency certification:

- Construction sites, buildings and parts of buildings leased for more than a year;
- Buildings with a heated area of more than 250 sq m, which house government agencies and receive citizens;
- Buildings undergoing thermal modernisation with state support aimed at achieving an energy efficiency class of the building not lower than the minimum requirements.

On 29 January 2020, the Cabinet of Ministers of Ukraine approved the Concept for the Implementation of the State Policy in the Field of Energy Efficiency of Buildings in terms of increasing the number of buildings with near-zero energy consumption and approved the National Plan for Increasing the Number of Buildings with Near-Zero Energy Consumption. The increase in the number of such buildings is aimed at reducing the overall primary energy supply and carbon dioxide emissions as one of the main objectives of Directive 2012/27/EU of the European Parliament and of the Council of 25 October 2012 on energy efficiency (Berzina et al., 2020).

In accordance with its obligations under the EU-Ukraine Association Agreement (Article 56), Ukraine has implemented EU Regulation 305. The transitional provisions of the Law of Ukraine "On the Provision of Construction Products on the Market" dated 02.09.2020, which entered into force on 01.01.2023, propose to amend the Law of Ukraine "On Construction Standards" by supplementing it with Article 7-2, which deals with the basic requirements for buildings and structures. "According to part 4 of this provision, the main requirements for buildings and structures are to ensure, in particular: hygiene, health and environmental protection, i.e. buildings and structures must be designed and constructed in such a way that throughout their life cycle they do not pose a threat to hygiene or health and safety, or have a significant impact on the quality of the environment or climate during their construction, operation and demolition, in particular as a result of any of the following factors:

(a) the release of toxic gas;
(b) emission of hazardous substances, volatile organic compounds, greenhouse gases or hazardous particles into the air inside or outside the premises;
(c) emission of hazardous radiation;
(d) release of hazardous substances into groundwater, sea water, surface water or soil;
(e) release of hazardous substances into drinking water or other substances that adversely affect drinking water;

(f) accidental discharge of wastewater, solid or liquid waste, emission of flue gases;
(g) dampness in parts of buildings or structures or on surfaces inside buildings or structures, as well as the possibility of using environmentally compatible raw and secondary materials in buildings and structures as a separate area (RADA, n. d.).

The list of national standards was approved by the Order of the Ministry of Communities and Territories Development of Ukraine dated 18 February 2022 No. 54 On Approval of the List of National Standards for the Purposes of Application of the Law of Ukraine "On Provision of Construction Products on the Market". These national standards are identical to the harmonised European standards in the framework of the implementation of Regulation (EU) No 305/2011 of the European Parliament. Starting from 2023, the declaration of indicators will be made in the "manufacturer's office" in the Unified State Electronic System in the field of construction.

In 2022, State Standards of Ukraine 9171:2021 "Guidelines for ensuring the balanced use of natural resources in the design of structures" was issued. This State Standards of Ukraine is revolutionary in certain provisions. In particular, it approves the reuse and recycling of materials and products at a level of at least 70%, which is part of the implementation of the agreement with the EU. The methods of economic and environmental life cycle assessment (LCA) provided in State Standards of Ukraine 9171 allow for an informed decision to be made when assessing different options for a building based on numerical indicators. It should be noted that almost all sustainability standards have already been implemented in Ukraine: State Standards of Ukraine ISO 14000 "Environmental Management", State Standards of Ukraine ISO 15686 "Life Cycle Planning", etc. (USCC, n.d.-a; Svitlana & Hanna, 2022).

The key determinant of a building's efficiency is environmental Life Cycle Assessment (LCA), an objective quantitative assessment of material and energy flows and environmental impacts associated with the life cycle of an activity, or some of these stages.

At the preliminary design or feasibility study (calculation) stage, a preliminary LCA assessment is sufficient. For other stages—design, detailed design or working documentation, when the volumes of basic materials and works related to the creation of an architectural object are known, a detailed, elemental life cycle analysis is applied. Such provisions of the State Standards of Ukraine 9171 were introduced in 2022 and in the State Construction Norms A.2-2:3. (USCC, n.d.-b).

The EU does not allow the construction of facilities that consume more than 60 kWh/m^2 per year (low-energy buildings). Since 2020, a massive transition to the construction of zero-energy buildings has begun. In the future, buildings will produce more energy than they consume (the standard is "energy plus building"). This is what we should focus on in the construction and renovation of buildings (Berzina et al., 2020).

Today, given the changes in the geopolitical landscape and the consequences of geopolitical crises, the relevance of energy efficient construction as an important component of Ukraine's environmental and energy security is being emphasized. This approach helps to reduce energy dependence, reduce greenhouse gas emissions and improve natural resource reserves. This contributes to the formation of a sustainable framework for the implementation of "green" and "ecological" practices in construction, which, in turn, contributes to the improvement of Ukraine's environmental and energy security in the context of global challenges and changes.

Green building is a principle of construction and operation of buildings, the main purpose of which is to reduce the consumption of energy and material resources throughout the entire life cycle of a building. This practice is used at every stage of building construction: from the selection of a site for design to its complete demolition. For a construction project to be called "green", certain standards and norms must be met at each of its stages. To adequately assess compliance with these principles in the implementation of real estate projects in the West, special market instruments have been developed—voluntary building certification systems, of which there are now several dozen in the world.

Green building certification in Ukraine has recently become an important issue, driven by the requirement to reduce the environmental impact of the construction industry and the efficient use of resources. Currently, there is a trend towards the spread of LEED and BREEAM methodologies in the practice of the construction industry in Ukraine, aimed at implementing environmentally friendly and energy efficient solutions.

Considering various national and international standards, such as BREEAM and LEED, it can be noted that their implementation not only contributes to solving environmental problems, but also promotes the development of energy efficient infrastructure and increases the value of construction projects. The point is not only that a building that meets the requirements of green standards becomes much more comfortable, environmentally friendly and economical (in terms of resource consumption), and therefore more profitable to operate. Such projects have a more attractive image and capitalisation, which means they are more interesting to investors, large tenants and the authorities.

Ukraine had taken its first steps towards energy efficiency before the full-scale Russian invasion. Every year, the number of companies operating in this segment grew steadily. Commercial real estate has begun to undergo international environmental certification. Well-known developers are gradually starting to build their new buildings using the following environmental trends.

The potential for further expansion of the number of buildings with green certificates is significant, and it is important to further develop infrastructure and promote business activity in the field of sustainable construction. The introduction of certification standards in construction is a step towards ensuring environmental sustainability and rational use of resources in Ukraine.

While some may perceive LEED or BREEAM certification as an additional cost, it is important to consider it from a strategic planning perspective. Projects with minimal scores may not make a significant difference to the project cost, while higher scores reflect the value of investing in high-quality construction and may help reduce overall costs in the future. The implementation of environmental approaches in the early stages of planning energy-efficient facilities is reflected in reduced additional costs and can have a significant impact on long-term operations.

Thus, a green certificate has an important integrated impact on the business and environmental aspects of construction, ensuring not only efficiency in resource use but also positive dynamics in investment and economic terms.

Analysis of the Best International Practices of Green Certification for the Reconstruction of Ukraine in the Post-war Period Based on the Principles of Green Certification and the Possibility of Their Adapted Application

Today, two building rating systems are the most well-known and widely used in the world. These are the BREEAM system developed by the British Bre Global Institute and the LEED system developed by the US Green Building Council. According to Western standards, buildings are assessed according to a set of formal criteria divided into several main groups. The more "points" a building receives for its documented environmental and other significant characteristics, the higher the level of the certificate it receives.

The American standard LEED (Leadership in Energy and Environmental Design) was developed in 1998. This standard embodies a comprehensive approach to measuring and assessing the environmental impact of construction projects, rational energy use and the use of environmentally friendly technologies.

BREEAM (Building Research Establishment Environmental Assessment Method) is the first environmental certification method for buildings and was developed in 1990. This assessment system takes into account a wide range of aspects of the environmental performance of buildings, including energy efficiency, water use, materials and other factors.

Properties that achieve LEED and BREEAM ratings demonstrate a higher level of compliance with modern environmental and energy sustainability requirements. This leads to an increase in its competitiveness in the real estate market, both for new construction and in the secondary market over time. Given the growing focus on sustainability and resource conservation, the importance of compliance with these standards is becoming increasingly relevant in the context of increased environmental requirements and strategic challenges in the construction industry.

The main differences between LEED and BREEAM are evident on several levels, making the two certification systems distinctly different in their approaches and emphasis. At first glance, they may seem to be just two different names for the same scheme, but a closer look reveals that there are some really significant differences that point to deep divergences.

LEED primarily focuses on energy and water management, and actively encourages the implementation of measures to improve the efficiency of their use. BREEAM, on the other hand, focuses on ecology, addressing environmental issues.

The rigor and uniformity of the requirements for LEED standards can be noted, but it is worth noting that facilities that have received BREEAM certification show significant differences in environmental parameters. This indicates an individual approach to assessment.

Another internationally recognized building certification system is the DGNB certification system (German Green Building Council). In 2009, the first buildings in Germany received the quality label from the DGNB, the German Green Building Council, founded in 2007. The DGNB developed its own certificate for Germany in order to fill gaps in existing systems and introduce additional quality criteria that take into account German standards and regulations. The system is based on a life-cycle approach and takes into account environmental, economic and socio-cultural aspects as the three pillars of sustainability. Technology, process and location also play a role in the planning and construction of a building. The certificate also takes into account regional characteristics and building materials. Achieving even the lowest level of such certification for a building implies a significant exceedance of legal standards.

Depending on the type of building, the assessment covers up to 40 sustainability criteria, which are constantly being developed by independent expert groups. The certificate is designed for all types of existing buildings and new construction, from commercial skyscrapers to family homes and infrastructure such as tunnels and bridges (GEZE, n.d.; Delehan et al., 2023).

Until recently, there were no scientifically based methods and criteria for determining the level of comfort and safety of indoor office space. In order to measure and objectively assess the compliance of buildings with established standards, scientists spent 7 years conducting comprehensive architectural and medical research. This lengthy process allowed the development of an exceptional technical approach known as the WELL Building Standard, which is designed to assess the level of "health" of a building. This standard focuses exclusively on those factors that directly affect the health and well-being of employees. The WELL Building Standard certification process is based on scientific evidence and technical requirements that modern office buildings must meet.

Obtaining the WELL Building Standard certificate is determined as follows:

- WELL Silver (50–59 points);
- WELL Gold (60–79 points);
- WELL Platinum (80–100 points).

There are several good reasons for implementing the WELL Building Standard certification: increasing the market value of real estate; market leadership; employee health and productivity; increased productivity; reduced health insurance costs; efficient use of resources; corporate and social responsibility.

The initial steps in the implementation of WELL certification in Ukraine in the post-war period may seem new and not clear to everyone, but 135 buildings have already been certified according to the Well Building standard worldwide, and about 1000 more are in the process of certification.

In recent years, the eco-building movement has become increasingly complex and large-scale, a good example of which is the trend towards the construction of entire eco-cities, where the environment, urban planning, development, communications and the lifestyle itself are in harmony with each other. In this case, any type of serialization can be applied. This approach could be used to rebuild from scratch the cities that were completely destroyed by the war, such as Bakhmut, Marinka, and Mariupol.

References

Berzina, S. V., Yareskovskaya, I. I., Perminova, S. Y., Buzan, G. S., Ignatenko, A. V., & Glushchenko, R. O. (2020). Recommendations on energy efficiency requirements for procurement of products by public authorities. Criteria for energy efficient procurement. Retrieved August 10, 2023, from https://iem.org.ua/images/2022/2022-11-20-rekomendacii.pdf [in Ukrainian].

Delehan, S., Melehanych, H., & Khorolskyi, A. (2023). The traditions and technologies of ecological construction in Portugal. *Eng. Proc., 57*, 23. https://doi.org/10.3390/engproc2023057023

Evensen, D., Sovakul, B., Dalton, N., Hlebova, K. (2022). Energy security, climate change, and the future of Ukraine's recovery. Institute for Global Sustainable Development, Boston University. Retrieved August 22, 2023, from https://www.bu.edu/igs/files/2022/10/Energy-Security-Climate-Change-and-the-Future-of-Ukraine-Reconstruction_FINAL_translation.pdf [in Ukrainian].

GEZE. (n.d.). Green construction is certified ecological construction. Retrieved August 11, 2023, from https://www.geze.ua/uk/cikavi-novini/temi/zelene-budivnictvo [in Ukrainian].

Konechenkov, A. (n.d.) Ukraine's renewable energy sector before, during and after the war. Retrieved August 20, 2023, from https://razumkov.org.ua/statti/sektor-vidnovlyuvanoyi-energetyky-ukrayiny-do-pid-chas-ta-pislya-viyny [in Ukrainian].

Livingplanet. (n.d.). Following the seminar on the implementation of energy-efficient public procurement for green reconstruction in Zhytomyr. Retrieved August 15, 2023, from https://livingplanet.org.ua/novuny/za-pidsumkami-seminaru-po-vprovadzhennyu-energoefektivnikh-publichnikh-zakupivel-dlya-zelenoji-vidbudovi-v-zhitomiri [in Ukrainian].

Malinovska, O. Y., Vysochenska, M. Y. (2023) Energy security of Ukraine as the main criterion of efficiency of the national economy functioning. Agroecological Journal. Retrieved August 20, 2023, from http://journalagroeco.org.ua/article/view/276723 [in Ukrainian].

Paryzjka ughoda. (n.d.) Oficijnyj pereklad/Verkhovna Rada Ukrajiny. https://zakon.rada.gov.ua/laws/show/995_l61#Text [in Ukrainian].

RADA. (n.d.) On the main principles (strategy) of the state environmental policy of Ukraine for the period until 2030: Law of Ukraine dated February 28, 2019 No. 2697-VIII. Retrieved August 10, 2023, from https://zakon.rada.gov.ua/laws/show/2697-19#Text [in Ukrainian].

Sukhodolya, O. M., Kharazishvili, Y. M., Bobro, D. G., Ryabtsev, G. L., & Zavhorodnia, S. P. (2021). In O. Sukhodolia (Ed.), *Determination of the level of energy security of Ukraine: Analytical supplement*. NISS. 71 c. Retrieved August 10, 2023, from https://www.researchgate.net/publication/358988588_VIZNACENNA_RIVNA_ENERGETICNOI_BEZPEKI_UKRAINI [in Ukrainian].

Svitlana, D., & Hanna, M. (2022). Regulations and plans to reduce climate change in Ukraine. 3(12), 1471–1477. https://doi.org/10.37871/jbresjbres1621, Article ID: JBRES1621. https://www.jelsciences.com/articles/jbres1621.pdf

USCC. (n.d.-a). DSTU 9171:2021 Instructions regarding ensuring balanced use of natural resources in building design. Retrieved August 12, 2023, from https://uscc.ua/dstu-nastanova-sodo-zabezpecenna-zbalansovanogo-vikoristanna-prirodnih-resursiv-pri-proektuvanni-sporud [in Ukrainian].

USCC. (n.d.-b). The revival of the construction industry in the conditions of war. Retrieved August 11, 2023, from https://uscc.ua/news/vidrodzenna-budivelnoi-galuzi-v-umovah-vijni [in Ukrainian].

Study of the State of Environmental Information Security of Ukraine in the Pre-war Period and Assessment of the Consequences of Environmental Information Manipulations in View of Changes in the Geopolitical Landscape and New Strategic Risks

Svitlana Delehan, Oksana Malychkovych, and Hanna Melehanych

Abstract This research investigates the media landscape in Ukraine amidst the backdrop of the Russian full-scale aggression, focusing on environmental issues. Analyzing data from 2019 to 2023, a notable surge in online publications, particularly on popular Ukrainian platforms, is observed, indicating sustained interest in environmental news despite the conflict. Recording the impact of Russia's full-scale aggression against Ukraine on the environment and assessing the damage remains one of the priority topics in the Ukrainian media. The full-scale war has shown that the threat to the environment is not limited to any local areas. Emissions of harmful substances affect at least the entire continent. The study underscores the importance of accurate and reliable information dissemination to avoid panic and misinformation. It highlights the role of media in keeping environmental concerns at the forefront of public discourse, potentially leading to increased awareness and civic engagement in sustainable development. Furthermore, the research delves into the concept of "ecocide" and its resonance in the media following environmental disasters linked to the conflict, emphasizing the need for public education and discourse. The analysis also explores the evolving media landscape, including the

Svitlana D. (✉)
Centre for Interdisciplinary Scientific Research, Uzhhorod National University, Uzhhorod, Ukraine
e-mail: svitlana.delehan-kokaiko@uzhnu.edu.ua

O. Malychkovych
Ukrainian Monitoring Research Agency LBI, Kiev, Ukraine

Hanna M.
Departmentof International Studies and Public Communications, Uzhhorod National University, Uzhhorod, Ukraine
e-mail: hanna.melehanych@uzhnu.edu.ua

S. Nate (ed.), *Ukraine's Journey to Recovery, Reform and Post-War Reconstruction*, Contributions to Security and Defence Studies,
https://doi.org/10.1007/978-3-031-66434-2_15

rise of social media platforms like Telegram, and the implications for communication strategies. Overall, the findings suggest a growing recognition of environmental issues amidst the conflict and underscore the pivotal role of media in shaping public opinion and fostering environmental stewardship.

Assessment of the State of Environmental Information Security of Ukraine in the Pre-war Period

The socio-cultural revolution of the second half of the twentieth century is characterised not only by an increase in the volume of information, but also by the creation of a space characterised by specific forms of behaviour and activity that differ from the previously existing ones. Today, the national information space is included in the list of important political concepts and can claim the second place after state independence in the value scale of social values. In the structure of state security, its information component comes to the fore in the light of recent events and global trends. Therefore, the state is obliged to ensure that its information field is used in the national interest [1].

The term "information space" has many interpretations today and is a key factor in social development. It is usually used to refer to a system of external and internal information flows, which, in turn, may have different characteristics in terms of content, methods, transmission and intensity of information exchange. It can also be used to refer to the relevant area of social activity covered by a particular system of information flows [2]. It is also used in context as a set of information, a set of relations arising from the use of information resources based on the search, accumulation, processing, analysis, storage, distribution and provision of access to data. The information space emerges with the development of society and communication, and it is the individual who is the main consumer of public information. The notion of national information space is associated with the state as a whole, with the reflection of events taking place on its territory at a particular time [3].

At present, there is no legally defined term "information space in the environmental sphere", but knowing the characteristics of the information space, we can identify the main features of the information space in the environmental sphere, including:

- formation of an information environment to provide citizens with reliable environmental information and access to it;
- creation of professional information resources or communities (in social networks) that will help develop and resolve relations between nature and humanity with the involvement of scientists;
- increasing the role of the issue and, therefore, the responsibility for the accuracy of the information disseminated, as environmental issues are becoming a sensitive topic in society, and manipulations around it can quickly spread panic;

- creating a system of free access to, dissemination and use of environmental information [4].

Environmental issues are particularly relevant, in particular for Ukrainian society, which suffered significant economic, environmental and social negative consequences from the accident at the Chernobyl nuclear power plant in the pre-war period, and today we have a fundamentally new term to describe the environmental disaster caused by Russia's full-scale war against Ukraine, namely ecocide. Obviously, the impact of the information space is significant and changes people's attitudes towards the environment and shapes environmental thinking. The media is one of the forms of influence on solving global environmental problems, reminding and demonstrating to society its interconnection with nature, the share of anthropogenic activity in the environment, and the fact that it is the individual who can prevent negative consequences that he or she has caused. The main areas of media activity in addressing environmental issues include the following:

- Informing citizens about the problems of today, about possible disasters and about the level of pollution of the biosphere components;
- identifying urgent environmental problems that have a negative impact not only on the environment but also on human health;
- monitoring the state of environmental components;
- formation of citizens' consciousness, independent opinion, involvement in various actions and conferences dedicated to solving environmental problems of mankind;
- providing the public with high-quality, reliable information on the state of the environment;
- involvement of public authorities and citizens in solving environmental problems and finding ways to minimise environmental impact;
- preventing the spread of fakes [5].

The results of the monitoring confirm the media's interest in environmental issues, which is manifested in the support of newsworthy events and coverage of both negative and positive news. The study of the Ukrainian media field (Ukrainian print and online media, TV and radio news blocks, social networks) for the period from 01.01.2019 to 30.06.2021 found that the total number of all publications in the database is about 60 million. The number of sources in the sample was 8760. The media field of social networks (Facebook, Instagram, Telegram, Youtube, Twitter, TikTok) was studied during 01.02.2021–30.06.2021. To create a representative sample, a spontaneous step-by-step non-repeated sample of 5651 publications was formed. The main purpose of the analysis was to identify the mouthpieces, topics, information topics of publications, and international donor institutions that support the implementation of practical environmental projects. Among the newsworthy sources are: state institutions, local authorities, experts, private business, international organisations, CSOs/activists, educational institutions, journalists, landfills (representatives of waste recycling sites) [6].

It was interesting to compare the percentage of publications on environmental issues with other topics in the media. For example, 31% of the information field of Ukraine in 2020–2021 was devoted to the fight against COVID-19, which is significantly higher than all other topics of resonance. A study was also conducted on the topic of cultural space in a broad sense and found that during this period, all publications related to the cultural component accounted for less than 1% of the total media field in Ukraine. Along with the overall increase in the number of publications in the Ukrainian information field, the number of environmental topics is also growing. At the same time, the average frequency and number of publications on environmental issues and the Green Deal for the entire period from 2019 to June 2021 is 2.3% of the media field of Ukrainian media [7].

Google Trends and the Role of Social Media in Shaping the Environmental Outlook of Ukrainian Citizens

Social networks play an important role in spreading environmental issues and shaping the environmental awareness of every citizen. The social network Facebook was the most popular, accounting for 98% of the topics shared. At the same time, Instagram and TikTok accounted for less than 1%, but some of the content may be lost when collecting retrospective data. Youtube accounted for 1% of the media field, i.e. 3125 stories with over 5.6 million views. The first place was taken by the Toronto Television channel in terms of the number of video engagements. According to the data of the PlusOne agency at the time, the social network Facebook stopped growing in Ukraine. In the first half of 2021, the audience remained at the level of 16 million users, decreasing in all major cities of Ukraine and increasing in small towns [6]. This social network was most actively used in Kyiv, Lviv, and Zakarpattia regions. The percentage of use was 58%, 49%, and 45%, respectively. The lowest percentage was in Kharkiv region (35%).

Educational institutions (school and extracurricular), government agencies, local authorities, NGOs, and business representatives were the mouthpieces of news stories on social media that raised the topic of environmental protection. They actively supported the topic of environmental protection. This was evidenced by the analyzed data. One of the most relevant topics, which had a constant steady trend on both Facebook and Google Trends, was waste sorting and waste management. At the same time, it was the main topic of school initiatives: 65% of posts contained information about waste management. In addition to the traditional speakers in this area (NGOs and government institutions), the voice of church communities was unexpectedly clear on the eve of Easter [6].

Study of Cases of Information Environmental Manipulations and Consequences of Environmental Disasters in Ukraine in 2023

As a result of military aggression in Ukraine, significant and, one might say, irreversible obstacles to the fulfillment and exercise of fundamental human and civil rights and freedoms have arisen. In this context, attention should be paid to the mechanism of ensuring the right to free access to environmental information and its dissemination. It is worth noting that this right is guaranteed by the Constitution of Ukraine and is defined in Article 50 of the Basic Law of the country. According to the constitutional provision, everyone is guaranteed the right to free access to information on the state of the environment, the quality of food and household items, as well as the right to disseminate it, and no information may be hidden from public access. Ensuring this right of access to environmental information plays an important role in guaranteeing fundamental human rights in peacetime, in particular, the right to a healthy and safe environment for life and health [7]. It should be noted that in the context of conflict, the realization of the right to access environmental information is an extremely important legal tool that can save lives and preserve human health. Obtaining information in advance about the threat of attack, occupation and other events can help to evacuate the population in time, prevent humanitarian and environmental disasters, and prevent the commission of crimes against humanity, genocide, ecocide and other terrible crimes. In this regard, in the context of military conflict, ensuring high-quality and prompt access to public environmental information is an integral part of the normal functioning of both state and public institutions, as well as the preservation of the environment, which directly affects the quality of life, safety, life and health of people [8]. Today, there are no full-fledged studies on access to environmental information, especially in the context of the war in Ukraine caused by the full-scale invasion that began in February 2022.

Undoubtedly, the conditions of a full-scale invasion and military aggression make it difficult to create effective prerequisites and mechanisms for ensuring free access to environmental information, compared to peacetime. Sometimes, in the occupied territories, this becomes an almost impossible task. In particular, we are talking about:

- Developing opportunities for free access to statistical data, archival materials, library and museum collections, as well as other information resources and databases.
- Informing the public and the media about environmentally important events and decisions made by the authorities.
- Ensuring access to the necessary information for requesters.
- Exercising state and public control over the implementation of legislation on access to information and other aspects [9].

Thus, the right to free access to environmental information is enshrined in Article 50 of the Constitution of Ukraine, and this article is not among those subject to restrictions. This suggests that temporary restrictions on environmental rights, including the right to free access to environmental information, are possible under martial law.

Additionally, the Decree of the President of Ukraine "On the Introduction of Martial Law in Ukraine" of February 24, 2022 No. 64/2022 [10], in paragraph 3, also refers to temporary restrictions on constitutional rights and freedoms of man and citizen provided for in Articles 30–34, 38, 39, 41–44, 53 of the Constitution of Ukraine. However, this list again does not include Article 50 of the Constitution of Ukraine, which means that environmental rights are not subject to temporary restrictions under the law. In view of this, under martial law, the right to free access to information on the state of the environment and the quality of food and household items in general may be limited. However, in our opinion, it is unreasonable to restrict this right in times of war, since timely publication of public environmental information to the public can save lives and health of citizens, as well as prevent or avert other negative consequences for the environment and human life. By the way, the recommendation not to restrict the right of access to environmental information is also mentioned in the explanations of the Ukrainian Parliament Commissioner for Human Rights [9].

Thus, the restrictions set forth in the above provisions of the Decree of the President of Ukraine "On the Introduction of Martial Law in Ukraine" of February 24, 2022, No. 64/2022 [10] may significantly complicate or even prevent citizens from accessing environmental information. However, these restrictions are not aimed at limiting citizens' access to environmental information, but are necessary conditions for martial law in Ukraine due to military aggression.

Despite the war in Ukraine, to date, under martial law, a number of regulations have been developed to ensure free access to environmental information. In particular, this applies to the Law of Ukraine "On Waste Management" adopted on June 20, 2022 [11, 12].

Another guarantee of access to environmental information is the Law of Ukraine "On the National Register of Pollutant Emissions and Transfers" adopted on September 20, 2022, during the war in Ukraine, which will come into force on September 20, 2022 [13], which will enter into force on October 08, 2023.

Additionally, on November 16, 2022, the Verkhovna Rada of Ukraine adopted Resolution No. 2768-IX "On Adopting as a Basis the Draft Law of Ukraine on Amendments to Certain Legislative Acts of Ukraine on the State System of Environmental Monitoring, Information on the State of the Environment (Environmental Information) and Information Support for Environmental Management" [14]. This draft law defines the basic principles for the creation and functioning of the state environmental monitoring system and its subsystems, the national environmental automated information and analytical system for making management decisions and access to environmental information, as well as the interaction of its sectoral components.

The draft law enshrines the principle that the information needs of environmental management are the basis for the formation and functioning of the state environmental monitoring system. In addition, the draft law introduces systemic changes and additions to the resource and environmental legislation of Ukraine, defining terms and provisions on environmental information and mechanisms for ensuring access to it through information legislation [15].

In general, despite the military situation in Ukraine and its consequences, the need to ensure access to environmental information remains relevant. Access to this information is an important guarantee for the realization and protection of citizens' rights to a healthy and safe environment. Despite the restrictions and challenges caused by the military aggression, Ukraine continues to work on improving the mechanisms for ensuring access to environmental information, as it is critical to protecting citizens' environmental rights.

An analysis of the general media field of Ukrainian traditional media shows a decrease in the volume of publications in 2022–2023 [6] compared to the data of 2019, 2020 or 2021 [16]. In general, the EL.B.I. search engine has shown a decrease in publications in the overall media field of Ukrainian media by about 40% between 2021 and 2022. Among the main facts of the reduction of the Ukrainian media field:

- Cessation of publication activities in the occupied territories.
- Closure of publications after the full-scale invasion in February 2022. These are mostly regional publications. A review by the Institute of Mass Information in early 2023 noted more than 200 closed publications.
- A sharp decline in print media in February–March 2022, which did not resume publication or switched from weekly to monthly formats.
- Reduction of news in the pages of narrow-profile publications in the first 3–5 months after the full-scale Russian attack.
- The news in the Unified Telethon broadcasts are duplicated on six TV channels, which is technically a news feed of one channel, not six, as it was before February 2022.

In turn, the top publications with millions of audiences increased the number of news stories during the day, but this did not compensate for the losses due to the above factors. The sharp increase in traffic on such well-known TOP online platforms suggests that Ukrainians paid all their attention to these few resources. For example, in the first quarter of 2022, Ukrainska Pravda became the leader in terms of views with a record average of 136 million views per month. For comparison, a year ago, Censor was the leader with 41.2 million views.

According to the results of the study, for the period from 02/24/2022 to 06/30/2023, about 12–15% of articles in Ukrainian traditional media on environmental topics use the phrase "environmental impact" and/or a similar semantic range. However, it is worth noting that this terminology is most often used in connection with the environmental damage caused by Russia's full-scale attack on Ukraine.

Compared to the list of the TOP platforms that covered the environment in 2019–2021, we can observe a 57% increase in online publications. In addition, website visit statistics show that environmental news resonated on the most visited Ukrainian online platforms. The coverage of environmental news by popular online resources indicates that after the start of Russia's full-scale attack, the range of topics has changed, but environmental problems and environmental crises continue to resonate in the media no less actively than until February 2022. Potentially, this resonance leads to an increase in the number of readers, and thus in audience awareness and, potentially, in the involvement of a wider range of citizens in environmental protection and sustainable development in the future. The active resonance in the pages of well-known publications keeps environmental issues high on the agenda, and to some extent may put pressure on authorities and organizations to take environmental issues seriously in their plans for recovery and reconstruction of Ukraine after the victory. However, the growing sensitivity of environmental threats requires the dissemination of accurate and reliable information.

Recording the impact of Russia's full-scale aggression against Ukraine on the environment and assessing the damage remains one of the priority topics in the Ukrainian media. The full-scale war has shown that the threat to the environment is not limited to any local areas. Emissions of harmful substances affect at least the entire continent. However, this global nature of the problem brings environmental issues in the Ukrainian media to the national level.

The threat of an explosion at the Zaporizhzhia Nuclear Power Plant and the Russian explosion of the Kakhovka Hydroelectric Power Plant set perhaps the greatest precedent for ecocide in the twenty-first century, and therefore should be considered and investigated in the smallest detail. For example, in terms of the impact on the wildlife of Ukraine. The resonance of such materials in the media will only strengthen Ukraine's position in the international arena.

However, it should be borne in mind that in June 2023 alone, about 100,000 publications were found about the Kakhovka HPP. With such a dense media field, it is difficult to convey specific information on the same topic. For example, the discussion of whether to restore the dam received less than 1% of all mentions of the tragedy.

The publication on Censor.net "Archaism vs. modernization. Or why Kakhovka HPP should be restored" received 849 views, while the publication "The explosion of Kakhovka HPP seriously disrupted access to fresh water in the south of Kherson region and the north of Crimea" gathered 3030 views on the same resource. All of this shows that the discourse on restoration, a substantive study of the damage caused to all areas of the environment, will remain the focus of attention only for the professional community. Involving the entire society in the discussion will require an ongoing national communication campaign.

Today, Ukraine is investigating 15 cases that are classified as ecocide under the Criminal Code. Such precedents are virtually non-existent in the international justice system. "Ukraine is the first country to prosecute environmental war crimes and ecocide on such a large scale." In total, more than 200 war crimes against the environment and 15 cases are being investigated, which are classified as ecocide under the Criminal Code of Ukraine. The term "ecocide" is still new in the Ukrainian media field, and so far it resonates in search queries only in the context of the Kakhovka hydroelectric power plant, so additional materials explaining the term and its scientific basis could help raise public awareness.

In the international arena, the term "ecocide" was first used by Swedish Prime Minister Olof Palme at the 1972 UN Environment Conference in Stockholm, where he demanded the adoption of an international law against the mass destruction of ecosystems. Despite the loud call that was made half a century ago, the term "ecocide" is still not officially used in international criminal law. In November, the NGO UAnimals created an international petition on Change.org to the UN and the European Parliament calling for Russia to be punished for environmental crimes during the war. This became one of the information occasions that increased the presence of the term in the media. UAnimals also launched an international information campaign #StopEcocideUkraine with the involvement of celebrities. All of the above messages focus the audience's attention on ecocide as a legal phenomenon that entails liability, but do not disclose the scientific basis that could strengthen the demand for punishment of Russia for the crimes of "ecocide" in Ukraine. In addition, combating ecocide is one of the 10 points of the peace formula proposed by Volodymyr Zelenskyy during the G19 summit in November 2022. The relevance of discussing compensation for environmental damage caused by Russian aggression is only gaining momentum in the Ukrainian media field. That is why it is important to continue and intensify educational work among journalists of socio-political publications on the differences between the terms ecology and environment. Particular attention should be focused on the use of correct terms and concepts to avoid the spread of false and inaccurate information messages.

The constant presence of the term in articles and in statements/publications of professional environmental initiatives and CSOs will help to increase understanding of the serious consequences of environmental violations and increase pressure on the international community to recognize crimes of ecocide and impose new sanctions against Russia. For example, the active dissemination of the initiatives of the NGO UAnimals in the media indicates the important role played by civic activists and independent media in covering the issue of environmental crimes. We also assume that the steady resonance of the term "ecocide" in the media field helps to draw the attention of a wide audience to environmental problems. This is important for shaping public debate and promoting environmentally appropriate decision-making at all levels.

The analysis of Google Trends confirms the assumption that the Ukrainian audience has come into closer contact with the use of the term "ecocide" quite recently—at the time of the Russians' blowing up the Kakhovka hydroelectric dam. The Russians' dam explosion doubled the engagement on social media and influenced the number of views—961 million times the information about the Kakhovka explosion was viewed on Telegram (90%), Youtube (7%) or Tiktok (3%), which is 61% of all views on environmental issues. However, an analysis of social media until June 2023, without the Kakhovka HPP news story, shows that Facebook remains the main social media platform for disseminating information about the environment. Environmental topics resonate in news Telegram channels with a large number of subscribers.

It should be noted that the reach of these resources is many times, or rather hundreds of times, lower than that of news outlets. Therefore, the total audience of all these channels, according to the number of subscribers, reaches 3500–4000 readers. Facebook is still an important social network for maintaining and developing discourse. However, it is worth noting that the network has its limitations in terms of target audience. Recent studies show that the most active audience is the 37+ generation. This should be taken into account when planning communication campaigns. According to the latest Internews research, Facebook has lost ground in news consumption—from 43% in 2021 to 25% in 2022, but 51% of respondents still prefer Facebook for communication. At the same time, 43% of Ukrainians temporarily abroad receive news from Facebook. In 2022, the Ukrainian Facebook audience decreased by 2.05 million [9], according to a study by the PlusOne communication agency. After the drop, Facebook's audience is now 13.7 million users. A decline in social media use was recorded in almost all regions and regional centers, especially in frontline areas and those constantly under Russian fire. Western regions and cities also lost their audience. Today, Facebook is preferred by users aged 32+. The new realities of Ukraine also dictate new technical conditions. Today, for fast and urgent communication, it is worth using channels that require minimal mobile Internet quality: Twitter, messengers, etc.

The Ministry of Culture and Information Policy will insist on expanding the number of Russian TV companies and propagandists in the next EU sanctions packages. As previously reported, the leaders of the European Union agreed on the sixth package of sanctions against the Russian Federation and Belarus, which, among other things, provides for the suspension of broadcasting of three Russian state-owned media: "Russia RTR/RTR Planet, Russia 24/Russia 24, and the International TV Center. The sanctions also apply to the National State Broadcasting Company of the Republic of Belarus, Belteleradiocompany, and JSC Voentelecom, a leading telecommunications service provider of the Russian Ministry of Defense. In Europe, more than 30 countries are already blocking Russian propaganda, including the broadcasting of Russian TV channels. However, after the full-scale invasion, the Chesno civic movement launched a register of traitors, in which it singled out media professionals as a separate category. As of mid-March 2023, the registry includes 89 propagandists, bloggers, and journalists. Some of the media professionals on the Chesno register have been pretending to love Ukraine since the full-scale invasion, but continue to covertly spread hostile narratives.

References

Marushchak A.I. (2007). Information law: Access to information: educational guide. Kyiv: KNT, 532 p.

Tykhomyrov, O.O. (2014). Zabezpechennia informatsiinoi bezpeky yak funktsiia suchasnoi derzhavy: monohrafiia. Ed. By R.A. Kaliuzhnyi. Kyiv: Tsentr navch.-nauk. ta nauk.-prakt. vyd. NA SB Ukrainy, 2014. 196 p. http://bibliofond.ru/view.aspx?id=652263

Aristova, I. V. State information policy and its implementation in the activities of the internal affairs bodies of Ukraine: organizational and legal principles [Text]: Doctor of Laws degree: 12.00.07 / Aristova Iryna Vasylivna. - Kharkiv, 2002. - 476 p.

Grushkevych, T.V. Information and legal support of constitutional environmental rights [Text]: author's dissertation for the degree of Candidate of Law: specialty 12.00.07 "Administrative law and process; financial law; information law" / T. V. Grushkevich. Irpin, 2012. 20 p.

Board of the Ministry of Education and Science of Ukraine. Section 8. Informal environmental education // [Electronic resource]. Date of access: 05/15/2022. Access mode: https://zakon.rada.gov.ua/rada/show/v6-19290-01#Text.

Tender commissioned by the International Renaissance Foundation "Environmental issues in the public information space of Ukraine". Delean-Kokaiko S. Malychkovych O. Access mode: http://cabinet.lbicompany.com.ua/dashboard_climat/.

The Constitution of Ukraine. Bulletin of the Verkhovna Rada of Ukraine. 1996. No. 30. Article 141.

Antoniuk U.V. The right to environmental information in Ukraine under martial law: some aspects / Scientific research in the modern world. Proceedings of the 4th International scientific and practical conference. Editor Komarytskyy M.L. Canada, Toronto: Perfect Publishing. 2023. Pp. 614-617. URL: https://sci-conf.com.ua/wp-content/uploads/2023/02/SCIENTIFIC-RESEARCH-IN-THE-MODERN-WORLD-9-11.02.2023.pdf (accessed February 22, 2023).

Peculiarities of realization of the right to access to public information under martial law: The Ukrainian Parliament Commissioner for Human Rights (explanations prepared with the assistance of the expert on access to information O. Kabanov (NGO "Center for Access to Information"). URL: https://ombudsman.gov.ua/storage/app/media/rozyasnennya-shchodo-doderzhannya-prava-na-dostup-do-informatsii-v-umovakh-voennogo-stanu13042022.docx (accessed February 22, 2023).

On the introduction of martial law in Ukraine: Decree of the President of Ukraine of February 24, 2022 No. 64/2022. URL: https://www.president.gov.ua/documents/642022-41397 (accessed February 22, 2023).

On Waste Management: Law of Ukraine of June 20, 2022 No. 2320-IX. URL: https://zakon.rada.gov.ua/laws/show/2320-20#Text (accessed February 22, 2023).

Romanko S. Is the new law enough to implement the European waste management system in Ukraine? URL: https://dixigroup.org/comment/chi-dostatno-novogo-zakonu-dlya-vprovadzhennya-%D1%94vrope-jsko%D1%97-sistemi-upravlinnya-vidhodami-v-ukra%D1%97ni/ (accessed July 20, 2023).

On the National Register of Pollutant Emissions and Transfers: Law of Ukraine of September 20, 2022 No. 2614-IX. URL: https://zakon.rada.gov.ua/laws/show/2614-20#Text (accessed July 22, 2023).

On Adopting as a Basis the Draft Law of Ukraine on Amendments to Certain Legislative Acts of Ukraine on the State System of Environmental Monitoring,

Information on the State of the Environment (Environmental Information) and Information Support for Environmental Management: Resolution of the Verkhovna Rada of Ukraine of November 16, 2022, No. 2768-IX. URL: https://zakon.rada.gov.ua/laws/show/2768-20#Text (accessed July 25, 2023).

International charitable organization “Environment-Law-Human”: We analyze the activities and inactivity of the authorities even during the war. Ecorevizor. 2022. No. 8. May - July. URL: http://epl.org.ua/eco-analytics/ekorevizor-8-traven-lypen-2022/ (accessed July 27, 2023).

Ukraine's Contribution to Enabling EU's Resilient Green Energy Transition and Sustainability

Leonela Leca

Abstract Although the scenarios of the post-war Europe are still unfolding, there is one certainty—the world plunged into a new energy paradigm, one of the clean energy technologies. The last 2 years reshaped the global energy systems. These tectonic shifts are impacting the energy systems at all levels: from normative to technological; from changing fossil fuels flows to rerouting supply chains and critical raw materials; from expanding oil and gas infrastructure to enhancing the power grid networks, etc. As a response this global transformation toward the green transition and decarbonisation but also with the aim to address the climate change while mitigating the ongoing energy related risks of the Russian war, Ukraine undertook strategic decisions aiming to meet the European Green Deal agenda goals.

The post-war Ukraine, the second largest country in Europe, plays a key role in overcoming and balancing European geographic disparities of the green transformation. As a member of the Energy Community Treaty, and with the opening of European Union (EU) membership negotiations, but also in the context of the recently adopted international climate change targets within COP28, Ukraine has the potential and responsibility to become an important contributor to the regional and European green transition. This paper suggests that the ongoing war and the global energy shift creates momentum for Ukraine to become a regional and European driver of change within the new, multilayered energy security concept with the green agenda at its forefront.

The War and the New Energy Paradigm

The Russian aggression in Ukraine catalyzed the results of the previous crises that led to an unprecedented shift in the global energy systems. Although the war prompted a short-term scramble for oil and gas supply, as a result of this global

L. Leca (✉)
GLOBSEC, Bratislava, Slovakia

Global Studies Center, Lucian Blaga University, Sibiu, Romania

S. Nate (ed.), *Ukraine's Journey to Recovery, Reform and Post-War Reconstruction*, Contributions to Security and Defence Studies,
https://doi.org/10.1007/978-3-031-66434-2_16

energy systems change, the economic models across the globe are being redesigned. From technologies to policies, the change within the energy systems comes not as an option, but as the path to be followed and an opportunity for the visionary ones.

The war, followed by the energy upheaval, has sparked a rethink of how the international actors define and prioritize energy security and climate change. Due to the strategic importance of energy and its interconnected nature at physical, political and trade levels make the interaction between energy security, security and foreign policy inevitable. Russia using energy as a weapon and the repositioning of Europe in a world of great power competition, where climate impacts increasingly hit, has changed energy interests and how they relate to security.[1] To simultaneously address energy security and the climate crisis, the energy transition should be accelerated worldwide. Security, trade, economic and financial vulnerabilities were exposed by the war and made it obvious that we must overcome the fossil fuels paradigm. The present transformation is a clean energy and green transition crisis that is addressing the climate change as well. This shift will set the new economic and industrial models that will in their turn determine the global competition.[2]

Besides speeding up the complex processes of green transition and fighting against climate change, the war triggered the redefinition of the whole energy security concept. The subsequent export restrictions and sanctions, market asymmetries are exposing vulnerabilities to the security of the supply of raw materials critical for industrial production and for the green transition.

Against this backdrop, trade and globalization, driven by liberal concepts are challenged by protectionist measures set to ensure technological supremacy. As countries seek to strengthen their footholds in the emerging clean energy economy, global competition enables a more comprehensive energy security concept with a strong alignment of climate and a focus on industrial strategy.[3]

Within these developments, Ukraine, the second biggest country in Europe, has the opportunity to strengthen its standing as a resilient and reliable partner and become a green energy hub for the EU.

---

[1] Leca, L., Prandin, F., Van Schaik, L., & Cretti, G. (2023, June). *Repower Security: Rethinking European energy relations in times of crisis*. GLOBSEC. https://www.globsec.org/what-we-do/publications/repower-security-rethinking-european-energy-relations-times-crisis.

[2] Leca, L., (2023). *Diplomaţia energetică a UE: intre asigurarea rezilienţei energetice internă si exportul Pactului Ecologic European.* In Constantin-Bercean, I. (2023) *Secolul XXI sub lupa expertelor – Diplomatie, Securitate, Comunicare Strategica, Feminism, Drept si Economie*, (p. 84 – 98), Editura Institutului de Ştiinţe Politice şi Relaţii Internaţionale "Io I. C. Brătianu".

[3] International Energy Agency. (2023). *Overview and key findings – World Energy Investment 2023 – Analysis*. IEA. https://www.iea.org/reports/world-energy-investment-2023/overview-and-key-findings.

From Legislation to Implementation. The New Energy Frameworks

As a response to the ongoing shifts in the energy field, major international actors adopted new normative frameworks in an unprecedented rhythm. Two years after Russia started the full scale war against Ukraine, the implementation of the adopted provisions and approval of the newly established targets in the energy and climate change fields are ongoing on both sides of the Atlantic and beyond.

Across the Atlantic, the United States adopted in 2022 the Inflation Reduction Act (IRA) that promised massive investment by the US government in US-built green infrastructure and industry. The IRA contains $394 billions[4] in tax incentives, grants, and loans, most of which will flow to businesses. The funds will be directed to green investment in sectors like energy, transportation, and manufacturing, all to support US industry.[5] The IRA targets the diversification of supply chains from clean energy manufacturing to critical minerals and electric vehicles batteries. But while the law was born in D.C., the IRA is having a major global impact as it reshapes industry across the country and the world.

From Miami to Mumbai, Boise to Brussels, the IRA has been top of mind for policymakers, business leaders, and civil society. It will not only determine whether the U.S. meets its emissions reduction goals, but also shape the global economy for decades to come.[6] As a response to the IRA, Japan released a draft "Green Transformation Act" in February 2023. The act will see Japanese Government bonds fund $1 trillion in green investments over the next decade. In April 2023, Canada announced clean energy tax credits and sustainable infrastructure investments. France was another country that stimulated French companies developing solar panels, batteries and wind farms by new green tax credits.

In June 2023, the Australian government announced its plans to become a "renewable energy superpower", with a particular focus on renewable hydrogen and a program to track 'country of origin' of green energy to support Australian businesses.[7]

---

[4]McKinsey. (2022). *What's in the Inflation Reduction Act (IRA) of 2022 | McKinsey*. Www.mckinsey.com. https://www.mckinsey.com/industries/public-sector/our-insights/the-inflation-reduction-act-heres-whats-in-it.

[5]Barr, S. (2023, October 13). *Protectionism Is Back – But Not as You Know It: How the US Inflation Reduction Act Is Reshaping the Path to a Green Energy Transition | Wilson Center*. Www.wilsoncenter.org. https://www.wilsoncenter.org/article/protectionism-back-not-you-know-it-how-us-inflation-reduction-act-reshaping-path-green.

[6]Worland, J. (2023, August 11). *How the Inflation Reduction Act Has Reshaped the U.S.—And The World*. Time. https://time.com/6304143/inflation-reduction-act-us-global-impact/.

[7]Barr, S. (2023, October 13). *Protectionism Is Back – But Not as You Know It: How the US Inflation Reduction Act Is Reshaping the Path to a Green Energy Transition | Wilson Center*. Www.wilsoncenter.org. https://www.wilsoncenter.org/article/protectionism-back-not-you-know-it-how-us-inflation-reduction-act-reshaping-path-green.

At the level of the European Union, the Union managed to absorb the main shocks of the war, war that actually had the effect of speeding up the creation of the legislative framework of the green deal and the energy transition. Announced a few weeks after the Russian invasion of Ukraine as a plan to rapidly reduce dependence on Russian fossil fuels and fast forward the green transition, the REPowerEU[8] package is a testament to the EU's determination to seize the critical historical moment to advance dual goals of eliminating its reliance on Russian hydrocarbons while fostering progress towards green targets.

Since December 2019, the European Commission (EC) approved the European Green Deal (EGD)—an economic strategy of the EU aiming to transform Europe into a climate-neutral continent by 2050. The European Green Deal is instrumental in addressing some of the implications of the war in Ukraine. Food security, energy security, industrial supply chains and environmental protection needed to be addressed with due attention to immediate threats, and with a view to speeding up the sustainability transformation in order to avoid exacerbating future disruptions. To simultaneously address energy security and the climate crisis, the energy transition should be accelerated worldwide. This could be done by building strong international partnerships to assist other interested countries in their own energy transitions and support them to become key trading partners of renewable energy sources.[9]

Success in this paramount task requires the transition to a low-carbon circular economy not only within EU borders, but also in neighbouring regions that include the Western Balkan states, Eastern Partnership (EaP) countries and Russia. As stated in EC's communication on the EGD, "the ecological transition for Europe can only be fully effective if the EU's immediate neighbourhood also takes effective action". The EU acknowledges it "can use its influence, expertise and financial resources to mobilise its neighbours and partners to join it on a sustainable path".[10] Extended with consequent set of legislative proposals, the European Green Deal is a package of policies that define Europe's strategy to reach net zero emissions and become a resource-efficient economy by 2050. Policies include measures from cutting greenhouse gas emissions, to investing in cutting-edge research and innovation, to preserving Europe's natural environment. The Green Deal is in fact an economic development program of the European Union that aims to transform Europe into climate-neutral continent by 2050.

Building on the efforts of REPowerEU and European Green Deal, in 2023, the European Commission presented the Green Deal Industrial Plan to enhance the

---

[8]*REPowerEU Plan.* (2022). Europa.eu. https://eur-lex.europa.eu/legal-content/EN/TXT/?uri=COM%3A2022%3A230%3AFIN&qid=1653033742483.

[9]Brozou, M. (2022, October 11). *The European Green Deal and the war in Ukraine: Addressing crises in the short and long term.* ETTG. https://ettg.eu/publications/the-european-green-deal-and-the-war-in-ukraine-addressing-crises-in-the-short-and-long-term/.

[10]Holovko, I. (2021). *Ukraine and the European Green Deal Guiding Principles for Effective Cooperation.* https://eu.boell.org/sites/default/files/2022-02/E-Paper%20Ukraine%20and%20the%20European%20Green%20Deal_barrierefrei.pdf.

competitiveness of Europe's net-zero industry and support the fast transition to climate neutrality. The Plan aims to provide a more supportive environment for the scaling up of the EU's manufacturing capacity for the net-zero technologies and products required to meet Europe's ambitious climate targets. It has two major pillars: *The Critical Raw Materials Act*—focused on new internal set of rules and provisions, as well as new international engagements and *The Net-Zero Industry Act*, which aims to scale up the manufacture of key carbon-neutral technologies for clean energy supply chains. By accelerating the development and production of net-zero technologies, the Act also aims to reduce the risk of replacing our reliance on Russian fossil fuels with other strategic dependencies that might hinder our access to key technologies and components for the green transition.[11]

In addition to the above mentioned international frameworks, recent developments such as the EU's Electricity Market Reform and the shift towards consolidating the electricity grid networks, the newly adopted climate change targets at the United Nations Climate Change Conference (COP28) that signals the "beginning of the end" of the fossil fuel, and formal opening of the EU negotiations with Ukraine are creating an irreversible path for a post-war Ukraine that puts the green agenda as a priority of its economic development.

Future Opportunities Amid Inherited Challenges

Among the Eastern Partnership countries, Ukraine stands out as the biggest eastern neighbour, and at least two particularities of its energy system are of high importance for Ukraine's potential to contribute to the European Green Deal.

- Intensive trade with the EU. In 2019, the share of exports to the EU relative to total exports was 41.5% and amounted to USD 20.75 billion. Through intensive trade, Ukraine exports large amount of its emissions to the EU. Between 16–19% of Ukrainian exports to the EU in 2017–2020 comprise carbon-intensive products such as steel and steel products, chemicals and minerals, which will now become subject to the EU's forthcoming carbon border regulations.
- The country is heavily dependent on fossil fuels and high greenhouse gas emissions. High intensity of economy and high share of heavy industry along with poor modernisation of its industry made Ukraine responsible for 60% of the EaP region's greenhouse gas emissions. Coal has historically been central. Coal use has been falling since 2016, mainly due to Russian military aggression. Gas has also played a key role. The government has sought to reduce dependence on Russian gas, and there have been no direct imports since 2015.

[11] *The Net-Zero Industry Act*. (n.d.). Single-Market-Economy.ec.europa.eu. https://single-market-economy.ec.europa.eu/industry/sustainability/net-zero-industry-act_en.

Both the inherited reliance on fossil fuels, and the intensive trade with the EU create numerous challenges to the prospects of decarbonisation and the new economic and industrial plans of the EU. Still, engaging Eastern European partners and especially Ukraine in the EU's green transformation started long before the war. For well over a decade, Ukraine was engaged in broad collaboration on the climate and energy transition with the EU, its member states, and various international organizations. Before the full-scale Russian invasion in 2022, the country was making slow but steady progress. Signing of Kyoto Protocol in 2004, becoming the member of the Energy Community Treaty in 2011 were the first steps. Following the 2014 Revolution, and spurred on by the EU Association Agreement, successive governments worked to transform one of the most carbon-intensive countries in Europe: energy efficiency increased significantly, renewables gained ground, and new protected areas were added. Ukraine was among the first EU neighbours to announce their readiness to contribute to the European Green Deal.[12] The Ukrainian government announced in July 2020, the country's readiness to contribute to the Green Deal, stressing that "Ukraine sees itself as an integral contributor to the European Green Deal goals".[13]

Prior to the war, Ukraine was able to attract approx. EUR 10 billion in investment in the renewable energy industry. Ukraine ranked 8th out of 140 countries in terms of attractiveness for renewable energy investment. Following the introduction of policy supports in 2009, renewables accounted for 8% of the overall energy balance in electricity generation. In terms of the pace of green energy development, Ukraine was among the top ten economies in the world in 2019 and was in the top five European countries in terms of solar energy development in 2020. In the structure of electricity production before the war, renewable energy accounted for 8% of the overall energy balance. Solar power plants accounted for ca. 58% of renewable energy, wind power plants generated 32%, biomass about 3%, hydroelectric power plants approx. 2%, and biogas close to 5%.[14]

Damage to Ukraine's energy sector during the war is estimated at $12 billion, with more than 50% of Ukraine's power infrastructure damaged in the winter of 2022–2023. Electricity production of all types of generation from January to April 2023 decreased by 32.5% compared to the same period in 2021 due to missile attacks on energy infrastructure and a drop in electricity consumption, according to Ukrenergo, the electricity transmission system operator in Ukraine. Electricity generation increased by 9.7% in the first quarter of 2023 compared to the fourth quarter of 2022.

[12] Holovko, I. (2021). *Ukraine and the European Green Deal Guiding Principles for Effective Cooperation*. https://eu.boell.org/sites/default/files/2022-02/E-Paper%20Ukraine%20and%20the%20European%20Green%20Deal_barrierefrei.pdf.

[13] Idem.

[14] *The role of RES in the post-war reconstruction of Ukraine*. (2023, April 13). ZPP. https://zpp.net.pl/en/the-role-of-res-in-the-post-war-reconstruction-of-ukraine/.

According to UNDP, Ukraine's electrical generation capacity has been reduced to roughly half its pre-war state. Russia has occupied southern Ukraine's Zaporizhzhia Nuclear Power Station, the largest nuclear power plant in Europe, all six reactors have been shut down. Oil refineries have been destroyed and hydropower plants damaged. Most recently, Russian shelling of a thermal power plant near the south-eastern front in early December caused two power units to shut down.[15]

- The country is heavily dependent on fossil fuels and high greenhouse gas emissions. High intensity of economy and high share of heavy industry along with poor modernisation of its industry made Ukraine responsible for 60% of the EaP region's greenhouse gas emissions. Coal has historically been central. Coal use has been falling since 2016, mainly due to Russian military aggression.[16] Gas has also played a key role. The government has sought to reduce dependence on Russian gas, and there have been no direct imports since 2015.

The situation looks particularly grim for thermal power plants, which are fired by coal or gas and are a key element in Ukraine's energy mix to meet demand during peak consumption periods, the experts say.

Although the situation in the power system has been temporarily stabilized it is impossible to recover all of the assets that have been destroyed. As the winter 2023–2024 started, Russia has resumed its attacks, launched on colder days when electrical demand are highest, targeting Ukraine's ability to generate electricity and the infrastructure required to move it. And there are concerns that despite months of preparation, parts of that energy system may be more vulnerable than before.

Reconstruction of Ukraine. The Need to Implement the Leap Forward Vision

During the war, Ukraine became in many cases a show case example for innovative military and energy solutions. Moreover, the war made adjustments to green energy and the green energy transition of Ukraine. The value of renewable energy shifted from ecology to security, and then to economy. Even half a year ago, renewable energy sources were considered by the international community primarily as a tool for combating inevitable climate change and reducing carbon emissions. Today, wind, solar, bio, small hydro and hydrogen energy are key to national energy security and independence and cost significantly less than fossil fuels, although as of 2021, Ukraine's renewable energy sector was fighting for the right to work under fair conditions guaranteed by the state, in 2023 it became one of the foundations of

[15] Idem.

[16] Pirani, S. (2022, December). *Principles for Ukraine's post-war reconstruction in the energy system. Workers and social movements approach.* Commons. https://commons.com.ua/en/principi-povoyennoyi-vidbudovi-energetichnoyi-sistemi-ukrayini/.

the post-war reconstruction of Ukraine and is preparing for the further increase of the country's energy independence.[17]

Despite the fossil fuels having an increased importance once the war unfolded, the dynamics changed and in the long term these energy sources will be overrun by new ones. Conflict, particularly if it goes on for a long time, transforms a society, and a return to the past may not be possible or desirable.[18] Reconstruction does not signify a rebuilding of the socioeconomic framework that existed before the onset of conflict, but enabling new conditions for a functioning society within a secure and economically developing environment. As the reconstruction of Ukraine is supported by a multilateral format consisting of Western countries, the new conditions of the post-war consolidation of Ukrainian energy security will go in parallel with the priorities agreed by the partners, specifically, decarbonisation, green transition and climate goals.

Although the effort that the Ukraine's Government has to undertake is doubled by the mission to operate in emergency mode and risks of disruption while implementing the new ambitions plans, Ukraine's post-war reconstruction must prioritise renewables, for its own energy security and for the European integration process. Ukraine's reconstruction is estimated by Kiev at a cost of $750 billion to rebuild devastated cities and achieve 2032 economic targets. Recent estimate from the World Bank and European Commission place the cost of reconstruction at around $349 billion.[19] If successfully implemented while expanding and developing renewable energy generation, it will also enable greater market integration with the European Union.

Increasing the deployment of renewable power generation in Ukraine will be a strategically important step in the reconstruction of the country. While Ukraine has a high level of energy independence due to its nuclear generation capacity, expanding renewable energy will enable the country to reduce exposure to imports from Russia and Belarus. Additionally, increasing renewable and export capacity will further Ukraine's economic and security integration with the European Union and constrain Russia's ability to use energy as a weapon in war. Establishing a solid policy basis for renewable deployment and investment should be a key focus for Ukraine's reconstruction and energy future.

In 2021, Ukrainian Government set a goal to source increase up to 25% of its total energy mix from renewables by 2035—an ambitious target that would depend on sizable investments in wind and solar. The war has and will continue to motivate further action in renewable deployment as energy independence from Russia while

[17] Zvarych, R., & Masna, O. (2023). Green energy transition in the concept of post-war reconstruction of Ukraine. *Herald of Economics*, *0*(3), 170–181. https://doi.org/10.35774/visnyk2023.03.170.

[18] Holtzman, S., Elwan, A., & Scott, C. (1998). *Post Conflict Reconstruction*. https://doi.org/10.1596/0-8213-4215-0.

[19] Majkut, J., & Dawes, A. (2022, October 18). *Ukraine's post-war reconstruction must prioritise Renewables, for energy security and European integration*. Energy Post. https://energypost.eu/ukraines-post-war-reconstruction-must-prioritise-renewables-for-energy-security-and-european-integration/.

Ukraine's grid integration with the European Union has become critical to national security.

The government of Ukraine pledges for "building a new country" promising to introduce green technologies and make Ukraine a successful example of "green transition". These ambitions were presented initially at the international donor conference in Lugano in 2022 and continued at the Ukraine Recovery Conference in London in June 2023. Securing Ukraine's long-term economic future, including helping Ukraine "build back better", as a more resilient, greener, and more prosperous European nation were among the commitments undertaken in 2023 conference.

The principles of "build back better" and "build back greener" with an emphasis on renewable energy sources and energy-efficient technologies are the approach to the green recovery of the energy sector the Ukrainian government has already announced in early 2023. In April 2023, the Government of Ukraine has approved the National Energy Strategy of Ukraine. One of the goals of the Strategy is the pursuit of green transition and decentralization and further harmonisation with the EU. The Strategy also focuses on the development of nuclear and renewable power generation capacity and on the modernisation and automatisation of transmission and distribution systems, in order to achieve carbon neutrality in the energy sector by 2050.[20]

A positive development in Ukraine's energy sector is joining in December 2023 the European network of electricity transmission system operators (ENTSO-E). The ambition of integration with the European internal electricity market was in the Strategy launched this year and follows the recent completion of synchronization of Ukraine's electricity networks with the Continental European Network.

All the above stated bold plans and actions are part of the Governments leap forward vision and are important steps that are able to modernise Ukrainian's economy. Of course, as the war continues, the future scenarios are still unfolding, many factors are important for the success of the ambitious plans. Political resilience, cross-sectoral approach, consequence of policies, transparency and an optimized use of funds are only some of the requirements to be met. In terms of technical capabilities, the positive development is that despite the massive destruction of the war, Ukraine proved to an important extent its energy resilience and innovative character. Even during the harsh conditions, the country was able to adapt to the new environment, maintain its path of integration with the European internal market and even resume electricity exports to the EU after being halted for 6 months by the Russian attacks.

[20] *Ukraine's government approves the Energy Strategy of Ukraine until 2050 | Enerdata*. (2023, May 3). Www.enerdata.net. https://www.enerdata.net/publications/daily-energy-news/ukraines-government-approves-energy-strategy-ukraine-until-2050.html.

Ukraine's Role in the EU's Green Transition and Sustainability

As presented in the previous sections, the context, although burdened by the uncertainty of the war, creates the prerequisites of a major advancement of the Ukraine's energy system and economy. Ukraine's contribution to the EU's plans of decarbonisation and green transition could become a game changer of the future energy systems of the region and of the EU.

Despite the fossil fuels inertia, the deployment of renewables is happening at the global level at much higher speed than expected. A green reconstruction provides a chance to turn challenges into opportunities for building back better, particularly by adopting and effectively implementing new green practices, which have been already codified into international standards. Ukraine needs to immediately synchronize its priorities taking into consideration the country's potential. The following arguments are in favor of committing Ukraine to it's role of significant potential contributor to the EU's green transition and resilience.

First, as the green transition and climate change agenda are more and more interrelated, especially in the context of the war in Ukraine, a EU green transition without Ukraine is not a realistic ambition. A highly dependent on coal, second in size European country, with a high trade volume with the EU and obsolete economic and industrial models presents many vulnerabilities and challenges to the future EU Energy Security and climate agenda.

Second. Ukraine's hydrogen potential. The ongoing initiatives such as the one on the joint work on the production, trade, transportation, storage and use of renewable gases, including hydrogen and biomethane (February 2023) are key to the future consolidation of Ukraine's energy potential.

Third, the regional impact. Such a big country that has land borders with four EU countries, is important geographically for the existing and future interconnection projects. The Central and Eastern Europe region is still registering a gap between the level of interconnectors, especially when it comes to power grid interconnections. On a regional level, as the EU is committed to building one of its three planned import hydrogen corridors from Ukraine (the others being from the Mediterranean and the North Sea), it will trigger the cross-border infrastructure framework issues and will boost the modernisation of the region. A hydrogen market will facilitate not only the decarbonisation of Ukraine's energy sector and economy but will impact the overall region as well. Moreover, Ukraine's role in the EU's Green Deal policies support greater regional cooperation on renewables, in particular with neighbouring EU member states and will impact the non EU countries such as Republic of Moldova. This will allow to balance the regional disparities between EU and non-EU countries, as new infrastructure and energy projects will be developed.

Fourth, Ukraine has vast potential in terms of renewable energy. In view of their high untapped potential in the country, bioenergy, hydro, solar and wind generation could constitute the building blocks of Ukraine's future energy system, contributing up to nearly 80% of total energy generation by 2050. Provided key strategies and investments are put in place, and complemented by nuclear, renewables could propel Ukraine towards a carbon-neutral future.[21] The deployment of renewables will allow a more decentralized model of energy system. Such a system is more difficult to destroy and damage than to disable a single thermal power plant or nuclear power plant.

Additionally, the critical raw materials potential is strategically important for the functioning of the EU economy. The deposits of the raw materials listed by the EU as critical[22] on the territory of the EU are not sufficient to meet the EU's needs. Ukraine is among the top ten countries with the largest deposits of this critical raw material and a significant global supplier of titanium that can become a potential supplier of more than 20 elements from the list of critical raw materials to the EU.[23]

The innovative and technological capabilities of Ukraine will allow to jointly develop economies of scale as needed to roll out innovative technologies to decarbonize the energy sectors and the economies in Ukraine and EU.

Finally, the post-war reconstruction and the ongoing EU and Eastern Partnership policies are offering tools and financial mechanisms that can enable a visionary economic model for Ukraine.

Conclusions

Despite skepticism, critics and even reluctance of several states and private actors, the energy global systems entered a new era. Green energy ambitions and the climate change targets moved forward on the global agenda, even if the later at a lower speed. Nevertheless, the fact that COP 29 is to be held in Azerbaijan, a historic fossil fuels producer is not just a random location but a clear message to the international community. New normative frameworks that are enabling clean energy were already adopted across the globe and set the basis for near future new economic models and types of interaction between the states.

Even while recognizing the maintaining role that some classic fuels such as gas will be still having in the following decade, the world is entering a new paradigm in which the economy and competition of the countries is shaped by their green ambitions. Clean technologies will find a way to penetrate the traditional energy systems even in the countries that are heavily dependent on fossil fuels, as new

[21] *Renewables could power almost 80% of Ukraine's economy by 2050, says UN report | UNECE.* (n.d.). Unece.org. Retrieved December 22, 2023, from https://unece.org/sustainable-development/press/renewables-could-power-almost-80-ukraines-economy-2050-says-un-report.

[22] *Press corner.* (n.d.). European Commission - European Commission. https://ec.europa.eu/commission/presscorner/detail/en/ip_23_1661.

[23] *What are "critical raw materials", and what does Ukraine have to do with them?* (2023, April 17). Better Regulation Delivery Office. https://brdo.com.ua/en/news/chomu-krytychna-syrovyna-ye-takoyu-naspravdi-ta-do-chogo-tut-ukrayina/.

business models are created. The global dynamic of the past years clearly indicates that we are already in the phase of the implementation of the energy transition.

The next years will be shaped by an increased share and improved technologies in the field of renewable energy, hydrogen, and other clean technologies. New partnerships for securing critical raw materials and supply chains will be shaped. In any of the above mentioned fields Ukraine has a consistent potential.

The war, with its massive destruction and ongoing threats and damages on one hand, and on the other hand the already enabled and enhanced processes of the EU integration, leaves Ukraine with only one option to demonstrate a leap forward vision—using the momentum to set the basis for a new economic and industrial model. Increased renewable potential, hydrogen perspectives, nuclear capabilities, critical raw materials potential, along with high level of trade and already integrated with the EU energy networks, combined with international financial, technical and human resources capabilities provided by the reconstruction plans, offer Ukraine a unique momentum—to become a green energy provider and a driver that will balance the discrepancies between Central and Eastern Europe and Western Europe in terms of green transition and sustainability.

References

Barr, S. (2023, October 13). Protectionism is back – But not as you know it: How the US inflation reduction act is reshaping the path to a green energy transition | Wilson Center. *Www.wilsoncenter.org*. https://www.wilsoncenter.org/article/protectionism-back-not-you-know-it-how-us-inflation-reduction-act-reshaping-path-green

Brozou, M. (2022, October 11). The European Green Deal and the war in Ukraine: Addressing crises in the short and long term. *ETTG*. https://ettg.eu/publications/the-european-green-deal-and-the-war-in-ukraine-addressing-crises-in-the-short-and-long-term/

Collins, L. (2022, November 14). US and Ukraine to build nuclear hydrogen pilot project in war-torn country to help improve food security. *Hydrogen News and Intelligence | Hydrogen Insight*. https://www.hydrogeninsight.com/production/us-and-ukraine-to-build-nuclear-hydrogen-pilot-project-in-war-torn-country-to-help-improve-food-security/2-1-1353715

dhojnacki (2023, December 8). Ukraine in the EU would be a game-changer for Europe's decarbonization drive. *Atlantic Council*. https://www.atlanticcouncil.org/blogs/new-atlanticist/ukraine-in-the-eu-would-be-a-game-changer-for-europes-decarbonization-drive/

Holovko, I. (2021). *Ukraine and the European Green Deal guiding principles for effective cooperation*. https://eu.boell.org/sites/default/files/2022-02/E-Paper%20Ukraine%20and%20the%20European%20Green%20Deal_barrierefrei.pdf

Holtzman, S., Elwan, A., & Scott, C. (1998). Post conflict reconstruction. https://doi.org/10.1596/0-8213-4215-0

International Energy Agency. (2023). Overview and key findings – World Energy Investment 2023 – Analysis. *IEA*. https://www.iea.org/reports/world-energy-investment-2023/overview-and-key-findings

Leca, L. (2023). *Diplomația energetică a UE: intre asigurarea rezilienței energetice internă si exportul Pactului Ecologic European*. In I. Constantin-Bercean (Ed.), *Secolul XXI sub lupa expertelor – Diplomatie, Securitate, Comunicare Strategica, Feminism, Drept si Economie* (pp. 84–98). Editura Institutului de Științe Politice și Relații Internaționale "Io I. C. Brătianu".

Leca, L., Prandin, F., Van Schaik, L., & Cretti, G. (2023, June). Repower security: Rethinking European energy relations in times of crisis. *GLOBSEC*. https://www.globsec.org/what-we-do/publications/repower-security-rethinking-european-energy-relations-times-crisis

Majkut, J., & Dawes, A. (2022, October 18). Ukraine's post-war reconstruction must prioritise Renewables, for energy security and European integration. *Energy Post*. https://energypost.eu/ukraines-post-war-reconstruction-must-prioritise-renewables-for-energy-security-and-european-integration/

McKinsey. (2022). What's in the Inflation Reduction Act (IRA) of 2022 | McKinsey. *Www.mckinsey.com*. https://www.mckinsey.com/industries/public-sector/our-insights/the-inflation-reduction-act-heres-whats-in-it

Pirani, S. (2022, December). Principles for Ukraine's post-war reconstruction in the energy system. Workers and social movements approach. *Commons*. https://commons.com.ua/en/principi-povoyennoyi-vidbudovi-energetichnoyi-sistemi-ukrayini/

Press corner. (n.d.). European Commission - European Commission. https://ec.europa.eu/commission/presscorner/detail/en/ip_23_1661

Renewables could power almost 80% of Ukraine's economy by 2050, says UN report | UNECE. (n.d.). Unece.org. Retrieved December 22, 2023, from https://unece.org/sustainable-development/press/renewables-could-power-almost-80-ukraines-economy-2050-says-un-report

REPowerEU Plan. (2022). Europa.eu. https://eur-lex.europa.eu/legal-content/EN/TXT/?uri=COM%3A2022%3A230%3AFIN&qid=1653033742483

Rott, N., Harbage, C., & Palamarenko, H. (2023, December 13). Ukraine is trying to keep its lights on this winter. Russia aims to turn them off. *NPR*. https://www.npr.org/2023/12/13/1215994869/ukraine-energy-russia-attacks-winter

Samus, Y. (2023, June 20). UNDP energy damage assessment for Ukraine reveals continued vulnerabilities | United Nations in Ukraine. *Ukraine.un.org*. https://ukraine.un.org/en/237345-undp-energy-damage-assessment-ukraine-reveals-continued-vulnerabilities

The Net-Zero Industry Act. (n.d.). Single-Market-Economy.ec.europa.eu. https://single-market-economy.ec.europa.eu/industry/sustainability/net-zero-industry-act_en

The role of RES in the post-war reconstruction of Ukraine. (2023, April 13). ZPP. https://zpp.net.pl/en/the-role-of-res-in-the-post-war-reconstruction-of-ukraine/

Ukraine's government approves the Energy Strategy of Ukraine until 2050 | Enerdata. (2023, May 3). Www.enerdata.net. https://www.enerdata.net/publications/daily-energy-news/ukraines-government-approves-energy-strategy-ukraine-until-2050.html

What are "critical raw materials", and what does Ukraine have to do with them? (2023, April 17). Better Regulation Delivery Office. https://brdo.com.ua/en/news/chomu-krytychna-syrovyna-ye-takoyu-naspravdi-ta-do-chogo-tut-ukrayina/

Worland, J. (2023, August 11). How the inflation reduction act has reshaped the U.S.—And the world. *Time*. https://time.com/6304143/inflation-reduction-act-us-global-impact/

Zvarych, R., & Masna, O. (2023). Green energy transition in the concept of post-war reconstruction of Ukraine. *Herald of Economics, 0*(3), 170–181. https://doi.org/10.35774/visnyk2023.03.170

Reforming Intelligence in Ukraine: The Past, Present, and Future

Irena Chiru, Cristina Ivan, and Silviu Paicu

Abstract This chapter looks at the evolution of institutional frameworks and processes related to intelligence in Ukraine. By using the methodology provided to reform intelligence in new democracies, it analyzes the institutional changes within the intelligence services and the initiatives aiming to enforce coordination, improve professionalism, transparency, and trust—as crucial norms for intelligence under democracy. Within this comprehensive framework, it aims to investigate the mechanisms in place to ensure that intelligence services conduct intelligence activities in a manner that achieves the proper balance between the acquisition of essential information and protection of individual interests (intelligence governance and oversight). Last but not least, the most recent reconfigurations of "open secrets" and public intelligence inbuilding trust and obtaining strategic advantage are discussed in the light of the war in Ukraine.

After Three Decades: Intelligence Reform in Ukraine

Intelligence reform is one the most thorny topics when discussing the role and function of intelligence in relation to governance as it puts in a most elucidatory light the ingrained tension and equal need for balance between secrecy on one hand and democratic effectiveness, transparency, and accountability on the other. Accordingly, the existing literature states that maintaining agencies dedicated to protecting national security through the gathering and analysis of intelligence in the midst of a

I. Chiru (✉) · S. Paicu
Intelligence and Security Doctoral School, Mihai Viteazul National Intelligence Academy, Bucharest, Romania
e-mail: chiru.irena@animv.eu; paicu.silviu@animv.eu

C. Ivan
National Institute for Intelligence Studies, Mihai Viteazul National Intelligence Academy, Bucharest, Romania
e-mail: ivan.cristina@animv.eu

S. Nate (ed.), *Ukraine's Journey to Recovery, Reform and Post-War Reconstruction*, Contributions to Security and Defence Studies,
https://doi.org/10.1007/978-3-031-66434-2_17

generally open political culture is a challenge for any democracy (Boraz & Bruneau, 2006). In particular the discussion about intelligence reform in new or emergent democracies is of high relevance because: (1) it illustrates the attempt of transforming intelligence bureaucracies that previously served undemocratic regimes, and, consequently, (2) can be used as a benchmark for measuring the level of democratization and maturation of intelligence practices in line with the principles of democratic governance. From this perspective, for an informed debate about the post-war reconstruction of Ukraine, which will probably be the largest post-conflict rebuilding effort after World War Two, a look at the status quo of intelligence agencies, processes and legal frameworks is needed.

Intelligence reform is meant to improve the efficiency of the intelligence community in particular historical contexts (e.g. transition from totalitarianism, post conflict recovery), to provide adequate responses to specific intelligence failures (e.g. 9/11 2001) or to calibrate intelligence community requirements and structure (e.g. Post Cold War). In a nutshell, it aims to improve processes and apply corrections to misconducts and abuses. When is comes to new democracies, such as Ukraine along with all the other former Soviet Union countries, intelligence reform involves an integrated evaluation of four main pillars (O'Connell, 2004; Warner, 2009): (1) organisational—the number and structure of agencies, the quality of their internal communications, qualities of staff and managers and protective security; (2) resources—law, budget, buildings and technological equipment; (3) processes of collecting information and developing intelligence including any resulting action; (4) relationships—with other agencies, foreign and domestic, with consumers of their product, policy-makers, overseers and citizens. Obviously, such an evaluation is highly dependent on data which is most frequently scarce in new democracies by comparison to "old" ones. This is to be mentioned as a transversal limit in conducting such applied research that must be provided not just with direct observation-driven data (intelligence usually being an epistemological object not subjected to direct observation). In addition, the characteristics of the previous nondemocratic regimes and the cultural variables invisibly impacting intelligence practices and the transition paths towards consolidated democracies brings additional but meaningful analytic layers.

The intelligence community of Ukraine is composed of three intelligence agencies: the Security Service of Ukraine (*Sluzhba Bezpeky Ukrainy*—SBU), the Main Intelligence Directorate of the Ministry of Defense (*Golovne Upravlinnia Rozvidky*—GUR), and the Foreign Intelligence Service of Ukraine (*Sluzhba Zovnishnioyi Rozvidky*—SZR), considered to be "a political intelligence branch of the SBU" (Fluri & Polyakov, 2021), which was separated from the latter in 2005. The three services have followed different paths towards reform and this differentiation can be attributed to the roles they play at a societal and political level.

For example, when officially created in March 1992, SBU was conceived as an unique intelligence task force, entrusted with multiple responsibilities in both intelligence and counterintelligence, protection of statehood and counter-terrorism activities, military counterintelligence, fighting corruption and organised crime, government communications and special interventions. Since then, the service has been subjected to several calls for improving coordination, professionalism, transparency, and trust. One of the most systematic critiques was directed against the overlapping roles of SBU having both law enforcement and intelligence missions—e.g. in 2021 SBU was characterized as "a sprawling agency whose operations now extend beyond its nominal counterintelligence mandate" (Atlantic Council, 2021). In the public eye, SBU has constantly been characterized as *successful* in avoiding serious reform for decades, while remaining a huge agency with more than 35,000 staff, "close to the size of the US Federal Bureau of Investigation and eight times as big as MI5" (Galeotti, 2022).

When compared to SBU, GUR and SZR have not been so much in the public critical light. For example, GUR enjoys a better reputation among foreign partners, being considered "Ukraine's lead intelligence agency in prosecuting the war" and known for its deliberate effort to refashion itself for the times and circumstances, which includes an active social media profile and online footprint (London, 2022). This relatively positive and unchallenged profile can most probably be attributed to its very constitution being created from scratch once Ukraine became independent from the USSR, which allowed a clear mandate. However, the favorable public profile must not exclude a look at some aspects that were identified as problematic by reference to a democratic framework regulating intelligence—e.g. GUR's statutory position of serving three entities—the Minister of Defense and the general Commander-in-Chief of the Armed Forces and the President as the Supreme Commander-in-Chief of the Armed Forces (Fluri & Polyakov, 2021). Similarly, due to its clear mandate—a foreign intelligence service protecting Ukraine's interests by collecting, analyzing and disseminating intelligence from abroad, SZR has been perceived as less tributary to the Soviet legacy. More recently, in the context of the 2022 accusations against Ukrainian national security leadership, the systematic critique against the security sector in Ukraine included SZR and blamed it for its undue raising of its personnel to numbers exceeding the personnel of other well known intelligence services as the Canadian Security Intelligence Service or Secret Intelligence Service (Fitsanakis, 2022).

The reforming initiatives of intelligence in Ukraine have been part of larger projects aimed at reforming the entire security sector via NATO and EU reforming bodies or under the Geneva Center for Security Sector Governance (DCAF). For example, EUAM Ukraine was established in 2014 as an EU mission with the aim of assisting relevant Ukrainian authorities—including security services towards a sustainable reform of the civilian security sector through strategic advice and practical support for specific reform measures based on EU standards and international principles of good governance and human rights. Starting with 2016, NATO provided supportive measures through the *Comprehensive Assistance Package* which is designed to support Ukraine's ability to provide for its own security and to implement wide-ranging reforms, based on democratic principles and best practices, aimed at strengthening its capacity and resilience or countering hybrid threats (*Relations with Ukraine*, 2023). Last but not least, the various and systematic initiatives of DCAF are worth mentioning to the benefit of the topic: e.g. the 2006 *Perspectives on Ukrainian Security Sector Reform* reinforcing the need for a responsible, democratically accountable community of enforcement structures or the 2018 *Supporting Ukraine's Security Sector Reform: Mapping Security Sector Assistance Programmes* seeking to provide a comprehensive and up to date picture of all international security sector reform projects focusing on Ukraine. These illustrate both the steps taken and the hindrances in implementing a sustainable model for the intelligence sector which should not just ensure a clear division of intelligence and counterintelligence activities, while depriving counterintelligence of law enforcement powers.

One of the milestones is the adoption of Ukraine's new Law on National Security (2018), a law consistent with Western principles also providing a framework for increasing the Ukrainian Armed Forces' NATO interoperability. Also, in 2020 as part of the efforts to reform the law enforcement agencies, bring them into conformity with NATO and EU standards, and leave behind Soviet and post-Soviet legacies, the new law on Intelligence of Ukraine entered into force. The law provides the framework for the democratic alignment of intelligence processes performed by three main bodies defined as legitimate intelligence agencies: The Foreign Intelligence Service, The Main Intelligence Directorate of the Ministry of Defense, and The Intelligence Agency of the State Border Guard Service. Notably, the Security Service of Ukraine is not acknowledged as an intelligence agency, but as a member of the intelligence community that may conduct counterintelligence activities, but only after obtaining a special court order proving the necessity of such activities for the benefit of counterintelligence tasks (Ukraine: New Law on Intelligence Enters into Force, 2020).

Democratic Oversight of Intelligence Services in Ukraine

The existence of a normative tension between the culture of secrecy which defines the craft of intelligence and the core values of modern democracy has been acknowledged by the intelligence scholarship even since its inception as a research discipline. According to Mark Phythian, the academic study of intelligence as such, 'arose to a large extent in response to concerns about the operation of intelligence in a democratic polity' (2019, p. 502). The systematic examination of intelligence oversight, accountability and control has emerged as an important dimension of this intellectual framework. Intelligence oversight has gradually become almost a general feature of old and new democracies everywhere and "the idea of Parliament itself providing the core of oversight structures, if not the only one, is more or less universal" (Gill & Phythian, 2006, p. 158). Reflecting this tendency, the scholarship on intelligence oversight has expanded its focus beyond the Anglosphere to include democracies around the world (e.g. Born & Caparini, 2007; Gill, 2016; Goldman & Rascoff, 2016; Leigh & Wegge, 2019).

Parliamentary or legislative intelligence oversight is a standard practice for democracies and carries considerable symbolic weight. Parliaments oversee intelligence services via specialized or non-specialized parliamentary committees, being responsible for enacting intelligence legislation and for approving intelligence agencies' budgets. Given that intelligence agencies are large governmental bureaucracies operating mostly under a veil of secrecy, managing and controlling them is especially difficult (Caparini 2016, p. 17). Democratic oversight of intelligence has therefore emerged as a solution within the logic of checks and balances, to control the often-unchecked power derived from secrecy. Thus, oversight of intelligence encompasses a contest over power (Omand & Phythian, 2018, p. 215). While intelligence services exist in both democracies and non-democracies alike, intelligence oversight is associated with democratic systems only. The difference, therefore, resides in the objective of intelligence oversight: enhancing the power for its holders in a non-democratic system as opposed to distributing the power to publicly accountable bodies in government for more transparency, in a democracy (Nolan, 2010). For example, in Ukraine, the SBU has often been viewed as an instrument of power for the president. As Gressel observed, "due to its wide array of competences and direct subordination to the president, the SBU can act as a weapon well suited to political wars and personal enrichment" (2019, p. 1).

In Ukraine, one could observe some formal attempts to establish parliamentary oversight of the intelligence services. Under the Law No. 912-IX on Intelligence of Ukraine, which had entered into force on 17 September 2020, the president of Ukraine is granted with the power of "general oversight of intelligence agencies" (art.11). Although stipulated in the new law, the principle of subordination of intelligence agencies to parliamentary oversight has been overshadowed in practice by the reference, within the same law, to subordination of intelligence services to presidential control (Fluri & Polyakov, 2021). The same law foresees the creation of a special parliamentary committee with intelligence oversight attributions over SBU and SZR. The Deputy Head of the European Union Advisory Mission to Ukraine astutely observed the terminological ambiguity in Ukraine's legislation on the use of "control" and "oversight", two distinct concepts that are often employed interchangeably (Wesslau, 2021). Although it has an important role in ensuring the accountability of intelligence activities, the mechanism of executive and internal control does not qualify, technically speaking, as a component of an oversight system. Hence, the presidential control over the intelligence community is not enough for achieving effective democratic oversight of intelligence services in Ukraine. In this context, the establishment of a credible and effective parliamentary oversight becomes a crucial goal in the attempt to successfully reform the Ukrainian security sector. Although foreseen in a series of laws, such as the 2018 Law on National Security, the 2020 Law on Intelligence and in the 2021 Draft Law on SBU, a special parliamentary committee dealing exclusively with intelligence matters is yet to be created. The parliamentary body responsible for the oversight of the secret services of Ukraine remains the Committee on National Security, Defence and Intelligence comprising five sub-committees, one of them dedicated to intelligence issues.

SBU as the "Rogue Elephant" That Needs to be Contained

Another attempt to consolidate the parliamentary intelligence oversight in Ukraine is the adoption in the first reading by the Parliament of the Draft Law 3196-D "On the Security Service of Ukraine" in January 2021, a bill addressing the reform of SBU. Among other provisions, the reform bill aims to regulate the issue of parliamentary oversight for SBU, stipulating the obligation of the SBU's head to report to the Parliament four times a year. In Ukraine, establishing robust parliamentary oversight is particularly important to contain the extensive power of SBU, an agency that could match the image of a "rogue elephant" (Born & Caparini, 2007). Frequently used in the specific literature, the analogy describes a secret service that is acting without restraint in the use of its authority, sometimes abusing citizens' civil rights and liberties and damaging the relationship of trust between the public and the intelligence community. The Draft Law on SBU has been under constant review, suffering multiple revisions since its initial form, mainly due to criticism coming from civil society organizations such as Human Rights Watch. They criticized the Draft provisions granting SBU wide surveillance and detention powers and pointed out the lack of safeguards for the protection of individual rights like freedom of speech and privacy (Human Rights Watch, 2021).

Improving Intelligence Oversight in Ukraine: Possible Answers

Oversight practices together with oversight innovation represent the dynamic core of democratic governance of intelligence. Specifically, in the context of rapidly evolving collection technologies deployed by security and intelligence agencies, oversight practices can come up with solutions for a more effective containment of intelligence agencies through the innovative use of technology. As Wetzling and Vieth (2018) put it,

> a court will not design new rules or prescribe specific accountability mechanisms. This is the difficult and necessary work of democratic governance, and it needs to be done by the principled members of the different oversight bodies that understand the critical importance of their work (p. 10).

In the case of Ukraine, a frequently invoked argument against parliamentary oversight of intelligence is the legislators' lack of expertise and adequate understanding of this exceptional field of government (Fluri & Polyakov, 2021). A potential solution to address this issue would be the creation of an external expert oversight body complementing the activity of parliamentary scrutiny. The creation of a permanent expert oversight body was also proposed in 2021 by the Secretary of the Parliamentary Committee on National Security, Defence, and Intelligence, the Ukrainian MP Roman Kostenko, who offered as a potential model the Norwegian experience in this field.

The Norwegian standing committee for the overseeing of the secret services-EOS Committee is a permanent and independent expert body, whose members are elected by the Parliament on the basis of their political and professional background-5 members, and their judicial and technological expertise-2 members (EOS Committee, 2022). However, its activity and work are separated from the Norwegian Parliament, and its members cannot act simultaneously as MPs. Thus, such an oversight body would have distinct functions from the Ukrainian parliamentary committee in charge of intelligence agencies. Because the degree of access to classified information is a central element in the process of intelligence accountability, members of such an expert oversight body would need a high-level security clearance. The access to classified information and reliance on experts combined with the possibility to engage with civil society, would place it in an optimal position for increasing the Ukrainian public trust in the intelligence services. In this sense, expert oversight bodies are "ideally placed to provide credible and reliable information and to educate the public about the activities and role of intelligence services" (Fundamental Rights Agency [FRA], 2017, p. 87). An effective intelligence oversight system could enhance Ukrainian citizens' trust and understanding of the agencies' practices and can also educate the public about the activities and role of the intelligence community. In other words, a credible oversight body engaging with civil society organizations like NAKO in Ukraine and other watchdogs such as media, academia and whistle-blowers, can act as a liaison between the intelligence community and the community of citizens.

Because of the vast power the practice of secrecy generates, oversight of intelligence services is unique in its modus operandi, with no equivalent among other types of oversight to be found in the workings of a democratic polity. Moreover, the oversight of intelligence is exceptional because it affects key dimensions such as separation of powers and national security and so the contest over power involved by oversight has significant implications for a young democracy like Ukraine. The ongoing war with Russia and the multiple threats to Ukraine's internal and external security make the continuation of the SBU reform a complicated task, slowing down any significant progress in this field (Soldatiuk-Westerveld et al., 2023). However, in the post-war context, the leadership of Ukraine will have to resume and even restart in some respects the process of building an effective oversight system. The parliamentary component of intelligence oversight can be improved through the establishment of a specialized committee and through a clearer delineation of its area of authority over intelligence services, as separate from the realm of presidential control. Moreover, the creation of an independent expert oversight body, also acting as a liaison between the intelligence community and civil society, would be beneficial to Ukrainian democracy. Intelligence oversight can be seen as a critical component not only for the architecture of a democratic state, but also for its national security, and while "getting [intelligence oversight] right is hard [. . .], getting it wrong is dangerous" (Zegart, 2011, p. 5).

Ukrainian Intelligence Communication in the "Open Secrets" Paradigm

In the days and months prior to and following the Russian invasion, similar to its allies (the US and UK), Ukraine used intelligence assessments communicated to European allied countries and the general public to forewarn on the invasion, thus enhancing awareness and support to diplomatic and political actions aimed to mitigate the crisis. The success of these measures was undoubtedly proven by the way skepticism was reduced among political stakeholders across Europe and support enhanced, public solidarity also acting as a leverage for shared action.

Deterrence on the other hand, an expected outcome of intelligence going public, was one of the effects that never materialized. What intelligence led strategic communication did however manage to obtain was an effective steering of the public communication agenda away from the narratives generated and multiplied by the Russian propaganda and disinformation machine. Public dissemination of strategic intelligence assessments has since become rule of thumb and are disseminated daily by social media channels of the intelligence communities (Dylan & Maguire, 2022). Nevertheless,

> public disclosure of intelligence involves significant risk to sources and methods. Sometimes the sources are based on technology, and publishing the information attained through them could lead to their discovery and removal, and later also to closure of the technological gap between the disclosure and the disclosed. Sometimes they are human sources with access to limited decision-making circles, so that exposing pieces of information based on their reports could easily lead to their discovery, and of course harm to their personal security. A reputation of revealing information and endangering sources can even lead to difficulty recruiting human sources in the future. (Riemer, 2022)

Such limitations make dissemination of intelligence-led strategic communication a difficult task, one that needs to be constantly pondered in terms of risks and benefits. Yet, it also remains a necessary endeavor. The constant noise created by propaganda and disinformation creates a necessity for proactive communication and framing of the public agenda. As stated also elsewhere, "this decision of the West to share intelligence with stakeholders and the public happens in a security environment where the Russian Federation and other actors have been making use of the instruments of information warfare like disinformation and propaganda to justify their actions and create confusion about their intentions before the aggression" (Arcos et al., 2023, p. 54).

In contrast, for understandable reasons, Ukrainian security and intelligence services have remained, in a time of war, rather cautious in sharing their own strategic intelligence. Intelligence leadership has rarely gone public on wartime operations involving intelligence. The public sites of both SSU and GUR maintain a strictly sanitized communication on public documents and laws governing intelligence activities. The Foreign Intelligence Service nevertheless, focuses much of its public communication on historical documents and declassified archives that highlight the fight of the Ukrainian people for independence and the special operations designed against it by Soviet authorities. Between the legal framework and the historical documents made available via electronic archives, the public communication of domestic and foreign intelligence services centers on the consolidation of an ontological narrative dedicated to the preservation of national identity and maintaining the classic tone adopted by similar institutional endeavors.

Alternately, The Defence Intelligence of the Ministry of Defence of Ukraine seems to take a different stand. More modern in design and with enhanced interaction, the military intelligence site engages the public in active support of offensive intelligence operations which are presented throughout articles dedicated to special forces units and their raids, videos of documented operations and guerrilla attacks, motivational clips, and a patriotic presentation of "glorious intelligence units". Its website also has an ongoing counter of days, hours and minutes since "Ukraine defends the world". A sort of communication by proxy channels approach was also created, in which intelligence communities in strategic partner countries combined expertise to produce accurate assessments disseminated online to the public, hence occupying the public arena with balanced estimates and not allowing Russian propaganda to flourish.

In Ukraine, significant statements have been made by the intelligence community leadership that seem to play an important role in power projection mechanisms on the public arena. One such example is Vasil Maliuk, the head of the Ukrainian Security Service, appointed by the Ukrainian Parliament in February 2023, after 6 months of interim management and the replacement of Ivan Bakanov, former head of SBU. His appointment put an end to a tumultuous period in which SBU was shaken by scandals related to espionage accusations made against former heads of intelligence departments in Harkiv and Crimeea, Roman Dudin and Oleg Kulinich (Dumitrache, 2023). Both Vasil Maliuk and Kirillo Budanov, the Head of the Military Intelligence Direction, have long careers inside the intelligence community and have risen to top management after many years of service. Maliuk's public narrative is built around successful special operations, such as the repeated attacks on the Crimean Kerch bridge in October 2022 and July 2023, or attacks on Russian ships which are post-event claimed and detailed in a narrative aimed to project power, efficiency, and determination.

Without embracing a proactive approach in communicating real time intelligence and maintaining a rather conservatory, centralized tone of communication, based on projecting strong leadership and indomitable courage, Ukrainian intelligence community nevertheless used strategic communication on niche topics (already implemented intelligence operations) as a way of building trust, keeping the morale of its citizens and debunking Russian disinformation. The focus was placed on military intelligence special operations which came to be reported and celebrated as deeds of valor during war. Operations such as the attacks and partial destruction of the Kerch bridge or landing of paratroopers in Crimea on Independence Day have become landmark stories keeping up the national morale (Meduza, 2023; Visit Ukraine, 2023). Such stories make use of "open secrets" and public intelligence to communicate strategic messages to domestic and foreign audiences alike, pinpointing "the ability to infiltrate enemy territory" (Segura, 2023) and thus obtaining strategic advantage.

Interestingly, in a more modern and unconventional approach, the story behind such operations, as well as the story of the special "glorious intelligence units" (as described by UKRPOSHTA) has also become subject of two issues of the postal series "Glory to the Defence and Security Forces of Ukraine!: Main Directorate of Intelligence of the Ministry of Defence of Ukraine", made available by the Ukrainian Postal Office, Ukrposhta. The latest charity stamp, created by artist Oleksandr Okhapkin, celebrates the Kraken, Shaman and International Legion special forces and was put in circulation on June 30th, 2023. Not coincidentally, June 30th is also the day in which Snake Island was liberated from the Russian troops and hence, the work of the Ukrainian artist makes an intertextual reference to another successful stamp issue after an iconic image illustration signed by Boris Groh, entitled "Russian warship, go...!", depicting a Ukrainian defender facing a Russian ship in full defiance and which sold in millions. The Boris Groh stamp depicts a soldier from behind, arm in hand lowered to the ground and displaying a defying gesture cursing the Russian military ship that threatens the small Ukrainian army with destruction. It is a symbolic image of courage and vulnerability in front of an aggressor, a refusal to accept surrender and a dignified way of awaiting death. The stamp showcases the contrast between the aggressor and the defender. A similar stamp, dated a month after, May 2022, with the ship gone and the soldier standing, is entitled "Russian ship... DONE!" celebrates the sinking of the Moskva cruiser the next day after the first stamp was issued. One year ahead, the new series, issued June 2023 and dedicated to the main directorate of intelligence reconnects to the depiction, as it was put into circulation on June 30, 2023, the day declared by the Ukrainian authorities as the day the Serpent Island was liberated from Russian invaders. This time, the stamp displays a fully geared soldier aiming his gun at an unseen enemy, in waiting. This contrasting image, connected to the heroic figure of the Serpent Island stamp, seems to invite a very different interpretation. In line with the main narrative advanced by the military intelligence service, it conveys the image of a prepared, fully geared, patient soldier, alert and ready to defend his position.

Without fully emerging into disseminating strategic intelligence, the intelligence community, with the help of other state institutions, like the Ukrainian Postal Office, succeeds in diversifying communication and addressing target audience at home and abroad with unconventional, intertextual messages, based on a combination of art, pop culture representations, and even graffiti, one stamp being dedicated to the Banksy graffiti representation of a judoka child putting down Putin in combat—another symbolic contextualization of Ukraine and its military in the framework of David and Goliat mythical plot. In fact, a compared analysis of the different wartime postage stamps issued since February 2022 shows that the collection embeds powerful pop art images created by popular artists, textual references to impactful events and successful military operations, stylized images of mythical figures in the Ukrainian lore, re-writings of pop culture iconic images, such as the image of the Titanic lovers on the Crimean bridge, common people preserving heroically light, electricity, water, train transportation etc. (https://www.ukrposhta.ua/en/marky-voiennoho-chasu).

Coming back to intelligence representations, the dedicated stamp series only adds to an entire array of communication tools used to create personalized depictions of successful operations. Video documentaries and clips of special units daily lives and interventions, photojournalistic stories and social media accounts create a framework in which strategic communication to both home audience and public abroad can be channeled into powerful ontological narratives that multiply and cross-pollinate with cultural productions, grassroot, collective art performance and public statements in graffiti representations (as the one created on the main bridge in Vilnius, Lithuania), memes, video games etc.

These combined interventions, some visibly the work of the intelligence community, some adding layers though anonymous interventions, collective authorship, grassroot reinterpretations and art, seem to be part of a larger, nascent trend in strategic communication, seamlessly integrating everyone and everyman, in a level of societal mobilization that speaks volumes about how co-creating narratives and opening unconventional channels of communication and mainstreaming them in the battle of narratives can become powerful tools for resilience building.

Conclusions and Way Ahead

Ukraine has been subject to successive and multiple initiatives of reforming its security sector in the years after the fall of Soviet Russia. Some of these endeavors have also tackled intelligence as an integral part of the security sector equipped with powers that need to be regulated by democratic control, effective oversight, and public accountability. One of the main conclusions that can be formulated based on existing developments is that although several steps have been taken, the process has so far proved to be less efficient in reforming the inherently secretive SBU. One of the significant variables that needs to be considered in this respect is certainly provided by the context of war. On one hand, it can be understood as a hindering variable impeding further democratic reforming as such reforming processes require many resources (diagnosing, planning, time, human resources etc.) currently being directed towards sustaining the war efforts against Russia. On the other hand, the war has already provided a framework for the civil society to act as an active intermediary between the authorities and the public, advocating and educating the public about the dilemmas and strategic choices faced by the authorities. This is one of the goals generally aimed by any intelligence sector reform and, in the case of Ukraine, one can easily observe an incipient reversed pattern of traditional mutual distrust of the citizenry in the security sector. Thinking in a post-conflict paradigm, capitalising on the general ‘rallying around the flag’ effect in wartime (which has already produced several results in the increase of trust in Ukraine’s government institutions) and allowing the full participation of non-state oversight actors can serve the objective of melting the long-standing resistance to change of Ukrainian intelligence.

References

Arcos, R., Ivan, C., & Buluc, R. (2023). Unprecedented use of intelligence instrumentalized by strategic communication. *Dominoes Project*. https://wordpress.projectdominoes.eu/wp-content/uploads/2023/07/DOMINOES-Handbook.final.pdf

Atlantic Council. (2021). *Securing the home front: SBU reform in Ukraine*. https://www.atlanticcouncil.org/event/securing-the-home-front-sbu-reform-in-ukraine/

Boraz, S. C., & Bruneau, T. C. (2006). *Reforming intelligence: Democracy and effectiveness*. https://apps.dtic.mil/sti/citations/ADA483968

Born, H., & Caparini, M. (Eds.). (2007). *Democratic control of intelligence services: Containing rogue elephants*. Ashgate.

Caparini, M. (2016). Controlling and Overseeing Intelligence Services in Democratic States in Hans Born (ed.) *Democratic Control of Intelligence Services*. Routledge.

Dumitrache, C. (2023, February 7). *Ucraina aplică "modelul Budanov" și în cazul SBU. Vasil Maliuk vine din zona operativă a structurilor de forță.* https://www.defenseromania.ro/serviciul-de-securitate-al-ucrainei-are-un-nou-sef-vasil-maliuk_621008.html

Dylan, H., & Maguire, T. (2022, September 27). *Why are governments sharing intelligence on the Ukraine war with the public and what are the risks?* https://www.kcl.ac.uk/why-are-governments-sharing-intelligence-on-the-ukraine-war-with-the-public-and-what-are-the-risks

Fitsanakis, J. (2022). *Analysis: The West should not trust Ukrainian spy agencies. Neither should Ukrainians*. https://intelnews.org/tag/foreign-intelligence-service-ukraine/

Fluri, P. H., & Polyakov, L. (2021). Intelligence and security services reform and oversight in Ukraine – An interim report. *Connections: The Quarterly Journal, 20*(1), 51–59. https://doi.org/10.11610/Connections.20.1.03

FRA. (2017). *European Union Agency for Fundamental Rights, Surveillance by intelligence services: fundamental rights safeguards and remedies in the EU, Volume II: field perspectives and legal update*. https://fra.europa.eu/sites/default/files/fra_uploads/fra-2017-surveillanceintelligence-services-vol-2_en.pdf

Galeotti, M. (2022). *Why Zelensky is purging the security services of Ukraine*. https://www.spectator.co.uk/article/why-zelensky-is-purging-the-security-services-of-ukraine/

Gill, P. (2016). *Intelligence governance and democratization*. Routledge.

Gill, P., & Phythian, M. (2006). *Intelligence in an insecure world*. Polity.

Goldman, Z. K., & Rascoff, S. J. (Eds.). (2016). *Global intelligence oversight. Governing security in the twenty-first century*. Oxford University Press.

Gressel, G. (2019, August 29). *Guarding the guardians: Ukraine's security and judicial reforms under Zelensky*. ECFR Policy Brief. https://ecfr.eu/publication/guarding_the_guardians_ukraine_security_and_judicial_reforms_under_zelensky/

Horbulin, V. P., Fluri, P. H., & Pirozhkov, S. I. (2006). *Perspectives on Ukrainian security sector reform*. https://www.dcaf.ch/perspectives-ukrainian-security-sector-reform

Human Rights Watch. (2021). Ukraine: Security agency reform bill risks undermining human rights. https://www.hrw.org/news/2021/10/08/ukraine-security-agency-reform-bill-risks-undermining-human-rights

Leigh, I., & Wegge, N. (2019). *Intelligence oversight in the twenty-first century accountability in a changing world*. Routledge.

London, D. (2022). *The intel on Zelensky's troubles with Ukrainian intelligence*. https://thehill.com/opinion/national-security/3572381-the-intel-on-zelenskys-troubles-with-ukrainian-intelligence/

Meduza. (2023, August 19). *Head of Ukraine's Security Service details how agency carried out Crimean Bridge explosion in October 2022*. https://meduza.io/en/news/2023/08/19/head-of-ukraine-s-security-service-details-how-agency-carried-out-crimean-bridge-explosion-in-october-2022

Nolan, C. M. (2010). Intelligence oversight in the USA. In *Oxford research encyclopedia of international studies*.

Norwegian Parliamentary Oversight Committee on Intelligence and Security Services [EOS Committee]. (2022). *Brief overview of intelligence and security oversight bodies in certain countries.* https://eos-utvalget.no/wp-content/uploads/2023/05/Overview-of-different-countries-oversight-bodies-v.-1.01.pdf
O'Connell, K. (2004). Thinking about intelligence comparatively. *Brown Journal of World Affairs, 11*, 1, 189–199.
Omand, D., & Phythian, M. (2018). *Principled spying – The ethics of secret intelligence.* Oxford University Press.
Phythian, M. (2019). Framing the challenges and opportunities of intelligence studies research. In S. Coulthart, M. Landon-Murray, & D. Van Puyvelde (Eds.), *Researching national security intelligence: Multidisciplinary approaches.* Georgetown University Press.
Relations with Ukraine. (2023). https://www.nato.int/cps/en/natohq/topics_37750.htm
Riemer, O. (2022, March 27). Intelligence and the war in Ukraine: The limited power of public disclosure. *Institute for National Security Studies Insight* (1577). https://www.inss.org.il/publication/ukraine-russia-intelligence/
Segura, C. (2023, August 23). From a truck bomb to a nautical drone: Ukraine details how it attacked bridge linking Crimea and Russia. *El Pais.* https://english.elpais.com/international/2023-08-23/from-a-truck-bomb-to-a-nautical-drone-ukraine-details-how-it-attacked-bridge-linking-crimea-and-russia.html
Soldatiuk-Westerveld, J., Deen, B., van Steenbergen, A. L. (2023). Work in progress: Ukraine's State-Civil Partnership to Reform the Security Sector, Clingendael Report, Netherlands Institute of International Relations. https://www.clingendael.org/sites/default/files/2023-09/work-in-progress.pdf
Ukraine: New Law on Intelligence Enters into Force. (2020). https://www.loc.gov/item/global-legal-monitor/2020-11-30/ukraine-new-law-on-intelligence-enters-into-force/
Visit Ukraine. (2023, September 7). Ukrainian Intelligence Day: Top of the most successful operations of the Defence Ministry's GUR fighters in recent times. *VisitUkraine.com.* https://visitukraine.today/blog/2549/ukrainian-intelligence-day-top-of-the-most-successful-operations-of-the-defence-ministrys-gur-fighters-in-recent-times
Warner, M. (2009). Building a theory of intelligence systems, in Gregory Treverton and Wilhelm Agrell (eds), National Intelligence Systems: Current research and future prospects, Cambridge: Cambridge University Press, 11–37.
Wesslau, F. (2021). Guarding the guardians: Reforming Ukraine's security service. *Security and Human Rights Monitor.* https://www.shrmonitor.org/guarding-the-guardians-reforming-ukraines-security-service/
Wetzling, T., & Vieth, K. (2018). *Upping the ante on bulk surveillance an international compendium of good legal safeguards and oversight innovations.* Heinrich-Böll-Stift.
Zegart, A. B. (2011). *Eyes on spies: Congress and the United States Intelligence Community.* Hoover Pres.

Free and Open Spaces: The Global Impact of Ukraine Reconstruction

James Jay Carafano and Silviu Nate

Abstract The reconstruction of Ukraine has far-reaching global implications. It presents an opportunity to reshape Eurasia's geopolitical and economic landscape, potentially rewiring the pathways of worldwide commerce and connectivity. Ukraine's strategic location makes it a pivotal link in integrating Central Asia, the Caucasus, and Eastern Europe with Western Europe and the broader transatlantic community. Rebuilding Ukraine must be approached not as a traditional foreign aid endeavor but as a private sector-driven economic integration effort. Harnessing global capital and expertise can deliver real growth, in contrast to past schemes of foreign assistance that have failed to sustain Ukraine's economy.

Crucial prerequisites include developing Ukraine's domestic defense capabilities, insulating the reconstruction effort from great power competition, and continuing anti-corruption reforms. The reconstruction should not only empower small and medium enterprises and leverage regional companies, but also utilize international private financing for large infrastructure projects, making all stakeholders feel included and valued in this effort.

If successfully implemented, this model could be a game-changer across the post-Soviet space, transforming the Eurasian landscape. It would not only create new trade and investment opportunities and foster greater regional integration and stability but also significantly diminish Russia's influence, providing a sense of empowerment and security for future geopolitical competition.

After World War II, modernisation theories experienced a new enthusiasm and competition between capitalist and communist perspectives. Still, each in its version

J. J. Carafano
The Heritage Foundation, Washington, DC, USA
e-mail: James.Carafano@heritage.org

S. Nate (✉)
Faculty of Social Sciences and Humanities, Department of International Relations, Political Science and Security Studies, Lucian Blaga University of Sibiu, Sibiu, Romania
e-mail: silviu.nate@ulbsibiu.ro

S. Nate (ed.), *Ukraine's Journey to Recovery, Reform and Post-War Reconstruction*, Contributions to Security and Defence Studies,
https://doi.org/10.1007/978-3-031-66434-2_18

aimed at economic growth, social progress, and modernisation, eventually leading to broader mass participation in politics.[1] Although previous versions of modernisation theory were deficient in many respects, scientific evidence indicates that socioeconomic development brings significant changes in society, culture, and politics. By processing four survey datasets from more than eighty societies, Inglehart and Welzel demonstrate that socioeconomic development tends to transform people's core values and beliefs—and it does so in an approximately predictable way.[2]

While modernisation is not linear, and certain predominant historical value landmarks of a society can delay modernisation processes, the result promises a shift from survival to self-expression values. Consequently, increasing emancipation from authority transforms modernisation into a process of human development that increases human freedom and choice by favouring the emergence of democracy.

The persistence of an obstruction unable to generate modernisation, the absence of viable regional alternatives, and the dependence on Russia of the states of the Caucasus and Central Asia determine their aspirations to embrace change and economic progress to some extent.

However, research shows that changes in the economic and political environment influence each other with changes in worldview; they occur with a generational gap and have considerable autonomy and momentum.[3]

We can conclusively admit that the prospect of positive economic change influences generational transformation and can induce at a slower or faster pace, depending on the traditionalist variable of the respective society, to the ideological break with the past that generated the feeling of survival at the expense of that of human autonomy.

Digital networks and improved access to information are vectors for accelerating transformative processes, especially among younger populations, if they experience substantially greater economic security.

Rebuilding Ukraine will impact a global transformation of economic, security, and diplomatic relationships. The collapse of Russian influence across the post-Soviet space, paired with the declining influence of China, has created an opportunity to restructure the face of Eurasia.

A free, strong, and prosperous Ukraine will play a key role in the future Eurasian political economy and a future security architecture that ameliorates competition and conflict. That development in and of itself is deeply significant. There is more.

Means and ways of reconstruction that effectively harness private sector investment, delivering real growth, will serve as a model that can be replicated across the Eurasian space. This is a different development pathway, transcending and replacing traditional schemes of foreign aid, international financing, and over dependency on

[1] Barrington Moore, *Social Origins of Dictatorship and Democracy: Lord and Peasant in the Making of the Modern World* (Beacon Press, 1993), CCLXVIII.

[2] Ronald Inglehart and Christian Welzel, *Modernization, Cultural Change, and Democracy: The Human Development Sequence* (Cambridge, UK: Cambridge University Press, 2005).

[3] Inglehart and Welzel.

contracting with traditional International Non-Governmental Organizations (NGOs). This model could serve well across Eurasia.

As long as Moscow has held levers of political control over Kyiv while maintaining Ukraine's dependence on Russia's weak economy, the Kremlin's campaign has focused exclusively on political and economic issues, with no security, civilisational or historical arguments committed. Following the loss of political control over Ukraine and the removal of President Yanukovych from power in 2014, the Kremlin's rhetoric toward Ukraine's EU integration effort has been aggressively extended to the theme of Russia's security interest and invocation of the common nation.

The Unattractive History of Russian Modernisation

Russia's lack of modernisation, failure to meet many of its political and economic commitments, and projection of Ukraine's total energy dependence were an unattractive offer, accentuating Kyiv elites' scepticism about Russia's capacity and intentions. Therefore, the Eurasian integration plan focused on the so-called economic "synergies" between Russia and Ukraine was a drawback from the Ukrainian perspective.

A state like Russia, unable to have democratic traction for the Ukrainian people, with a high GDP per capita predominantly supported by the export of energy resources but in urgent need of modernisation, was not an attractive development path.[4]

Similarly, regarding democratisation, Putin's Russia would have made an insignificant contribution to Ukraine, especially compared to the EU, which has a different attitude towards state and public institutions' quality, nature, and substance.[5] At the same time, participation in Russia's Eurasian integration would have further deepened Ukraine's asymmetric interdependence.

Low energy prices and an existing opaque trading system have discouraged investment, modernisation, and reduction of Ukraine's energy dependence on Russia while creating massive rent-seeking opportunities for ruling elites in both countries.[6]

The Soviet inheritance was a real impediment to the modernisation of the region, paving the way in the 1990s for the emergence of "opaque groups",[7] invisible

---

[4]Rilka Dragneva-Lewers and Kataryna Wolczuk, *Ukraine between the EU and Russia: The Integration Challenge* (Springer, 2015), p. 71.

[5]Dragneva-Lewers and Wolczuk.

[6]Margarita Mercedes Balmaceda, *The Politics of Energy Dependency: Ukraine, Belarus, and Lithuania between Domestic Oligarchs and Russian Pressure* (University of Toronto Press, 2013), XL.

[7]Verena Fritz, 'State Weakness in Eastern Europe: Concept and Causes', 2004, p. 11.

networks of patronage and clientelism operating between the state and private sectors. This way of undermining and simulating economic freedom has intrinsically captured the potential of societies to aspire to economic security and democracy.

This "modernised" form of neopatrimonialism[8] operated intensively in the first two post-Soviet decades through the back door of state institutions, which became much more self-sufficient to the needs of society and superficially modern. This widely used practice in the post-Soviet space shaped the options available to economic and political actors to determine the rules of the game,[9] parasitising and subsequently slowing down the reform of public administration in Ukraine with the support of international technical assistance.[10]

Strategic Context

The most significant importance of Ukraine reconstruction is the strategic implications of this endeavor. Before delving into the specifics of why, when, and how the global community should partner in the reconstruction of the country, it is crucial to understand the stakes—the world changing implications which such a successful effort might trigger.

After the two world wars, the term reconstruction was used for rebuilding infrastructure and services, but also for political and security reconstruction, where the economic dimension is relegated to a minor role.[11] One of the most serious challenges in economic reconstruction is to design and implement an economic program supported by other multilateral organisations and donors—within the framework of reconciliation efforts resulting from peace agreements. If the political agreement and economic programme are not integrated, the country will most likely plunge back into conflict or face regime change.

According to the UN,[12] resources spent on implementing peace agreements and peacebuilding are one of the best investments that can be made in conflict prevention, while approximately 50% of countries in the transition from war to peace return to conflict and in the early stages of peace implementation societies are most vulnerable.

[8]Oleksandr Fisun, 'Developing Democracy or Competitive Neopatrimonialism? The Political Regime of Ukraine in Comparative Perspective', *Institution Building and Policy Making in Ukraine*, 2003, p. 3.

[9]Verena Fritz, *State-Building: A Comparative Study of Ukraine, Lithuania, Belarus, and Russia* (Central European University Press, 2007), p. 57.

[10]Duncan Leitch, *Assisting Reform in Post-Communist Ukraine, 2000? 2012: The Illusions of Donors and the Disillusion of Beneficiaries* (Columbia University Press, 2016), p. 213.

[11]Graciana Del Castillo, *Rebuilding War-Torn States: The Challenge of Post-Conflict Economic Reconstruction* (OUP Oxford, 2008), p. 29.

[12]General Assembly, 'Report of the High-Level Panel on Threats, Challenges and Change', 2004.

The high risk of relapse in conflict makes short-term reconstruction necessary and demanding, and in the case of Ukraine, connecting to regional economic and trade opportunities can sustain resilience and robustness progressively or concurrently with long-term sustainable policies and programmes. The institutional, economic, commercial, energy, and infrastructure interconnection represent opportunities that accelerate reconstruction, implicitly generating increased security.

What's in a Name?

Due to interdependencies with Moscow, Central Asian countries are also experiencing the effects of Russia's geopolitical and economic weakening. Amid the background of the decreasing attractiveness of Russia's offers and the desire for modernisation, the EU should deepen bilateral economic and political relations with countries incorporated into the Eurasian Union[13] by exploring future alternatives. Although the effect of sanctioning Russia was not the one expected to determine hostilities ending in Ukraine, the strategic and economic competition of the West in Central Asia and the Caucasus may impose additional markers, making the Kremlin think that its strategy to Europe is not a winning one, requiring rethinking its approach and attitude, while avoiding at the same time the pitfalls of ambiguous negotiations.

Offering concessions to Russia, such as those under the Minsk Agreements, would legitimise Russia's current and future attacks, replicating the model by rekindling frozen conflicts in the wider Black Sea region, such as Transdniestria in the Republic of Moldova, Abkhazia and South Ossetia in Georgia, Nagorno Karabakh in Armenia and Azerbaijan, forcing these states to amend their constitutions while granting special status to Russian controlled areas.

Historically, the United States has not promoted a clear vision of their interests in "distant and unknown" Central Asia.[14] The concept of "Inner Asia", advanced by Robert Legvold two decades ago, could suggest a more favourable context for increasing the region's importance on the Western agenda in view of Central Asia's economic unlocking and modernisation.[15]

Today, Russia must confront its geopolitical fragility that has inevitably branched out to the five republics of Inner Asia. The tendency to weaken the buffer zone between Russia and the rest of the Islamic world, historically artificially maintained by Moscow, may today be the opportunity to rearrange broader principles and

[13] Janusz Bugajski and Margarita Assenova, *Eurasian Disunion: Russia's Vulnerable Flanks* (Jamestown Foundation Washington, DC, 2016), p. 485.

[14] Eugene B Rumer, Dmitriĭ Trenin, and Huasheng Zhao, *Central Asia: Views from Washington, Moscow, and Beijing* (ME Sharpe, 2007), p. 23.

[15] Robert Legvold, *Thinking Strategically: The Major Powers, Kazakhstan, and the Central Asian Nexus* (MIT Press, 2003).

functions of economic interdependence that favour their modernisation and connection with other geographical spaces.

Labeling the state of contemporary global conflict and confrontation is a major controversy all on its own. There is no question, there is consensus the forces driving the present are different from what they were perceived just decades ago. After the September 11, 2001 terrorist attacks on New York and Washington, DC, combating extremism, protecting homelands and managing failed and ungovernable spaces was the most recent effort to define geopolitical dynamics in a post-Cold War world. Like other efforts to define the post-Cold War World, 20 years on that conceptualization is considered outdated. Today, the focus of attention is on relationships between the U.S., Europe, Russia, Iran, and China, as well as the place of and impact on other regions, such as the Global South.[16] This condition has been called everything from Great Power Competition to a New Cold War.[17]

Whatever this new world disorder is called, one of its defining characteristics is the collapse of regional spheres of influence in the post-Soviet space across the Eurasian land mass. In part, this reflects the decline of Russian power and influence, particularly after the onset of the war against Ukraine. In addition, after years of isolation and sanction, Iran's regional dominance has never been shakier. Meanwhile, China's expansionist policies such as the Belt and Road Initiative are less attractive than they were after decades of empty promises of investment, and the poor state of partner nations such as Pakistan, Ethiopia, and Sri Lanka which have seen declines in governance, public safety, economic performance, and a rise in unsustainable debt. As a result, "from the Arctic Circle bordered by the Nordic nations in Europe to the steppes of Central Asia, the peoples that live and work across the breadth of the world's oldest trade routes have an opportunity to secure their own future, dictated not by the whims of great powers, but by a common bond, seeking shared prosperity, security derived from stability and peace, and respect for national sovereignty."[18] One of the consequences of great power competition has been give greater space for small and medium size nations to chart their own course.[19]

The Eurasian space is, of course, not the only world region up for grabs. Africa, the Middle East, and Latin America have emerged as theaters where external

[16] James Jay Carafano, "The U.S. and the new great power paradigm," Geopolitical Information Service, September 5, 2019, https://www.gisreportsonline.com/r/great-power-competition/; "America's response to the Global South," Geopolitical Information Service, August 3, 2023, https://www.gisreportsonline.com/r/great-power-competition/.

[17] See, for example, James Jay Carafano, et al., "Winning the New Cold War: A Plan for Countering China," Heritage, March 28, 2023, https://www.heritage.org/asia/report/winning-the-new-cold-war-plan-countering-china.

[18] James Jay Carafano and Anthony B. Kim, "Sovereignty, Security, Prosperity, and the Future of the Eurasia Project," The Market for Ideas, https://www.themarketforideas.com/sovereignty-security-prosperity-and-the-future-of-the-eurasia-project-a789/.

[19] James Jay Carafano, "Why Small Nations Matter to Great Powers," The National Interest, August 10, 2018, https://nationalinterest.org/feature/why-small-states-matter-big-powers-28362.

regional powers have vied for influence. However, Competition in Eurasia is unique in that it could disrupt traditional notions of spheres of influence and restore the historic and natural geographic connectivity that has dominated commerce for most of human history. "These pathways," writes historian Peter Frankopan, "serve as the world's central nervous system, connecting peoples and places together."[20] Thus, in terms of shifting the course of future geopolitical competition, the fate of the Eurasian space looms particularly large.

Eurasia's New Map

Russia's dominant aspirations in Central Asia are not motivated by physical reintegration but present themselves as soft formulas. Rather, Moscow wants to ensure favourable conditions in this region for a high degree of Russian political influence, guaranteeing loyalty.[21] However, Central Asia has become an area of competing external influences, which include China, the US, the European Union, and India. The intensification of economic and infrastructure connections of Western powers with Central Asian states will lead to tempering Russia's ambitions to use this region as a "gate" for executing the southern strategy.

Russia's interest is to become an indispensable player in the mediation group of the Israeli-Palestinian conflict,[22] seeking to deepen relations with the Persian Gulf states to protect its status as a major energy supplier in the energy market. Russia's dominant strategy towards Central Asia is aimed directly at managing the Russian-Chinese interaction, instrumenting its files in the Middle East such as the conflict in Syria, the growing relationship with Iran—a proxy to support Hamas and the Houthi rebels, controlling the energy market and its interests, blocking East-West economic and security prospects from Central Asia to the Black Sea and the Baltic Sea.

The potential for connectivity across the Eurasian space is unprecedented, conditions that have not existed since before the outbreak of World War I (1914–1918). With the addition of Finland and Sweden to NATO, Europe has an integrated frontier of political, economic, and security integration that reaches from the High North to the Mediterranean Sea. The consolidation of Europe's Arctic frontier is noteworthy not only for the region's full integration into NATO but because of the increasing importance of Nordic energy and high-end-manufacturing to the European industrial base. In addition, the High North is an anchor for the future

---

[20] Peter Frankopan, *The Silk Roads: A New History of the World* (New York: Vintage Books, 2015), p. xvi.

[21] Rumer, Trenin, and Zhao, p. 82.

[22] 'Israel-Hamas War: What Is Russia's Role as Mideast Mediator? – DW – 02/26/2024' <https://www.dw.com/en/israel-hamas-war-what-is-russias-role-as-mideast-mediator/a-68340753> [accessed 29 February 2024].

development of the North-South pathways of economic, infrastructure, and digital integration that could form the new backbone of the European economy.

The most visible expression of the effort to develop North-South architecture integrating Central and Southern European states that were formerly under the dominance of the Soviet Union is the Three Seas Initiative. Although Central Europe's democracies have joined NATO and the European Union, they remain hampered by the legacy of the Cold War. Most of Europe's roads and rail lines run east-to-west and peter out in Central Europe. Economic evolution, long retarded by Soviet overlords that segregated the region from the rest of Europe, still lags the West, and there are no major north-south economic corridors. The legacy consists of fragmented markets, inadequate, outdated, and insufficient infrastructure that makes for a poor conduit for North-South economic activity across Europe. According to a study by the International Monetary fund, "CESEE [Central, Southern and Eastern European] countries lag in terms of infrastructure compared to the EU [European Union] 15, and deficient infrastructure is often cited as a constraint to growth and convergence."[23] In 2016, the countries launched the Three Seas Initiative to accelerate development of cross-border energy, transport, and digital infrastructure in the region. Austria, Bulgaria, Croatia, the Czech Republic, Estonia, Hungary, Latvia, Lithuania, Poland, Romania, and Slovakia pioneered the effort. The established a joint public-private investment fund to underwrite projects.[24]

Indeed, the task of making the Three Seas Initiative more practical operationally has gained greater urgency and necessity. In part, the lack of energy security, shortfalls in infrastructure, border security challenges, and inadequacies in collective defense were all highlighted as consequence of the Russian invasion of Ukraine. Putin's war was a stress test, clearly showing the need for more robust infrastructure and resilience in the heart of Europe. Nowhere was the need for North-South connectivity important than in the case of energy security. The war prompted a number of initiatives for new energy pathways such as importing gas from Azerbaijan.[25] The formation of the initiative predates the war in Ukraine, but the war in Ukraine demonstrably proves how crucial it is to deliver a more secure and prosperous Europe.

Concomitant with the development of Europe's North-South corridor is the importance of a free and open Black Sea, where commercial traffic can move unimpeded by conflict. The Black Sea is lynchpin that connects several pathways

---

[23] Anil Ari, et al., "Infrastructure in Central, Eastern, and Southeastern Europe: Benchmarking, Macroeconomic Impact, and Policy Issues," Departmental Papers, September 18, 2020, https://www.imf.org/en/Publications/Departmental-Papers-Policy-Papers/Issues/2020/09/25/Infrastructure-in-Central-Eastern-and-Southeastern-Europe-Benchmarking-Macroeconomic-Impact-49580.

[24] Unless otherwise noted, this section adopted from James Jay Carafano, "America Should Help Transform Central Europe," The Heritage Foundation, January 31, 2020, https://www.heritage.org/europe/commentary/america-should-help-transform-central-europe; Carafano and Kim, "Sovereignty, Security, Prosperity, and the Future of the Eurasia Project."

[25] "European countries to boost gas imports from Azerbaijan" in EuroNews, April 4, 2023, https://www.euronews.com/2023/04/25/european-countries-to-boost-gas-imports-from-azerbaijan.

of Eurasian commerce together. Russia's grain embargo of Ukrainian exports via the Black Sea. This crisis, which has impact global grain prices and supplies demonstrated the fragility of supply chains dependent on transit of the Black Sea.[26] While Ukraine, Poland, Romania, and Latvia have partnered to provide alternative routes this initiative has also shown that the region could benefit from more robust, resilient, and redundant transportation infrastructure.

Another post-Soviet Space open for development extends from the Black Sea to the East—The Middle Corridor.[27] The Middle Corridor, officially known as the Trans-Caspian International Transport Route (TITR), runs from Europe to Kazakhstan, the Caspian Sea, Azerbaijan, and Georgia, and from there, via the Black Sea, to Turkey. Connecting the Caucasus and Central Asia to Europe and other regions via the Mediterranean could deliver new sources of energy, alternative supply routes, and new sources of materials and manufacturing capacity.

Development of the Middle Corridor is particularly critical to reshaping the face of Eurasian commerce. China's ambition to dominate global markets and supply chains, grandiosely envisioned as a "New Silk Road," recalls the Eurasian routes that dominated global trade from Roman times to the fifteenth century. Then, as now, goods travel along one of three routes: the northern corridor, which winds through Russia to the West; the middle corridor, which makes its way through Central Asia, the Caspian Sea, the Caucuses and the Black Sea; and a southern corridor, which crosses the Indo-Pacific to Africa and then moves upward through the Middle East and the Mediterranean. But after many years of press releases and unrealized promises, Beijing's belts and roads mostly look like bridges to nowhere.

Russia's war on Ukraine has triggered a flurry of sanctions against Moscow and has hamstrung the northern corridor.[28] Nations in the middle corridor, the countries of Central Asia and the Caucuses, have been reluctant to sign big ticket infrastructure deals with China after watching Beijing saddle countries like Pakistan and Sri Lanka with massive amounts of debt that have stymied economic growth and led to bankruptcy.

As for the southern corridor, China simply doesn't have enough strength to dominate the Indo-Pacific, the Middle East, and the Mediterranean—all key links in one of the world's most vital maritime corridors.

Thus, the Middle Corridor represents not another path for connecting China to the West, but for connecting Central Asia to the rest of the world. Even Asian partners

---

[26] See, for example, Eckart Woertz, "The Russian War against Ukraine: Middle East Food Security at Risk," German Institute for Global and Area Studies (GIGA) - Leibniz-Institut für Globale und Regionale Studien, Institut für Nahost-Studien, 2023.

[27] This section adapted from James Jay Carafano, "Time for Central Asia To Create Its Own New Silk Road," Heritage, June 6, 2023, https://www.heritage.org/asia/commentary/time-central-asia-create-its-own-new-silk-road and James Jay Carafano and Silviu Nate, "The West Should Welcome the Middle Corridor," The National Interest, October 1, 2022, https://nationalinterest.org/feature/west-should-welcome-middle-corridor-205085.

[28] Kornel Mahlstein, "Estimating the economic effects of sanctions on Russia: An Allied trade embargo," *The World Economy* (45/11, November 2022): 3344–3383.

like India, South Korea, Taiwan, and Japan will likely find the most robust route connecting to Central Asia across the Southern Corridor to the Black Sea.

West from the Black Sea, pathways lead to the Eastern Mediterranean which provide global access. From the Mediterranean through the Middle East and the Suez Canal runs the Southern Corridor which provides Access to the Indo-Pacific. There is also connectivity to energy and other resources and markets in North, East and West Africa. In addition, the Mediterranean offers connections to the broader transatlantic community including North and South America.

Pivot Point

The opportunities to reshape the map of Eurasian commerce, security and connectivity could potentially rewire the pathways of global intercourse. This is important context for the discussion of Ukraine's recovery and rebuilding. Ukraine is an important picot point in connecting all the links that could transform the post-Soviet space. Ukraine, for instance, has already been granted participating partner status in the 3SI. Some 3SI could contribute directly to the reconstruction of Ukraine as well is accelerating the nation's integration with Europe.

Ukraine will also play a crucial role in building a free and open Black Sea. Black Sea security and assurance of freedom of navigation can only be practically assured by building up the capacity of littoral states, including Ukraine, expanding their capacity to conduct anti-mine and anti-submarine warfare, expand maritime and air situational awareness, protect shipping and conduct anti-area denial maritime operations.[29]

In turn, the viability of the other pathways of the Eurasia network depends in great part on the successes of these pivotal projects. So the question should not be if there is much for the world to gain from a revived Ukraine—but when and how to start this great project. Let's take each of those questions in turn.

Estimate of the Situation

There is endless speculation of how war against Ukraine will end; what will be the countries boundaries; and what will be the future relations between Ukraine, Russia, and the transatlantic community? There is no sound strategic logic to think it wise to wait until all these questions are resolved before planning and beginning the reconstruction of Ukraine's economy. In contrast, there are several compelling

[29] James Jay Carafano, "The contest over the Black Sea in the new Cold War," Geopolitical Information Service, August 16, 2022, https://www.gisreportsonline.com/r/black-sea-security/.

reasons to start now on supporting the campaign for the future peace and prosperity of Ukraine's people.

First, waiting cedes all initiative to Russia. That would be a strategic blunder. The more Moscow believes Ukraine's friends and partners are holding-off long-term support for the country, the more likely the Russian regime will be encourage to persist in armed conflict hoping Western resolve will crack, creating an opportunity for future military successes through continuing the war.[30] The more Moscow believes Ukraine's friends and partners are holding-off long-term support for the country, the more likely the Russian regime will be encouraged to persist in armed conflict hoping Western resolve will crack, creating an opportunity for future military successes through continuing the war.[31]

Second, progress of the war suggests Russian conventional military forces have been significantly degraded, and when considered against the significant build-up of Ukrainian military capability over the last year, Russia lacks the capacity in the near term to achieve its maximalist goal of eliminating a free and independent Ukraine.[32]

Third, issues concerning other initiatives which would speed Ukrainian integration with the West, specifically entry into NATO or the European Union (UN) are unlikely to be resolved anytime soon. Thus, the future of Ukraine in the near-term will be dependent on its ability to both rebuild its economy and provide conventional forces for self-defense, both of which will require substantial engagement with friends and partners.[33]

Fourth, the cases of both Israel and Ukraine demonstrate through the development of air and missile defenses, robust cyber capabilities, electronic warfare countermeasures, enhanced energy security, and the exploitation of space-based infrastructure, modern nations can be made resilient, protecting both civilian populations and infrastructure, against persistent threats including drone, missile, and cyber-attacks. This establishes conditions facilitating economic recovery, physical safety, and public security even in the face of persistent conflict.[34]

[30]This argument was made by Ukrainian Foreign Minister Dmytro Kuleba. See, Jeyhun Aliyev, "West should turn to 'proactive strategies' when dealing with Russia: Ukraine," AA, February 2, 2022, https://www.aa.com.tr/en/europe/west-should-turn-to-proactive-strategies-when-dealing-with-russia-ukraine/2492322.

[31]This argument was made by Ukrainian Foreign Minister Dmytro Kuleba. See, Jeyhun Aliyev, "West should turn to 'proactive strategies' when dealing with Russia: Ukraine," AA, February 2, 2022, https://www.aa.com.tr/en/europe/west-should-turn-to-proactive-strategies-when-dealing-with-russia-ukraine/2492322.

[32]See, for example, Office of the Director of National Intelligence, "Annual Threat Assessment of the U.S. Intelligence Community," February 6, 2023, pp. 13–14.

[33]James Jay Carafano, "Forging the Future of NATO," Real Clear World, May 19, 2023, https://www.realclearworld.com/2023/05/19/forging_the_future_of_nato_900640.html.

[34]In Israel, for instance, protection against missile attacks has not only protected populations and physical infrastructure but improved mental health outcomes. See, Yaakov Hoffman, et al., "Confidence in the 'Iron Dome' Missile Defense System Combined With a Sense of Resilience Reduced the Effect of Exposure on Posttraumatic Stress Disorder Symptoms After Missile Attacks,"

Fifth, historically there is an advantage to advanced planning and action. For instance, before the end of World War II, the liberation of territories in France, Italy, and Austria and the occupation of Germany, the U.S. began planning for post-conflict activities. Though incomplete and imperfect, they set conditions for operations that helped deal with masses of displaced persons, public safety challenges, health, welfare, and governance issues. This activity established the preconditions for the establishment of political stability and security and implementation of the Economic Recovery Plan (popularly known as the Marshall Plan).[35] In contrast, the U.S. did almost no post-conflict planning for the occupation of Iraq after the Second Iraq War. The lack of proactive effort without question contribute to the instability and violence that followed.[36]

Sixth, a stable and prosperous Ukraine is an important interest for the transatlantic community. If the war was won, but the peace was lost, the West would squander a significant strategic advantage in limiting Russian threats to destabilize Europe and counter the expansion of malicious Chinese influence. While investing and partnering in Ukraine is not without risks, a future Ukraine that lacks the capacity for self-defense, political stability, and economic resilience risks repeating the conditions that precipitated previous Russian incursions in 2014 and 2021. In contrast, a strong Ukraine would both a military deterrent to future Russian military operations and a net contributor to the transatlantic economy and regional political stability—one step closer the vision of a Europe whole, free, prosperous and at peace.[37]

There are, of courses, risks attendant in making commitments now in the face of many unknowns. Major endeavors, however, always include future uncertainty. The art of strategic planning is to include measures to mitigate future risks. The alternative is to be lulled into inaction.

Psychiatrist.Com, March 23, 2016, https://www.psychiatrist.com/jcp/trauma/ptsd/confidence-iron-dome-missile-defense-system-combined/.

[35] For the specific example of the application to the liberation of Austria see, James Jay Carafano, *Waltzing into the Cold War: The Struggle for Occupied Austria* (College Station: Texas A&M University Press, 2002).

[36] James Carafano, Dana Dillion, and James Roberts, "Winning the Peace: Principles for Post-Conflict Operations," Heritage Backgrounder, June 13, 2005, https://www.heritage.org/defense/report/winning-the-peace-principles-post-conflict-operations.

[37] James Jay Carafano, "Democracy's Journey East Continues," in Sławomir Dębski and Daniel S. Hamilton, eds. *Europe Whole and Free: Vision and Reality* (Warsaw: The Polish Institute of International Affairs/Transatlantic Leadership Network, 2019), p. 55.

How to Rebuild

The claim we need another Marshall Plan is frequently bandied about.[38] While useful as metaphor for the strategic scale of effort required, the plan has little relevance, as the conditions in Ukraine differ so markedly from those of postwar Europe. Indeed, there were calls for a Marshall Plan for Iraq that were equally misplaced because postwar reconstruction has to be structured for the conditions on the ground not based on a formula developed for another time and place.[39]

The key to getting the scale and speed needed to reconstruct Ukraine is harnessing the tremendous power, expertise, and wealth of private sector investment. As Max Primorac, an expert in post conflict reconstruction declared: Ukraine's post-war reconstruction strategy should not rely on donor-centered reconstruction that wastes taxpayer money—and which has repeatedly failed to raise countries out of poverty and dependence. Instead, Ukraine should radically break away from the Soviet legacy and conduct reconstruction efforts based on private sector-driven economic integration into Western institutions.[40]

For three decades Ukraine has been the recipient of billions of dollars of traditional foreign assistance which have consistently failed to deliver outcomes needed to establish a strong and resilient Ukrainian economy.

Crucial to attracting and sustaining investments are four prerequisites.

First, Ukraine must continue to develop and expand its capacity for self defense, including developing a robust domestic defense industrial base. This is an activity which partner nations must support.

Second, Ukraine must be insulated from the buffeting distractions of great power competition. China must be completely excluded from reconstruction projects.

Third, Ukraine must continue to expand anti-corruption efforts.

Fourth, partner nations ought to provide the political and diplomatic support for the effort. This should be G7 plus project including regional allies such as the Baltic States, Poland, Romania as full partners.

With these in place the essential steps for a private-sector centered reconstruction effort must include the following.[41]

First, eliminating obstacles to small and medium enterprises. Small business activity could be the first part of the economy to recover and generate many tens of billions of dollars of economic growth. Indeed, many small and medium

[38] See, for example, Heather A. Conley, "A Modern Marshall Plan for Ukraine," The German Marshall Fund, https://www.gmfus.org/sites/default/files/2022-10/A%20Modern%20Marshall%20Plan%20for%20Ukraine.pdf.

[39] James Jay Carafano, "Marshall Plan Won't Work in Iraq," Heritage, October 13, 2003, https://www.heritage.org/middle-east/commentary/marshall-plan-wont-work-iraq.

[40] Max Primorac, "Ukraine's Post-War Reconstruction: Taking the Path Toward Strategic Victory," July 27, 2023, https://www.heritage.org/defense/lecture/ukraines-post-war-reconstruction-taking-the-path-toward-strategic-victory.

[41] Ibid.

enterprises have found means to sustain themselves through the war. That ingenuity and innovation must be nurtured and empowered.

Second, local regional companies that have operated in with and Ukrainians for years ought to be the first and first supported. Indeed, Ukraine's neighbors ought to serve as platforms for rebuilding and reestablishing business, incubating to them be ready to move back to Ukraine, partnering in reconstruction, and building out regional connectivity and enterprise in Central Europe.

Third, rely on international private sector financing for big projects. "Ukraine's large infrastructure and industrial-size project needs can be financed by global capital through privatization schemes."[42]

The implications of this structure of development beyond Ukraine. While the Marshall Plan may not be a good model, the conditions in Ukraine are similar to those present in many states in the post-Soviet space. Thus, the Ukraine model potentially could be expanded to the Caucuses, Central Asia, and parts of North, West and East Africa.

[42] Ibid.

A Critical Infrastructure Protection Perspective on the Conflict in Ukraine: Recommendations for a Resilient Post-war Ukraine

Alexandru Georgescu

Abstract Russia's actions before and after its invasion of Ukraine in February 2022 can be analyzed using the framework of Critical Infrastructure Protection. The task of shoring up Ukrainian resilience to Russian hybrid attacks against its critical infrastructures can also be analyzed and planned using this framework. This article proposes a Critical Infrastructure Protection perspective of the conflict in Ukraine and makes recommendations to enhance the resilience of Ukraine in all potential phases of the conflict, including during post-ceasefire reconstruction efforts. Lastly, the authors highlight the role of Romania in Ukrainian resilience through a trans-border critical infrastructure perspective, suggesting also potential future contributions.

Introduction

In parallel with Russia's initial advance into Crimea in 2014, a campaign of cyber attacks against Ukrainian critical energy infrastructures, especially its electricity grid, commenced. The hackers, whether belonging to or sponsored by the Russian state, utilized their knowledge of the Ukrainian electricity grid, as developed during the Soviet era and the close ties afterwards, as well as other forms of specific knowledge regarding industrial control systems, in order to disrupt the functioning of the Ukrainian energy system (European Parliament, 2022). The main purpose was not only to distract the Ukrainian society from the illegal annexation of Crimea and its subversive actions in the so-called separatist republics, but also to degrade the Ukrainian economy, to impose costs and uncertainties on businesses, to reduce quality of life for Ukrainian citizens and to reduce the confidence in the authorities on the part of citizens, partner states and investors. This set the trend for the next

A. Georgescu (✉)
Cyber Security and Critical Infrastructure Department, National Institute for Research and Development in Informatics - ICI Bucharest, Bucharest, Romania
e-mail: alexandru.georgescu@ici.ro

S. Nate (ed.), *Ukraine's Journey to Recovery, Reform and Post-War Reconstruction*, Contributions to Security and Defence Studies,
https://doi.org/10.1007/978-3-031-66434-2_19

8 years, during which conventional kinetic attacks along a stalemated frontline were accompanied by attacks on institutions, power plants, banks and other key assets. Along with disinformation campaigns and other forms of warfare, these constituted a Russian approach to hybrid warfare (Fox, 2021). The invasion of Ukraine in February 2022 represented a transformation of this warfare, placing greater emphasis on kinetic strikes and conventional military actions, but did not see the repudiation of these other forms of attack with coercive intent.

Russia's actions in Ukraine can, in many ways, be interpreted through the framework of Critical Infrastructure Protection (CIP) theory. It is a comprehensive framework which provides concepts, tools and knowledge regarding the secure functioning of socio-technical systems called critical infrastructures (CI) which produce critical goods and services and perform critical functions on which all societies are reliant (Bucovețchi & Simion, 2015). These infrastructures are critical if their destruction or disruption would cause significant loss of human life, material losses, environmental impact and, just as important in the case of Ukraine, loss of prestige and confidence, especially on the part of its people and partners in the West. CIP theory is at the basis of legislative and administrative frameworks, as well as operational planning, in the United States, in the EU Member States, in the EU and in NATO, that aim to increase the resilience of a particular society or collectivity of nations to all hazards. These hazards can be natural or man-made, accidental or deliberate, low intensity but continuous or in the form of high impact—low frequency events (Gheorghe et al., 2018). The framework is influential enough to have been utilized also by international organizations such as the OSCE, which tries to increase resilience to terrorism, or aid organizations looking to allocate scarce resources.

If we flip the framework around, it becomes a blueprint for a potential adversary to employ a wide variety of methods, both conventional and unconventional, kinetic or hybrid, in order to degrade their target's capabilities in the civilian or military realm, and to coerce them in order to achieve particular goals such as political decisions, territorial submissions and more. The pattern of Russia's actions in Ukraine actively suggests CIP-related planning, and Ukraine initially responded by engaging in the transfer of best practices and knowledge from the West and by launching its own CIP legislative and administrative framework.

This chapter proposes to describe the application of CIP theory to Russia's actions in Ukraine both pre- and post- invasion, as well as to Western responses to Ukraine's requests for assistance. It also suggests actions that can be taken by Ukraine and its partners to increase the resilience of Ukraine in the context of near-certain continuation of hybrid warfare by the Russian Federation regardless of a ceasefire or another form of political agreement being reached. This conforms to a pattern of disruptive and coercive use of "gray zone" threats against Ukraine, its partners (especially the United States and the Eastern Flank nations), and countries in Russia's near abroad over the years. These actions are frequent, deniable, difficult to attribute and located below the threshold of armed response. Their logic also frequently conforms to that of economic warfare and is therefore amenable to analysis through the CIP framework.

The chapter is structured as follows. The section "Critical Infrastructure Protection" presents an overview of CIP theory and concepts useful for the discussion on Ukraine. The section "Russian Hybrid Action Against Ukrainian CIs" provides interpretations of Russian tactics and strategy according to CIP theory both pre- and post- invasion. The section "Western Contributions to Ukrainian Resilience, from a CIP Perspective" lists some Western interventions, including some contributions by Romania, and analyzes them from the perspective of CIP theory. The section "Recommendations on Increasing Ukrainian Resilience" lists recommendations from Ukraine's partners as well as Romania in order to assist in the increase of Ukrainian resilience to Russian hybrid warfare. The section "Conclusions" concludes the article.

Critical Infrastructure Protection

As mentioned before, CIs encompass a wide variety of technical systems and the organizations which run them. Various national taxonomies include as CI sectors energy, finance, transport, chemical and nuclear industry, ICT, healthcare, drinking water, wastewater, food supply, education, public administration, space, public order and national security in various combinations. What they have in common is their criticality—the fact that the impact of their disruption or destruction exceeds key thresholds established and measured according to specific measuring methodologies (Mureşan & Georgescu, 2016). Once identified and designated, the operator of that CI, who can be a private company, a public authority, or a state-owned enterprise, has to comply with a series of regulations on periodic protection planning, investment in resilience and information sharing with the competent authorities, while the various authorities have to coordinate to achieve national resilience (Gheorghe et al., 2006). Because of the transborder nature of many critical infrastructures, especially in energy, transport or finance, there are many instances where cooperation between states with common (inter) dependencies is necessary. Within the European Union, this cooperation is formalized within the European Programme for Critical Infrastructure Protection (EPCIP), which establishes minimum mandatory national frameworks for Member State (MS) protection of national CIs, while also defining European CIs (ECI). These affect two or more MS and have a European and multilateral dimension to their security governance, requiring communication and coordination across various jurisdictions. In recent years, EPCIP has grown steadily more complex, having started with just transport and energy ECIs. The most recent Directive, the Critical Entities Resilience Directive (European Commission, 2022a) (approved politically in June 2022, with national implementation by 17 October 2024) contains ten ECI sectors and introduces the concept of critical entity, while simultaneously lowering the threshold for criticality. This is a result of the experience of recent years, including through the war in Ukraine and the pandemic, which proved that regionalization and globalization have generated far more interdependencies than previously considered and with many more transborder couplings that

Table 1 The various sectors in the CER Directive and the NIS 2 Directive (source: legislative texts)

<table>
<tr><th></th><th>Critical entities
CER Directive</th><th>High criticality or essential entities
NIS 2 Directive</th><th>Other critical or important entities
NIS 2 Directive</th></tr>
<tr><td rowspan="2">Entity sector</td><td colspan="2">1. Energy sector
2. Transport sector
3. Banking sector
4. Financial market infrastructure sector
5. Health sector
6. Drinking water sector
7. Waste water sector
8. Digital infrastructure sector
9. Public administration sector
10. Space sector</td><td rowspan="2">1. Postal and courier services
2. Waste management
3. Manufacture, production, and distribution of chemicals
4. Production, processing, and distribution of food
5. Manufacturing
6. Digital providers
7. Research</td></tr>
<tr><td>11. Production, processing, and distribution of food sector</td><td>11. ICT service management (business-to-business)</td></tr>
</table>

make even smaller infrastructures potentially critical in terms of the larger effects of their disruptions.

An important aspect of the new CER Directive is its accompaniment by the updated Network and Information Security Directive (NIS 2) (European Commission, 2022b), with their taxonomies of critical and very important entities converging, meaning that digitalization has permeated every one of these critical infrastructure sectors and one cannot discuss security and protection without cybersecurity. Table 1 emphasizes this overlap. This has important consequences for the surface contact area with an increasingly chaotic and dangerous cyberspace, which is relevant for our discussions on hybrid warfare in Ukraine, since Russian "new generation warfare" has come to rely heavily on low cost, low risk and low chance of attribution actions such as cyber-attacks (Adamsky, 2015).

Russian Hybrid Action Against Ukrainian CIs

Russia enacted a near continuous hybrid campaign starting in 2014 against Ukrainian CI, for a host of reasons, as seen in Fig. 1. Just like we speak, more and more, about dual use technologies as being the norm, so too are dual-use critical infrastructures the norm, motivating an attacker to try and disrupt them.

Russia did not initiate the targeting of Ukrainian CI or those of other countries in 2014. While a full list of such interventions is beyond the scope of this chapter, we can identify numerous prior instances of the use of hybrid warfare targeting critical infrastructures in order to harass, punish, coerce and threaten others (Adamsky, 2015). The list includes the 2007 Estonian cyber-attacks, the 2009 shutdown of

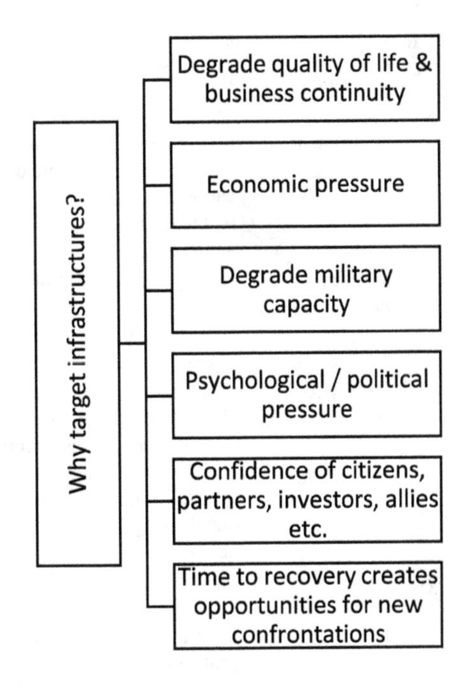

Fig. 1 Reasons for targeting civilian critical infrastructures

Russian energy exports to the West through Ukrainian pipelines and many instances of cyber-attacks attributed to Russia.

Starting in 2014, Russia stepped up attacks on the Ukrainian energy system and on Ukrainian state institutions (also a critical infrastructure as providers of public services in EU and US frameworks). Its tactics and motivation in the takeover of Crimea (securing key assets on the peninsula and the military infrastructure of Sevastopol military port) also indicate CI-based thinking, as does the later construction of the Kerch Strait Bridge that provides road, rail, water and electricity connections between the Russian mainland and the illegally annexed peninsula. In fomenting separatism in various regions of Ukraine, there was also a logic in depriving Ukraine of key resources, key industrial assets (in aerospace, metallurgy and more) and critical infrastructures such as multimodal transport hubs. Should the Novorossiya project have succeeded, Ukraine would have become landlocked and would have lost its maritime critical infrastructures which mediate much of its trade with the rest of the world. Even with the failure of the Novorossiya project, the existence of the so-called separatist republics and the possibility of their reintegration dangled before Ukraine, and the critical infrastructures and resources on their territory became a tool for the coercion of Ukraine to achieve political ends such as the country's federalization and abandonment of European integration. Table 2 summarizes some characteristics of the Ukrainian CIP environment.

The 2015–2016 period saw a major transfer of know-how and best practices from the West to Ukraine in setting up a Western-style CIP framework, initially focused on energy and cyber. This included the Green Book on Critical Infrastructure Protection in Ukraine (Fig. 2), resulting in 2016 from an effort which included

Table 2 Characteristics of the Ukrainian CI environment

Characteristic	Explanation
Complex impoverishment	Though a relatively poor country by European standards, Ukraine has a highly complex economy with a large stock of inherited and more recently built infrastructure, including in energy, transport, high technology fabrication (aerospace). The normal life of Ukraine is therefore critically reliant on the exploitation of these CI, which become a natural target for would-be aggressors.
Maintenance decline	Rapid degrowth following USSR dissolution and problems with reform have led to issues with the maintenance and upgrade of existing infrastructures, increasing vulnerabilities and making crises related to spontaneous or targeted malfunctions more likely.
CI legibility for Russia	From the perspective of standards and technology, Ukrainian CI are very aligned or compatible with those Russia, through the USSR and common supplier ecosystems. Ukrainian CI are highly "readable" to Russian state or Russian-backed aggressors. Systems are familiar to them, their location is well known, their supply chains for components can be similar. This gives an advantage to Russia as a hybrid attacker (and to Ukraine in counter-attacks).
Ancillary vulnerabilities	Factors such as corruption and organized crime can affect resilience because they are enablers for terrorists and other hybrid actors, undermining and increasing the fragility of state institution and their protection efforts, and even providing valuable assistance to hostile actors (resources, false IDs, compromised insiders, inside information and plans etc.).
Dual-use CI	The distinction between civilian and military targets is often blurred when it comes to CIs. No country can afford to have complete parallel systems for their civilian society and for their military, so the military relies on civilian transport, energy, food, telecom CIs and more. Alternatives are limited to short-term disruption responses (such as back-up generators or stockpiles of rations and medical supplies). In targeting Ukrainian CI, Russia was also both directly and indirectly targeting the capabilities of the Ukrainian military.

also NATO Advanced Research Workshops within the Institute for Strategic Studies under the President of Ukraine, to which the author of this chapter contributed (Mureşan & Georgescu, 2016).

With the commencement of the invasion and the failure of Russia's initial decapitation strike, which proved to be too optimistic, the conflict entered a phase of strong conventional activity that nevertheless saw a lot of unconventional actions against Ukrainian infrastructures. Russia sought to physically occupy and secure critical infrastructures such as the Zaporozhe Nuclear Power Plant (the largest in Europe, with six reactors), Russia reportedly trying to integrate it within its own grid. Alarm regarding the prospect of damage to the nuclear facility was utilized by Russia to mobilize global opinion against conventional action in its area that could have dislodged Russia (Rzheutska, 2022).

Overall, Russia tried to disrupt the functioning of Ukrainian-held CI, but this action had two periods. In the early stages of the invasion, the intent was to reduce

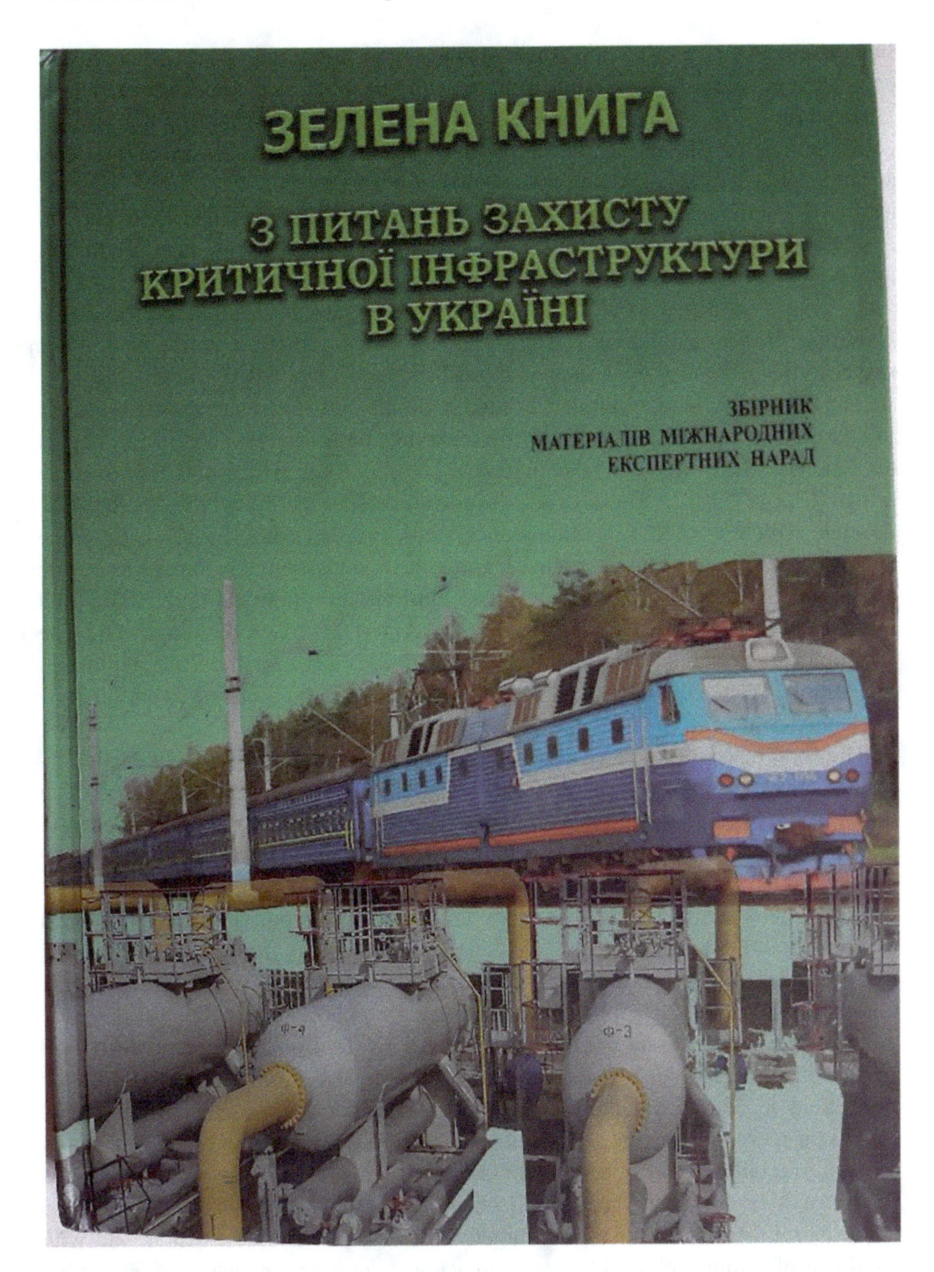

Fig. 2 Green book on critical infrastructure protection in Ukraine

the capacity to supply critical goods and services and temporarily damage or disrupt the CIs of Ukraine to assist in the Russian invasion. However, Russia nevertheless sought a quick victory, which would have offered the possibility of the exploitation of captured CIs by Russia and the version of the Ukrainian state that it would have implemented. By causing repairable damage and temporary disruptions, Russia could reverse its offensive hybrid actions with minimum cost after the war. In the latter phase of the war, faced with escalating Western support for Ukraine and the achievements of Ukraine in preventing Russian advancement, Russia switched to strong kinetic attacks or debilitating cyber and other types of destructive action against Ukrainian CIs, even at the risk of permanently degrading Ukrainian economic and functional capacity. As shown in Fig. 1, the purpose of such destructive action was to degrade the capability of the Ukrainian military, to generate hardship for the population that would translate into political and humanitarian pressure on Ukrainian leadership and its Western partners and to remove Ukraine as a viable player in the long-term, including as a prospective EU and NATO member.

The best example of systemic CI thinking on the part of Russia was the blockade of Ukrainian ports that prevented its grain exports, an action with significant impact on food insecurity in vulnerable regions such as North Africa and Sub-Saharan Africa (Chibani, 2022). This was also leveraged by Russia through the "grain deals" through which it tried to obtain concessions on sanctions. In blockading the Ukrainian sea access, Russia denied Ukraine its few economic resources to ensure a measure of fiscal self-sufficiency, given the long-term political unreliability and unsustainability of Western and especially American macroeconomic aid. The Ukrainian government deficit stood at 5 billion dollars a year in mid-2022, optimized to 3 billion by late 2022, of which approximately 1.5 billion dollars was provided by the United States.[1].

The food insecurity engendered by the conflict in Ukraine was accompanied by similar effects in energy markets, with uncertainty over supply driving spikes in prices that also endangered the viability of the artificial fertilizer industry needed to keep agricultural yields high. A combination of food and energy crisis could have triggered real hunger.

Lastly, it is worth noting that, both for financial reasons and out of political calculus, both Ukraine and Russia continued to trade energy throughout the conflict, using Ukraine's pipelines to supply Western consumers who had received exceptions from the sanctions applied to Russian energy exports in the EU.

In parallel with Russia's actions in Ukraine, we find other examples of hybrid warfare against CIs, such as the constant cyber-attacks on CI systems and public institutions in countries such as Poland, Romania, the Baltics and the US. Noted attacks on energy CI operator Solarwinds in the US was linked to Russia. Attribution problems remain both for cyber and for other types of attacks. An aspect that sets this period of hybrid warfare apart from others is the extent to which offshore and undersea infrastructures have been targeted for disruption or destruction, and with the threat of future such attacks meant to act as a deterrent against the West taking action against Russia. Examples include the Nord Stream 1 and 2 gas pipeline sabotage in the Baltic Sea, the cutting of the fiber optics cables connecting Norway to its satellite communication center on the island of Svalbard (Humpert, 2022), the

[1]Figures from interview by authors of USAid representative, November 2022.

cutting (and disappearance) of 4.3 km (and ten tons) of undersea cable from a maritime surveillance network in the North Sea (Kulha, 2021). Reports about Russian ships mapping undersea infrastructure for potential sabotage highlight the concern that this issue engenders, given EU determination to create more offshore energy infrastructure (wind power farms, electricity interconnectors, new pipelines) and the current uncertainties regarding their protection within but especially beyond territorial waters.

Western Contributions to Ukrainian Resilience, from a CIP Perspective

In addition to the macroeconomic aid, as well as the military equipment, munitions and training received by Ukraine, we see numerous cases of CIP-related action. The attempted transfer of experience, best practices and assistance for implementation in the sectors of cybersecurity and energy security before the invasion commenced is a good example, both through NATO, the EU and individual states such as Romania.

Another example has been the attempted supplying of Ukraine with energy from the West through pipeline reversal and through electricity interconnections. An additional example is the support given to Ukraine in order to repair damage to its electricity grid and to setup generators to support critical functions such as healthcare in the context of frequent Russian rocket artillery attacks. Several Western nations contributed to this, with USAid in particular having a program to facilitate the transfer of key components and equipment from the inventories of American energy infrastructure operators to Ukraine.[2] The attempted patching of Ukrainian infrastructure while under fire is certainly a spectacular example of increasing resilience, although it ran into compatibility issues between Western equipment and the Soviet and Russian type equipment in use in Ukraine.

Possibly the best example of Western assistance to Ukraine which can be analyzed from a CIP perspective is the attempted rerouting of Ukrainian grain exports through neighboring friendly states. Prior to the war, Ukraine had been one of the great grain exporters of the world as part of the global critical food infrastructure. Its attempted exclusion did not lead to famine, because of a certain flexibility of supply, but it did lead to price volatility in the food markets that intensified macroeconomic imbalances in grain importers such as Egypt, which faced unrest and possible political upheaval and tried to counter through unsustainable food subsidies which deteriorated the government's fiscal situation. The failure of the grain deals made the alternate routes even more important (European Council, 2023a).

Poland seemed initially to be more important than Romania as a logistics partner to Ukraine. Polish infrastructure is more developed than Romania's, its border with

[2] From interview by author of USAid representative, November 2022.

Ukraine is longer and the border infrastructure more developed, and Polish authorities mobilized quicker to create infrastructure at the border, such as a grain hub, in addition to hubs for humanitarian aid and other necessities. The preference of Ukrainian refugees to leave Ukraine through and towards Poland attests the better communication and coordination that Poland can achieve in its relationship with Ukraine.

However, over time, Romania's still secure position on the Black Sea cuts maritime transport costs and times by a great deal, and Romanian authorities took decisive steps to enhance the capacity of critical transport infrastructure to facilitate the transport of Ukrainian grain. By late 2023, Romania was mediating 70% of Ukrainian grain exports through partner countries (Agerpres, 2023) and Romanian capacity had grown from 300,000 tons per month in March 2022 to over 3 million tons in December 2023, with 4 million tons per month as a target in 2024 (Reuters, 2024), even though Romania itself is an agricultural exporter and its own farmers have to move harvests to market in the same periods as Ukraine. Moreover, Romania experienced the least amount of internal farmer lobby pressures against Ukrainian grain, by comparison to Poland, Hungary and Slovakia, which is another factor in trade flow reorientation (Reuters, 2023). This is enabling a rapid drawdown of accumulated Ukrainian grain stocks which have not been destroyed and enables a critical financial lifeline to Ukraine. As a result of this process, the port of Constanța entered the top ten list for European ports by tonnage, having already been the largest Black Sea container port and also by tonnage.

The gradual success of the Romanian route for grain transport, based on its strategic position on the Black Sea and in proximity to the Middle Eastern—North African and Sub-Saharan markets for Ukrainian grain, is the result of the rapid revamp and enhancement of pre-existing transport that connects Romania to Ukraine.

This infrastructure includes river ports, Soviet-gauge rail lines, multimodal transport facilities (for grain and for energy, the latter being transported towards Ukraine) and road infrastructure. This infrastructure was previously underutilized because of the fall in economic relations between Romania and Ukraine following Romania's orientation towards Western markets, the failure of common Romanian-Ukrainian projects such as in Krivoi Rog, the Ukrainian emphasis on energy exports towards Western markets (based on pre-existing pipeline infrastructure) and, not least, the chilly relations between Romania and Ukraine. This does not mean that the infrastructure was not utilized at all—as early as 2013, before the Russian invasion of Ukraine, Chinese companies were utilizing the rail infrastructure connecting Ukraine to the river-maritime port of Galați on the Danube to transport grain to Romania and then, from the private Galați New Port, to transport by barges to Constanța where the Chinese company COSCO owns a grain silo and terminal and perform maritime transport from there, in addition to Ukrainian ports like Odessa. Such transport route diversifications are in keeping with CIP governance and resilience enhancing measures.

The problem with the Romania-Ukraine infrastructure was that, being underutilized, it had also not been a priority for investment in maintenance and capacity enhancement. This is a general factor in Romanian infrastructure in several sectors, which has had several decades of underinvestment, especially the rail and energy infrastructure. The road infrastructure has received much more attention as a result of access to European funding and the visibility of the issue among Romanian society resulting in pressures on the political class. The Romania-Ukraine infrastructure was, therefore, in a degraded state, especially the rail component which was nevertheless one of the main vectors of bulk transport of grain. Examples of the unpreparedness of the infrastructures include the use of the rail lines near Constanța as a storage site for Soviet-gauge rolling stock and their general degradation.

Recommendations on Increasing Ukrainian Resilience

Having proven that the CIP framework is a relevant tool for analysis of the conflict in Ukraine, we can also use it to formulate policy recommendations on increasing CI resilience. Obviously, current commitments should continue, while adapting them to the new requirements on the ground in terms of repairing, hardening, and rerouting Ukrainian CIs. Other options should be explored, keeping in mind that planning must concern the build-up of resilience for an eventual post-armistice era, when kinetic strikes against CIs will have ceased, but hybrid warfare will likely continue, in lined with the 2014–2022 pattern. The civilian governance aspect of CIP will take center stage at that time.

Prioritize the Rapid Implementation of the European CIP Framework

Having opened accession talks with Ukraine, a series of reforms and legal and administrative convergences must take place before Ukraine can join the EU. Ukraine should prioritize the implementation of the CIP framework of the EU at national level, translating into national legislation both the CER Directive and the NIS2 Directive, as well as taking heed of other relevant documents of reference (ex: "the blueprint for resilience"—European Council, 2023b). As seen in the EU, there is ample scope for Ukraine to adapt the European framework to its needs and perspectives. Romania can be an important technical partner, given its commonalities with Ukraine and having experienced one of the best adoptions of the Directive 114/2008 on the identification and designation of CIs (Lazari & Simoncini, 2016), which was superseded in 2023 by the CER Directive. The EU should make available substantial aid for implementation, through the formation of a Pre-Accession Assistance Instrument dedicated to CIP, while understanding that some forms of Security Sector Reform have to wait until after the shooting has stopped. The EU can assist in the setting up of local CIP certification programs or the setting up of key technical secretariats and interministerial bodies. This is not just about the allocation of new resources, but it is also a principle for the reorganization of part of the current aid in order to maximize resilience. It would also be useful if the EPCIP were to evolve towards a European Agency for Critical Infrastructure Protection which could undertake more significant cross-sector efforts at increasing the collective European resilience.

Integrate Ukraine into EPCIP

Certain steps have already been taken, such as the cooperation between Ukraine and the European Security and Defence College of the European External Action Service on, among others, the participation of Ukrainian military personnel in trainings on the Common Security and Defence Policy. However, given the systemic threat facing EU MS and EU critical infrastructures, the integration of Ukraine into EPCIP should take place, as far as possible, as if Ukraine had already joined the EU. This is something that should be done with the Republic of Moldova and, where possible, also in the Western Balkans, with a lighter version of such cooperation throughout the EU vicinity, including in North Africa. This integration enables the functioning of the security liaison officer system, the two-way structured flow of information regarding security issues, access to specialized infrastructures such as the Critical Infrastructure Warning Information Network (CIWIN) or the labs and other facilities of the European Reference Network for CIP (ERNCIP). As they are being set up, Ukraine can be integrated into the EU networks for ISAC (Information Sharing and Analysis Centers), for national cyber competence centers and more. Through this effort, it can then access other forms of support available to EU MS in case of European CI disruption, especially the new category of aid for ECI affecting six or more MS. In this way, there will also be a tangible resilience dividend for the EU MS which feature dependencies on Ukraine or pathways to CI disruption propagation. A thorough review of the possibilities for Ukrainian inclusion into CIP and CIP-related efforts should be made. As an ancillary example, Ukraine could be invited to participate in certain European Defence Agency (EDA) activities, similar to Norway and Serbia. This is relevant to the discussion at hand, because the EDA has CIP-related initiatives, including for transfer of knowledge and best practices. The various Captechs (capability technology areas) of the EDA provide CIP opportunities in cyber, energy, environmental issues, simulation capabilities. The EDA also has other initiatives, such as the Consultation Forum on Sustainable Energy in the Security and Defence Sectors, the largest energy and defense community in Europe, with a Working Group on defence-related critical energy infrastructure protection. Recent topics of interest include offshore CI protection. Since EU MS can register objections to inviting outside participants to individual EDA activities, it will not be difficult to tailor Ukrainian involvement in the EDA to the level with which MS are comfortable.

The Inclusion of Ukraine in Other CIP-Related Initiatives

All opportunities to contribute to greater Ukrainian resilience should be taken. One area of potential development is the inclusion of Ukraine as a strategic partner in the Three Seas Initiative, during the September 2023 Bucharest Summit. The initiative is oriented towards North-South infrastructure development in transport, energy and cyber, but its activities are fundamentally resilience enhancing, especially in the logic of regional interconnectedness, and a component of CIP is gradually going to emerge especially in order to secure the digital and physical protection dimensions of new infrastructures, which will become critical. Other initiatives can also be developed, such as a formalized and recurring regional conference on CIP issues, attended not just by state leaders or ministers, but also by the main coordinators of CIP at the level of each participating state, including Ukraine. This would parallel the NATO Defense Ministers reunions. Another permutation could be a NATO-EU-Ukraine cooperation format, given that the NATO-EU cooperation agenda has an important CIP component that could be developed further, through the common declarations setting 42 recommendations in 7 areas, with 32 concrete actions. Priority areas of interest include hybrid threats, maritime issues, common exercises, cyber defence and security etc. The formalized cooperation between CERT-EU (the EU Computer Emergency Response Team) and the NATO Cyber Security Center (formerly NCIRC) on cybersecurity can also provide opportunities a common approach to cybersecurity capacity building with Ukrainian partners.

Develop a European Infrastructure Reorientation Plan for the EU Vicinity of Ukraine

Whatever the result of the ongoing conflict, unless it is a total Ukrainian loss, it is highly unlikely that Ukraine will want to risk systemic exposure to dependence on Russia or Belarus, while also contending with the permanentizing of hybrid warfare against its CI through deniable assets. Therefore, the EU should already begin assisting Ukraine's neighbors in expanding border and near border infrastructure in order to accommodate Ukraine's future normal flows of goods, data and people, as well as assisting in reconstruction efforts when they will be feasible. Romania has already taken an individual first step through the planned purchase of the Moldovan port of Giurgiulești to support logistics for reconstruction efforts (Marinescu, 2023). However, piecemeal action so far on energy, transport, humanitarian issues such as water access and food security, should be Europeanized and coordinated accordingly.

Conclusions

In this chapter, we have analyzed the Ukrainian conflict through a Critical Infrastructure Protection perspective. CIP is the premier resilience and systemic governance framework utilized by the states in the West, as well as the EU. It enables a better understanding of the dynamic and complex interactions between interdependent CIs at national, regional, and global levels across multiple sectors while providing the toolbox for identifying, designating, and protecting these systems. We used the CIP framework to analyze Russia's actions in Ukraine prior and during the invasion, as well as various aspects of Western aid. CIP turns out to be a strong instrument for explaining the conflict in Ukraine starting in 2014 and provides insight into future issues. We concluded by formulating some recommendations mainly on enhancing the CIP governance cooperation between Ukraine and its Western partners, starting with its neighbors, and followed by the EU, NATO and others. An important conclusion is that many economic and governance initiatives can have a CIP component insofar as they address a particular infrastructure sector or contribute to resilience. Coupled with the possibility of a rapid and as complete as possible adoption of the EU framework on CIP, Ukraine can be we positioned to become a more resilient actor, not only weathering the hybrid warfare organized against it, but also ensuring in the future business continuity and quality of life for its citizens, while contributing to those of its partners.

References

Adamsky, D. (2015). Cross-domain coercion: The current Russian art of strategy. Proliferation Papers 54, Institut Français des Relations Internationales (IFRI), ISBN: 978-2-36567-466-9. https://www.ifri.org/sites/default/files/atoms/files/pp54adamsky.pdf

Agerpres. (2023, December 13). Currently, 70% of our grains are exported through Romania. *Agerpres, Romanian Press Agency*. https://www.agerpres.ro/english/2023/12/13/currently-70-of-our-cereals-are-exported-through-romania-says-ukrainian-pm%2D%2D1218781

Bucovețchi, O., & Simion, C. P. (2015). Importance of interdependencies in critical infrastructures' protection. *U.P.B. Sci. Bull., Series C, 77*(1), ISSN 2286-3540.

Chibani, A. (2022, April 27). Grains and hydrocarbons: The Middle East and the war in Ukraine. Viewpoints Series. *Wilson Center*. https://www.wilsoncenter.org/article/grains-and-hydrocarbons-middle-east-and-war-ukraine

European Commission. (2022a). Directive (EU) 2022/2557 of the European Parliament and of the Council of 14 December 2022 on the resilience of critical entities and repealing Council Directive 2008/114/EC (Text with EEA relevance). Brussels. https://eur-lex.europa.eu/eli/dir/2022/2557/oj

European Commission. (2022b). Directive (EU) 2022/2555 of the European Parliament and of the Council of 14 December 2022 on measures for a high common level of cybersecurity across the Union, amending Regulation (EU) No 910/2014 and Directive (EU) 2018/1972, and repealing Directive (EU) 2016/1148 (NIS 2 Directive) (Text with EEA relevance). Brussels. https://eur-lex.europa.eu/eli/dir/2022/2555

European Council. (2023a). Infographic - Ukrainian grain exports explained. 22 December 2023. https://www.consilium.europa.eu/en/infographics/ukrainian-grain-exports-explained/

European Council. (2023b). Council recommendation of 8 December 2022 on a Union-wide coordinated approach to strengthen the resilience of critical infrastructure (Text with EEA relevance) 2023/C 20/01, 20 January 2023. https://eur-lex.europa.eu/legal-content/EN/TXT/?uri=CELEX:32023H0120(01)

European Parliament. (2022). Russia's war on Ukraine: Timeline of cyber-attacks. Briefing for the European Parliament. https://www.europarl.europa.eu/RegData/etudes/BRIE/2022/733549/EPRS_BRI(2022)733549_EN.pdf

Fox, A. C. (2021). Russian hybrid warfare: A framework. *Journal of Military Studies, 10*(1). eISSN 1799-3350. https://sciendo.com/it/article/10.2478/jms-2021-0004

Gheorghe, A., Vamanu, D. V., Katina, P., & Pulfer, R. (2018). *Critical infrastructures, key resources, key assets: Risk, vulnerability, resilience, fragility, and perception governance* (Topics in safety, risk, reliability and quality). Springer. https://doi.org/10.1007/978-3-319-69224-1

Gheorghe, A. V., Masera, M., de Vries, L., & Weijnen, M. (2006). *Critical infrastructures at risk - Securing the European electric power systems*. Springer. isbn:978-1-4020-4306-2.

Humpert, M. (2022, September 29). Nord stream pipeline sabotage mirrors Svalbard cable incident. *High North News*. https://www.highnorthnews.com/en/nord-stream-pipeline-sabotage-mirrors-svalbard-cable-incident

Kulha, S. (2021, November 11). 4.3 Kilometers of subsea cable vanished off north Norwegian coast. *The Drive*. https://nationalpost.com/news/world/norways-strategic-underwater-research-observatory-has-cables-cut-removed-in-suspicious-act

Lazari, A., & Simoncini, M. (2016). Critical infrastructure protection beyond compliance. An analysis of national variations in the implementation of Directive 114/08/EC. *Global Jurist, 16*(3), 267–289. https://doi.org/10.1515/gj-2015-0014

Marinescu, G. (2023, December 14). Romania - Logistic hub for the reconstruction of Ukraine. *Bursa.ro*. https://www.bursa.ro/romania-logistic-hub-for-the-reconstruction-of-ukraine-07174155

Mureşan, L., & Georgescu, A. (2016). Critical infrastructure protection - Romanian contributions and experiences. In O. Sukhodolia (Ed.), *Green book for critical infrastructure protection in Ukraine* (pp. 93–107). ISBN 978-966-554-258-2.

Reuters. (2023, August 7). Explainer-How does central Europe's ban impact Ukrainian grain exports? *US News*. https://www.usnews.com/news/world/articles/2023-08-07/explainer-how-does-central-europes-ban-impact-ukrainian-grain-exports

Reuters. (2024, January 10). Ukraine grain pushes Romanian Constanta port to record volumes in 2023. *Reuters*. https://www.reuters.com/markets/commodities/ukraine-grain-pushes-romanian-constanta-port-record-volumes-2023-2024-01-10/

Rzheutska, L. (2022, July 11). Zaporizhzhia plant no longer connected to Ukraine grid. *Deutsche Welle*. https://www.dw.com/en/zaporizhzhia-power-plant-no-longer-connected-to-ukraine-grid/a-62976178

Formation of Competencies for Managers of Sustainable Development in Ukraine

Oleksandra Humenna , Yuriy Dyachenko , and Mariia Vasylets

Abstract The relevance of training management specialists in sustainable development and the formation of "tomorrow's" competencies in them is determined by the need to be included in the world's global space. After all, there is no alternative to the Millennium Goals (Sustainable Development Goals) today. The need to develop policies embodied in best practices, particularly at the local level, determines the necessity of creating new educational programs and components focusing on sustainable development management, which should be based on a balance of economic, social, and environmental dimensions, as well as the measurement of management efficiency. Therefore, it is imperative to consider all stakeholders' interests in achieving progress in the country's sustainable development.

This chapter examines and substantiates the methodology and algorithm for forming a set of competencies of a modern manager of sustainable development based on the balance of interests and considering the challenges/risks that managers of this new type face. Additionally, it was determined that the understanding of people of different generations regarding the concept of sustainable development is a crucial aspect in the formation of educational programs. Attitudes towards sustainable development differ between generations due to their distinct life experiences, socio-cultural influences, and perceptions of global issues.

The methods of comparative analysis were employed in the literature review and the evaluation of existing educational programs on sustainable development management worldwide and the competencies they provide.

O. Humenna (✉)
Department of Scientific Research, State Scientific Institution Institute of Education Content Modernization, NaUKMA, Kyiv, Ukraine
e-mail: gumenna@ukma.edu.ua

Y. Dyachenko
Graduate Department of Social Sciences and Humanities, Kyiv School of Economics, Kyiv, Ukraine
e-mail: ydyachenko@kse.org.ua

M. Vasylets
Association of Sustainable Development Experts, Zurich, Switzerland

S. Nate (ed.), *Ukraine's Journey to Recovery, Reform and Post-War Reconstruction*, Contributions to Security and Defence Studies,
https://doi.org/10.1007/978-3-031-66434-2_20

Introduction

One of the UN Sustainable Development Goals is to ensure inclusive and equitable quality education and promote lifelong learning opportunities (Agenda for SD, 2015).

Higher education today faces certain challenges, such as high competition in the market of educational services, growing risks, and lack of predictability. Managing education as a service is a process aimed at improving the structure of educational service providers and the educational structure of society. To build this structure, we need to consider actions related to a particular system and ensure its sustainable development. Implementation of such actions requires management through strategy setting and coordination of efforts. To achieve the goals, we need to have a certain predictability of the system. But due to the unpredictability of human behavior, we will still face some uncertainty in the future. This makes it impossible to build a closed system that could provide an opportunity to obtain predetermined results of intellectual activity (including artificial intelligence). This becomes a source of instability and potential danger. On the other hand, the next generation will have to deal with climate change, pandemics, and other global problems that are complex and can be solved through a system approach.

Sustainable economic development is a major concern of scholars (Gryshova et al., 2019). In this context, it is worth mentioning the 2018 Report to the Club of Rome (Ulrich von Weizsäcker & Wijkman, 2018). The authors paid a lot of attention to various aspects of sustainable development, and did not ignore global challenges in the education system. Particularly emphasized the development of students' ability to solve problems and engage in critical, independent, and creative thinking.

Understanding the meaning of education today is to expand the kinds of knowledge, skills, and abilities that will be needed to adapt and creatively respond to an uncertain future. So today, society needs a new agreement, an agreement between society and the future, which meets the current conditions and no longer prepares young people for a future that is generally a copy of the past. The requirements of this agreement provide that education must: be active and cooperative; be based on relationships; have a valuable character; pay more attention to the topic of sustainability; to encourage content pluralism.

Today, the state policy of post-war recovery and renovation in Ukraine should focus on implementing mechanisms that ensure the stability and continuity of the national economy's development, as well as the development and restoration of human potential, ensuring and restoring their well-being, and assuming responsibility for decisions before current and future generations. This is outlined in the Sendai Framework Program for Disaster Risk Reduction, whose fourth priority—"Build Back Better"—calls for algorithms for Ukraine's recovery from a systemic perspective, based on the principles of Industry 5.0, specifically human-centeredness, stability, and sustainability. These concepts are meant to complement each other. Today, Ukraine must become a "fast state," ensuring the speed and efficiency of management decisions. The recovery of Ukraine's economy is based on achieving key performance indicators in the implementation of the Sustainable Development Goals, namely overcoming hunger, providing decent employment, infrastructure, responsible consumption, and cooperation to achieve these goals, that is, unification.

Thus, the formation of sustainable development management skills in the conditions of uncertainty, and post-war reconstruction of Ukraine is relevant for future education.

Competency Approach in Higher Education

The International Bureau of Education (UNESCO) defines the concept of competence as the basis of curriculum development and the driving force of the change process (UNESCO, 2019).

The Bologna Agreement, signed in 1999, aimed to synchronize European education systems, promoting a unified educational space and facilitating mobility for students, educators, and researchers across borders. It emphasized the adoption of a competence-based approach, focusing on developing essential skills and knowledge transcending traditional disciplinary boundaries.

The commitment to a competence-based education system reflected a broader vision of not only enhancing the quality of education but also promoting greater collaboration and integration among European countries. The emphasis on competencies underscored the need for learners to acquire versatile skills that are applicable across diverse contexts, preparing them for the complexities of the contemporary global landscape. Some authors rightly point out that connections to competence development, to performance motivation theories and to entrepreneurship form a multifaceted theoretical construction that allows for a variety of interpretations (Brauer, 2021; Mulder & Winterton, 2017).

The competencies approach is playing a fundamental role, and is being used to design new syllabuses to enable comparability throughout Europe by standardizing the way student performance is assessed (Lozano et al., 2012).

We define competence as a dynamic symbiosis of knowledge, abilities and skills, professional, worldview and civic qualities, moral and ethical values, which determines a person's ability to successfully carry out professional and further educational activities and is the result of training at a certain level of education. At the same time, knowledge is a theoretically generalized socio-historical experience, the result of students' mastery of reality, its knowledge. A skill is a student's readiness to successfully perform a certain activity based on knowledge and skills. The ability is formed in the process of students performing various tasks. Skills are considered as an action brought as a result of repeated exercises to the perfection of performance based not on automation, but on the improvement of the quality of the performance of the action.

Some researchers define competence as mastery, which sounds like a synonym for perfection. For example, Curry and Docherty (2017) identify that mastery in a defined competency is demonstrated according to pre-set criteria. As noted by

(Holmes et al., 2021), true mastery of competencies should be determined by examining a student's capabilities with a set of skills, understanding of basic concepts, and ability to work over a period of time, rather than peak performance on a single test.

Today, the formation of competencies based on knowledge, abilities and skills is implemented by applying various technologies and methodological techniques (problem-based learning, programmed learning, practical training, etc.) in the educational process.

An important aspect of preparing for such interaction is the creation and mastery of certain models of reality through education, which forms the necessary skills and abilities. Let us consider the requirements for these skills and abilities that should be formed in higher education institutions.

Education for Sustainable Development

While sustainable development cannot be exclusively realized through education, the pivotal role that education plays in shaping societal systems renders it a cornerstone in the pursuit of almost all Sustainable Development Goals (SDGs). Education functions as a powerful catalyst and system-forming force, wields the potential to instigate far-reaching changes in societal attitudes, behaviors, and structures. In Ukraine 2030: The Doctrine of Sustainable Development, education is defined as the basis for the formation of the country's human and social capital, and one of the key mechanisms of Ukraine's sustainable development (Kharlamova et al., 2018).

The significance of education in the context of sustainable development extends beyond the mere transmission of knowledge; it encapsulates the cultivation of a mindset that embraces environmental stewardship, social equity, and economic viability. A well-rounded and inclusive education system has the capacity to foster awareness, critical thinking, and a sense of responsibility among individuals, qualities that are essential for the attainment of various SDGs.

Education acts as a conduit for disseminating information about environmental conservation, social justice, and economic empowerment. It empowers individuals with the knowledge and skills needed to address complex challenges such as poverty, inequality, climate change, and environmental degradation. By integrating sustainable development principles into curricula, education becomes a transformative force capable of shaping a generation of change-makers and advocates for a more sustainable and equitable world. Furthermore, education plays a pivotal role in achieving goals related to health, gender equality, and economic development. It contributes to the eradication of poverty by equipping individuals with the skills necessary for gainful employment and entrepreneurship.

In essence, education serves as a linchpin in the intricate web of strategies required to address the multifaceted challenges outlined in the SDGs. By nurturing informed and engaged citizens, education becomes a catalyst for positive societal change, fostering the values and capabilities needed to build a sustainable future.

Therefore, while not a sole solution, education emerges as an indispensable factor in the collective pursuit of the Sustainable Development Goals, laying the foundation for a more enlightened, equitable, and sustainable global society.

However, educational services are intangible, non-proprietary, and must play an important role in filling a gap in an industry or country (Gryshova et al., 2019).

The aforementioned Club of Rome report mentions the fact that during the years 2005–2014, UNESCO began implementing initiatives and measures to integrate the principles, values and practices of sustainable development into all aspects of education. The main goal of these activities is to initiate changes in the behavior of youth and future generations to create an environmentally safe, economically viable and socially just world of the future (Ulrich von Weizsäcker & Wijkman, 2018).

One of the ways to achieve this goal is to expand learning opportunities with the help of technologies that provide decision support in learning and education management. In this framework, we consider the possibility and conditions of using information and communication technologies in student learning and human resource development.

Education in the field of sustainable development is represented in the world mainly by master's level programs. In total, there are more than 200 educational programs on sustainable development (this is a Master's Program or Master in Science) in the world—in many countries and on all continents. At the same time, there are no more than a dozen purely educational programs on the management of sustainable development. Some of them with a detailed description of the competencies obtained as a result of training are presented in Table 1.

At present, Ukraine lacks specialized educational programs designed for the comprehensive training of managers in the field of sustainable development, both within the formal academic curriculum and through informal learning pathways. The foundational educational route usually entails pursuing a degree in fields such as "ecology" or "economics." However, the current educational landscape lacks specific courses or programs that holistically address the multifaceted aspects of sustainable development management.

Equally important is the formation of an educational environment or an educational landscape of sustainable development.

In our opinion, it represents a combination of external conditions, factors, social objects necessary for the successful functioning of the education system of sustainable development, where economic, social, and environmental management components will be combined. It is not just the largest integrated system within a society or country. It also has a number of derivatives. Depending on how the organization of a sustainable educational process is carried out, it is possible to determine the directions of qualitative development of social relations. To form an effectively functioning landscape of sustainable development education, it is necessary to:

- consider it in two aspects: (a) integration of education for sustainable development into educational disciplines, programs and courses; (b) organization of separate courses and programs on sustainable development;

Table 1 Existing educational programs in the field of sustainable development management in the world[a]

№	City, country, university	Name of the program	General characteristics of the program	Basic competences acquired
1	Modul University, Vienna, Austria	Sustainable Development, Management and Policy	The Master program equips a fresh cohort of professionals with the skills needed to address upcoming global sustainability dilemmas with confidence.	– understanding of public, private, and non-profit sectors. This competence involves gaining knowledge about how sustainability affects various sectors. – understanding and analyzing sustainability-related policies and governance structures, including their impact and aftereffect. – managing environmental resources sustainably and implementing sustainable practices. – understanding the economic aspects of sustainability, including how sustainable practices in the particular sectors can contribute to economic development. – being able to lead sustainably the organizations and projects of the particular sector; – recognizing and prioritizing sustainability as a central element of decision-making and strategy in various organizations.
2	Sunway University, Shah Alam, Malaysia	Sustainable Development Management	The Master program strives to cultivate a fresh cohort of cross-disciplinary professionals skilled in both management and analytical problem-solving, applying systems thinking guided by global issues.	– developing creative and innovative solutions to solve complex challenges related to Sustainable Development Goals (SDGs). – being able to manage projects effectively, including aspects of leadership, sustainable decision-making, and resource allotment. – developing and

(continued)

Table 1 (continued)

№	City, country, university	Name of the program	General characteristics of the program	Basic competences acquired
				implementing sustainable strategies; – managing financial aspects related to sustainable initiatives and projects. – growing the understanding of social entrepreneurship and its role in achieving SDGs. – understanding comprehensively of sustainability areas, which include climate change, waste management, energy systems, agriculture and food systems, forestry, and biodiversity.
3	University for Peace, Jan Jose, Costa Rica	Responsible Management and Sustainable Economic Development	The Master Program places a strong emphasis on exploring the economic and managerial aspects of peace, all the while concentrating on the principles of sustainability and ethical responsibility.	– understanding deeply of the economic and management aspects with a focus on sustainable practices. – developing interdisciplinary competence, allowing students to bridge the gap between economics, management, and sustainability. This interdisciplinary perspective enables students to work effectively in diverse sectors, from corporate to public and social, and in various countries, including both industrialized and developing nations. – developing problem-solving skills to contribute to political-economic stability and social cohesion.
4	Dublin City University, Dublin, Ireland	Management for Sustainable Development	The Master program primarily offers a program for people seeking to enhance their professional skills in	– comprehension of the theoretical, practical, and legal dimensions of contemporary environmental approaches.

(continued)

Table 1 (continued)

№	City, country, university	Name of the program	General characteristics of the program	Basic competences acquired
			sustainable management through remote, part-time study.	– developing the proficiency in the fundamental management responsibilities essential in the business realm, such as strategic management, project management, and risk evaluation. To empower students to conduct research on various specific subjects, encompassing activities like data gathering, critical examination, interpretation, and the ability to present their findings in a report structure. – developing skills to effectively manage business' assets as environmental, economic and social resources, from a sustainable, global approach.
5	CNAM The International Institute of Management Paris, France	Management in Sustainable Development	The program is the Master in Management program, specialized in Sustainable Development and Quality Management. The program is designed for students who want to have a management or business career mainly in the private sector.	– assessing the organization's capacity through the application of appraisal and auditing techniques derived from quality and sustainability methodologies. – understanding the Innovating Managerial Behavior, in QHSE (Quality, Health, Security, and Environment) – understanding the worldwide economic and social landscape, considering trade-offs between human and natural resources – mastering the contemporary principles and tools designed for business unit managers, tailored to address current management challenges

(continued)

Table 1 (continued)

№	City, country, university	Name of the program	General characteristics of the program	Basic competences acquired
				within the actual business landscape
6	Queen's University of Belfast, Belfast, United Kingdom	Leadership for Sustainable Development	The Master program created for future leaders in sustainable development in all fields. Students will learn diverse areas such as leadership, management, environmental and sustainability science, social studies, economics, and more. The program encourages students to tailor their studies when feasible, allowing them to build upon their existing knowledge, experiences, and personal interests.	– understanding of sustainability, encompassing leadership, management, environmental science, social studies, and economics. – developing critical-thinking and systems-thinking skills, allowing them to analyze complex issues, identify root causes, and develop effective solutions within the framework of sustainable development. – gaining hands-on experience in applying sustainability principles through practicals, site visits, work placements, and community-based projects

[a]*Prepared on the basis of the service: https://www.masterstudies.com.au/*

- to spread positive experience in education, which will contribute to changes in behavior in favor of sustainability (Vysotska, 2011);
- to strengthen the cooperation and partnership of teachers with other participants in the process;
- promote understanding of the essence of global, national and local environmental problems with an emphasis on their socio-economic consequences;
- introduce new approaches to education: discussions, round tables, encourage self-education.

As part of the preparations for the second national voluntary report on Ukraine's achievement of the Sustainable Development Goals, some of the authors of this study conducted a survey of young people at the Universities of Ukraine (a total of 432 questionnaires were collected). The vast majority of students note the need to study sustainable development management. At the same time, 91.4% of respondents noted the need to increase state support in various forms to such educational programs.

Understanding the attitudes of individuals from various generations towards the concept of sustainable development is a crucial aspect in shaping educational

Table 2 The attitude of different generations to the concept of sustainable development (*author's design*)

Generation	Birth period	Attitude towards the principles of sustainable development
X	Approximately between 1965 and 1980	– often adopt a pragmatic stance towards sustainable development, having witnessed environmental crises and societal transformations during their lifetimes; – display an interest in conserving natural resources, albeit with a degree of caution and skepticism
Y	Approximately between 1981 and 1996	– typically exhibit a strong inclination towards sustainable development, having grown up amidst escalating environmental challenges and a burgeoning global consciousness; – frequently base their decisions on social responsibility and environmental concerns, manifesting in product choices, support for environmental initiatives, and active participation in community engagements
Z	Approximately from the mid-1990s to around 2010	– generally demonstrate a heightened interest in sustainable development, given their upbringing in a world where environmental issues and sustainable practices are increasingly pertinent; – actively engage in social movements and initiatives advocating for ecological preservation and sustainable development
Alpa	After 2010	– while their attitudes towards sustainability remain nascent due to their young age, this generation appears to be cultivating environmental consciousness from early developmental stages; – likely to demonstrate a predisposition to acquiring knowledge and understanding of environmental issues and sustainable development, facilitated by the widespread availability of information through digital platforms and social media

programs. This notion has been highlighted notably in studies cited as references (Nichols, 2023; Senegacnik et al., 2017).

Attitudes toward sustainable development vary across generations due to their distinct life experiences, socio-cultural influences, and perceptions of global issues. Here are generalized characteristics of how each generation—X, Y, Z, and Alpha—might approach sustainability (Table 2).

It's important to note that these observations represent overarching tendencies, and individual beliefs and attitudes may significantly vary within each generational cohort.

The findings of a survey conducted among undergraduate students from National University of Kyiv-Mohila Academy, aged 19–21 and representing various academic disciplines, revealed intriguing insights regarding the significance of educational activities in sustainable development. Consequently, these results are pivotal for developing an effective competency framework. Presented below are the key questions from the survey, where participants had the option to select multiple answers:

Question 1: Key Steps for Achieving Sustainability

- Raise awareness: 25%
- Offer educational programs on sustainable development: 81.3%
- Implement best practices (e.g., waste sorting, energy-efficient technologies): 56.3%
- Encourage student research and projects on sustainable development: 50%

Question 2: Role of Students/Youth in Sustainable Development Goals

- Adhere to sustainable principles and promote them: 87.5%
- Conduct educational outreach: 25%
- Create societal demand for sustainability training: 62.5%
- Advocate for sustainability in workplaces: 68.8%

And all 100% of students indicate that they would like to know more about how to implement sustainable development in Ukrainian companies and how to manage companies in modern conditions.

Are Managers of Sustainable Development Needed Today and What Competencies Are Required for Them?

A Sustainable Development Manager strategically establishes and sustains social and environmental responsibility within organizations. Engaging stakeholders, they formulate and execute sustainable strategies to ensure economic prosperity. Operating on dual fronts of responsibility and business, they oversee enduring practices, considering profitability alongside environmental and social impact. This involves decision-making and implementation for environmental preservation and company growth. They empower companies by adhering to conservation norms, implementing policies for responsibility, educating stakeholders on sustainable practices, and enhancing corporate reputation through best practices.

The scope of a Manager of Sustainable Development extends beyond the private sector to encompass governmental bodies, consulting firms, and non-governmental sectors. Their responsibilities, depend on the company's requirements, the specific position, and the organizational structure, may include:

- Developing and implementing a corporate sustainable strategy.
- Identifying key sustainability indicators for the enterprise.
- Monitoring corporate sustainability indicators.

- Analyzing and auditing environmental, social, and corporate activities.
- Drafting reports, including non-financial and sustainable development reports, detailing research results, and presenting this information to management with recommendations for modifications based on research.
- Establishing guiding principles governing the company's interaction with the environmental and social environment.
- Collaborating with various company departments to incorporate sustainable practices and set sustainable development goals.
- Conducting training and seminars on sustainable development practices and policies for company employees.
- Disseminating knowledge about sustainable development among human resource managers, colleagues, leadership, media, and other stakeholders.
- Attracting green investments from international donors.

In the realm of the creative economy, where production is grounded in individual talents and unconventional ideas, the role of a sustainable development manager becomes exceptionally crucial. The sustainable development manager in the creative economy plays a pivotal role in facilitating the effective resolution of socio-economic challenges. They are responsible for the development and implementation of strategies aimed at balanced and sustainable production, aligning with the fundamental principles of the creative economy. Currently, the creative economy is becoming a foundation for the world economy. Present fast-paced changes in global creation processes and the introduction of inventions indicate that all of the future economies will be creative. The economic measurement for creativity is its impact on business and the ability to generate and promote innovation, productivity, and economic growth (Kharlamova & Gumenna, 2018).

In light of the projected macro trends over the next 5 years, the sustainable development manager emerges as an even more pivotal player. The green transition of businesses, widespread adoption of environmental and social standards are the directions where the manager must initiate and implement strategies to ensure sustainable development.

The anticipated increase in job positions by 40% for sustainable development specialists underscores the growing importance of this role (Future of Jobs Report, 2023). In the context of the creative economy, where innovation and socio-environmental responsibility are paramount, the sustainable development manager acts as a strategic agent, supporting and ensuring the effective functioning of organizations.

By the results of the evaluation of the study programs in sustainable development at the University of Bern, the competency "Communicating in a comprehensive and target group-oriented manner" was considered the most important competency by all three surveyed groups according to the proportions of "very important" responses. Similarly, the two competencies "Recognizing and reflecting on one's own perspective on a situation and problem" and "Interconnected, foresighted and thinking in system-dynamic contexts" were also estimated to be of above-average importance (Table 3 and Fig. 1) (Hammer & Lewis, 2023).

Table 3 Average importance of the sustainability competencies by the survey from (Hammer & Lewis, 2023)

Competences	Very important	Rather important	Partly	Rather unimportant	Very unimportant
Students					
Discipline-independent knowledge of SD	24	42	25	9	–
Methodological expertise, as well as inter- and transdisciplinary approaches	38	38	18	5	1
Interconnected, foresighted, and thinking approaches in systemdynamic contexts	61	30	7	2	1
Accessing knowledge from other disciplines	40	35	20	5	–
Graduates					
Discipline-independent knowledge of SD	22	46	19	2	1
Methodological expertise, as well as inter- and transdisciplinary approaches	28	45	22	5	1
Interconnected, foresighted, and thinking approaches in systemdynamic contexts	55	30	9	7	–
Accessing knowledge from other disciplines	38	38	20	3	1

For the professional field, the competency "Communicating in a comprehensive and target group-oriented manner" is rated most important by all three groups (Hammer & Lewis, 2023).

Authors of research make the conclusion that "in order to ensure that lecturers align respective learning outcomes, as well as teaching/learning arrangements and assessments in their educational elements, there will need to be a greater focus on competency development across a program of study" (Hammer & Lewis, 2023).

The evaluation and favorability ascribed to outcomes emanating from a company's initiatives in sustainable development can exert influence on various facets, including the competitive standing of the company; the reputational capital of the company; the sustenance of morale support.

According to the analysis of the "Future of Jobs Report 2023", conducted by the World Economic Forum, an evolution of the skills required for workers is anticipated over the next 5 years. Key competencies encompass analytical and creative thinking, technological literacy, skills for continuous learning, and mindfulness.

In 2018, a novel four-tiered skills model was delineated, which incorporates:

- Existential skills—fundamental abilities aimed at developing character and life strategies, encompassing aspects supporting willpower, health, emotional self-regulation, self-awareness, self-reflection, and the capacity for self-development.

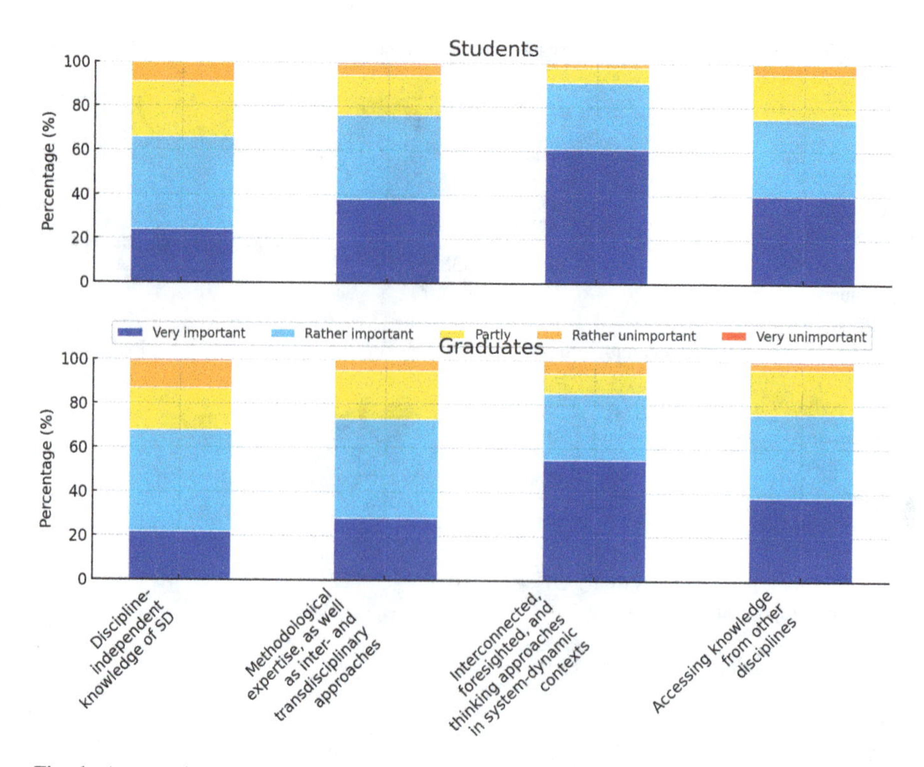

Fig. 1 Average importance of the sustainability competencies by the survey from (Hammer & Lewis, 2023)

- Meta-skills—means of managing objects in the mental or physical realm, including various types of intelligence and creativity.
- Cross-contextual skills—knowledge and abilities applied in broader social-economic or personal spheres, such as reading, writing, time management, collaboration, and others.
- Contextual skills—professional knowledge and abilities, specific physical skills, or unique social skills pertaining to a particular professional domain (Luksha et al., 2018).

With the goal of preparing qualified managers in the field of sustainable development, this study aims to identifying the necessary competencies that students acquire through the development of skills, knowledge, and abilities, utilizing the concept of the four-tiered model (Fig. 2).

Context skills can vary depending on the position held, organizational structure, and area of responsibility (expertise).

Establishing a competency framework for sustainable development in modern youth education is crucial. It equips them with the necessary skills to tackle pressing global challenges effectively, fosters holistic thinking, and empowers them to become proactive contributors to a more sustainable future.

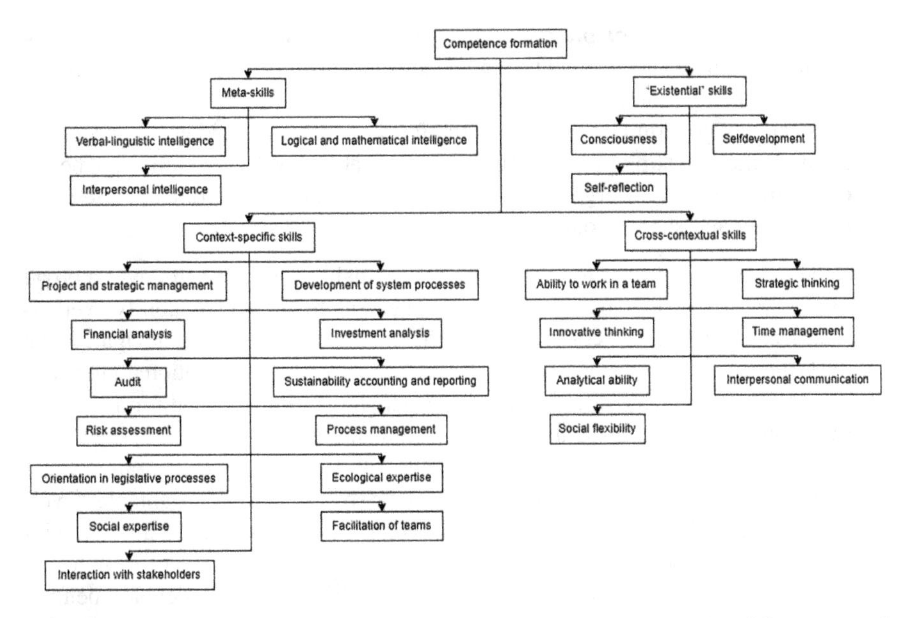

Fig. 2 Competence formation for managers of sustainable development based on different types of skills (*author's design*)

Conclusion

The imperative for managers of sustainable development in the context of the creative economy is undeniable. As the creative economy plays a pivotal role in addressing socio-economic challenges through innovation, the sustainable development manager becomes a strategic force. Their role extends beyond traditional business practices, incorporating socio-environmental responsibility and ensuring balanced and sustainable production.

The anticipated rise in demand for sustainable development specialists underscores the growing significance of this role. The World Economic Forum's "Future of Jobs Report 2023" emphasizes the evolution of skills required for workers, emphasizing analytical and creative thinking, technological literacy, continuous learning, and mindfulness. This aligns with the proposed four-tiered skills model, encompassing existential, meta-skills, cross-contextual, and context-specific skills.

To address the current lack of specialized programs for sustainability managers in Ukraine, it is imperative to adopt a comprehensive approach involving educational institutions, policymakers, and industry stakeholders. Here are some of our suggestions:

- encourage research initiatives focused on sustainable development and the creative economy;

- design interdisciplinary programs that draw from fields such as ecology, economics, business management, and social sciences to provide a holistic understanding of sustainable development;
- advocate for government support in the form of grants, subsidies, or incentives for institutions that pioneer programs in sustainable development management.
- create student clubs or organizations focused on sustainability to foster a sense of community and shared goals.

The competencies essential for managers in sustainable development cover a broad spectrum. From project and strategic management to analytical ability, verbal-linguistic intelligence, and consciousness, these skills are integral to navigating the complexities of the creative economy. The lack of specialized educational programs in Ukraine for sustainable development managers highlights the need for a comprehensive curriculum to address the multifaceted nature of this role.

In essence, as we navigate the intricate landscape of the creative economy, where individual talents and unconventional ideas flourish, the role of sustainable development managers becomes instrumental. By championing strategies that align with environmental and social standards, these professionals contribute not only to the economic prosperity of organizations but also to the sustainable development of society at large. Their ability to navigate the green transition and implement effective sustainable practices positions them as key agents in shaping a resilient and innovative future.

References

Brauer, S. (2021). Towards competence-oriented higher education: A systematic literature review of the different perspectives on successful exit profiles. *Education + Training, 63*(9), 1376–1390. https://doi.org/10.1108/ET-07-2020-0216

Curry, L., & Docherty, M. (2017). Implementing competency-based education. *CELT Collected Essays on Learning and Teaching, X,* 61–73.

Gryshova, I., Demchuk, N., Koshkalda, I., Stebliuk, N., & Volosova, N. (2019). Strategic imperatives of managing the sustainable innovative development of the market of educational services in the higher education system. *Sustainability, 11*, 7253.

Hammer, T., & Lewis, A. L. (2023). Which competencies should be fostered in education for sustainable development at higher education institutions? Findings from the evaluation of the study programs at the University of Bern, Switzerland. *Discover Sustainability, 4*(1), 19. https://doi.org/10.1007/s43621-023-00134-w

Holmes, A. G. D., Tuin, M. P., & Turner, S. L. (2021). Competence and competency in higher education, simple terms yet with complex meanings: Theoretical and practical issues for university teachers and assessors implementing Competency-Based Education (CBE) Educational Process. *International Journal, 10*(3), 39–52. https://doi.org/10.22521/edupij.2021.103.3

Kharlamova, G., Aynonyuk, L., Chala, N., & Humenna, O. (2018). Ukraine 2030. The Doctrine of Sustainable Development. ADEF-Ukraine PH.

Kharlamova, G., & Gumenna, O. (2018). Creative economy and competitiveness: Case of Ukraine. In S. Mărginean, C. Ogrean, & R. Orăştean (Eds.), *Emerging issues in the global economy* (Springer proceedings in business and economics). Springer. https://doi.org/10.1007/978-3-319-71876-7_18

Lozano, J. F., Boni, A., Peris, J., & Hueso, A. (2012). Competencies in higher education: A critical analysis from the capabilities approach. *Journal of Philosophy of Education, 46*(1), 132–147. https://www.researchgate.net/publication/230545715_Competencies_in_Higher_Education_A_Critical_Analysis_from_the_Capabilities_Approach
Luksha, P., Cubista, J., Laszlo, A., Popovich, M., & Ninenko, I. (2018). Global education futures report: Educational ecosystems for societal transformation. *Global Education Futures*. https://drive.google.com/file/d/1zmxNZpeitzDgQ7hVtj1u0FCm3EsXKk-t/view
Mulder, M., & Winterton, J. (2017). *Competence-based vocational and professional education. Bridging the worlds of work and education* (pp. 1–43). Springer.
Nichols, B. S. (2023). A comparison of sustainability attitudes and intentions across generations and gender: A perspective from U.S. consumers. *Cuadernos de Gestion*. https://www.researchgate.net/publication/367243538
Senegacnik, M., Borojevic, T., Petrovic, N., & Maletic, M. (2017). Youth attitudes towards goals of a new sustainable development agenda. Problemy Ekorozwoju. https://www.researchgate.net/publication/317767876
Transforming our world: the 2030 Agenda for Sustainable Development. United Nations. https://web.archive.org/web/20171205210925/https://sustainabledevelopment.un.org/post2015/transformingourworld
Ulrich von Weizsäcker, E., & Wijkman, A. (2018). *Come on! Capitalism, short-termism, population and the destruction of the planet*. A Report to the Club of Rome.
UNESCO. (2019). Competency-based approaches. Retrieved July 24, 2020, from http://www.ibe.unesco.org/en/topics/competency-based-approaches
Vysotska, O. E. (2011). *Education for sustainable development: A scientific and methodological manual* (200 p.). Royal Print.
World Economic Forum. (2023). Future of Jobs Report 2023 INSIGHT REPORT. *World Economic Forum*. https://www3.weforum.org/docs/WEF_Future_of_Jobs_2023.pdf?_gl=1*x0g234*_up*MQ..&gclid=CjwKCAjw69moBhBgEiwAUFCx2HMCMudgZMZUXju8tgllkXZEDFMryBReso4W7xXCKv8dlqSgHfbGTxoCgKMQAvD_BwE

War-Related Moral Damage: Ukrainian and International Practice

Bohdan Karnaukh

Abstract Moral damage is a negative psychological experience endured by a person, consisting of mental pain and anguish. War brings with it an inconceivable amount of such experience. However, not all such experience can be compensated through legal mechanisms. There is a certain threshold of severity of moral damage below which compensation is not provided. Such a 'threshold' of compensability is often dependent on the functioning and purpose of a particular compensation mechanism. The chapter aims to explore the practice of Ukrainian courts, the UN Compensation Commission, and the ECtHR in matters concerning compensation for war-related moral damage. The chapter addresses evidentiary matters (burden of proof, standard of proof and presumptions) and provides some guidance on the calculation of monetary compensation for mental pain and anguish. The author concludes that the awarded sum should not be viewed as a precise monetary representation of the ordeal. Rather, it serves as a relative indication of the severity and duration of the pain and suffering endured. Determining the monetary unit of measurement hinges on various political, economic, and practical factors, such as the nature and responsibilities of the adjudicating body, the socioeconomic conditions in the applicant's country, and the resources available to the responsible entity.

Introduction

Tort law aims to rectify damage caused by wrongful actions, seeking to restore the injured person to the pre-incident state (restitutio in integrum). Ideally, compensation should strive to "revert" the injured individual to the position they would have been in but for the harmful event.

However, time cannot actually be "rewound" in the literal sense of the word. So, even when the negative consequences in the physical world are repaired (the

B. Karnaukh (✉)
Department of Civil Law, Yaroslav Mudryi National Law University, Kharkiv, Ukraine
e-mail: b.p.karnauh@nlu.edu.ua

S. Nate (ed.), *Ukraine's Journey to Recovery, Reform and Post-War Reconstruction*, Contributions to Security and Defence Studies,
https://doi.org/10.1007/978-3-031-66434-2_21

damaged property is restored or replaced with a new one), the negative experience that the person has undergone—the painful feelings, emotions, and distress—remains with the person. And the fact that the property is now safe and sound does not negate the time spent in worry, anxiety, and stress.

This is even more true in cases of damage to life and limb. Even when the victim makes a full recovery and the economic consequences of their injury (such as medical expenses and lost earnings) are fully covered by the tortfeasor, the pain and suffering experienced remains unaddressed. This experience can be a depressing, indelible pain, and a trauma that stays for life.

Moral (non-pecuniary) damage is a legal term intended to provide compensation for adverse, traumatic experiences. Often, the same incident causes damage on two levels at the same time—on the economic and moral (non-pecuniary) levels. For example, if the victim's arm is broken, this entails economic damage in the form of treatment costs, loss of earnings (income) due to a decrease in professional or general ability to work, additional costs for prosthetics, third-party care, etc. and non-pecuniary damage in the form of pain, discomfort, inconvenience, etc. In order to fully restore the situation of the injured person, tort law provides for the possibility of claiming compensation for both economic and moral (noneconomic) damage.

However, with regard to non-pecuniary damage, there are a number of questions that remain problematic for lawyers and that have not received (and perhaps cannot receive) clear, unambiguous answers. These include the minimum threshold of compensable negative experience; determining the amount of monetary compensation for pain and suffering; the degree to which individual traits are taken into account when assessing the severity of the experience; and evidentiary standards for proving non-pecuniary damage.

Russian aggression against Ukraine has affected every Ukrainian without exception. There is not a single Ukrainian who has not been touched by this war as a deeply distressing ordeal. The conflict touches everyone: at the very least, it instills constant fear for their own lives and those of their loved ones, erodes confidence in the future, and disrupts established routines and life plans. However, these are just the 'lightest' of the adversities brought about by the war. It claims lives, causes injuries, destroys homes and entire cities, decimates cultural heritage, and damages the environment.

Among all those affected by this conflict, who can seek compensation for the emotional harm they've endured? Whose psychological suffering is significant enough to warrant legal recognition and compensation? And what might be the appropriate amount for such compensation? To address these questions, we propose an examination of both national and international precedents regarding compensation for the moral damage inflicted by war and egregious violations of universally acknowledged human rights and freedoms.

Ukrainian Practice

In April 2022, the Supreme Court passed a landmark ruling[1] according to which the Russian Federation cannot invoke jurisdictional immunity in cases concerning compensation for war-related damage (previously, claims against the Russian Federation could be tried by Ukrainian courts only upon the consent of the Russian Federation itself).[2] This finding enabled Ukrainian citizens to sue the aggressor state in Ukrainian courts. As a result, a new category of cases has emerged in Ukrainian jurisprudence—cases concerning compensation for war-related damage, in which the Russian Federation is the defendant.

In almost every case of this kind plaintiffs seek compensation for moral (non-pecuniary) damage. In claims brought by individuals (as opposed to legal entities) moral damage is usually the only type of damage sought. And that is not because no other harm has been suffered, but rather due to the difficulties of proving the pecuniary damage (and its exact amount) with the precision demanded by the Ukrainian courts. Therefore, seeking compensation for the moral damage may often be seen by the plaintiffs as a way to overcome hurdles of proving their financial losses according to the demanding evidentiary standards.[3]

The definition of moral damage and general rules for its compensation are set forth in **Article 23 of the Civil Code of Ukraine**. Many clarifications regarding moral damage were provided by the highest courts.[4] Particularly significant was the legal position of the Grand Chamber of the Supreme Court in case No. 216/3521/16-ц, in which compensation for moral damage was recognized as a universal remedy, i.e. one that applies to all legal relationships, and not only when it is expressly provided for a particular situation by a special statute or by contract between the parties.[5] It means that any time moral damage is inflicted, the victim is entitled to claim compensation without the need to rely on special provisions of legislation allowing such compensation in this fact setting or on the terms of the contract between the parties.

---

[1] See: Judgment of the Civil Court of Cassation of April 14, 2022 in case No. 308/9708/19. URL: https://reyestr.court.gov.ua/Review/104086064.

[2] For a detailed analysis of this case, see: Karnaukh B 'Territorial Tort Exception? The Ukrainian Supreme Court Held that the Russian Federation Could Not Plead Immunity with regard to Tort Claims Brought by the Victims of the Russia-Ukraine War' 2022 3(15) Access to Justice in Eastern Europe 165–177. https://doi.org/10.33327/AJEE-18-5.2-n000321.

[3] On the evidentiary standards applied by Ukrainian courts against the comparative background see: B Karnaukh 'Standards of Proof: A Comparative Overview from the Ukrainian Perspective' 2021 2(10) Access to Justice in Eastern Europe 25–43. https://doi.org/10.33327/AJEE-18-4.2-a000058.

[4] See: Resolution of the Plenum of the Supreme Court of Ukraine No. 4 of 31.03.1995 "On Judicial Practice in Cases Concerning Compensation for Moral (Non-Pecuniary) Damage". URL: https://zakon.rada.gov.ua/laws/show/v0004700-95#Text.

[5] Judgment of the Grand Chamber of the Supreme Court, 1 September 2020, case no. 216/3521/16-ts. URL: https://reyestr.court.gov.ua/Review/91644731.

Thus, moral damage is always subject to compensation, provided that it is caused by unlawful decisions, actions or omissions (see Article 1167 of the Civil Code of Ukraine). However, the plaintiff in such cases must prove that he or she has actually suffered moral damage. And since the very concept of moral damage is evaluative (since not every negative experience is severe enough to give rise to the right to compensation), the case law on this issue remains heterogeneous.

All cases involving moral damage caused by the war can be divided into five categories: (a) cases where moral damage is caused by the loss of a family member; (b) cases where moral damage is caused by injury or other damage to the plaintiff's health; (c) cases where moral damage is caused by the destruction, impairment, loss of property or loss of access to property; (d) cases where moral damage is caused by internal displacement or the need to flee the country; and (e) cases where moral damage is caused by the fact of war per se.

As for categories (a), (b) and (c), the presence of moral damage is usually not in dispute, and the only challenging issue is the calculation of the amount of compensation. Instead, in categories (d) and (e), the courts sometimes take opposite views.

Thus, for the most part, the courts uphold claims where moral damage is caused by internal displacement or the need to flee the country (category (d)). However, there are also cases in which the courts arrive at the opposite conclusion.

It is noteworthy that in many cases where plaintiffs claim compensation for moral damage caused by the displacement, the amount of compensation is estimated at **35,000 euros.**[6] This figure comes from the case of *Loizidou v. Turkey*, which was considered by the European Court of Human Rights (ECHR) and will be discussed in detail below.

Category (e) cases involve plaintiffs citing Russia's invasion of Ukraine as a source of stress and asserting that moral damage they suffered stems from the intense experiences endured due to the war. They do not allege any other personal or financial harm, including the necessity for internal displacement.

In this type of cases plaintiffs allege that moral damage consisted of constant distress, anxiety, disruption of normal life ties, inability to lead life as usual and build relationships with others, fear for their lives, ruined life plans, decrease in vitality etc. In one of the cases the plaintiff claimed that her moral damage was related to her constant worrying about the state of environment affected by the war.

For the most part courts dismiss this type of claims. Often the courts substantiate the dismissal by finding that the plaintiff has not proven the damage.[7] In some other cases the courts emphasize that the plaintiff did not demonstrate what actions of the

[6]See, for example: Ruling of the Kropyvnytskyi Court of Appeal of 14 December 2023, case no. 398/3995/22, proceedings no. 22-c/4809/751/23; Ruling of the Belozersky District Court of Kherson Region of 18 March 2019, case no. 648/3345/18, proceedings no. 2/648/161/19; Ruling of the Rivne City Court of Rivne Region of 11 January 2019, case no. 569/20061/18.

[7]See: Decision of the Darnytsia District Court of Kyiv of October 04, 2022 in case No. 753/15426/20. https://reyestr.court.gov.ua/Review/106915823.

aggressor state were wrongful *vis-a-vis* him or her in particular.[8] In this letter type of reasoning the courts suggest that the plaintiff has to show how exactly the war affected him or her personally and the overall effects of the war on the population at large does not count as a cause of action for each particular member of population.

However, the plaintiffs are not disingenuous when saying that the war made them feel anxious—the war indeed affected every Ukrainian. Even people who have not suffered the bitter loss of loved ones, injury, or other bodily pain, did not lose their property, are still going through a psychologically difficult experience.

However, if this experience is recognized as legally compensable, then every person living in Ukraine would have the right to go to court. Moreover, the range of potential victims would not be limited to the physical borders of Ukraine—anyone who cares about Ukraine could be a victim, because they also experience hard feelings. Therefore, if tort law were to recognize the claims of such people as eligible, it would open the door to tens of millions of claims that the national judicial system could hardly handle.

Secondly, unlike other categories of cases where moral damage is incidental to other (bodily or economic) damage, in category (d) moral damage is the only type of damage claimed by the plaintiff. Is it possible for moral damage to occur on its own, and not as a "concomitant consequence" of some other (bodily or economic) damage? Yes. For example, in the case of humiliation of the honor and dignity of an individual (in the case of dissemination of false information about a person). However, even in such cases, moral damage must be the result of a violation of a concrete right enjoyed by a concrete person (the right to inviolability of honor, dignity and business reputation). In contrast, an aggressive war to seize territories is a violation of the sovereignty of a particular state, not a violation of the rights of a particular citizen of that state. Therefore, the mere fact of an aggressive war against Ukraine, in the absence of any other bodily or economic harm or other observable inconveniences (such as the need to leave one's home), does not entitle a Ukrainian citizen to claim compensation for moral damage under the rules of tort law.

The United Nations Compensation Commission's Practice

The United Nations Compensation Commission (hereinafter referred to as the Commission) was established in 1991 pursuant to UN Security Council Resolution 692[9] to consider claims and pay compensation for damage and losses caused by Iraq's illegal invasion of Kuwait and subsequent occupation of Kuwait in 1990–1991.

---

[8] See: Decision of the Zhovtnevyi District Court of Kryvyi Rih, Dnipro Region, of December 19, 2022, in case No. 212/3718/22. https://reyestr.court.gov.ua/Review/108199195.

[9] Resolution 692 (1991)/adopted by the UN Security Council at its 2987th meeting, on 20 May 1991. https://digitallibrary.un.org/record/113598?v=pdf.

The Governing Council defined six categories of claims. In addition to compensation for pecuniary losses, in designated cases, applicants were also entitled to claim compensation for moral damage, or—in the Commission's own terminology—compensation for mental pain and anguish (MPA). The list of such cases and the maximum amount of compensation were set out in Decision No. 8.[10] In particular MPA claims were available in the following categories of cases: death of a family member (category A); serious personal injury (Category B); sexual assault or aggravated assault or torture (category C); witnessing the intentional infliction of events described in Categories A, B or C on a family member (category D); being taken hostage or illegally detained for more than 3 days, or for a shorter period in circumstances indicating an imminent threat life (category E); on account of a manifestly well-founded fear for life or of being taken hostage or illegally detained, the individual was forced to hide for more than 3 days (category F); and the individual was deprived of all economic resources, such as to threaten seriously his or her survival and that of his or her spouse, children or parents, in cases where assistance from his or her Government or other sources has not been provided (category G).

With regard to the Commission's practice, it is important to note, first, that not in all cases of pecuniary damage, the victims were recognized as having the right to additionally claim compensation for non-pecuniary damage.

Second, in those specified cases in which the victims were entitled to compensation for non-pecuniary damage, no additional evidence was required to prove mental pain or suffering. Thus, applicants had to prove only the fact of a traumatic incident (serious bodily injury, sexual violence, torture, etc.), and the occurrence of non-pecuniary damage in such cases was accepted as an irrefutable presumption. There was no need to prove mental suffering separately, by means of an expert opinion.

At the same time, in Decision No. 3,[11] the Commission's Governing Council emphasized the need to distinguish between "mental pain and anguish" (i.e. non-pecuniary damage), on the one hand, and "mental injury", on the other. If the events of the war had such a severe impact on a person's mental state that he or she developed a condition that qualifies as a mental disorder (e.g., post-traumatic stress disorder), then such a disorder should be treated as an independent type of damage in category "B"—serious bodily injury, and it is subject to separate proof. In this case, the concept of mental disorder should be understood in accordance with the tenth edition of the International Classification of Diseases.

---

[10] Decision taken by the Governing Council of the UN Compensation Commission during its Fourth Session, at the 22nd meeting, held on 24 January 1992 "Determination of Ceilings for Compensation for Mental Pain and Anguish".

[11] Decision taken by the Governing Council of the United Nations Compensation Commission during its second session, at the 15th meeting, held on 18 October 1991 "Personal Injury and Mental Pain and Anguish".

The Report of the Panel of Experts appointed to assist the UN Compensation Commission in matters relating to mental pain and suffering[12] deserves special attention. This panel included leading psychiatrists whose task was to help the Commission determine guidelines for compensation for non-pecuniary damage.

It is noteworthy that in this Report, the experts specifically emphasized that the conclusions they made could be useful not only for the work of the Commission, but also for similar compensation mechanisms in the future, when it comes to assessing moral damage caused by armed conflicts.

Experts also noted that the maximum compensation limits set by the Compensation Commission are generally low. However, it should be realized that these amounts are not a universal and accurate measure of the suffering caused—they are the result of considering numerous political, economic and practical factors.

An important outcome of the experts' work was the development of "Modifying Factors," i.e., circumstances to be taken into account when determining the exact amount of compensation to be awarded within the maximum cap. The Modifying Factors served as guidelines to help determine whether the amount awarded in each case should be closer to the maximum or minimum limit.

Case Law of the European Court of Human Rights (ECtHR)

General principles on compensation for non-pecuniary damage applied by the ECtHR are set out in the Practice Directions on Just Satisfaction.[13]

The ECtHR notes that applicants are not required to submit additional evidence to prove their mental suffering—the conclusion that such suffering was present is a natural inference when a person has proven a violation of his or her fundamental rights.

Secondly, the ECtHR notes the impossibility of accurate calculation of non-pecuniary damage. At the same time, the Court emphasizes that the approach must be flexible and take into account all the relevant circumstances of the case.

Finally, the ECtHR holds that the amount of compensation is dependent on the overall economic situation in the respondent state. Effectively, this means that the amount of compensation for moral damages under the same circumstances will be different for applicants from different countries: in richer economies, the amount will be higher than in less wealthy ones. This is because just satisfaction is not intended to

[12] Annex VI. Expert Report on Mental Pain and Anguish (Prepared for the United Nations Compensation Commission, 14 March 1993). In Report and Recommendations Made by The Panel of Commissioners Concerning the First Installment of Individual Claims for Damages up to US$100,000 (CATEGORY "C" CLAIMS).

[13] Practice direction issued by the President of the Court in accordance with Rule 32 of the Rules of Court on 28 March 2007 and amended on 9 June 2022. https://www.echr.coe.int/documents/d/echr/pd_satisfaction_claims_eng.

equalize global economic inequality, but only to remedy the situation of a particular claimant living in concrete economic conditions.

As noted above, Ukrainians in their claims against the Russian Federation often refer to the ECtHR judgment in *Loizidou v. Turkey* (just satisfaction) [GC], no. 15318/89, which concerned Turkey's occupation of Northern Cyprus.

In this case the applicant, a Cypriot national, grew up in Kyrenia in northern Cyprus. She owned ten plots of land in Kyrenia. Prior to the Turkish occupation of northern Cyprus on 20 July 1974, work had commenced on one of the plots for the construction of a block of flats, one of which was intended as a home for her family. The applicant had entered into an agreement with the property developer to exchange her share in the land for an apartment of 100 sq. m. Yet, since1974 she had been prevented from gaining access to her properties in northern Cyprus and "peacefully enjoying" them as a result of the presence of Turkish forces there.

The ECtHR held that there had been a violation of Article 1 of Protocol No. 1, as the applicant had effectively lost any control over her property, as well as all possibilities to use and dispose of it. In addition to the pecuniary damage (300,000 Cypriot pounds) in the form of lost profits that the applicant could have received by leasing her land plots, the ECtHR awarded non-pecuniary damage in the amount of 20,000 Cypriot pounds, equivalent to 35,000 euros.

Despite the fact that Ukrainian courts often award the same amount to internally displaced persons, it is worth noting that this amount was determined by the ECtHR based on the specific circumstances of the case under consideration. Such circumstances include, in particular, the amount of property to which the applicant lost access (ten land plots), its value, the amount of financial damage (over half a million euros), and the duration of the violation (the Court took into account the period from 1990 to 1997). Therefore, this amount should not be considered as a "default rate" of moral damages for all internal displacement cases.

For the Ukrainian situation, the findings of the ECHR in the case of *Georgia v. Russia II* (just satisfaction) [GC], no. 3826308 may be helpful. This case concerned the detention, custody and expulsion from Russia of a large number of Georgian citizens from the end of September 2006 to the end of January 2007. According to the Georgian government, during this period, the Russian authorities issued more than 4600 expulsion orders against Georgian citizens, of whom more than 2300 were detained and forcibly expelled, and the rest left the country on their own. The Court found that the expulsion of Georgian nationals during the period under review was not based on a reasonable and objective consideration of the circumstances of each individual's case, but instead constituted an arbitrary administrative practice in violation of Article 4 of Protocol No. 4 to the Convention.

It was also held that the lack of effective and accessible remedies for Georgian citizens violated Article 5 § 4 of the Convention, while the conditions of detention in which Georgian citizens were placed (overcrowding, inadequate sanitary and hygienic conditions and lack of privacy) constituted an administrative practice in violation of Article 3 of the Convention. The Court also found a violation of Article 13 in conjunction with Article 5(1) and Article 3 of the Convention.

Regarding the compensation for non-pecuniary damage in this case, the ECtHR noted that in some cases, the mere recognition by the Court that the applicant's rights have been violated is sufficient to remedy non-pecuniary damage, but in other cases it is not enough, and compensation must be awarded. This case falls into the latter category.

As a result, the ECtHR ruled that Russia should pay Georgia EUR 10 million in compensation for the damage suffered by a group of at least 1500 Georgian citizens; this amount should be distributed among individual victims in the amount of EUR 2000 to Georgian citizens who were victims of a violation of Article 4 of Protocol No. 4 to the Convention (collective expulsion) only, and EUR 10,000 to 15,000 to those who were also victims of violations of Article 5, paragraph 1 (unlawful detention) and Article 3 (inhuman and degrading treatment) of the Convention, taking into account the length of their respective detention periods.

The damage caused by the armed conflict was also addressed in the case of *Chiragov and Others v. Armenia* (just satisfaction) [GC], no. 13216/05. The applicants in this case were Azerbaijani Kurds living in the Lachin region of Azerbaijan. They claimed that they could not return to their homes and property after being forced to leave them in 1992 during the Armenian-Azerbaijani conflict over Nagorno-Karabakh. The Court concluded that Armenia had violated Article 1 of Protocol No. 1 to the ECHR (right to peaceful enjoyment of possessions) and Article 8 of the ECHR (right to respect for private and family life).

Assessing the amount of both pecuniary and non-pecuniary damage in this case was complicated by a number of unknown or unconfirmed circumstances. In particular, the case file did not contain sufficient evidence to show that the applicants' houses still existed as of April 2002 and, if so, in such a condition that they could be taken into account for the purposes of awarding compensation. It was also extremely difficult to determine the value of the applicants' land. Therefore, the usual approach of calculating economic damage based on the expected rent for the relevant period and the income from agriculture and livestock cannot be applied in such circumstances.

No evidence, other than witness testimony, has been provided to support allegations of the loss of household items, cars, fruit trees, bushes and livestock. Furthermore, it is reasonable to assume that all of these items were probably destroyed or disappeared during the attack on the Lachin district or during the subsequent 10-year period until April 2002. If some items still existed as of that date, they most likely deteriorated, died, or were no longer usable over time. The loss of wages and other income was not related to the lack of access to the applicants' property and housing, but to the applicants' displacement from Lachin in 1992. In this context, it was impossible to determine what kind of job or income the applicants could have had in Lachin in 2002, 10 years after their flight.

Therefore, the ECtHR proceeded from the premise that a decision on compensation for pecuniary damage could be made only on two counts, namely, the loss of income from the applicants' land in Lachin and the increase in their living expenses in Baku. However, the assessment of the damage suffered depended on a large number of unknown circumstances, partly because the claims were generally based on a very limited evidentiary basis. As a result, the pecuniary damage suffered by the applicants could not be accurately calculated.

With regard to non-pecuniary damage, the ECtHR concluded that the circumstances of the case had clearly inflicted emotional suffering and stress on the applicants due to the prolonged and unresolved situation that separated them from their homes and property in the Lachin district and forced them to live as internally displaced persons in Baku in presumably worse living conditions. In such circumstances, the mere recognition of a violation is not sufficient satisfaction for the moral damage suffered.

As a result, the ECtHR awarded each applicant EUR 5000 in compensation for pecuniary and non-pecuniary damage combined.

The case of *Chiragov and Others v. Armenia* (just satisfaction) [GC], no. 13216/05 shows that even the lack of reliable evidence and documentary proof of the amount of damage suffered is not an insurmountable obstacle to awarding compensation. The approach to the standards of proof should be flexible and take into account the realities in which applicants find themselves (armed conflict, prolonged occupation, the passage of time, etc.). All of these circumstances make proving the amount of damage significantly more difficult, if not impossible. In such circumstances, demanding standards of proof that would otherwise be fully justified may turn out to be excessive and unfair.

Conclusions

Moral damage is a negative psychological experience endured by a person, consisting of mental pain and anguish. War brings with it an inconceivable amount of such experience. However, not all such experience can be compensated through legal mechanisms. First, in any legal mechanism, there is a certain threshold of severity of moral damage below which compensation is not provided. For example, the mere fact of the Russian Federation's invasion of Ukraine does not automatically entitle everyone living in Ukraine to claim compensation for moral damages (despite the fact that it is no exaggeration to say that the war has indeed affected everyone). Secondly, such a "threshold" of compensability is often dependent on the functioning and purpose of a particular compensation mechanism. For example, the UN Compensation Commission did not award compensation for non-pecuniary damage caused by forced displacement or loss of access to property. This can probably be explained by the fact that a fixed amount of compensation was awarded for forced displacement, which in turn was necessitated by the need to promptly review a large number of applications (the Commission received 2.7 million applications). Instead, the ECtHR practices awarding significant amounts of compensation for non-pecuniary damage resulting from forced displacement and loss of access to property.

According to the established practice of international institutions, a person claiming compensation for non-pecuniary damage does not have to provide special evidence to prove his or her mental suffering. It is enough for a person to prove the traumatic event (injury, assault, torture, death of a loved one, etc.), and the existence of non-pecuniary damage is then presumed. Moreover, the standards for proving a traumatic event should be flexible and take into account the realities in which victims find themselves (passage of time, loss of documents due to war and occupation, etc.) The burden of proof, which would be justified in other circumstances, may be excessive in times of war. With this in mind, international institutions establish special, lowered requirements for proving non-pecuniary damage for victims of war.

Mental pain and anguish should be distinguished from mental disorders, which are equivalent to physical illnesses and as such are subject to separate proof and give a separate right to compensation.

The peculiarity of non-pecuniary damage is that it cannot be accurately calculated. Difficulties in determining the amount of compensation do not deprive the victim of the right to receive it. Nor do these difficulties relieve the court of its obligation to take into account all the circumstances of the case relevant to determining the amount of just satisfaction. The amount of the award should not be taken as a universal measure and an exact monetary equivalent of the experience. The awarded amount only relatively reflects the intensity and duration of the pain and suffering experienced, so that deeper and longer suffering requires bigger compensation than less deep and shorter suffering. However, the unit of measurement in monetary terms has not been established and depends on many political, economic and practical considerations. In particular, it depends on the characteristics and tasks of the specific body considering the application, the level of welfare and economic conditions in the applicant's country, the capabilities and resources of the responsible entity, etc.

Printed in the USA
CPSIA information can be obtained
at www.ICGtesting.com
CBHW071915181124
17601CB00002B/12

9 783031 664335